D1372876

Using
Microprocessors
and
Microcomputers

The
6800
Family

Electronic
Technology Series

Using Microprocessors and Microcomputers

The 6800 Family

JOSEPH D. GREENFIELD
Rochester Institute of Technology

WILLIAM C. WRAY
Motorola Microsystems

JOHN WILEY & SONS

New York · Chichester · Brisbane · Toronto · Singapore

Library of Congress Cataloging in Publication Data:

Greenfield, Joseph D   1930-
    Using microprocessors and microcomputers.

    (Electronic technology series)
    Includes index.
1. Motorola 6800 (Computer)   I. Wray,
William C., joint author.   II. Title.

QA76.8.M67G75   001.64'04   80-18090
ISBN 0-471-02727-8

Printed in the United Sates of America

20 19 18 17 16 15 14 13

Preface

Microcomputers (μCs) and their principal component, the microprocessor (μP), have generated a great deal of interest and enthusiasm among students, teachers, and practicing engineers. Writing a book on this subject is difficult, however, because students need to know both digital hardware and software techniques to thoroughly understand the μC.

The object of this book is to explain the uses and operation of the **6800** family of microcomputer components to electronic technology and engineering students. We have assumed that students have had some introduction to digital electronics, but we cover programming as needed, so one need not have had a prior programming course to understand this book. We have also assumed that the μC will be used primarily in applications where it controls external "real world, real time" devices and that "number crunching" still remains the province of larger computers. Therefore, we have included several chapters on hardware, interfacing, and interrupts. Our goal is to familiarize readers with all aspects of the μC, so that they can assume responsibility for a complete μC project and debug both the hardware and software to get it running.

Some earlier textbooks tried to cover several μPs. We rejected this approach feeling that it led to a summary description with no depth. Indeed, some of these texts were merely a rehash of the manufacturer's literature. We have strived to improve upon this approach by giving detailed explanations and many examples. We have selected the popular and widely used **6800** family of μC components and, as Mr. Wray works for Motorola on projects involving the **6800** and its compatible relatives—the **6801, 6809,** and **6805**—our information is correct and authentic.

The first four chapters are a general introduction to computers for students who have no prior experience with them. Students conversant with computers can read these chapters very rapidly.

In Chapters 5 and 6 the **6800** instruction set is discussed in detail. Many examples are presented to illustrate the use of each instruction. As with many computer texts, however, seemingly simple problems sometimes lead to long programs. We tried to keep the programs as short and compact as possible.

Chapter 7 introduces assembly language programming as a software aid, and it is used with examples presented in the later chapters of the book. A machine language program from Chapter 6 is converted to an assembly language program so the student can thoroughly examine the process.

Chapters 8, 9, and 10 are hardware oriented. These chapters cover the bus structure and control signals for the **6800** μP; the two most commonly used interfacing ICs, the PIA and ACIA; and the use of interrupts. Timing circuits and time control of events are also discussed. These chapters explain how to interface the μC to external peripherals so that it can communicate with the outside world.

Chapter 11 discusses rudimentary and advanced development systems. For the simple systems, we emphasized the MEK6800-D2 kit that is used by many schools. The EXORciser, an advanced μC development system widely used in industry, is also discussed in detail.

Chapter 12 discusses other microprocessors such as the **6809** and introduces microcomputers such as the **6801.** The newer more powerful μPs, like the **6809,** seem to be destined to replace the **6800** in new designs in the coming years. The newer μPs, while more powerful, are also more complex. Since these new designs are extensions of the **6800,** we feel the background and concepts gained by studying the **6800** are indispensable for any understanding of the newer μPs. A thorough introduction to the most promising of these μPs, the **6809,** is presented so that the student may understand its advantages and incorporate it in new designs.

Chapter 13 presents some of the problems that the student may encounter when interfacing a μP in a real world environment. It also introduces A/D and D/A converters and gives several commercial applications of the μPs.

Chapter 14 is devoted to a typical CRT terminal application of a μP. We feel we have given a balanced presentation of the hardware, software, and interfacing in this book.

We thank Dr. Irving Kosow for his help and encouragement. We also thank the critics who reviewed the book before publication. Many of their constructive comments were incorporated in the final text.

We are grateful for the cooperation of the Motorola Technical Information Center, Phoenix, Arizona. With their permission we have reproduced many figures found in this book from manuals and other literature. We would like to acknowledge that many of the terms used in the text are trademarks of Motorola Inc.; These include EXORciser®, EXORterm, EXbug, MINIbug, JBUG, MICRObug, MIKBUG, MDOS, EXORdisk, and Micromodule. We also thank Lothar Stern, Manager of the Technical Information Center, for his encouragement, and Bill Crawford, of Motorola Microsystems Marketing, and Don Kesner, Engineering Manager, for their criticism. Above all, we thank our wives, Gladys and Dorothy, for their understanding, their sympathy, and their typing. Without them nothing would be possible.

Joseph D. Greenfield
William C. Wray

Contents

Using Microprocessors and Microcomputers

The 6800 Family

Chapter 1 Introduction to Microcomputers

**1-1
Introduction**

The introduction of the digital computer in the early 1950s revolutionized methods of computing and manipulating data. The development of the *microcomputer* (one or more integrated circuit chips that provide all the functions of a computer) is revolutionizing the computer industry and many other industries as well. Because of their low cost, small size and versatility, microcomputers (μCs) are surely destined to play an increasingly important role in the technologies of the future.

A μC system is generally built around a microprocessor (μP). The μP chip contains within it most of the control and arithmetic functions of a computer. To become a complete μC, it is augmented by other integrated circuit (IC) chips, such as RAMs (random access memories), ROMs (read only memories) and peripheral drivers. The most popular μPs at present are the Intel **8080** and **8085**, the Zilog **Z80**, the **6502** and the Motorola **6800**.

The purpose of this book is to introduce μC integrated circuit (IC) components and to help the reader understand how they work and how they can be used. This is not a simple task because many μC families are available; each has its own *set of instructions* and *unique hardware configuration*. If we attempted to describe each μP, we could not discuss any one in enough depth to enable the reader to build or use a system containing a specific family. Therefore, this book focuses primarily on the popular and extensively used Motorola **6800** family of μC components. The **M6800** microprocessor (μP) has features that are common to most μPs (multibyte instructions, interrupts, stacks, clocks, etc.). If the reader understands how these operations work on the **6800**, he or she will have little trouble understanding the operation of other μCs that also use these features.

One chapter is devoted to other μCs (including bit-slices) where the emphasis is on the similarities and differences to the **6800**. We believe that this concept works well and results in text that is practical and easily understood.

This introductory chapter presents an overview of microcomputers (μCs). A detailed explanation of μC construction and operation begins in Chapter 2. After reading this chapter, the student should be able to:

1. Decide whether to use a μC in a given application.
2. Describe the differences between NMOS, PMOS, or CMOS technologies.
3. List the differences between a minicomputer and a μC.

1-2
Self-Evaluation Questions

Watch for the answers to the following questions as you read the chapter. They should help you to understand the material presented.

1. What are the advantages of a μC over a minicomputer? What are the disadvantages?
2. How does programmability give the μC an advantage over hard-wired electronic controllers?
3. What are the most important characteristics of a μC?
4. Explain why displays and switches (the equivalent of a computer front panel) are not required in many μC applications.
5. Why is it important to design test connections into a μC system?
6. What is the major cost in developing a μC system?
7. What is the major disadvantage of compiler languages for a μC?

1-3
Historical Background

In the last three decades electronics has made tremendous strides progressing from vacuum tubes to transistors to integrated circuits (ICs). ICs are very small electronic circuits that contain miniature transistors and their associated components diffused into a silicon wafer or chip. The science of placing these electronic components on a tiny semiconductor chip is called *semiconductor technology*. In recent years, highly complex circuits have been fabricated on a single wafer. The most complex, and perhaps the most useful of these, is the μC.

1-3.1
Recent Developments in Semiconductor Technology

The complexity of electronic circuits that can be incorporated into one integrated circuit chip (IC) has been doubling each year for the last few years. Since the basic raw materials used in ICs are very inexpensive, the cost of digital ICs has been declining rapidly. The first ICs used bipolar technology, which eventually resulted in the availability of families of circuits, such as the **7400** TTL (Transistor-Transistor Logic) series. Each of these ICs contains just a few gates; this is called *small scale integration* (SSI). Improvements in this process have resulted in bipolar medium-scale-integration (MSI) devices that use many gates on each IC and produce complex circuits, such as shift registers and multiplexers.

Digital integrated circuits using MOS (metal-oxide-semiconductor) technology were introduced around 1969. MOS technology (Sec. 1-5.2) has several advantages over bipolar:

1. MOS devices require fewer manufacturing cycles.
2. MOS gates dissipate less power per gate.
3. MOS gates require less space on the silicon wafer.

Because of these advantages, far more MOS circuitry can be placed on a single IC.

Bipolar TTL ICs continue to dominate in SSI and MSI because of their high speed, wide acceptance, and long history of reliable operation. Most LSI (large-scale-integration) devices, including memories and μPs that require hundreds or even thousands of gates in a single IC, use MOS, rather than bipolar technology.

1-3.2
Recent Developments in
Computer Hardware

Many minicomputers and larger computers were built in the 1960s and 70s using bipolar or TTL ICs. A computer consists of an *arithmetic logic unit,* which performs the required arithmetic operations, a *memory, input/output circuits,* and gates and registers to control and coordinate the sequence of operations of these circuits. A computer is different from other electronic circuits because its operation is controlled by a *program,* or *software,* and can be changed by *changing the program,* instead of *rewiring the circuits.* A more detailed explanation of computer organization and operation is given in Chapters 2, 3, and 4.

By 1969 (when MOS was first introduced), semiconductor technology had progressed to the point where all of the individual μC circuits (e.g., gates, registers, and arithmetic/logic units) existed as individual ICs. About that time, the IC manufacturers started to combine these individual ICs into a single IC to produce a microprocessor (μP). This chip included most (but not all) of the functions of the complete computer.

The first practical IC μP, the Intel **4004**, appeared in 1971. The **4004** is a 4-bit μP that is slow and difficult to use. Later in the same year, Intel also introduced the **8008**, an 8-bit μP with a more sophisticated instruction set.

Two of the most popular μPs in current use, the Intel **8080** and the **M6800**, were introduced in 1974. In 1977 and 1978, several one chip microcomputers, such as the Fairchild **F8**, the TI **TMS1000**,

Table 1-1
Microprocessor Types

uP TYPE	MFGR	TCHNGLY	ARCHITECTURE	INTRO DATE	UNIQUE CHARACTERISTICS
4004	Intel	PMOS	4-bit	'71	12-bit multiplxed address
4040	"	"	"		Updated 4004 14 added inst + intrpt
8008	"	"	8-bit	'72	Mltplxed 14 bit addr - 48 instr
8080	"	NMOS	8-bit uP 16-bit addr 16-bit stk ptr	'74	40 pin non-mltplx
8080A	"	"	"		updated 8080
8048	"	"	8-bit uC ROM- RAM I/O-Timer	'78	Sngl chip uC EPROM version unique instr set
8085	"	N chnl depl. load	8-bit uP int clk vect intrpts 5 V Only		8080 compatible
6800	Motorola	NMOS	8-bit uP 16-bit addr 16-bit stk 5 V only	'74	40-pin, unlm stack
6802	"	"	6800 uP 128 RAM Int clk	'77	32 byte Lo-pwr RAM for standby. 6800 object compatible
6801			8-bit uC 2K ROM 128 RAM internl clk timer- UART 4- I/O ports	'78	Enhanced instrns faster thruput 6800 object code compatible
6803	"	"	8-bit uC same as 6801 except no ROM	'78	Enhanced instrctns 6800 obj code compatible
6809	"	"	8-bit uP Int or Ext clk 3 interrupts 2 index regs 2 index/SP regs	'78	Hi-performance uP Enhanced instrns faster thruput 16 bit instrns 6800 source code compatible

and the Motorola **6801** were introduced. Table 1-1 lists the currently available μPs and μCs, their characteristics, technology, and date of introduction. This information was correct at the time of writing, but the field is progressing so rapidly it is difficult to keep it up to date.

Table 1-1 (continued)
Microprocessor Types

141000 141200	"	CMOS	4-bit static 1K ROM 64x4 RAM 11 or 16 I/O	'77	0-700 kHz clk Sngl chip uC TMS1000 compatible
3870	"	NMOS	8-bit uC 2K ROM 64 bytes RAM Timer-int clk		F8 type map not expandble
IMP-16	Nat.	PMOS	4-bit slice	'73	multi chp 16-bit
SC/MP	"	"	8-bit uP	'75	
PACE	"	"	16-bit uP	'76	1st 16-bit system not TTL cmptbl
2650	Sig- netics	NMOS-I	8-bit uP	'75	
CDP 1801	RCA	CMOS	8-bit uP	'75	
PPS-8	Rock- well	PMOS	8-bit uP	'75	
PPS-4	Rock-	PMOS	4-bit uP	'72	
6502	MOS- tech.	NMOS	8-bit uP int clk	'75	Diffrnt pinouts Like 6800 2nd index reg
F8	Fair child	"	8-bit RAM int clock I/O	'74	
3850	Mostec	"	8-bit uP		F8 type
9900	Texas Inst.	"	16-bit	'76	64 pin pkg
TMS- 1000	TI	PMOS	4-bit uC 1Kx8 ROM 64x4 RAM Int clk 11 I/O lines		28-pin -15 V only
TMS- 1200	TI	PMOS	same except 16 I/O lines		40-pin
Z80	Zilog	NMOS	8-bit CPU 5 V only int clk	'76	Dual register like 8080 175 instructions

Note: NMOS-D denotes depletion load and NMOS-I denotes ion-
implantation.

1-4
µC Families

The original µC developments placed the major elements of the computer on one chip but, because of the combination of functions provided, they were described as microprocessors (µPs). Microprocessors cannot function by themselves because they only include parts of a computer. Other components, such as RAM, ROM, and input/output (I/O) devices are required. These can also be placed on IC chips. Together with the μP, they form a family of μC components. Recently, the manufacturers have succeeded in placing small RAMs, ROMs, I/O and even a clock on one chip, along with the CPU (central processing unit), and have truly produced a single chip computer. These μCs are generally suitable for very simple applications and must be augmented by additional RAM, ROM, and I/O chips for bigger jobs.

1-4.1
Microprocessors (μPs) and
Microcomputers (μCs)

Strictly speaking, the term microprocessor should refer to the *central processing unit* of a microcomputer. The CPU contains within it the arithmetic/logic unit, registers, and counters that are the majority of the functions necessary for the operation of a computer. The term microcomputer (μC) refers not only to the CPU, but to the other functions needed for the operation of the computer. All these functions, including the CPU, are available in individual ICs or in various combinations and are provided in dual-in-line (DIP) packages. Figure 1-1 shows the **6800** μP in a DIP package and also shows a block diagram of the μP and the other functions necessary to complete the

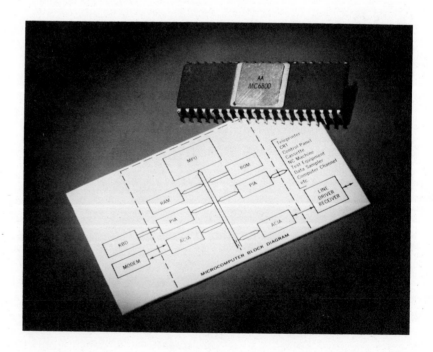

Figure 1-1 The **6800** μP and its associated family of ICs.

Figure 1-2 The **6800** µC on a single card.

µC. These other functions are also available in similar packages. By using them an entire computer can now be placed on a single printed circuit module. Figure 1-2 shows such a module. It contains a **6800** µP, plus the associated RAMs, ROMs, clock, and SSI chips required to make a complete functioning µC. Recently, all these functions have been incorporated onto a single chip. Single-chip computers are discussed in Chapter 12.

1-4.2
Microcomputer Memories

A computer memory consists of RAMs (random-access-memory) ROMs (read-only-memory), or PROMs (field programmable-read-only-memory). Memory is essential to the operation of the µC and is discussed in detail in Chapter 3. The ROM or PROM is used to store the program instructions, and the RAM saves all variable data used in the course of program operation. In general, the more functions performed, the more memory required, but this addition does not affect the cost of the µP chip, the clock or even Input/Output (I/O) operations. Memory ICs are available in a wide variety of configurations; several of them are provided in the **6800** family specifically designed for small µC systems. These and other hardware aspects of the **6800** family are discussed in Chapter 8.

1-4.3
Testing μC Systems

The difficulties of developing and testing μC systems led to the need for *system development test instruments*. Microprocessor manufacturers introduced these specialized instruments that are used with the μC family of components for both hardware and software troubleshooting. Intel's development system is called the *Intellec*. Motorola's *EXORciser* was developed in 1974. Other semiconductor manufacturers also make similar μC test instruments. A growing list of companies that do not manufacture ICs have introduced a variety of specialized analyzers for general purpose use in μC system design. The explanation of the need and the techniques for using these and other test instruments is included in Chapter 11.

1-5
Microcomputer Component
Manufacture

This book is primarily concerned with the *use* of μC components. It is important, however, to have a basic understanding of semiconductor manufacture to be aware of performance differences, to plan future products, and to anticipate cost trends.

Semiconductor technology involves photography, chemistry, materials science, metallurgy, physics, and electronics. Progress is rapidly being made in all these disciplines, resulting in continual improvements in the semiconductors themselves.

The first step in the process of making μPs is to grow *silicon crystals* and slice them into *thin wafers*. The electrical circuits are then chemically deposited on the silicon wafers by treating them with a photosensitive material and exposing them through a *mask* of the desired pattern. These masks are photographically reduced almost 500 times and made into multiple images on each wafer. The wafers are subsequently subjected to processes of diffusion or ion implantation, deposition of oxide or metal, and are chemically etched. After many such steps, the wafer is ready to be cut up (diced) into "chips," usually less than 6 mm (¼ inch) square. The chips are tested to select the good ones, which are then mounted into the familiar plastic or ceramic packages (DIPs). The silicon crystals, which were originally less than 5 centimeters (2 inches) across, are now being grown in even larger sizes. This increases the yield of good chips or dies/wafer. Using presently available photographic improvements, hundreds of dies are now being cut from each wafer. As the technology improves, the yield of good dies/wafer also increases. This has caused the price of ICs to come down to the point where even μCs are inexpensive. The **M6800** silicon wafer is shown in Fig. 1-3.

Figure 1-3 The **6800** silicon chip.

1-5.1
Microprocessor Characteristics

Microcomputers are frequently compared on the basis of several main characteristics. Among them are, *speed* (the rate at which μCs execute instructions), the number of power supplies used, TTL compatibility, and the number of chips needed to form a complete μC. In specialized designs, the power dissipation may be important. The operation of most μCs is controlled by a digital clock (see Sec. 8-7). If the basic semiconductor technology allows high speed performance, the clock can be run at a higher frequency. This permits the μC to execute more instructions per second, making it more useful.

1-5.2
PMOS, NMOS, and CMOS
Technologies

MOS technology is divided into two types, PMOS, which is based on *p*-doped silicon, and NMOS, which is based on *n*-doped silicon. These two types of implementations can be used individually or can be combined to effectively form a third category known as CMOS (complementary MOS). Each of these technologies have much in common, but each also exhibits some unique characteristics.

PMOS was perfected originally and the first μPs were designed using this process. The Intel **4004** and **8008** are examples of PMOS technology. The circuit speed of PMOS was nearly an order of magnitude (one tenth) slower than bipolar devices, but because of the reduced geometry and lower power dissipation per gate, much more complexity was possible on a chip.

However, *n*-type silicon is basically three times faster than *p*-type silicon (because mobility of electrons is three times that of holes). As a result, and because of TTL compatible voltages, NMOS has emerged as the most popular process for μP production. It is the process used for the **6800**, the **8080**, the Fairchild **F8**, and Zilog **Z80**.

The newest category, CMOS, combines an *n*-channel and a *p*-channel MOS transistor in each gate. It has the advantage of extremely low power dissipation when it is static (not being switched). CMOS has an added advantage of considerable latitude in supply voltage. Consequently, it is advocated as a good choice for automotive (12 V) use.

1-6 Microprocessors and Hard-Wired Logic

In the past decades, industry has made use of *industrial controllers* to control machines, manufacturing processes, and appliances. These controllers are primarily electronic devices. The method of building controllers has progressed from electromechanical to electronic (frequently analog) and now to digital integrated circuits. These are called *hard-wired* devices because their operation is determined by the circuits and wires contained within them. At each step in the progression, controllers became smaller, yet more sophisticated. They were capable of performing more diverse operations and responding to a larger number of inputs.

The home washing machine is a common example of electromechanical control. Relays and timers within the machine determine the sequence of operations (wash, rinse, spin dry) and the time of each operation.

The μC is a great leap forward in this evolutionary chain. Its operation is determined primarily by its *program,* instead of its components and its wires. This makes the μC more flexible and amenable to change.

Any function that can be implemented using hard-wired digital ICs can also be implemented or performed by a μC. The converse is also true. Hard-wired logic still maintains the following advantages over MOS μCs.

1. It is faster. It can execute a function in perhaps one-tenth of the time required by a MOS μC, because the execution time for computer instructions is much longer than for TTL ICs. (Where speed is needed, the bit-slice μP should be considered. See Chapter 12.)
2. For small devices requiring just a few ICs the hard-wired approach is less costly, because the more complex (and higher cost) chips and their associated connections are not required.
3. No programming costs are incurred.

As the size and complexity of the devices increase, μCs become more attractive for two reasons.

1. The hard-wired approach requires adding ICs to perform more complex tasks; μCs usually require only a longer program.
2. Microcomputers are more versatile. Any change in a hard-wired system usually involves replacing ICs and rerouting wires. Most modifications to a μC system are made simply by changing the program. For example, a modification can frequently be accomplished by replacing a ROM, which can easily be done in the field by nontechnical users.

Microcomputers are very useful where many decisions or calculations are required. It is easier to use the *computational power* of a computer than to use discrete logic. One example is TV games where the controller must keep track of the position of the ball and paddles, determine when a point is scored, and keep score. Most of the controllers for these games include a μC.

Microcomputers are now being considered for many new designs (and are often used to replace existing designs) because they are far simpler to use than conventional IC logic. Since the μC approach is programmable, many additional features are possible with little or no added cost. Programmability makes possible multiple use of a common piece of hardware (i.e., only the ROM control program needs to be changed).

**1-7
Computers and
Minicomputers**

Large computers (such as the IBM 360 or 370) are used to solve highly sophisticated problems or to handle operations that require large volumes of output data. Most corporations, for example, use large computers to print their payrolls and write their bills.

A minicomputer is a scaled-down version of a larger computer resulting in reduced computational power. It is much smaller and less expensive, and is an ideal solution for problems of medium complexity. In the early 1970s, minicomputers were used primarily to control industrial processes. Now μCs are replacing minicomputers as industrial controllers. Similarly, minicomputers, which are becoming more sophisticated, are taking over some tasks formerly performed by large computers.

Microcomputers cost less than minicomputers, but μC performance is still far short of a minicomputer. Minicomputers are generally faster than μCs and can generally execute more complex programs. Since minicomputers are often less than fully utilized, however, μCs have become a viable alternative for many uses. Each year μC costs drop and performance improves so that more and more applications are being found where the μC is able to substitute for larger computers.

**1-7.1
Minicomputers**

Minicomputers were the first step in the miniaturization of computers. They are available from several manufacturers as basic general purpose computers that can be adopted for a variety of uses, usually by plugging in various modular cards. The cards usually include a complete function, such as an input module, output module, or memory module. As a rule, the modules are assembled using discrete components.

**1-7.2
Minicomputers vs. μCs**

A μC is often used to perform a specific task and contains only the ICs necessary for that specific application (i.e., processor, clock, memory, and I/O). A minicomputer, on the other hand, is usually a very complete assembly of these same functions and also includes displays, registers, entry switches, plug-in accessory modules, software, and instruction manuals. It is a general purpose package capable of a variety of uses without hardware modifications. Another distinction between a μC and a minicomputer is in the type of memory provided. Practically all minicomputers have only read/write memory, but some units have a small ROM (read-only-memory) bootstrap program to permit easy loading of the RAMs. Minicomputers usually require either a disc, cassette, or similar device to reload the memory in the event of a power interruption. This unit is either permanently associated with the minicomputer, or is transported to it in order to get the minicomputer restarted. The μC, on the other hand, usually has the majority of its memory as ROM or PROM for program instruction storage. It also uses a small RAM for variable data, such as the stack and for scratch-pad calculations. Because the operating program is *nonvolatile* (permanent), restarting the program after power has been off is quickly and easily accomplished. If the RAMs are equipped with a "battery backup" circuit, and the necessary software routines are included in the ROMs, recovery from a power failure without loss of data is possible. This auto-restart capability is one of the μCs most valuable features.

The real advantage of the μP and its companion LSI components is that it can be assembled with as few or as many parts as needed to do the required task. It is not necessary, for example, to include register/display entry switches or terminal input/output facilities in most systems, because the μC is often built into machinery where the operator is not skilled in computer discipline, or where the equipment is unattended in normal operation. In these cases, the design, debugging, and maintenance is accomplished by plug-in or transportable test equipment.

Of course the μC system must be designed to accommodate this test equipment. Methods of *testing* a computer system should be considered *during*, not after, the system is designed, or the final product may be difficult or impossible to test.

1-8
Software Control of
Electronic Systems

The technique of substituting software (computer programs) for hardware logic is largely responsible for the acceptance of μCs. A μC can completely control any system, but it is necessary to provide the appropriate interface. Consider a μC built to control a device that includes motors or solenoid valves. The electronic circuitry external to the μC would consist of solid-state relays or power transistor amplifiers, and the TTL level signals from the μC I/O lines would control them. (A $+5$ V ON signal could make a motor run, or open a valve, and a 0 V OFF signal could halt the action.) The problems of timing, limiting, or interlocking would be provided in software. This is not always safe, so mechanical limit switches or pressure relief valves can be added to the hardware, providing that the reliability of the electromechanical devices is adequate. These design decisions are often referred to as the *hardware/software trade-offs*, and must be made by the system designer. Mechanical and hydraulic logic devices, such as mechanical interlocks or speed controlling governors, are being replaced by appropriately designed μC systems. *Electronic control is faster, cleaner, more accurate, more reliable, and electronic components do not wear out.* Such systems contain electrical or electronic sensors (transducers) and their outputs are connected to μC input lines so that the information can be processed by the software routines. In the automotive field, for example, ignition spark advance mechanisms, which were vacuum controlled, and transmission control, which has been universally hydraulic, are being replaced by μPs. These advances are possible today because of the low cost of the μC. They can be justified on the basis of the increased reliability, accuracy, or ease with which a feature can be added to a μC controller.

1-9
The Future of μCs

If the future of μCs is based on projections, it would appear that the material cost of the ICs themselves will virtually disappear. Since the raw materials are abundant, it can logically be assumed that the cost of each chip will level off at a few dollars. As more functions are included in each package, the total hardware costs become *insignificant* compared with the *design* and *programming* costs. Although many people are alarmed at the apparent rising costs of programming, what is occurring is really just a shift in costs because *software is being substituted for hardware.*

New concepts and techniques are necessary to handle the tasks to be performed and therefore new methods of cost analysis must be used. Since the price of each system sold is determined by the cost of the hardware, plus the cost of development divided by the number of systems sold, high volume production can result in very low-priced equipment. The importance of keeping the development costs low should not be overlooked. Selection of a μP that is easy to program, as well as the use of good systems development tools, are both advisable. Good development tools include not only software editing and debugging aids, but also the means to troubleshoot the hardware quickly and easily, and to monitor the interface between the μC and its peripherals.

Most μP manufacturers provide support tools for software development, but not all of them provide the necessary hardware debugging assistance required. Compilers and other high level languages are being used, but even though program writing is easier than when using assembly language, the additional debugging time required may outweigh much of the gain and may result in excessive memory requirements. Currently, Fortran, Basic, and versions of PL/1 are in use. Compilers in general are oriented toward simplifying mathematical calculations and are notoriously poor at *bit* manipulations that are needed in most control system applications, which are a large segment of μC uses. Improvements in compilers, editors, assemblers, and other development aids continues to occur and should serve to decrease development time and costs.

1-10 Summary This chapter provides an introduction and brief history of μPs. The configuration of a μC system and the areas where μCs should and should not be used were discussed.

At this point, the reader should review the self-evaluation questions (Sec 1-2). If any of them seem unclear, he should reread the appropriate sections of the text.

1-11 Glossary **Clock** A fixed frequency square wave source that synchronizes the operation of a microprocessor.

Controller A device (usually electronic) that controls the operation of a machine or process.

Hardware The actual electronic circuits in a computer.

Integrated circuit (IC) A small silicon chip that contains many electronic circuits.

Metal oxide semiconductor (MOS) A form of transistor used in an IC.

Microcomputer (μC) A computer consisting of a microprocessor and other associated chips, such as memories, necessary to form a complete computer.

Microprocessor (μP) A single integrated circuit containing most of the elements of a computer.

Programmability The ability to change the operation of a device by changing a program.

Semiconductor Generally silicon doped with p or n material to form resistors and transistors. Semiconductor material is the basis of transistors and ICs.

Software The programs that control the operation of a computer or microprocessor.

1-12 References **Bylinsky, Gene** *Fortune Magazine,* Vol. XCII, No. 5, November, 1975, "Here Comes the Second Computer Revolution."

Motorola Monitor, Vol. 9, No. 2, October, 1971.

Osborne, Adam *An Introduction to Microcomputers,* Volumes 1 and 2, Adam Osborne & Associates, Inc., P.O. Box 2036, Berkeley, California 94702.

Chapter 2 Binary Numbers and Logic Operations

2-1
Instructional Objectives

This chapter introduces the binary number system and gives the student some facility in handling binary numbers. The 2s complement system of arithmetic and the logical operations performed by a computer are also introduced. After reading this chapter, the student should be able to:

1. Convert binary numbers to decimal numbers.
2. Convert decimal numbers to binary numbers.
3. Find the sum and difference of two binary numbers.
4. Convert negative binary numbers to their 2s complement form.
5. Add and subtract numbers in 2s complement form.
6. Complement a word.
7. Find the logical AND, OR, and EXCLUSIVE OR of two words.

2-2
Self-Evaluation Questions

Watch for the answers to the following questions as you read the chapter. They should help you to understand the material presented.

1. What are the advantages of digital circuits?
2. What is the difference between a bit and a decimal digit? How are they similar?
3. How are binary addition and subtraction different from decimal addition and subtraction? How are they similar?
4. How are bits, bytes, and words related?
5. What are the advantages of long word lengths? Why do microprocessors use short words?
6. How is the sign of a 2s complement number determined by inspection?
7. What is the major advantage of 2s complement notation?
8. How can the positive equivalent of 2s complement negative numbers be found?

2-3
The Binary Number System

Computers and microprocessors are built from a large number of digital electronic circuits that are carefully interconnected to perform the operations necessary to properly execute each of the computer's instructions.

At the present time, *standard* computers are built of many ICs. Each IC contains some of the digital circuits that make the computer work.

The output of a digital electronic circuit is a *single binary digit* commonly called a *bit*. *A single bit has one of only two possible values, 0 or 1*. In digital circuits a certain *range* of voltages is defined as a logic 1 and another voltage range is defined as a logic 0. In TTL (transistor-transistor logic) circuits, for example, any voltage between 0 and 0.8 V is a logic 0, and any voltage between $+2$ and $+5$ is a logic 1. Digital circuits have a range of *undefined* or *forbidden* voltages that separate logic 1s from logic 0s. For TTL this range is from 0.8 to 2.0 V. If a circuit should produce an output voltage in the undefined range, it is malfunctioning and should be investigated.

Two advantages are gained by restricting the output of an electronic circuit to one of two possible values. First, it is rarely necessary to make fine distinctions. Whether an output is 3.67 or 3.68 V is immaterial; both voltages correspond to a logic 1. Well-designed logic circuits produce voltages near the middle of the range defined for 1 or 0, so there is no difficulty in distinguishing between them. In addition, a digital circuit is very tolerant of any drift in the output caused by component aging or changes. A change in a component would almost have to be catastrophic to cause the output voltage to drift from a 1 to a 0 or an undefined value. The second advantage of digital circuits is that it is far easier to remember a 1 or a 0 than to remember an analog quantity like 3.67 V. Since computers are required to remember many bits, this is a very important consideration.

The output of a single digital circuit, a single bit, is enough to answer any question that has only *two* possible answers. For example, a typical job application might ask, "What is your sex?" A 1 could arbitrarily be assigned to a male and a 0 to a female, so that a single bit is enough to describe the answer to this question. A single bit is all the space a programmer needs to reserve in his computer for this answer.

However, another question on the job application might be, "What is the color of your hair?'' If the possible answers are black, brown, blonde, and red, a single bit cannot possibly describe them all. Now several bits are needed to describe all possible answers. We could assign one *bit* to each answer (i.e., brown = 0001, black = 0010, blonde = 0100, red = 1000), but if there are many possible answers to the given question, many bits are required. The coding scheme presented above is not *optimum*; it requires more bits than are really necessary to answer the question.

It is most economical to use as few bits as possible to express the answer to a question, or a number, or a choice. So the crucial question arises:

''*What is the minimum number of bits required to distinguish between n different things?*''

Whether these *n* things are objects, or possible answers, or *n* numbers is immaterial. To answer this question, we realize that each bit has two possible values. Therefore k bits would have 2^k possible values. This gives rise to theorem 1.

Theorem 1

The minimum number of bits required to express n different things is k, where k is the smallest number such that $2^k \geq n$.

A few examples should make this clear.

Example 2-1

What is the minimum number of bits required to answer the hair color question, and how could they be coded to give distinct answers?

Solution

There are four possible answers to this question; therefore $2^k = 4$. Since 2 is the smallest number such that $2^2 \geq 4$, $k = 2$, and 2 bits are needed. One way of coding the answers is 00 = brown, 01 = black, 10 = blonde, 11 = red.

Example 2-2

How many bits are needed to express a single decimal digit?

Solution

There are 10 possible values for a single decimal digit (0 through 9); therefore $2^k \geq 10$. Since $k = 4$ is the smallest *integer* such that $2^k \geq 10$, 4 bits are required.

Example 2-3

A computer must store the names of a group of people. If we assume that no name is longer than 20 letters, how many bits must the computer reserve for each name?

Solution

To express a name, only the 26 letters of the alphabet, plus a space and perhaps a period, are needed. This is a total of 28 characters. Since $2^k \geq 28$, $k = 5$ and 5 bits are required for each character. Since space must be reserved for 20 such characters, 100 bits are needed for each name.

2-3.1
Bits, Bytes, and Words

For use in computers, bits are grouped into *words*. The *word length* of a computer is the *number of bits involved in each memory data transfer*. While word lengths vary from computer to computer, each has a definite word length and its registers are built to accommodate words of that length.

Large computers generally use long words. The IBM 360/370 series, for example, uses 32-bit words. Minicomputers use intermediate word lengths; 16 bits is the most popular minicomputer word size. Microprocessors generally use 8-bit words, although 4-bit and 16-bit microprocessors exist.

There are two advantages to using long word sizes.

1. Larger numbers can be accommodated within a single word.
2. Instruction words are larger and more flexible; they allow the instructions to contain more options.

Unlike large computers, microprocessors are rarely used to solve complex mathematical problems. They are most often used to control physical processes and can use shorter word lengths that keeps the cost of the microprocessor and memory down, and allows the user to adjust the size of his system to fit the job requirements. Shorter word lengths complicate the programming, and the additional effort required to program microprocessors must be compensated for by the low cost of the hardware.

Example 2-4

How many numbers can be represented by:

a. A single IBM 360/370 word?
b. An 8-bit microprocessor word?

olution

a. Since an IBM 360/370 word contains 32 bits, any one of $2^{32} = 4,294,967,296$ numbers may be represented in a single word.

b. For the microprocessor word of 8 bits, $2^8 = 256$ numbers may be represented by a single word.

2-3.2
Bytes and Nibbles

A group of 8 bits is called a *byte*. This is a convenient size for storing a single *alphanumeric character* (a character from a teletype or typewriter that could be an alphabetic character, a number, a punctuation mark, or a control character). For the many microprocessors that have an 8-bit word size, the words byte and word are used interchangeably.

Groups of four bits are sometimes called a *nibble*. They also comprise a *hexadecimal digit* (see Sec. 4-3). In addition, 32-bit computers use the terms *half word* and *double word*. Thus we have the following conversion table:

$$4 \text{ bits} = 1 \text{ nibble}$$
$$2 \text{ nibbles} = 1 \text{ byte}$$
$$2 \text{ bytes} = 1 \text{ half word} = 16 \text{ bits}$$
$$4 \text{ bytes} = 1 \text{ word} = 32 \text{ bits}$$
$$2 \text{ words} = 1 \text{ mouthful (double word)} = 64 \text{ bits}$$

2-4
Binary-to-Decimal
Conversion

Because computer operation is based on the *binary* (base 2) number system and people use the *decimal* (base 10) number system, it is often necessary to convert numbers given in one system to their equivalents in the other system. To eliminate any possible confusion, a subscript is used to indicate which number system is employed. Thus, 101_{10} is the decimal number whose value is one hundred and one, while 101_2 is a binary number whose decimal value is five. Of course, any number containing a digit from 2 to 9 is a decimal number.

The value of a decimal number depends on the *magnitude* of the decimal digits expressing it and on their *position*. A decimal number is equal to the sum $D_0 \times 10^0 + D_1 \times 10^1 + D_2 \times 10^2 + \cdots$, where D_0 is the least significant digit, D_1 the next significant, and so on.

Example 2-5

Express the decimal number 7903 as a sum to the base 10.

Solution

Here D_0, the least significant digit is 3, $D_1 = 0$, $D_2 = 9$, and $D_3 = 7$.
Therefore 7903 equals:

3×10^0	3
$+\ 0 \times 10^1$	0
$+\ 9 \times 10^2$	900
$+\ 7 \times 10^3$	7000
	7903

Similarly, a group of binary bits can represent a number in the binary system. The binary base is 2; therefore the digits can only be 0 or 1. However, a binary number is also equal to a sum, namely $B_0 \times 2^0 + B_1 \times 2^1 \cdots$, where B_0 is the least significant bit, B_1 the next significant bit, and so on. The powers of 2 are given in the *binary boat* or table of Appendix A. In this table, n is the exponent and the corresponding positive and negative powers of 2 are listed to the left and right of n respectively.

A binary number is a group of ones (1s) and zeros (0s). To find the equivalent decimal number, we simply add those powers of 2 that correspond to the 1s in the number and omit those powers of 2 that correspond to the 0s of the number.

Example 2-6

Convert 100011011_2 to a decimal number.

Solution

The first bit to the left of the decimal point corresponds to $n = 0$, and n increases by one (increments) for each position further to the left. The number 100011011 has 1s in positions 0, 1, 3, 4 and 8. The conversion is made by obtaining those powers of 2 corresponding to these n values (using Appendix A, if necessary) and adding them:

n	2^n
0	1
1	2
3	8
4	16
8	256
	283

Therefore, $100011011_2 = \mathbf{283}_{10}$.

Example 2-7

In the PDP-8 computer, each word consists of 12 bits, that is, $k = 12$. How many numbers can be represented by a single PDP-8 word?

Solution

Since 12 bits are available, any one of 4096 (2^{12}) numbers can be expressed. These numbers range from a minimum of twelve 0s to a maximum of twelve 1s, which is the binary equivalent of 4095. Therefore, the 4096 different numbers that can be expressed by a single word are the decimal numbers 0 through 4095.

2-5
Decimal-to-Binary
Conversion

It is often necessary to convert decimal numbers to binary. Humans, for example, supply and receive decimal numbers from computers that work in binary; consequently, computers are continually making binary-to-decimal and decimal-to-binary conversions.

To convert a decimal number to its equivalent binary number, the following *algorithm* (or procedure) may be used:

1. Obtain N. (The decimal number to be converted.)
2. Determine if N is odd or even.
3a. If N is odd, write 1 and subtract 1 from N. Go to step 4.
3b. If N is even, write 0.
4. Obtain a new value of N by dividing the N of step 3 by 2.
5a. If $N > 1$, go back to step 1 and repeat the procedure.
5b. If $N = 1$, write 1. The number written is the binary equivalent of the original decimal number. The number written first is the least significant bit, and the number written last is the most significant bit.

This procedure can also be implemented by following the flowchart of Fig. 2-1. Computer programmers often use *flowcharts* to describe their programs graphically. For the rudimentary flowcharts drawn in this text, the square box is a command, which must be obeyed unconditionally. The diamond-shaped box is a decision box. Within the decision box is a question that must be answered *yes* or *no*. If the answer is yes, the *yes* path must be followed; otherwise the *no* path is followed. The flowchart of Fig. 2-1 starts with the given number N and since K equals 0, initially we are writing B_0, the least significant digit. Note that equations in a flowchart are programmer's equations, not algebraic equations. The "equation" $N = N - 1$ makes no sense mathematically. What it means here is that N is *replaced* by $N - 1$.

On the initial pass through the flowchart, B_0, the least significant bit, is written as 0 or 1, depending on whether N is even or odd.

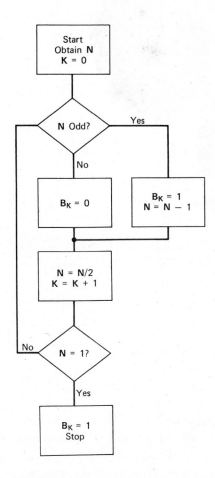

Figure 2-1 Flowchart for decimal-to-binary conversion of whole numbers.

Next N is divided by 2 and K is incremented so that on the following pass, B_1, the second least significant bit (LSB) will be written. We continue looping through the flowchart and repeating the procedure until $N = 1$. Then the most significant bit (MSB) is written as a 1, and the process stops. The bits written are the binary equivalent of the decimal number.

Example 2-8

Find the binary equivalent of the decimal number 217.

Solution

The solution proceeds according to the algorithm or flowchart. When an odd number is encountered, a 1 is written as the binary digit and subtracted from the remaining number; when the remaining number is even, 0 is written as the binary digit. The number is then divided by 2. The process continues until the number is reduced to 1.

Remaining number		Binary Digit or Bit
217	Odd—subtract 1	1
216	Divide by 2	
108	Even—divide by 2	0
54	Even—divide by 2	0
27	Odd—subtract 1	1
26	Divide by 2	
13	Odd—subtract 1	1
12	Divide by 2	
6	Even—divide by 2	0
3	Odd—subtract 1	1
2	Divide by 2	
1	Finish	1

Note that the *least significant bit* (LSB) was written first. Therefore 217_{10} = $\mathbf{11011001_2}$. To check this, convert back from binary to decimal.

$$11011001 = 128 + 64 + 16 + 8 + 1 = 217_{10}$$

2-6
Addition and Subtraction of
Binary Numbers

The binary number system is a valid system, and mathematical operations such as addition, subtraction, multiplication, and division can be performed on binary numbers. In this section, the most commonly performed arithmetic operations, addition and subtraction, will be discussed. These are the arithmetic operations performed by a microprocessor or minicomputer. The reader should consult more specialized texts (Sec. 2-11) for multiplication, division, squares, square roots, and other arithmetic operations.

2-6.1
Addition of Binary Numbers

The addition of binary numbers is similar to the addition of decimal numbers, except that $1 + 1 = 0$ with a carry out to the next significant place. A carry into a more significant position acts like an additional 1.

Example 2-9
Add the binary numbers $A = 11101100$ and $B = 1100110$.

Solution

Column	9 8 7 6 5 4 3 2 1	(Decimal addition)
A	1 1 1 0 1 1 0 0	(236)
B	1 1 0 0 1 1 0	(102)
	1 0 1 0 1 0 0 1 0	(338)

The above addition proceeded as follows:
1. Column 1 (least significant digit) $0 + 0 = 0$

2. Column 2 $0 + 1 = 1$

3. Column 3 $1 + 1 = 0$ plus a carry output

4. Column 4 $0 + 1$ plus a carry input from Column 3 sums to a 0 and produces a carry out to Column 5.

5. Column 5 $0 + 0 = 0$, but the carry input from Column 4 makes the sum 1.

6. Column 6 $1 + 1 = 0$ and a carry output to Column 7.

7. Column 7 $1 + 1$ plus a carry input results in a sum of 1 and a carry output.

8. Column 8 B does not have an 8th bit; therefore a leading 0 can be assumed. Here $0 + 1$ plus a carry input yields a 0 sum plus a carry output.

9. Column 9   Neither A nor B has a 9th digit so leading 0s are written for both. In Column 9 we have $0 + 0$ plus a carry in from Column 8 that gives a sum of 1. Since there is no carry out of column 9, the addition is complete.

The sum of Example 2-9 can be checked by converting the numbers to their decimal equivalents. These numbers are shown in parenthesis beside the sum.

2-6.2
Subtraction of binary numbers

The rules for the subtraction of binary numbers are:

1. $1 - 1 = 0$
2. $0 - 0 = 0$
3. $1 - 0 = 1$
4. $0 - 1 = 1$ with a *borrow out*

In order to borrow, change the next 1 in the minuend to a 0 and change all intervening 0s to 1s.

Example 2-10
Subtract 101101001 from 100011010011.

Solution

Column	12 11 10 9 8 7 6 5 4 3 2 1	(Decimal Subtraction)
	1 0 0 0 1 1 0 1 0 0 1 1	(2259)
	1 0 1 1 0 1 0 0 1	− (361)
	1 1 1 0 1 1 0 1 0 1 0	(1898)

1. **Column 1** $1 - 1 = 0$
2. **Column 2** $1 - 0 = 1$
3. **Column 3** $0 - 0 = 0$
4. **Column 4** $0 - 1 = 1$ The 1 in Column 5 is changed to a 0 due to the borrow out generated in Column 4.
5. **Column 5**   This is now $0 - 0 = 0$
6. **Column 6** $0 - 1 = 1$ The 1 in Column 7 is changed to a 0.
7. **Column 7**   Due to the borrow from Column 6, this now becomes $0 - 1$ or 1 with a borrow out that changes the 1 in Column 8.
8. **Column 8**   This becomes $0 - 0 = 0$
9. **Column 9** $0 - 1 = 1$ Columns 10 and 11 are 0 so the borrow must be from Column 12. Columns 10 and 11 contain intervening 0s so they change to 1s and Column 12 changes to a 0.
10. **Column 10**   This is now $1 - 0 = 1$
11. **Column 11**   This is now $1 - 0 = 1$
12. **Column 12** $1 - 1 = 0$

The results were checked by converting the binary numbers to their decimal equivalents, which are shown in parentheses beside the numbers.

**2-7
2s Complement Arithmetic**

When building hardware such as computers to accommodate binary numbers, two problems arise:

1. The number of bits in a hardware register is finite.
2. Negative integers must also be represented.

These problems do not arise in conventional pencil-and-paper arithmetic. If additional bits are needed, the number can always be extended to the left and negative numbers can always be represented by a minus sign.

Since a hardware register consists of a finite number of bits, the range of numbers that can be represented is finite. An n-bit register can contain one of 2^n numbers. If positive binary numbers are used, the 2^n numbers that can be represented are 0 through $2^n - 1$ (a string of n 1s represents the number $2^n - 1$).

The simplest approach to the problem of representing negative integers is to use the MSB to denote the *sign* of the number. Normally an *MSB of 0 indicates a positive number, and an MSB of 1 indicates a negative number*. The remaining bits denote the *magnitude* of the number. This is called *sign-magnitude* representation.

Example 2-11

What range of positive and negative numbers can be represented in sign-magnitude notation by a 16-bit computer?

Solution

Since the 16th bit is reserved for the sign, the largest number that can be represented is a string of fifteen 1s, which is $2^{15} - 1$, or 32,767.

Therefore 32,767 positive and 32,767 negative numbers can be represented. Zero, of course, can also be represented for a total range of 65,535 different numbers. There are two representations for 0; a positive 0 (all 0s) and a negative 0 (an MSB or sign bit of 1 followed by all 0s).

Some computers use sign-magnitude representation. The vast majority, however, use the *2s complement* method of representing numbers. It does not have the double representation of 0, and has other advantages that will soon become clear.

2-7.1
2s Complement Numbers
As in sign-magnitude representation, the *MSB of a 2s complement number denotes the sign* (0 means the number is positive, 1 means the number is negative), but *the MSB is also a part of the number*. In 2s complement notation, positive numbers are represented as simple binary numbers with the restriction that the MSB is 0. Negative numbers are somewhat different. To obtain the representation of a negative number, use the following algorithm:

1. Represent the number as a positive binary number.
2. Complement it (write 0s where there are 1s and 1s where there are 0s in the positive number).
3. Add 1.
4. Ignore any carries out of the MSB.

Example 2-12

Given 8-bit words find the 2s complement representation of:

  a. 25
  b. -25
  c. -1

Solution

a. The number $+25$ can be written as 11001. Since 8 bits are available, there is room for three leading 0s, making the MSB 0.

$+25 = 00011001$

b. To find -25, complement $+25$ and add 1.

$$\begin{array}{r} +25 = 00011001 \\ \overline{(+25)} = 11100110 \\ +\ 1 \\ \hline -25 = 11100111 \end{array}$$

Note that the MSB is 1.

c. To write -1, take the 2s complement of $+1$.

$$\begin{array}{r} +\ 1 = 00000001 \\ \overline{(+1)} = 11111110 \\ +\ 1 \\ \hline -\ 1 = 11111111 \end{array}$$

From this example, we see that a solid string of 1s represents the number -1 in 2s complement form.

To determine the magnitude of any unknown negative number, simply take its 2s complement as described above. The result is a positive number whose *magnitude equals that of the original number*.

Example 2-13

What decimal number does 11110100 represent?

Solution

Complementing the given number, we obtain:

$$\begin{array}{r} 00001011 \\ \text{Adding 1} \qquad +\ 1 \\ \hline 00001100 \end{array}$$

This is the equivalent of $+12$. Therefore, **11110100 = -12**.

2-7.2
The Range of 2s Complement Numbers

The *maximum positive* number that can be represented in 2s complement form is a single 0 followed by all 1s, or $2^{n-1} - 1$ for an n-bit number. The *most negative* number that can be represented has an MSB of 1 followed by all 0s, which equals -2^{n-1}. Therefore, an n-bit number can represent any one of $2^{n-1} - 1$ positive numbers, plus 2^{n-1} negative numbers, plus 0 which is 2^n total numbers. Every number has a *unique* representation.

Other features of 2s complement arithmetic are:

1. Even numbers (positive or negative) have an LSB of 0.
2. Numbers divisible by 4 have the two LSBs equal to 0 (see Example 2-13).
3. In general, numbers divisible by 2^n have n LSBs of 0.

Example 2-14

What range of numbers can be represented by an 8-bit word (a byte) using 2s complement representation?

Solution

The most positive is 01111111 = 127.

The most negative number in 8 bits is 10000000 = -128.

Therefore, any number between $+127$ and -128 can be represented by an 8-bit number in 2s complement form. There are 256 numbers in this range, as expected, since $2^8 = 256$. Note also that the 7 LSBs of -128 are 0, as required, since -128 is divisible by 2^7.

2-7.3
Adding 2s Complement Numbers

Consider the simple equation $C = A$ plus B. While it seems clear enough, we cannot immediately determine whether an addition or subtraction operation is required. If A and B are both positive, addition is required. But if one of the operands is negative and the other is positive, a subtraction operation must be performed.

The major advantage of 2s complement arithmetic is:

If an addition operation is to be performed, the numbers are added regardless of their signs. The answer is in 2s complement form with the correct sign. Any carries out of the MSB are meaningless and should be ignored.

Example 2-15

Express the numbers 19 and -11 as 8-bit, 2s complement numbers, and add them.

Solution

The number $+19$ is simply 00010011. To find -11, take the 2s complement of 11.

$$11 = 00001011$$
$$(\overline{11}) = 11110100$$
$$-11 = 11110101$$

Now $+19$ plus (-11) equals:

```
  1111 111              Carry
  00010011                 19
+ 11110101               - 11
  00001000               + 8
```

Note that there is a carry out of the MSB that is ignored. The 8-bit answer is simply the number $+8$.

Example 2-16
Add -11 and -19.

Solution
First -19 must be expressed as a 2s complement number:

$$19 = 00010011$$
$$(\overline{19}) = 11101100$$
$$-19 = 11101101$$

Now the numbers can be added:

```
    1     111111 1      Carry
 (-19)    11101101
+(-11)    11110101
          11100010      Answer (-30)
```

Again, a carry out of the MSB has been ignored.

**2-7.4
Subtraction of Binary Numbers** Subtraction of binary numbers in 2s complement form is also very simple and straightforward. The *2s complement of the subtrahend is taken and added to the minuend.* This is essentially subtraction by changing the sign and adding. As in addition, the signs of the operands and carries out of the MSB are ignored.

Example 2-17
Subtract 30 from 53. Use 8-bit numbers.

Solution
Note 30 is the subtrahend and 53 the minuend.

$$53 = 00110101 \quad \text{(minuend)}$$
$$30 = 00011110 \quad \text{(subtrahend)}$$

Taking the 2s complement of 30 and adding, we obtain:

$$(\overline{30}) = 11100001$$
$$-30 = 11100010$$
$$+53 = 00110101$$
$$\overline{}\ 00010111 = 23$$

Example 2-18
Subtract -30 from -19.

Solution

Here $-19 =$ 11101101 (See Example 2-16.)
$-30 =$ 11100010 (subtrahend)

Note: -30 is the subtrahend. 2s complementing -30 gives $+30$ or 00011110.

$$
\begin{array}{rl}
-19 & 11101101 \\
+30 & \underline{00011110} \\
& \mathbf{00001011} \quad = \; +11
\end{array}
$$

The carry out of the MSB is ignored and the answer, $+11$, is correct.

2-8 **Logical Operations**	Besides addition and subtraction, computers must be able to execute a variety of *logical* instructions. These logical operations are performed between words or bytes, on a bit-by-bit basis. There is no interaction (such as borrows or carries) between the bits.
2-8.1 **The Logical OR Operation**	*If two words are ORed together, the result, or output word, has a 1 in each bit position where either or both of the input words had a 1.* The logical OR of two operands, A and B, is expressed as $A + B$. Note that this is different from A *plus* B, which means the arithmetic *sum* of A and B.

Example 2-19
Given two words, $A = 10111001$ and $B = 11011010$, find $A + B$.

Solution
The words are lined up as follows:

Bit Position	**7 6 5 4 3 2 1 0**
A	1 0 1 1 1 0 0 1
B	1 1 0 1 1 0 1 0
$A + B$	**1 1 1 1 1 0 1 1**

For all bit positions except position 2, either word A or word B, or both, contain a 1. Therefore the logical OR $(A + B)$ results in a 1 in all bit positions except position 2.

2-8.2 **The Logical AND Operation**	*When two words are ANDed, the output word is a 1 only in those bit positions where both input words are 1.* Since the operation is analogous to multiplication, $Y = AB$ means that Y is logical AND of words A and B.

Example 2-20

If the two words of Example 2-19 are ANDed, what is the output word?

Solution

The words are ANDed bit-by-bit:

Bit Position	7 6 5 4 3 2 1 0
A	1 0 1 1 1 0 0 1
B	1 1 0 1 1 0 1 0
AB	**1 0 0 1 1 0 0 0**

A and B are both 1 only in bit positions 3, 4, and 7 as the answer shows.

2-8.3
The EXCLUSIVE OR Operation
Another logical operation that has many uses (parity checking is one example), is the *EXCLUSIVE OR* (XOR) operation. The symbol for the XOR operation is $\oplus$. If two words are XORed, the bits of the output word are a 1 if *either, but not both,* of the corresponding bits of the input words are 1.

Example 2-21

Find the XOR of words A and B of Example 2-19.

Solution

The words are XORed on a bit-by-bit basis.

Bit Position	7 6 5 4 3 2 1 0
A	1 0 1 1 1 0 0 1
B	1 1 0 1 1 0 1 0
$A \oplus B$	**0 1 1 0 0 0 1 1**

The output word is seen to be 1 wherever exactly one of the input words contain a 1.

2-8.4
Complementation
The *complement* of a word is obtained simply by *inverting each bit of the word.* Because complementation is often used in computer arithmetic, most microprocessors contain a complementation instruction.

Example 2-22

Complement word A of Example 2-19.

Solution

Complementation is obtained simply by changing each bit of the word.

$$A = 10111001$$
$$\overline{A} \text{ (the complement of } A) = 01000110$$

**2-9
Summary**

In this chapter, basic binary arithmetic used in computers was introduced. The binary number system was explained and examples of binary addition, binary subtraction, and binary-to-decimal conversion were presented.

The 2s complement system, used in most computers, was then introduced and arithmetic examples in this system were presented. The organization of a computer word and the basic computer logic operations were also explained.

**2-10
Glossary**

Alphanumeric character A character that may be either an alphabetic, numeric, or a punctuation character.

Analog quantity A continuously variable quantity; one that may assume any value usually within a limited range.

Binary system A number system with 2 as the base.

Bit A single digital quantity; a 1 or a 0.

Byte A group of 8 bits.

Complementation The process of taking the difference between a given number and an input number.

Digital quantity A variable that has one of two possible values.

Integrated circuit (IC) A small electronic package usually containing several circuits.

LSB Least significant bit.

MSB Most significant bit.

2s complement A representation of numbers where negative numbers are obtained by complementing their equivalent and adding 1.

Word A group of bits that constitute the basic unit of information within a computer.

**2-11
References**

Barna, Arpad, and Dan I. Porat, *Integrated Circuits in Digital Electronics,* Wiley, New York, 1973.

Hill, Frederick J., and Gerald R. Peterson, *Introduction to Switching Theory and Logical Design,* Second Edition, Wiley, New York, 1974.

Kostopoulos, George K., *Digital Engineering,* Wiley, New York, 1975.

Nashelsky, Louis, *Introduction to Digital Computer Technology,* Second Edition, Wiley, New York, 1977.

**2-12
Problems**

2-1 How many bits are required to distinguish between 100 different things?

2-2 A major league baseball teams plays 162 games a year. Before the season starts, how many bits must be reserved to express the number of games the team will win and how many bits to express the number of games the team will lose?

2-3 A line printer is capable of printing 132 characters on a single line and each character is 1 of 64 symbols (26 alphabetics plus 10 numbers plus punctuation). How many bits are needed to print an entire line?

2-4 Express the following decimal numbers as a sum.
a. 4,507
b. 137,659
c. 8,897,061

2-5 Convert the following binary numbers to decimal.
a. 10111
b. 110101
c. 110001011

2-6 Convert the following decimal numbers to binary.
a. 66
b. 252
c. 5795
d. 106,503

2-7 For each of the following pairs of numbers, find $A + B$ and $A - B$, completing the third and fourth columns below:

	A	B	$A + B$	$A - B$
a.	11011	1001		
b.	111001	101010		
c.	111000111	100101		
d.	101111011	1000101		

2-8 Find $A + B$ and $A - B$ by converting each number to binary and doing the additions and subtractions in binary. Check the results by converting back to decimal.

	A	B	$A + B$	$A - B$
a.	67	39		
b.	145	78		
c.	31,564	26,797		

2-9 A PDP-11 is a minicomputer with a 16-bit word length. What range of numbers can a single word contain?

2-10 How high can you count using only your fingers?

2-11 Find the 8-bit 2s complement of the following numbers.
a. 99
b. −7
c. − 102

2-12 Determine by inspection which of the following 2s complement numbers are divisible by 4.
   a. 11011010
   b. 10011100
   c. 01111000
   d. 00001010
   e. 01000001
   f. 01010100

2-13 A PDP-8 is a computer with a 12-bit word length that uses 2s complement arithmetic. What range of numbers can be expressed by a single PDP-8 word?

2-14 Express each of the following numbers in 9-bit, 2s complement form and add them.

   a.   85   **c.**   −85
              + 37   +37

   b.   85   **d.**   −85
          +(−37)   +(−37)

2-15 Do the following subtractions after expressing the operands in 10-bit, 2s complement notation.

   a.   36   **c.**   −450
         −(23)   −(−460)

   b.   835   **d.**   316
       −(214)   −(−579)

2-16 A number in 2s complement form can be inverted by subtracting it from −1. Invert 25 using this procedure and 8-bit numbers.

2-17 Given two bytes:
   $A = 10001101$
   $B = 01001011$
   Find:
   $A + B$
   AB
   $A \oplus B$
   $\overline{A}$
   $\overline{B}$

    After attempting to solve the problems, try to answer the self-evaluation questions in Sec. 2-2. If any of them still seem difficult, review the appropriate sections of the chapter to find the answers.

Chapter 3

**The
Basic
Computer**

**3-1
Instructional Objectives**

The basic principles of operation of a microprocessor are identical to those that control the operation of any larger computer. In this chapter we discuss the basic parts of a rudimentary computer, and how they work together to execute a simple program.

After reading this chapter, the student should be able to:

1. List each basic part of a computer and describe its functions.
2. Explain the steps involved in reading or writing a memory word.
3. Determine the result of a *shift* or *rotate* instruction.
4. List the registers and flip-flops required by the control section of a computer and explain their operation.

**3-2
Self-Evaluation Questions**

Watch for the answers to the following questions as you read the chapter. They should help you understand the material presented.

1. What are the MAR and MDR? What is their function?
2. Are the contents of a memory location changed when it is written? When it is read?
3. What is the difference between a ROM and a RAM? State an advantage of each.
4. What is the advantage of a PROM over a ROM? When would each be used?
5. What is the PC? Why is it incremented during each instruction?
6. Is there any distinction between data and instructions when they are in memory? How does the computer tell the difference?

**3-3
Introduction to the Computer**

A computer consists of four basic parts, as shown in Fig. 3-1.

1. The memory
2. The arithmetic-logic unit (ALU)
3. The input-output system
4. The control unit

The *memory* is an indispensable part of a computer. It contains the *data* used in a program as well as the *instructions* for executing the program. A *program* is a group of instructions telling the com-

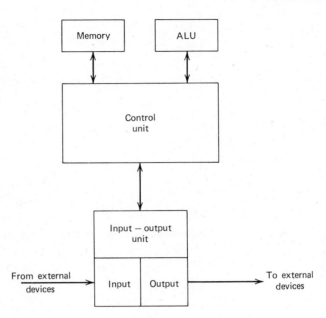

Figure 3-1 Block diagram of a basic computer.

puter what to do with the data. An extremely simple program might instruct the computer to add two numbers in its data area; another program might command the computer to subtract the same numbers. Obviously, completely different results can be obtained from the same data by applying different programs.

The *arithmetic-logic unit* (ALU) is the part of the computer that performs those arithmetic or logic operations required by the routine or program, and generates the status bits (condition codes) that are the heart of the decision-making capabilities of any computer.

The *input-output system* controls communication between the computer and its external devices. The computer must receive data and status information from external devices such as sensors, A/D (analog-to-digital) converters, or disc or tape units. It must also produce outputs that depend on its program and the data it receives. If the computer is solving a problem, the output is usually a printout of the results. In this case it must issue commands to a printer to cause the results to be printed for the user to read. If the function of the computer is to control a physical process, however, its output will be electronic pulses that are translated into *commands* (open a valve, reduce the air flow, etc.) to regulate a process.

The *control unit* consists of a group of flip-flops (FFs) and registers that regulate the operation of the computer itself. The function of the control unit is to cause the proper sequence of events to occur during the execution of each computer instruction.

In this chapter the construction and operation of the ALU, memory, and control unit are described in detail for a rudimentary computer. A discussion of the input-output system is found in Chapter 9.

3-4
The Memory

Even the smallest minicomputer or microprocessor system requires a memory of several thousand bits to store its programs and data. Large-scale memories for computers are constructed of magnetic cores or integrated circuit flip-flops. A flip-flop (FF) is an electronic circuit that can be placed in one of two states (SET or RESET), and remains there until commanded to change states. Thus a single FF functions as a one-bit memory. It remembers whether it was last SET or RESET.

Many FFs (presently up to 65,536) can be placed within a single IC. These ICs constitute one type of *semiconductor memory* (static) and are available from many manufacturers (see Sec. 3-5).

3-4.1
Memory Concepts

The binary bits of a block of memory can be organized in various ways. It is usual for most computers to be arranged so that the bits are grouped into *words* of 4, 8, or 16 bits each. In most present-day microcomputers, such as the **6800**, an 8-bit word length (or byte) is used. Modern computers are *word oriented* in that they transfer one byte (or word) at a time by means of the data bus. This bus, the internal computer registers, and the ALU (arithmetic logic unit) are *parallel* devices that handle all the bits of a word *at the same time*. The memory can be thought of as a post office box arrangement with each location containing a word. The boxes are set up in an orderly sequence so that they can be addressed easily. Each instruction or data word is *written* into a specific location in memory (a word at a selected address) *when it must be preserved* for future use, and read at a later time *when the information is needed*. During the interval between writing and reading, other information may be stored or read at other locations.

Microprocessor instructions require 1, 2, or 3 bytes (or words) and typical routines include 5 to 50 instructions. Since IC memories are physically small and relatively inexpensive, they can include thousands of words and thereby provide very comprehensive computer programs.

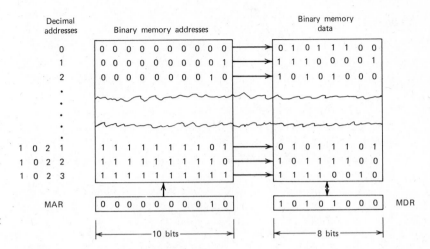

Figure 3-2 A typical 1024 word by 8-bit memory.

A typical microcomputer memory size is 1K to 4K words. Unlike standard engineering terminology, where K is an abbreviation for kilo, or 1000, $K = 2^{10}$ or 1024 when applied to memories. This value of K is used because normal memory design leads to sizes that are even powers of 2.

Each word in memory has *two parameters*; its *address,* which locates it within memory, and the *data,* which is stored at that location. The process of accessing the contents of the memory locations requires two registers, one associated with address and one with data. The MEMORY ADDRESS REGISTER (MAR) holds the *address of the word currently being accessed,* and the MEMORY DATA REGISTER (MDR) holds the *data being written into or read out of the addressed memory location*. These registers can be considered part of the memory or of the control unit (see Sec. 3-7).

A block diagram of a typical 1K word by 8-bit IC RAM memory is shown in Fig. 3-2. The address information in the MAR selects 1 of the 1024 words in memory.

Example 3-1

The 1K by 8-bit memory of Fig. 3-2 is used as part of a μP system with a 16-bit address bus. Find:

a. How many bits are required to address all locations in this IC?
b. How many address bits are used for the whole μP system?
c. How many bits are required in the MDR?
d. How many data bits are contained in this memory IC?

Solution

a. A memory specification of $1K \times 8$ means 1024 (2^{10}) words of 8 bits each. The MAR must hold an address value between 0 to 1023 (1024 total locations) to select any word in this IC. Thus, 10 bits are needed to address the memory.

b. The μP uses 16 address lines (or bits in the MAR). Since 10 are used to select the locations in this memory IC, the other 6 are available to select other ICs.

c. Each memory location contains 8 bits. Consequently, the MDR must be 8 bits long to accommodate one data word.

d. A $1K \times 8$ memory contains 2^{10} words times 2^3 (8) bits per word = 2^{13} or 8192 bits. For a microcomputer, this is a relatively small memory and several such ICs would typically be used.

In Fig. 3-2 the MAR is shown to contain address 2 and the MDR register contains the value that is in that location.

3-4.2
Reading Memory

Memories operate in two basic modes: READ or WRITE. A memory is read when the information at a particular address is required by the system. To *read* a memory:

1. The location to be read is loaded into the MAR.
2. A READ command is given.
3. The data is transferred from the addressed word in memory to the MDR, where it is accessible to the system.

Normally, *the word being read must not be altered by the READ operation,* so the word in a particular location can be *read many times.* The process of reading a location without changing it is called *nondestructive readout.*

3-4.3
Writing Memory

A memory location is written when the data must be preserved for future use. In the process of writing, the previous information in the specified location is *destroyed* (overwritten). To write into a memory:

1. The address (the memory location where the data is to be written) is loaded into the MAR.
2. The data to be written is loaded into the MDR.
3. The WRITE command is then given (by means of the READ/WRITE line), which transfers the data from the MDR to the selected memory location.

3-5
Semiconductor Memories

Microcomputers use memories built of semiconductor ICs. These are packaged in a dual-in-line package (DIP) as is the μP and the rest of the components in the system.

Most μCs use at least some RAM memory. Literally speaking, the term RAM means *Random Access Memory,* but it generally means a Read/Write memory, a memory that can both be *read* and *written into.*

Semiconductor RAMs are built primarily of MOS gates and store their information in FFs or capacitors within the IC. These two implementations are designated as *static* or *dynamic.* Static RAMs use FFs and are the simplest to understand and use, but require more circuitry on the chip for each cell (bit). Dynamic memories use capacitors to store their information and require constant clocking (pulsing) to refresh them. Because of the simpler geometry, however, they can contain significantly more memory in a given size. Both of these types are said to be *volatile,* since the circuits lose their information whenever power is turned OFF or inadvertently fails. To overcome this drawback, well developed μP programs are written in ROMs (read only memories) or PROMs (programmable ROMs) which are *nonvolatile.*

In most μPs, the memory consists of two parts with different memory addresses, a *ROM area* used to hold the *program, constant data,* and *tables,* and a *RAM area,* used to hold *variable data.* Generally, the data on which the program operates must be rewritten every time the system is started again (restarted), and the system must always be restarted (going through a start-up procedure) after any power failure occurs. This is not a severe drawback because data is usually invalid after a power failure. Fortunately, the program, if it is contained in ROM, can be restarted immediately because a power failure does not affect a ROM. The internal structure of the FFs and gates comprising a memory are not considered in this book. Instead, we concentrate on the input/output (I/O) characteristics that must be understood if one is to use a memory.

3-5.1
Interfacing with a RAM Memory

A semiconductor RAM normally has pins for the following inputs and outputs.

1. m output bits
2. m input bits
3. n address bits (for 2^n words)
4. READ/WRITE input
5. CHIP SELECT or ENABLE input

To read a location in a static semiconductor memory, the READ/ WRITE line is set to the READ level. The memory chip is then *selected* or *enabled*. The memory contents at the addressed location are transferred to the output, and continue to be present until the address, READ/WRITE line or CHIP SELECT signals change. Reading is *nondestructive* (it does not change the information in the memory cells); the state of the internal memory cells at the selected address is simply brought to the outputs.

Writing into a memory requires that the address of the desired location be in the MAR and the data be in the MDR prior to the enabling of the memory. These registers (MAR and MDR) are connected to the memories by means of bus lines. When the READ/ WRITE line is switched to WRITE and the memory is enabled, the data on the bus lines is entered into the memory at the addressed location. The data on the input lines is then entered into the memory at the addressed location. One must be careful about changing the input data while in WRITE mode. Any change of data is gated into the memory and overwrites the previous contents of the memory, which are lost.

The CHIP SELECT or ENABLE inputs are used to turn the memory ON or OFF and, more importantly, to disconnect it from the bus. This allows the μP designer to multiplex several memory or I/O devices onto a common bus.

Example 3-2

The **MC6810** is the RAM usually used in **6800** μCs. It is a 1024-bit memory organized as 128 bytes (128 words by 8 bits). What input and output lines are required?

Solution

This memory requires:

1. 7 address bits to select 1 of 128 words.
2. 8 data input lines, one for each bit of the word.
3. 8 data output lines, one for each bit of the word.
4. 1 Read/Write line.
5. 1 CHIP SELECT or ENABLE.
6. Power and ground.

Actually the **6810** has 6 CHIP SELECT lines to make decoding easier, and the data input and output lines are on a common bidirectional data bus. Details of the **6810** are given in Sec. 8-8.

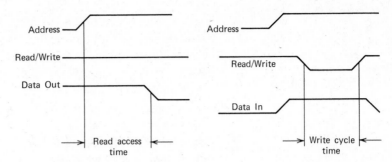

Figure 3-3 Memory timing.
(a) Read cycle
(b) Write cycle

3-5.2
Memory Timing

For high speed systems, memory timing is very important. A READ cycle is limited by the access time of a memory, and a WRITE cycle is limited by the cycle time.[1]

Access time is the time required for the memory to present valid data after the address and select signals are firm. *Cycle time* or WRITE time is the length of time the address and data must be held constant in order to write the memory.

Access time and cycle time are illustrated in Fig. 3-3. Similar figures with specific times are supplied by the manufacturers of IC memories.

Figure 3-3*a* shows the normal situation where the memory is constantly in READ mode. The output data will change in response to an address change and the time for this response, the access time, is clearly visible.

Figure 3-3*b* shows the WRITE cycle. Note that the address and data are firm before the WRITE pulse occurs on the R/W line and do not change while the memory is in WRITE mode. This is necessary to prevent spurious writes that could enter unwanted information into the memory.

3-5.3
Read-Only Memories (ROMs)

As its name implies, a *read-only memory* is read but not written into during the course of computer operation. Data is *permanently written* into a ROM when it is manufactured. Usually μP users write their programs into ROM because it is permanent and nonvolatile. With its program in ROM, a μP can be restarted after a power failure with no need to reload or bootstrap its program.

The most popular manufacturing process involves generating a special mask from the user's program with which to make the chips.

[1]A more complete discussion of memory timing is given in Leucke, Mize, and Carr, *Semiconductor Memory Design and Application*, Sec. 9-3, McGraw-Hill, 1973.

This is economically feasible only when a production run of a thousand or more ROMs are manufactured.

The operation of a ROM is identical to the READ mode of a RAM; the user supplies an address and the ROM provides the data output of the word prewritten at that address. As with RAMs, ROMs are organized on an n word by m bit basis. Supplying the proper address results in an m bit output. Access time for a ROM is the time between the setting of the address input and the appearance of the resulting data word on the output pins.

Example 3-3

A memory has dimensions of 8K words by 8 bits. What input and output lines are required if the memory is:

  a. a RAM?
  b. a ROM?

Solution

  a. A RAM of this size requires:
    1. 8 data input bits
    2. 8 data output bits
    3. 13 address bits ($2^{13} = 8192$)
    4. A READ/WRITE line
  b. An 8K by 8 ROM requires:
    1. 8 data output bits
    2. 13 address bits

Since a ROM cannot be written into, the data input and READ/WRITE lines are not required.

Programs for μPs are generally developed using RAMs or PROMs (see Sec. 3-5.5), because programs are changed many times during development and debugging. Once their programs are fully developed and not expected to change, users may order a custom built ROM from a manufacturer. They must supply the manufacturer of the ROM with the code they wish each word to contain. The manufacturer then builds a mask that is used to produce the ROM. Because of the custom programming involved, a mask costs about $1000. Users should be sure of their inputs before they incur the masking charge, because the ROM is normally useless if a single bit is wrong. Once the mask is made, identical ROMs can be produced inexpensively.

3-5.4
Programmable Read Only
Memories

Programmable read only memories (PROMs) are designed to be programmed by the users at their facility, instead of being programmed by the manufacturer. Most of these PROMs come with all outputs at 0. By following the programming procedure specified by the manufacturer, users can change bits at selected locations to a 1. Often this is done by driving high current through the IC that opens fusible links. Each open link provides a 1 instead of a 0 output. Thus users must open a link for a 1 in every location of their programs. Again, a mistake may cause the PROM to be useless. A 0 can always be changed to a 1, but a 1 cannot be changed back to a 0. If only a small quantity of identical ROMs is required, it is less expensive to use fusible link PROMs than a custom-masked ROM.

3-5.5
Erasable PROMs

Some PROMs can be *erased* and *reprogrammed* in the field if users have the proper equipment. The **1702A**, or **2708**, manufactured by Intel, Inc., or the **MC68708** made by Motorola, can be erased by exposing them to ultraviolet light. Because these are erasable and reprogrammable, they are very popular for developing programs for μPs, where programming mistakes are common, or changes in program occur frequently.

3-6
The Arithmetic Logic Unit
(ALU)

The ALU performs all the arithmetic and logical operations required by the computer. It accepts two operands as inputs (each operand contains as many bits as the basic word length of the computer) and performs the required arithmetic or logical operation upon them. ALUs are readily available as ICs (the **74181** is an ALU that provides for a variety of operations on two 4-bit operands), but μPs contain their ALUs within the μP chip.

Most ALUs perform the following arithmetic or logical operations.

1. Addition
2. Subtraction
3. Logical OR
4. Logical AND
5. EXCLUSIVE OR
6. Complementation
7. Shifting

In the **6800** a 6-bit Condition Code Register is also associated with the ALU. The Condition Code Register is discussed in Sec. 5-6.

Computers are capable of performing more sophisticated arithmetic operations such as multiplication, division, extracting square roots, and taking trigonometric functions; however, in most computers these operations are performed as *software subroutines*. A multiplication command, for example, is translated by the appropriate subroutine into a series of add and shift operations that can be performed by the ALU. A multiplication subroutine is written in Sec. 6-6.

3-6.1
The Shift Operation

The ALU used in the **6800** is a 2s complement 8-bit parallel register that performs the arithmetic and logic operations described in Chapter 2. It also performs shift and rotate operations. The ASL (arithmetic shift left), ASR (arithmetic shift right), and LSR (logical shift right) instructions are shown in Fig. 3-4. Note that the Carry FF that is part of the condition code register (see Sec. 5-6.2) is used in the shift operations.

In the ASL operation, the MSB is shifted out of the data word and into the Carry FF. The LSB is filled with a 0.

The ASR operation shifts each bit to the right and moves the LSB into the Carry FF. The MSB, however, is retained and also shifted into bit 6. If the bits in the register are considered as a 2s complement number, this method of shifting *preserves the sign of the number*. The ASR is equivalent to dividing the number in the register by 2, regardless of the sign of the number.

Figure 3-4 The **6800** shift instructions.
(a) Arithmetic Shift Left (ASL)
(b) Arithmetic Shift Right (ASR)
(c) Logical Shift Right

The LSR operation simply shifts each bit one position to the right. The MSB becomes a 0 and the LSB goes into the Carry FF.

Bit positions

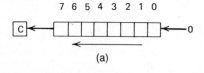 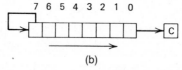 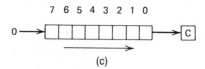

| (a) | (b) | (c) |

Example 3-4

An 8-bit word contains the bit pattern 10011010 (Hexidecimal 9A).

  a. What is the contents of the word after two shifts to the right (ASR, ASR)?

  b. What is its contents after 3 arithmetic shifts to the left (ASL, ASL, ASL)?

  c. What is its contents after 2 logic shifts to the right (LSR, LSR)?

Solution

a. Here every bit is moved 2 places to the right, except bit 7. Since the rightmost bits are shifted through the carry register, bit 0 is lost and bit 1 becomes the carry bit. After execution of these two instructions, the word is:

$$11100110$$

Note that bits 7, 6, and 5 are 1s because bit 7 was originally 1.

b. The bits are shifted 3 positions to the left and the two most significant bits are lost. Since bit 5 was 0, the carry is now 0. The least significant bit positions are filled with 0s; the word is now:

$$11010000$$

c. After two LSRs the word becomes:

$$00100110$$

and the carry bit is a 1. Note that 0s are shifted into the MSBs in an LSR.

Example 3-5

a. If the number in an accumulator is 50, show that an ASR is equivalent to a division by 2.
b. Repeat for -50.

Solution

a. Since $+50 = 00110010$, an ASR causes the accumulator to become 00011001, or $+25$.

b. Since $-50 = 11001110$, an ASR causes the accumulator to become 11100111, or -25. Again, division by 2 has occurred. This would not have been so if a 0 had been shifted into bit 7, instead of a 1.

3-6.2
Rotations

Two additional shifting instructions are ROL (rotate left) and ROR (rotate right), shown in Fig. 3-5. These are special forms of circular shifting where the bits coming off one end of the word are inserted into the Carry FF, while the contents of the Carry FF are transferred into the vacated bit position.

Bit position

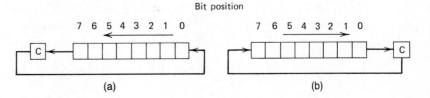

Figure 3-5 The **6800** Rotate instructions.
(a) Rotate Left (ROL)
(b) Rotate Right (ROR)

(a)   (b)

Example 3-6
If a computer word is 11011100, what is it after the following commands?

a. Rotate right three times (ROR, ROR, ROR). Assume the Carry FF is CLEAR.

b. Rotate left twice (ROL, ROL). Assume the Carry FF is SET.

Solution
a. In response to three ROR instructions, the three LSBs are moved through the Carry FF to the other end of the word. The word becomes

00011011

and the Carry FF contains the 1 that was originally in bit 2.

b. In rotating left twice, the carry now contains the original bit 6 (1) and the 1 that was bit 7 is now the LSB of the word. The result is

01110011

The 1 that was originally in the Carry FF has been shifted through bit 0 and appears in bit 1 of the result.

There are many uses for ROTATE instructions. One application is to determine the *parity* of a byte. If the bits of the byte are successively shifted into the carry FF, the number of 1s in the byte can be counted and its parity can be determined.

**3-7
The Control Section**

The function of the *control section* is to regulate the operation of the computer. It decodes the instructions and causes the proper events to occur in the correct order.

The control section of a computer consists of a group of registers and FFs and the timing circuitry necessary to make them operate properly. In a rudimentary computer the following registers might be part of the control section.

1. **The MAR and MDR.**
2. **The program counter (PC).** This is a register that contains as many bits as the MAR. *It holds the memory address of the next instruction word to be executed.* It is usually *incremented* during the execution of an instruction so that it contains the address of the next instruction to be executed.
3. **The instruction register.** This register holds the instruction while it is in the process of being executed.
4. **The instruction decoder.** This decodes the instruction presently being executed. Its inputs come from the instruction register.
5. **The accumulator.** The accumulator is a register containing as many bits as the MDR. It contains the basic operand used in each instruction. In

ALU operations where two operands are required, one of the operands is stored in the accumulator as a result of previous instructions. The other operand is generally read from memory. The two operands form the inputs to the ALU and the result is normally sent back to the accumulator.

3-7.1
Control Unit FFs

A FF is an electronic circuit that can function as a 1-bit memory. A FF can be set into the 1 or 0 state and remain there until another command causes it to change states. Large computer memories are frequently made up of many thousands of integrated circuit FFs.

Individual FFs are used where small quantities of data (several bits) must be remembered and changed frequently.

The control unit usually contains several FFs. The flags or condition codes (see Chapter 5) are FFs. Most μPs also have FETCH and EXECUTE FFs.

The FETCH and EXECUTE FFs determine the state of the computer. The instructions are contained in the computer's memory. *The computer starts by FETCHing the instruction.* This is the FETCH portion of the computer's cycle. *It then EXECUTES, or performs, the instruction.* At this time, the computer is in EXECUTE mode. When it has finished executing the instruction, it returns to FETCH mode and reads the next instruction from memory. Thus *the computer alternates between FETCH and EXECUTE modes* and the FETCH and EXECUTE FFs determine its current mode of operation.

3-8
Execution of a
Simple Routine

A μP starts to execute instructions by fetching the byte at the address contained in the PC. Most μPs use this first byte as an 8-bit OP code (short for operations code). The OP code tells the μP what to do (what instruction to execute). Since μPs have an 8-bit OP code, they can execute up to 256 different instructions.

In most cases the μP then executes a second fetch cycle[2] to get the address required by the instruction. It then has both the OP code and the address and can execute the instruction. When execution is complete the μP proceeds to execute the next instruction. The **6800** μP has no HALT instruction as such. Once started it continues to execute instructions until it is halted by an external signal. An instruction can also be used to halt the μP (see Chapter 6), but this

---

[2]The number of bytes and cycles required for each instruction depends upon the instruction itself and the mode of the instruction. This is discussed thoroughly in Chapter 5.

instruction does not truly stop the computer; it reexecutes itself over and over again.

As a simple example, let us consider what a μP must do to add two numbers. Before starting the μP, both the numbers to be added and the program must be written into memory. Suppose we are trying to add the numbers 2 and 3. We can arbitrarily set aside location 80 to hold the number 2 and location 81 to hold the number 3. Location 82 is also set aside to hold the result.

The program, or set of instructions, required to add the numbers might be this:

LOAD 80	First instruction
ADD 81	Second instruction
STORE 82	Third instruction

The first instruction LOADs or takes the contents of location 80 (2 in this example) and stores it into the accumulator. Note that it leaves the contents of 80 unchanged.

The second instruction reads the contents of 81 (3) and adds it to the accumulator, which contains a 2 because of the first instruction. The sum, 5, is then placed in the accumulator.

The third instruction causes the contents of the accumulator to be written to memory. Thus, 5 is written into location 82 and the program is complete.

This section describes how the registers and ALU within the μP are coordinated and work together to execute the above program. The instructions must reside at specific locations in memory. Let us assume that location 10 is set aside for the start of the program. Thus, location 10 contains the LOAD, location 11 contains 80, location 12 contains the ADD instruction, etc. The contents of the registers and memory are shown in Fig. 3-6.

Before starting execution, the starting address of the program (10 in this example) must be written into the PC. Program execution then proceeds as follows.

1. The 10 is transferred from the PC to the MAR and the memory is read at location 10.

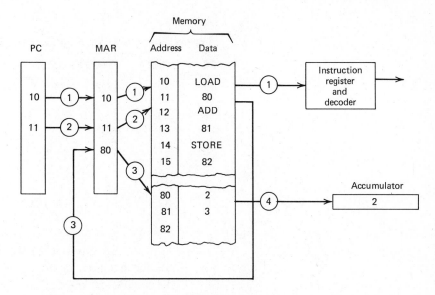

Figure 3-6 Execution of a Load instruction of a rudimentary μP.

2. Since this is the first part of the FETCH cycle, the data read is placed in the instruction register and the instruction decoder determines that it is a LOAD instruction. Note that the μP cannot actually read the word LOAD in location 10. It reads a byte of 1s and 0s that are decoded as a LOAD command.

3. The μP then increments the PC and MAR and reads the contents of 11 (80), which it places in the MAR.

4. The μP is now ready to execute the LOAD instruction. It does so by reading the contents of 80, which is already in the MAR, and placing it in the accumulator. The accumulator now contains the contents of 80 (the number 2).

5. The instruction execution is now finished and the FETCH mode for the next instruction is entered. The PC is again incremented to 12 and placed in the MAR.

6. The code for ADD is fetched from location 12 and decoded.

7. The PC is again incremented and 81 is read from memory and placed in the MAR.

8. The execute portion of the ADD instruction is entered. The contents of 81 (3) are read and added to the contents of the accumulator. This uses the ALU within the μP. The results (5) are written to the accumulator and the ADD instruction is complete.

9. The PC is again incremented and transferred to the MAR. The OP code for the STORE instruction is fetched and decoded.

10. The address for the store instruction (82) is fetched from location 15 and placed in the MAR.

11. The store instruction is now executed by taking the contents of the accumulator (5) and writing them to memory at location 82.

Table 3-1

Register Changes as the Example of Sec. 3-8.2 Progresses

PC	MAR	MEMORY DATA	ACCUMULATOR	
10	10	LOAD	X	LOAD instruction
11	11	80	X	
11	80	2	2	
12	12	ADD	2	ADD instruction
13	13	81	2	
13	81	3	5	
14	14	STORE	5	STORE instruction
15	15	82	5	
15	82	5	5	

The hardware execution of the LOAD instruction is shown in Fig. 3-6, where the numbers in the circles indicate the step number. In Step 1 the contents of the PC (10) are transferred to the MAR and the LOAD OP code is read from memory to the instruction register and decoded. The PC is then incremented (Step 2), sent to the MAR and 80 is read. In Step 3 the 80 is transferred to the MAR and the number 2 is read, which is sent to the accumulator in Step 4. Thus, LOAD 80 placed the contents of location 80 in the accumulator.

Table 3-1 shows the contents of the registers at each step in the program. It correlates with the outline description of the program's progress.

**3-9
Summary**

In this chapter, the operation of a basic computer was described. First the major parts of the computer were listed and the function of each was explained briefly. In subsequent paragraphs, the operation of the memory, ALU, and control sections were described in detail. Particular attention was paid to the μP execution of shift and rotate instructions.

Finally an example of the execution of a simple program was presented. We showed how the hardware and software work together in a step-by-step manner to solve a simple problem.

**3-10
Glossary**

Access time The time required to read a memory.

Accumulator A register or registers in a computer that hold the operands used by the instructions.

Address The memory location where data is stored.

Arithmetic-logic unit (ALU) The part of the computer that performs the required arithmetic and logic operations.

Bus A group of interrelated wires; generally a bus carries a set of signals from one digital device to another.

Control unit The internal parts of a computer that control and organize its operations.

Cycle time The time required to read and write a memory.

Destructive readout Destroying data in the process of reading it.

EPROM Erasable programmable read only memory.

EXECUTE The portion of an instruction cycle where the instruction is executed.

FETCH The portion of an instruction cycle where the instruction is sent from memory to the instruction register.

Flip-flop (FF) An electronic circuit that functions as a 1-bit memory.

Increment To add 1 to a number.

Input-Output (I/O) system The part of a computer that communicates with external devices.

Instruction A command that directs the computer to perform a specific operation.

Instruction register The register in a computer that holds the instruction currently being executed.

MAR Memory *address* register. It contains the address of the memory location currently being accessed.

MDR Memory *data* register. A register that contains the data going to or coming from the memory.

OP CODE The portion of an instruction that tells the computer what to do.

Program A group of instructions that control the operation of a computer.

Program counter (PC) A register in a computer that contains the address of the next instruction to be executed.

RAM Random access memory. A memory capable of both READ and WRITE operations.

Register A group of related bits usually containing a character, command, or number.

Restart The act of starting up the computer. A restart is performed when the computer is first turned on and after most power failures

ROM Read only memory. A memory that is not written into during the normal course of operations.

Rotate A circular shift where the bits from one end of the word move to the opposite end of the word.

Routine A short program.

Shift operation Shift all bits of a register to a different position in the register.

Software Refers to the programs used in a computer.

Subroutine A small specific routine or program.

Volatility Characteristic of a memory that loses data when power is interrupted.

**3-11
References**

Bartee, Thomas C., *Digital Computer Fundamentals,* Fourth Edition, McGraw-Hill, New York, 1977.

Greenfield, Joseph D., *Practical Digital Design Using ICs,* Wiley, New York, 1977.

**3-12
Problems**

3-1 The dimensions of a memory are 16K words by 32 bits. How many bits are:
   a. In the MAR
   b. In the MDR
   c. In the memory

3-2 Repeat Problem 3-1 for an 8K by 24 bit memory.

3-3 In Problem 3-1 and 3-2, list the input and output lines required for the memory if:
   a. The memory is a RAM.
   b. The memory is a ROM.

3-4 Explain how a memory can be addressed sequentially.

3-5 A 16-bit computer contains the following word in its accumulator:
$$1011100111000111$$
What will the accumulator contain after the following instructions?
   a. Shift left 2 bits.
   b. Shift right 4 bits.
   c. Rotate left 5 bits.
   d. Rotate right 3 bits.

3-6 Write a program to add 50 and 75 and then subtract 25. Select memory areas for your data and instructions. Describe the progression of your program and list the contents of each pertinent memory location before and after its execution.

3-7 Write a program to add 25, 35, 45, and 55 and then shift the results two bits to the right. Explain the significance of your answer.

3-8 Prepare a chart similar to Fig. 3-7 for the programs of Problems 3-6 and 3-7.

After attempting to solve the problems, try to answer the self-evaluation questions in Sec. 3-2. If any of them still seem difficult, review the appropriate sections of the chapter to find the answers.

Chapter 4 Elementary Programming

This chapter covers some additional material that must be mastered before starting Chapter 5, the study of the **6800** microprocessor. It introduces hexadecimal notation, flowcharts, and programs involving branches and loops. After reading it, the student should be able to:

1. Convert between hexadecimal, binary, and decimal numbers.
2. Add and subtract hexadecimal numbers.
3. Explain the meaning of the symbols used in flowcharts.
4. Construct a flowchart for a problem.
5. Write programs involving branch instructions and loops.

Watch for the answers to the following questions as you read the chapter. They should help you understand the material presented.

1. What is the advantage of hexadecimal notation over binary notation?
2. Why is it necessary to use the letters A through F as hex digits?
3. In hex addition, what is the numerical equivalent of a carry?
4. What decisions must be made during program planning?
5. What action is necessary prior to starting execution of an actual program?
6. What instructions allow a program to make decisions? How does it do it?
7. How do loop counting and event detection determine when to end a loop?

Most μPs, including the **6800**, the **8080/85**, the **6502** and the **Z80**, use 16 address lines and 8 data lines. They therefore can use a memory of up to 64K bytes. To express the 16 bits needed for an address (or the 8 bits needed for a data byte) as 1s and 0s results in a long string of bits and is very tedious. In most literature and documentation today, the convention of using *hexadecimal notation* has been adopted.

The hexadecimal system is a *base 16* arithmetic system. Since such a system requires 16 different digits, the letters A through F are added to the ten decimal digits (0–9). The advantage of having 16 hexadecimal digits is that each digit can represent a unique combination of 4 bits, and that any combination of 4 bits can be repre-

55

sented by a single hex[1] digit. Table 4-1 gives both the decimal and binary value associated with each hexadecimal digit.

4-3.1
Conversions between Hexadecimal and Binary Numbers

To convert a binary number to hexadecimal, start at the least significant bit (LSB) and divide the binary number into groups of four bits each. Then replace each 4-bit group with its equivalent hex digit obtained from Table 4-1.

Table 4-1

Hexadecimal Digit	Decimal Value	Binary Value
0	0	0000
1	1	0001
2	2	0010
3	3	0011
4	4	0100
5	5	0101
6	6	0110
7	7	0111
8	8	1000
9	9	1001
A	10	1010
B	11	1011
C	12	1100
D	13	1101
E	14	1110
F	15	1111

Example 4-1

Convert the binary number 110000010111111101 to hex.

Solution

We start with the LSB and divide the number into 4-bit nibbles. Each nibble is then replaced with its corresponding hex digit as shown:

$$0011 \quad 0000 \quad 0101 \quad 1111 \quad 1101$$
$$3 \quad\quad 0 \quad\quad 5 \quad\quad F \quad\quad D$$

When the most significant group has less than 4 bits, as in this example, leading 0s are added to complete the 4 bit nibble.

[1]The word hex is often used as an abbreviation for hexadecimal.

To convert a hex number to binary, simply replace each hex digit by its 4-bit binary equivalent.

Example 4-2

Convert the hex number 1CB09 to binary.

Solution

We simply expand the hex number:

$$
\begin{array}{ccccc}
1 & C & B & 0 & 9 \\
\overbrace{0001} & \overbrace{1100} & \overbrace{1011} & \overbrace{0000} & \overbrace{1001}
\end{array}
$$

Thus the equivalent binary number is:

$$11100101100001001$$

It is not necessary to write the leading 0s.

4-3.2
Conversion of Hex Numbers to Decimal Numbers

The hex system is a base 16 system; therefore any hex number can be expressed as:

$$H_0 \times 1 + H_1 \times 16 \times H_2 \times 16^2 + H_3 \times 16^3 \ldots$$

where H_0 is the least significant hex digit, H_1 the next, etc. This is similar to the binary system of numbers discussed in Sec. 2-4.

Example 4-3

Convert 2FC to decimal.

Solution

The least significant hex digit, H_0, is C or 12. The next digit (H_1) is F or 15. This must be multiplied by 16 giving 240. The next digit, H_2, is 2, which must be multiplied by 16^2, or 256. Hence, 2FC = 512 + 240 + 12 = 764.

An alternate solution is to convert 2FC to the binary number 1011111100 and then perform a binary to decimal conversion.

Decimal numbers can be converted to hex by repeatedly dividing them by 16. After each division, the remainder becomes one of the hex digits in the final answer.

Example 4-4

Convert 9999 to hex.

Solution

Start by dividing by 16 as shown in the table below. After each division, the quotient becomes the number starting the next line and the remainder is the hex digit with the least significant digit on the top line.

Number	Quotient	Remainder	Hex Digit
9999	624	15	F
624	39	0	0
39	2	7	7
2	0	2	2

This example shows that $(9999)_{10} = (270F)_{16}$. The result can be checked by converting 270F to decimal, as shown in Example 4-3. By doing so we obtain:

$$(2 \times 4096) + (7 \times 256) + 0 + 15 = 9999$$
$$8192 + 1792 + 0 + 15 = 9999$$

4-3.3
Hexadecimal Addition

When working with μPs, it is often necessary to add or subtract hex numbers. They can be added by referring to hexadecimal addition tables, but we suggest the following procedure.

1. Add the two hex digits (mentally substituting their decimal equivalent).
2. If the sum is 15 or less, it can be directly expressed in hex.
3. If the sum is greater than or equal to 16, subtract 16 and carry 1 to the next position.

The following examples should make this procedure clear.

Example 4-5

Add D + E.

Solution

D is the equivalent of decimal 13 and E is the equivalent of decimal 14. Together they sum to 27 = 16 + 11. The 11 is represented by B and there is a carry. Therefore, D + E = **1B**.

Example 4-6

Add B2E6 and F77.

Solution

The solution is shown below.

Column	4 3 2 1
Augend	B 2 E 6
Addend	F 7 7
Sum	C 2 5 D

Column 1 $6 + 7 = 13 = $ D. The result is less than 16 so there is no carry.

Column 2 $E + 7 = 14 + 7 = 21 = 5 + $ a carry because the result is greater than 16.

Column 3 $F + 2 + 1$ (the carry from Column 2) $= 15 + 2 + 1 = 18 = 2 + $ a carry.

Column 4 $B + 1$ (the carry from Column 3) $= $ C.

Like addition, *hex subtraction* is analogous to decimal subtraction. If the subtrahend digit is larger than the minuend digit, one is borrowed from the next most significant digit. If the next most significant digit is 0, a 1 is borrowed from the next digit and the intermediate digit is changed to an F.

Example 4-7
Subtract 32F from C02.

Solution
The subtraction proceeds as follows:

Column	1 2 3
Minuend	C 0 2
Subtrahend	3 2 F
Difference	8 D 3

Column 1 Subtracting F from 2 requires a borrow. Because a borrow is worth 16, it raises the minuend to 18. Column 1 is therefore $18 - F = 18 - 15 = 3$.

Column 2 Because Column 2 contains a 0, it cannot provide the borrow out for Column 1. Consequently the borrow out must come from Column 3, while the minuend of Column 2 is changed to an F. Column 2 is therefore $F - 2 = 15 - 2 = 13 = $ D.

Column 3 Column 3 can provide the borrow out needed for Column 1. This reduces the C to a B and $B - 3 = 8$.

As in decimal addition, the results can be checked by adding the subtrahend and difference to get the minuend.

4-3.4
Negating Hex Numbers
The negative equivalent of a positive hex number can always be found by converting the hex number to binary and taking the 2s

complement of the result (Sec. 2-7). A shorter method exists, how-ever.

1. Add to the least significant hex digit the hex digit that makes it sum to 16.
2. Add to all other digits the digits that make it sum to 15.
3. If the least significant digit is 0, write 0 as the least significant digit of the answer and start at the next digit.
4. The number written is the negative equivalent of the given hex number.

This procedure works because the sum of the original number and the new number is always 0.

Example 4-8
Find the negative equivalent of the hex number 20C3.

Solution
The least significant digit is 3. To make 16, D must be added to 3. The other digits are 2, 0, and C. To make 15 in each case, we add D, F, and 3, respectively. The negative equivalent of 20C3 is therefore **DF3D**. This example can be checked by adding the negative equivalent to the positive number. Since X plus $-$X always equals 0, the result should be 0.

$$
\begin{array}{r}
20C3 \\
+\,DF3D \\
\hline
0000
\end{array}
$$

The carry out of the most significant digit is ignored.

4-3.5
Octal Notation

Octal notation is an alternate form of concise notation used by many minicomputer manufacturers. It divides binary numbers into 3-bit groups and each group represents the particular digit (0 through 7) that corresponds to the value of the 3-bit group.

Octal notation is a base 8 system. The rules for conversions and addition and subtraction in octal are analogous to those for hexa-decimal.

Octal is not as convenient as hex when expressing two bytes as a bit word. For example, compare these three ways to describe the same 16 bits of information:

Octal	2	6	5		3	0	6
Binary	1 0 1	1 0 1 0 1			1 1 0 0	0 1 1 0	
Hexadecimal		B	5			C	6

When expressed as a 16-bit address, these same bits would be:

	132706	in octal
or	B5C6	in hex

It is obvious that the hex version is much easier to use when combining groups of 8-bit words because the hex notation is simply the linking of the two 8-bit notations, while octal requires conversion to different numbers to express the 16-bit value. Because hex is far more popular among μP users, it is used exclusively throughout this book.

4-4
Flowcharts

Flowcharts are used by programmers to show the progress of their programs graphically. They are a clear and concise method of presenting the programmers approach to a problem. They are often used as a part of programming documentation, where the program must be explained to those unfamiliar with it. Since good documentation is essential for proper use of any computer, the rudiments of flowcharts are presented in this section.

4-4.1
Flowchart Symbols

The flowchart symbols used in this book are shown in Fig. 4-1.

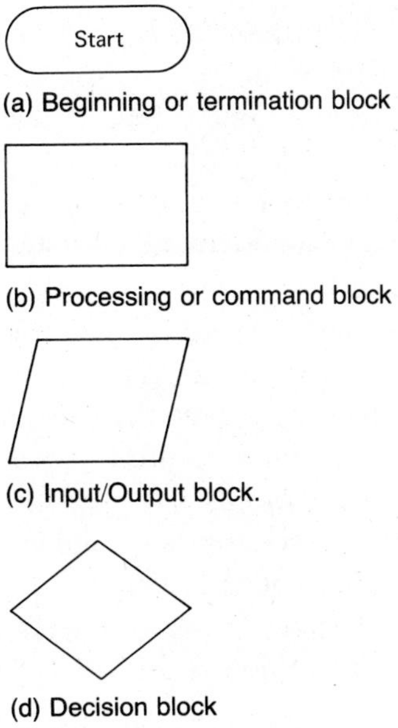

Start

(a) Beginning or termination block

(b) Processing or command block

(c) Input/Output block.

(d) Decision block

Figure 4-1 The most common standard flowchart symbols.

1. The *oval* symbol is either a *beginning* or *termination* box. It is used simply to denote the start or end of a program.
2. The *rectangular block* is the *processing or command block*. It states what must be done at that point in the program.
3. The *parallelogram* is an *input/output block*. Such commands as READ or WRITE, especially from an external device such as a disc or card reader, are flowcharted using these boxes.
4. The *diamond box* is a *decision box*. It usually contains a question within it. There are typically two output paths; one if the answer to the question is yes, and the other if the answer is no. Sometimes when a comparison between two numbers is made, there might be three exit paths corresponding to the greater than, less than, and equal, possibilities.

Example 4-9

Draw a flowchart to add the numbers 1, 4, 7, and 10 together.

Solution

The solution is shown in Fig. 4-2. It consists simply of a start box, four command boxes, and a stop box. This is an example of straight-line programming since no decisions were made. It was also assumed that the numbers 1, 4, 7, and 10 were available in the computer's memory and were not read from an external device.

4-4.2
Elementary Programming

To introduce the concepts of programming in this chapter, we use a rudimentary computer, such as that described in Sec. 3-8. The instructions are really binary data words stored in various memory locations. Each instruction is assumed to consist of words that contain the OP code and the address of the data. The OP codes used in this section are ADD, SUBTRACT, MULTIPLY, DIVIDE, LOAD, and STORE.

For example, consider the problem of writing instructions for the flowchart of Fig. 4-2. The first problem is to allocate memory areas for the instructions and the data. All these words must be in memory before the program can be started. The methods to actually write or LOAD these words into memory are described in Chapters 7 and 11, where assembly language programming and system test equipment are described in detail.

As in Chapter 3, assume we are using a μP where the first byte of each instruction is the OP code and the next byte is the address

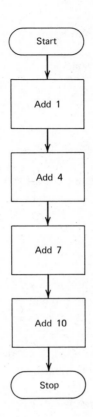

Figure 4-2 Flowchart for Example 4-9.

of the data. Again we arbitrarily decide to start the program at location 10 and the data at 80. The program would then be as follows:

Location	Instruction
10	LOAD
11	80
12	ADD
13	81
14	ADD
15	82
16	ADD
17	83
18	STORE
19	84
1A	HALT

The operation of the LOAD, ADD, and STORE instructions was explained in Sec. 3-8.1.

The data might then be this:

Location	Contents
80	1
81	4
82	7
83	10
84	Reserved for result

Once the data areas and all the required constants are written in memory, the code can be executed by starting at location 10. Note that the data could be changed and the same program executed any number of times.

4-5
Branch Instructions
and Loops

The program of the previous section is extremely simple; indeed, the user can compute the answer more quickly than he can write the program. Suppose, however, the program is expanded so that we are required to add the numbers 1, 4, 7, 10, . . . , 10,000.[2] Conceptually, this could be done by expanding the program and flowchart of Sec. 4-4. However, the program and data areas would then require 3333 locations each and just writing them would become very tedious. Obviously, something else must be done.

4-5.1
Branch Instructions

Branch instructions provide the solution to the above problem. *A branch or jump instruction alters the normal sequence of program execution and is used to create loops that allow the same sequence of instructions to be executed many times.*

As we have seen in Sec. 3-8, in the normal course of program execution the program counter (PC) is incremented during the execution of each instruction and contains the location of the next instruction to be fetched. A branch instruction might look like this:

BRANCH 500

where BRANCH is the OP code and 500 is the branch address. It causes the branch address to be written into the PC. Thus the location of the next instruction to be executed is the branch address (500 in this case), rather than the sequential address.

[2]Since the object of this section is to teach programming and not mathematics, we ignore the fact that this is an arithmetic progression whose sum is given by a simple formula.

There are two types of branch instructions, unconditional and conditional.

The unconditional branch always causes the program to jump to the branch address. It is written as BRA, which stands for BRANCH ALWAYS.

The conditional branch causes the program to branch only if a specified condition is met. For this introductory chapter only two of the **6800**'s sixteen conditional branch instructions are used:

> BPL—branch on positive (0 is considered as a positive number.)
> BMI—branch on negative.

Therefore, should the computer encounter one of these instructions, it simply tests the negative bit of the CCR. The state of this bit (which is established during the execution of the previous instructions), determines whether the branch should be taken. (See Sec. 6-3.4).

Example 4-10
A computer is to add the numbers 1, 4, 7, 10, . . . , 10,000.[3] Draw a flowchart for the program.

Solution
The flowchart is shown in Fig. 4-3. We recognize that we must keep track of two quantities. One is the number to be added. This has been labeled N in the flowchart and progresses 1, 4, 7, 10. . . . The second quantity is the sum S, which progresses 1, 1 + 4, 1 + 4 + 7, . . . or 1, 5, 12. . . . The first box in the flowchart is an initialization box. It sets N to 1 and S to 0 at the beginning of the program. The next box ($S = N + S$) sets the new sum equal to the old sum plus the number to be added. The number to be added is then increased by 3. At this point the flowchart loops around to repeat the sequence. This is accomplished by placing an unconditional branch instruction in the program. The quantities S and N will progress as specified.

4-5.2
Decision Boxes and Conditional Branches
The reader has probably already realized that there is a serious problem with Example 4-10; the loop never terminates. Actually, putting a program into an endless loop is one of the most common programming mistakes.

[3]For the introductory problems of this section we have ignored the fact that decimal 10,000 cannot be contained within a single byte.

There are two common ways to determine when to end a loop; *loop counting* and *event detection*. Either method requires the use of decision boxes in the flowchart and corresponding conditional branch instructions in the program. Loop counting is considered first.

Loop counting is done by determining the number of times the loop should be traversed, counting the actual number of times through and comparing the two.

Example 4-11

Improve the flowchart of Fig. 4-3 so that it terminates properly.

Solution

The program should terminate not when $N = 10{,}000$, but when $10{,}000$ is added to the sum. For the flowchart of Fig. 4-4, N is increased to $10{,}003$ immediately after this occurs. At the end of the first loop $N = 4$, the second loop $N = 7$, etc. It can be seen here that $N = 3L + 1$ where L is the number of times through the loop. If N is set to $10{,}003$, $L = 3334$. The loop must be traversed 3334 times.

The correct flowchart is shown in Fig. 4-4. The loop counter L has been added and set initially to -3334. It is incremented each time through the loop and tested to see if it is positive. After 3334 loops, it becomes 0. Then the YES path from the decision box is taken and the program halts.

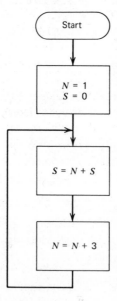

Figure 4-3 Flowchart for Example 4-10.

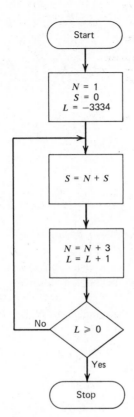

Figure 4-4 Flowchart for Example 4-11.

Example 4-12
Write the code for the flowchart of Fig. 4-4.

Solution
As in Sec. 4-4.2, the program is started at location 10 and the data area at location 80. In the data area three variables, N, S, and L are needed. These should be initialized to 1, 0, and -3334, respectively, before the program starts. In addition, two constants, 1 and 3, are needed during the execution of the program. Before the program starts, the data area should look like this:

Location	Term	Initial value
80	N	1
81	S	0
82	L	-3334
83	Constant	3
84	Constant	1

The program can now be written directly from the flowchart.

Locations	Instruction	Comments
10,11	LOAD 81 ⎤	
12,13	ADD 80 ⎬	$S = N + S$
14,15	STORE 81 ⎦	
16,17	LOAD 80 ⎤	
18,19	ADD 83 ⎬	$N = N + 3$
1A,1B	STORE 80 ⎦	
1C,1D	LOAD 82 ⎤	
1E,1F	ADD 84 ⎬	$L = L + 1$
20,21	STORE 82 ⎦	
22,23	BMI 10	
24,25	HALT	

Each instruction takes two bytes as it could in a µP. Two locations are therefore assigned to each instruction and the addresses are in hex.

Note that the instructions follow the flowchart. The decision box has been implemented by the BMI instruction. The program loops as long as L remains negative.

Check: as a check on the program, we can write the contents of N, S, and L at the end of each loop in the following table.

Times through the Loop	N	S	L
1	4	1	−3333
2	7	5	−3332
3	10	12	−3331

The chart shows that each time around the loop:

$$\frac{N - 1}{3} + |L| = 3334$$

Therefore, when $N = 10{,}003$, L indeed equals 0 and the loop terminates.

Event detection terminates a loop when an event occurs that should make the loop terminate. In Example 4-12, that event could be the fact that N is greater than 10,000. Using event detection, locations 1C through 21 could be replaced by:

1C,1D	LOAD N
1E,1F	SUBTRACT 105
20,21	Not needed (NOP)
22,23	BMI 10

where location 105 contains 10,001. This program branches back until $N = 10{,}003$. In this problem, the use of event detection is conceptually simpler and saves one instruction.

As a final introductory programming example, consider the problem of adding together all the numbers in memory between locations 100 and 200. This problem has practical applications. If, for example, a firm has 101 debtors, it can store the amount owed by each debtor in one of the locations. The sum of these debts is the firm's accounts receivable.

The flowchart for this example is shown in Fig. 4-5. At the start the sum is set to 0 and the loop counter to 101 because there are 101 addresses between 100 and 200.[4] The loop counter and the addresses are then incremented. Note the box $S = S + (A)$. The parenthesis around A means that the contents of location A are being added to the sum.

The difficult part of this problem is to find a way to increment the addresses. One way to do this is to increment the ADD instruction. This is done in Example 4-13.

_____

[4]In this introductory problem, decimal addresses are assumed for simplicity.

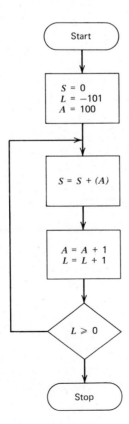

Figure 4-5 Flowchart for adding together the contents of locations 100 to 200.

Example 4-13

Write the code for the flowchart of Fig. 4-5.

Solution

Again, the program is started at location 10. Because locations 100 to 200 contain data, the constant area is set up at 300. It looks like this:

Location	Term	Initial Value
300	S	0
301	L	−101
302	Constant	1

The coding can then proceed as follows.

Location	Instruction		Comments
10	LOAD	300	
11	ADD	100	$S = S + (A)$
12	STORE	300	
13	LOAD	11	
14	ADD	302	Increment address portion of instruction
15	STORE	11	11 and resume
16	LOAD	301	
17	ADD	302	$L = L + 1$
18	STORE	301	
19	BMI	10	
20	Halt		If minus, branch back to 10

Note particularly instructions 13, 14, and 15. These instructions treat location 11, which contains an instruction, as data. The assumptions are that the instructions consist of an OP code and address, and the address occupies the LSBs of the instruction, and that adding 1 to the instruction increments the address without affecting the Op Code or other parts of the instruction. These assumptions are valid for most computers.

This method of solving this problem is not generally used, nor do we recommend it, because more powerful methods, such as indexing (see Sec. 5-5.4) are preferable. It was presented, however, to emphasize that instructions occupy memory space and can be treated as data. In this example, the instruction in location 11 is treated as data when the instructions in locations 13, 14, and 15 are executed. This is a *self-modifying program,* which means it *changes its own contents as it executes.* Most programmers *avoid* self-modifying programs. They are complex and difficult to document or understand, and the program cannot be run successively without reentering the initial values between each run. Also, they cannot be used in ROM.

Problem 4-12 requires that the reader write a self-modifying program but, in general, these programs should be avoided, and they can be avoided with techniques such as indexing. Nevertheless the reader should understand these programs even if cautioned not to write them.

4-6 Summary

In this chapter, hexadecimal numbers (which are used with many computers and μPs) were introduced. Conversions between hexadecimal and binary or decimal numbers and hexadecimal arithmetic were discussed.

Elementary programming was further explored. Flowcharts and their uses were introduced, and simple problems involving loops and branches were presented.

4-7 Glossary

Branch instruction An instruction that alters the normal course of a program by causing it to branch or jump to another instruction.

Conditional branch An instruction that causes the program to branch only if a certain condition is met.

Event detection Using the occurrence of an event to terminate a loop or program.

Flowchart A graphic method used to outline or show the progress of a program.

Hexadecimal A base 16 system that uses the numbers 0 to 9 and letters A to F to express 4-bit binary nibbles with one digit.

Initialization The clearing or presetting of RAM locations and the programming of the peripheral adapters prior to program execution.

Load An instruction that causes data to be brought from memory into an accumulator register.

Loop Returning to the start of a sequence of instructions so that the same instructions may be repeated many times.

Store An instruction that causes data in the accumulator to be moved to memory or a peripheral register.

4-8 References

Bartee, Thomas C., *Digital Computer Fundamentals,* Fourth Edition, McGraw-Hill, New York, 1977.

Boillot, Gleason, and Horn, *Essentials of Flowcharting,* William C. Brown, Dubuque, Iowa, 1975.

4-9

Problems

4-1 Convert the following binary numbers to hexadecimal.
  a. 11111011
  b. 1011001
  c. 10000011111100
  d. 10010101100011101

4-2 Convert the following hex numbers to binary.
  a. 129
  b. 84C5
  c. 5CF035
  d. ABCDE2F

4-3 Convert the numbers in Problem 4-2 to decimal numbers.

4-4 Convert the following numbers to hex.
  a. 139
  b. 517
  c. 2,000
  d. 105,684

4-5 Perform the following hex additions.

  a.   99   **b.**   CB
          + 89   DD

  c.   15F02   **d.**   2CFB4D
            3C3E   5DC98B

4-6 Perform the following hex subtractions.

  a.   59   **b.**   1CC
             F   DE

  c.   1002   **d.**   5F306
            5F8   135CF

4-7 Find the negative equivalent of the following hex numbers.
  a. 23
  b. CB
  c. 500
  d. 1F302
  e. F5630

4-8 Your alarm always goes off at 8 o'clock. You then get up, except on Tuesdays, when you can sleep an extra hour. You then eat breakfast. If it's raining, you take an umbrella. If your car starts, you go to work; otherwise you go back to bed. Draw a flowchart showing this portion of your day's activities.

4-9 Your friends are: Alice, George, Cindy, and Arthur in that order. You ask one of them to the ballgame. If it's raining, or if none of your friends can make it, you stay home and watch television. Draw a flowchart to show this portion of your activities.

4-10 Write a program to add the numbers 1, 5, 9, 13, . . . , 20,001.

4-11 The number N is in location 40. Write a program to put N! in location 41.

4-12 There are 101 numbers in locations 100 to 200. Some of them are 5. Write a program to count the number of times 5 appears in these locations.

After attempting to solve the problems, try to answer the self-evaluation questions in Sec. 4-2. If any of them still seem difficult, review the appropriate sections of the chapter to find the answers.

Chapter 5 Accumulator and Memory Referencing Instructions

5-1
Instructional Objectives

This chapter first introduces the software features of the **6800**, the mnemonics or assembly language concept, and then the accumulator and memory referencing instructions. After reading it, the student should be able to:

1. Explain the function of each register in the **6800** μP.
2. Realize the need for mnemonics and assembly language.
3. Write and use instructions that use the immediate, direct, extended, indexed, and implied addressing modes.
4. List each bit in the Condition Code Register and explain its function.
5. Perform multibyte additions and subtractions using the carry bit.
6. Write programs to add and subtract BCD numbers.
7. Use logic instructions.
8. SET or CLEAR specific bits in a register.
9. Test specific bits in a register.

5-2
Self-Evaluation Questions

Watch for the answers to the following questions as you read the chapter. They should help you to understand the material presented.

1. Why are mnemonics easier to use than machine language?
2. What is one advantage of having two accumulators?
3. Which memory locations can be accessed by *direct instructions*? Why can't *all* memory locations be accessed by direct instructions?
4. What is the difference between an ADD and an ADD-WITH-CARRY instruction? Give an example of the proper use of each.
5. Why is it necessary to worry about overflow or underflow?
6. What is the significance of the H bit? Why is it only used in BCD operations?
7. Why doesn't the *carry bit* have any effect on logic operations?
8. Why do INCREMENT, DECREMENT, and CLEAR instructions require many memory cycles?
9. What are the advantages of using the carry bit in conjunction with the SHIFT and ROTATE instructions?

5-3
Programming the 6800
Microprocessor

In Chapters 3 and 4 we have shown how a rudimentary computer works and is programmed. The **6800** μP is much more complete than the simple processor that has been discussed and it will now be described from a functional point of view. The diagram of Fig. 5-1 shows the registers contained within the **6800** and identifies the flag bits in the Condition Code Register (CCR).

Most of the functions necessary for total system operation are included in the **6800** IC itself. At this point, the features of the **6800** μP that determine the software characteristics will be described, and the hardware aspects will be discussed in later chapters.

5-3.1
Arithmetic/Logic Unit (ALU)

As a complete processor, the **6800** contains within it all of the registers necessary for the operation of a computer, such as the instruction register and decoder, the input and output buffers, and the ALU. These are shown in the expanded block diagram of Fig. 5-2.

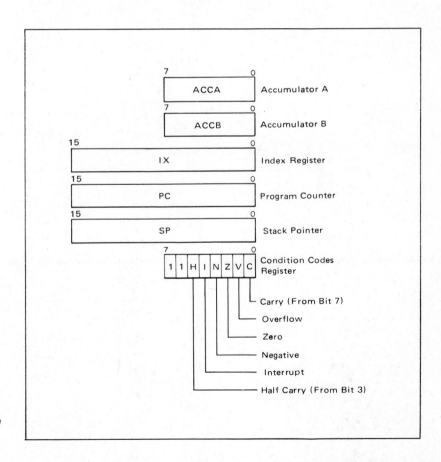

Figure 5-1 Programming model of the microprocessing unit.

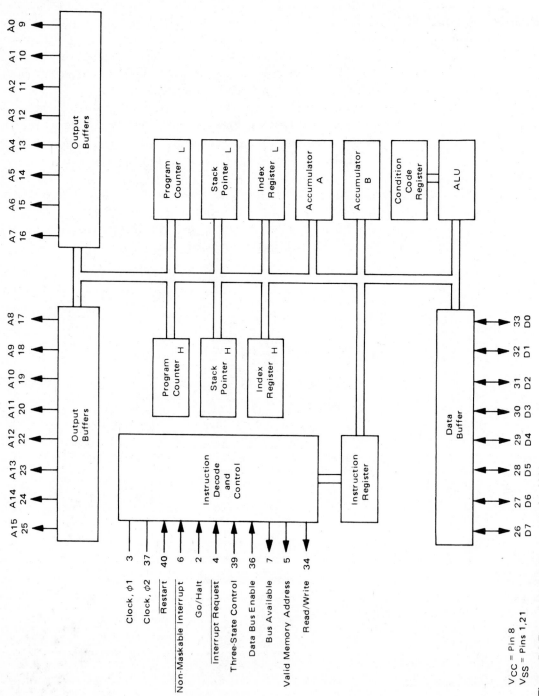

Figure 5-2 Expanded block diagram of the **6800**.

The **6800** ALU performs the arithmetic operations of addition, subtraction, complementation, negation, and shifting. Multiplication and division are performed by programs (subroutines) that use these functions (shifts with additions or subtractions). The ALU also performs the Boolean algebra functions of AND, OR, and EXCLUSIVE OR.

The _Condition Code Register_ (CCR) is a part of the ALU and its bits are altered as a result of each arithmetic or logic instruction. The bits of this register are then used by the _conditional branch instructions_ to select alternate paths for the program. These are the decision-making functions that distinguish a computer and are described in Sec. 6-3.

5-3.2
Registers and Accumulators

The registers and accumulators within the **6800** are all 8-bits wide and, as shown in Fig. 5-2, are interconnected by an 8-bit internal bus. Because the **6800** is designed to work with 65536 (2^{16}) bytes of memory, a 16-bit address bus is used and those registers in the μP that are associated with addresses (program counter [PC], index [X] and stack pointer [SP]) have a high (H) and low (L) byte. The μP also contains two 8-bit accumulators (A and B) and an 8-bit Condition Code Register (CCR).

As explained in Chapter 3, the PC keeps track of the location in memory where the next instruction byte is to be fetched. The bytes are then loaded into the instruction register and the instructions are executed. The operation of the X and SP registers are explained in Secs. 5-5.4 and 6-4, respectively.

5-3.3
The 6800 Instruction Set

The first byte of each instruction is called the _operation code_ (OP code) because its bit combination determines the operation to be performed. The second and third bytes of the instruction, if used, contain address or data information. They are the _operand_ part of the instruction. The OP code also tells the μP logic how many additional bytes to fetch for each instruction. There are 197 unique instructions in the **6800** instruction set. Since an 8-bit word has 256 bit combinations, a high percentage of the possible OP codes are used.

When an instruction is fetched from the location in memory pointed to by the program counter (PC) register, and the first byte is moved into the instruction register, it causes the logic to execute the instruction. If the bit combination is 01001111 (or 4F in hex), for example, it CLEARs the A accumulator (RESETs it to all 0s), or if the combination is 01001100 (4C), the processor increments the A accumulator (adds 1 to it). These are examples of *one-byte* instructions that involve only one accumulator. An instruction byte of 10110110 (B6) is the code for the *extended addressing mode* of LOAD A (see Sec. 5-5). It also commands the logic to fetch the *next two bytes* and use them as the *address* of the data to be loaded into the A accumulator.

5-3.4
Understanding the 6800 Instructions

When the OP codes for each instruction are expressed in their binary or hex format, as in the previous paragraph, they are known as *machine language instructions*. The bits of these OP codes must reside in memory and be moved to the instruction decoder for analysis and action by the μP.

Programs and data can be entered into a μP in machine language using data switches or keyboards. It is easier, however, as explained in Chapter 11, to use a control ROM and a terminal to enter the hexadecimal forms of the same words.

Writing programs in machine language is very tedious, and trying to follow even a simple machine language program strains the ability of most people. As a result, various techniques have evolved in an effort to simplify the program documentation. The first step in this simplification is the use of *hexadecimal notation* to express the codes. This reduces the digits from 8 to 2 (10100011 = A3, for example) or, in the case of an address, from 16 binary digits (bits) to 4 hex digits. Even this simplification, however, is insufficient and the concept of using *mnemonic language* to describe each instruction has therefore been developed. *A mnemonic is defined as a device to help the memory.* For example, the mnemonics LDA A (load A) and STA A (store A) are used for the LOAD and STORE instructions instead of the hex OP codes of 86 and B7 because the *mnemonics are descriptive and easier to remember.*

5-4
Assembly Language

Not only are mnemonics easy to remember, but the precise meaning of each one makes it possible to use a computer program to translate them to the machine language equivalent that can be used by the computer. A program for this purpose is called an *assembler* and the mnemonics that it recognizes constitute an *assembly language program*. A number of different assemblers exist for the **6800**, each with its own mnemonics. The mnemonics described here are used by Motorola for the **6800** μP instruction set. The mnemonics for each machine language instruction code and its hexadecimal equivalent are shown in Table 5-1.

Table 5-1

Mnemonics and Hexadecimal Values for the **6800** Machine Codes.

Hex	Mnem	Acc	Mode	Hex	Mnem	Acc	Mode	Hex	Mnem	Acc	Mode	Hex	Mnem	Acc	Mode
00	·			40	NEG	A		80	SUB	A	IMM	C0	SUB	B	IMM
01	NOP			41	·			81	CMP	A	IMM	C1	CMP	B	IMM
02	·			42	·			82	SBC	A	IMM	C2	SBC	B	IMM
03	·			43	COM	A		83	·			C3	·		
04	·			44	LSR	A		84	AND	A	IMM	C4	AND	B	IMM
05	·			45	·			85	BIT	A	IMM	C5	BIT	B	IMM
06	TAP			46	ROR	A		86	LDA	A	IMM	C6	LDA	B	IMM
07	TPA			47	ASR	A		87	·			C7	·		
08	INX			48	ASL	A		88	EOR	A	IMM	C8	EOR	B	IMM
09	DEX			49	ROL	A		89	ADC	A	IMM	C9	ADC	B	IMM
0A	CLV			4A	DEC	A		8A	ORA	A	IMM	CA	ORA	B	IMM
0B	SEV			4B	·			8B	ADD	A	IMM	CB	ADD	B	IMM
0C	CLC			4C	INC	A		8C	CPX	A	IMM	CC	·		
0D	SEC			4D	TST	A		8D	BSR		REL	CD	·		
0E	CLI			4E	·			8E	LDS		IMM	CE	LDX		IMM
0F	SEI			4F	CLR	A		8F	·			CF	·		
10	SBA			50	NEG	B		90	SUB	A	DIR	D0	SUB	B	DIR
11	CBA			51	·			91	CMP	A	DIR	D1	CMP	B	DIR
12	·			52	·			92	SBC	A	DIR	D2	SBC	B	DIR
13	·			53	COM	B		93	·			D3	·		
14	·			54	LSR	B		94	AND	A	DIR	D4	AND	B	DIR
15	·			55	·			95	BIT	A	DIR	D5	BIT	B	DIR
16	TAB			56	ROR	B		96	LDA	A	DIR	D6	LDA	B	DIR
17	TBA			57	ASR	B		97	STA	A	DIR	D7	STA	B	DIR
18	·			58	ASL	B		98	EOR	A	DIR	D8	EOR	B	DIR
19	DAA			59	ROL	B		99	ADC	A	DIR	D9	ADC	B	DIR
1A	·			5A	DEC	B		9A	ORA	A	DIR	DA	ORA	B	DIR
1B	ABA			5B	·			9B	ADD	A	DIR	DB	ADD	B	DIR
1C	·			5C	INC	B		9C	CPX		DIR	DC	·		
1D	·			5D	TST	B		9D	·			DD	·		
1E	·			5E	·			9E	LDS		DIR	DE	LDX		DIR
1F	·			5F	CLR	B		9F	STS		DIR	DF	STX		DIR
20	BRA		REL	60	NEG		IND	A0	SUB	A	IND	E0	SUB	B	IND
21	·			61	·			A1	CMP	A	IND	E1	CMP	B	IND
22	BHI		REL	62	·			A2	SBC	A	IND	E2	SBC	B	IND
23	BLS		REL	63	COM		IND	A3	·			E3	·		
24	BCC		REL	64	LSR		IND	A4	AND	A	IND	E4	AND	B	IND
25	BCS		REL	65	·			A5	BIT	A	IND	E5	BIT	B	IND
26	BNE		REL	66	ROR		IND	A6	LDA	A	IND	E6	LDA	B	IND
27	BEQ		REL	67	ASR		IND	A7	STA	A	IND	E7	STA	B	IND
28	BVC		REL	68	ASL		IND	A8	EOR	A	IND	E8	EOR	B	IND
29	BVS		REL	69	ROL		IND	A9	ADC	A	IND	E9	ADC	B	IND
2A	BPL		REL	6A	DEC		IND	AA	ORA	A	IND	EA	ORA	B	IND
2B	BMI		REL	6B	·			AB	ADD	A	IND	EB	ADD	B	IND
2C	BGE		REL	6C	INC		IND	AC	CPX		IND	EC	·		
2D	BLT		REL	6D	TST		IND	AD	JSR		IND	ED	·		
2E	BGT		REL	6E	JMP		IND	AE	LDS		IND	EE	LDX		IND
2F	BLE		REL	6F	CLR		IND	AF	STS		IND	EF	STX		IND
30	TSX			70	NEG		EXT	B0	SUB	A	EXT	F0	SUB	B	EXT
31	INS			71	·			B1	CMP	A	EXT	F1	CMP	B	EXT
32	PUL	A		72	·			B2	SBC	A	EXT	F2	SBC	B	EXT
33	PUL	B		73	COM		EXT	B3	·			F3	·		
34	DES			74	LSR		EXT	B4	AND	A	EXT	F4	AND	B	EXT
35	TXS			75	·			B5	BIT	A	EXT	F5	BIT	B	EXT
36	PSH	A		76	ROR		EXT	B6	LDA	A	EXT	F6	LDA	B	EXT
37	PSH	B		77	ASR		EXT	B7	STA	A	EXT	F7	STA	B	EXT
38	·			78	ASL		EXT	B8	EOR	A	EXT	F8	EOR	B	EXT
39	RTS			79	ROL		EXT	B9	ADC	A	EXT	F9	ADC	B	EXT
3A	·			7A	DEC		EXT	BA	ORA	A	EXT	FA	ORA	B	EXT
3B	RTI			7B	·			BB	ADD	A	EXT	FB	ADD	B	EXT
3C	·			7C	INC		EXT	BC	CPX		EXT	FC	·		
3D	·			7D	TST		EXT	BD	JSR		EXT	FD	·		
3E	WAI			7E	JMP		EXT	BE	LDS		EXT	FE	LDX		EXT
3F	SWI			7F	CLR		EXT	BF	STS		EXT	FF	STX		EXT

Notes: 1. Addressing Modes: A = Accumulator A   IMM = Immediate
                      B = Accumulator B   DIR = Direct
                     REL = Relative
                     IND = Indexed
       2. Unassigned code indicated by "·"

When a program is written in mnemonic or assembly language, it is called a *source program*. After being assembled (or translated) by the computer, the machine language codes that are produced are known as the *object program*. An assembler also produces a *program listing*, which is kept as a record of the design.

The programmer must understand the differences between each mnemonic in order to write his program; the following sections and chapters are devoted to describing these differences. A detailed description of the assembler is given in Chapter 7.

5-4.1
Numerical Identifications

The **6800** assembler uses several symbols to identify the various types of numbers that occur in a program. These symbols are:

1. A blank or no symbol indicates the number is a *decimal* number.
2. A $ immediately preceding a number indicates it is a *hex* number. ($24, for example, is 24 in hex or the equivalent of 36 in decimal.)
3. A # sign indicates an *immediate* operand (see Sec. 5-5.1).
4. A @ sign indicates an *octal* value.
5. A % sign indicates a *binary* number (01011001, for example).

5-5
Addressing Modes

The accumulator and memory instructions available in the **6800** are given in Table 5-2.

The leftmost column indicates their operations and the mnemonic for each instruction. The accumulator and memory instructions can be broken down roughly into these categories.

1. Transfers between an accumulator and memory (LOADs and STOREs).
2. Arithmetic operations—ADDITION, SUBTRACTION, DECIMAL ADJUST ACCUMULATOR.
3. Logical operations—AND, OR, XOR.
4. Shifts and rotates.
5. Test operations—bit test and compares.
6. Other operations—CLEAR, INCREMENT, DECREMENT, and COMPLEMENT.

In order to reduce the number of instructions required in a typical program and, consequently, the number of memory locations needed to hold a program, the **6800** features several ways to address them. They are called *addressing modes* and many of them only use one or two bytes. The following paragraphs and examples illustrate how and when each mode is used.

The instructions of Table 5-2 can be addressed in one or more of the following modes: *immediate, direct, indexed, implied,* or *ex-*

Table 5-2
Accumulator and Memory Instructions

The accumulator and memory operations and their effect on the CCR are shown in Table 7. Included are Arithmetic Logic, Data Test and Data Handling instructions.

OPERATIONS	MNEMONIC	IMMED OP	~	=	DIRECT OP	~	=	INDEX OP	~	=	EXTND OP	~	=	IMPLIED OP	~	=	BOOLEAN/ARITHMETIC OPERATION (All register labels refer to contents)	H	I	N	Z	V	C
Add	ADDA	8B	2	2	9B	3	2	AB	5	2	BB	4	3				A + M → A	‡	•	‡	‡	‡	‡
	ADDB	CB	2	2	DB	3	2	EB	5	2	FB	4	3				B + M → B	‡	•	‡	‡	‡	‡
Add Acmltrs	ABA													1B	2	1	A + B → A	‡	•	‡	‡	‡	‡
Add with Carry	ADCA	89	2	2	99	3	2	A9	5	2	B9	4	3				A + M + C → A	‡	•	‡	‡	‡	‡
	ADCB	C9	2	2	D9	3	2	E9	5	2	F9	4	3				B + M + C → B	‡	•	‡	‡	‡	‡
And	ANDA	84	2	2	94	3	2	A4	5	2	B4	4	3				A · M → A	•	•	‡	‡	R	•
	ANDB	C4	2	2	D4	3	2	E4	5	2	F4	4	3				B · M → B	•	•	‡	‡	R	•
Bit Test	BITA	85	2	2	95	3	2	A5	5	2	B5	4	3				A · M	•	•	‡	‡	R	•
	BITB	C5	2	2	D5	3	2	E5	5	2	F5	4	3				B · M	•	•	‡	‡	R	•
Clear	CLR							6F	7	2	7F	6	3				00 · M	•	•	R	S	R	R
	CLRA													4F	2	1	00 → A	•	•	R	S	R	R
	CLRB													5F	2	1	00 → B	•	•	R	S	R	R
Compare	CMPA	81	2	2	91	3	2	A1	5	2	B1	4	3				A - M	•	•	‡	‡	‡	‡
	CMPB	C1	2	2	D1	3	2	E1	5	2	F1	4	3				B - M	•	•	‡	‡	‡	‡
Compare Acmltrs	CBA													11	2	1	A - B	•	•	‡	‡	‡	‡
Complement, 1's	COM							63	7	2	73	6	3				M̄ → M	•	•	‡	‡	R	S
	COMA													43	2	1	Ā → A	•	•	‡	‡	R	S
	COMB													53	2	1	B̄ → B	•	•	‡	‡	R	S
Complement, 2's	NEG							60	7	2	70	6	3				00 - M → M	•	•	‡	‡	①	②
(Negate)	NEGA													40	2	1	00 - A → A	•	•	‡	‡	①	②
	NEGB													50	2	1	00 - B → B	•	•	‡	‡	①	②
Decimal Adjust, A	DAA													19	2	1	Converts Binary Add. of BCD Characters into BCD Format	•	•	‡	‡	‡	③
Decrement	DEC							6A	7	2	7A	6	3				M - 1 → M	•	•	‡	‡	④	•
	DECA													4A	2	1	A - 1 → A	•	•	‡	‡	④	•
	DECB													5A	2	1	B - 1 → B	•	•	‡	‡	④	•
Exclusive OR	EORA	88	2	2	98	3	2	A8	5	2	B8	4	3				A ⊕ M → A	•	•	‡	‡	R	•
	EORB	C8	2	2	D8	3	2	E8	5	2	F8	4	3				B ⊕ M → B	•	•	‡	‡	R	•
Increment	INC							6C	7	2	7C	6	3				M + 1 → M	•	•	‡	‡	⑤	•
	INCA													4C	2	1	A + 1 → A	•	•	‡	‡	⑤	•
	INCB													5C	2	1	B + 1 · B	•	•	‡	‡	⑤	•
Load Acmltr	LDAA	86	2	2	96	3	2	A6	5	2	B6	4	3				M → A	•	•	‡	‡	R	•
	LDAB	C6	2	2	D6	3	2	E6	5	2	F6	4	3				M → B	•	•	‡	‡	R	•
Or, Inclusive	ORAA	8A	2	2	9A	3	2	AA	5	2	BA	4	3				A + M → A	•	•	‡	‡	R	•
	ORAB	CA	2	2	DA	3	2	EA	5	2	FA	4	3				B + M → B	•	•	‡	‡	R	•
Push Data	PSHA													36	4	1	A → MSP, SP - 1 → SP	•	•	•	•	•	•
	PSHB													37	4	1	B → MSP, SP - 1 → SP	•	•	•	•	•	•
Pull Data	PULA													32	4	1	SP + 1 → SP, MSP → A	•	•	•	•	•	•
	PULB													33	4	1	SP + 1 → SP, MSP → B	•	•	•	•	•	•
Rotate Left	ROL							69	7	2	79	6	3				M	•	•	‡	‡	⑥	‡
	ROLA													49	2	1	A	•	•	‡	‡	⑥	‡
	ROLB													59	2	1	B C b7 ← b0	•	•	‡	‡	⑥	‡
Rotate Right	ROR							66	7	2	76	6	3				M	•	•	‡	‡	⑥	‡
	RORA													46	2	1	A	•	•	‡	‡	⑥	‡
	RORB													56	2	1	B C b7 → b0	•	•	‡	‡	⑥	‡
Shift Left, Arithmetic	ASL							68	7	2	78	6	3				M	•	•	‡	‡	⑥	‡
	ASLA													48	2	1	A	•	•	‡	‡	⑥	‡
	ASLB													58	2	1	B C b7 b0 ← 0	•	•	‡	‡	⑥	‡
Shift Right, Arithmetic	ASR							67	7	2	77	6	3				M	•	•	‡	‡	⑥	‡
	ASRA													47	2	1	A	•	•	‡	‡	⑥	‡
	ASRB													57	2	1	B b7 b0 C	•	•	‡	‡	⑥	‡
Shift Right, Logic	LSR							64	7	2	74	6	3				M	•	•	R	‡	⑥	‡
	LSRA													44	2	1	A 0 → b7 b0 → C	•	•	R	‡	⑥	‡
	LSRB													54	2	1	B b7 b0 C	•	•	R	‡	⑥	‡
Store Acmltr.	STAA				97	4	2	A7	6	2	B7	5	3				A → M	•	•	‡	‡	R	•
	STAB				D7	4	2	E7	6	2	F7	5	3				B → M	•	•	‡	‡	R	•
Subtract	SUBA	80	2	2	90	3	2	A0	5	2	B0	4	3				A - M → A	•	•	‡	‡	‡	‡
	SUBB	C0	2	2	D0	3	2	E0	5	2	F0	4	3				B - M → B	•	•	‡	‡	‡	‡
Subtract Acmltrs.	SBA													10	2	1	A - B → A	•	•	‡	‡	‡	‡
Subtr. with Carry	SBCA	82	2	2	92	3	2	A2	5	2	B2	4	3				A - M - C → A	•	•	‡	‡	‡	‡
	SBCB	C2	2	2	D2	3	2	E2	5	2	F2	4	3				B - M - C → B	•	•	‡	‡	‡	‡
Transfer Acmltrs	TAB													16	2	1	A → B	•	•	‡	‡	R	•
	TBA													17	2	1	B → A	•	•	‡	‡	R	•
Test, Zero or Minus	TST							6D	7	2	7D	6	3				M - 00	•	•	‡	‡	R	R
	TSTA													4D	2	1	A - 00	•	•	‡	‡	R	R
	TSTB													5D	2	1	B - 00	•	•	‡	‡	R	R
																		H	I	N	Z	V	C

tended. Each mode occupies a column in Table 5-2 and the instructions that can be executed in each mode are listed in the appropriate column. The listing contains the OP code, the number of cycles, and the number of bytes required for the instruction. The number of cycles is listed under the ~ symbol, and gives the number of *clock cycles* each instruction uses. This information is used when analyzing the timing of the μP (Sec. 8-7.1). The number of *bytes* is listed under the # symbol and indicates the number of memory locations required by each instruction.

Example 5-1

How many cycles and bytes are required by:

a. A LOAD IMMEDIATE instruction?
b. A LOAD EXTENDED instruction?

Solution

a. Looking at the load accumulator instructions (LDAA means *load* the A accumulator and LDAB means *load* the B accumulator) in the IMMED column, we find that a LOAD IMMEDIATE takes **two cycles** and requires **two bytes**.

b. Moving over to the EXTND column, we see that a LOAD EXTENDED takes **four cycles** and the instruction occupies **three bytes**.

These modes are explained in the following paragraphs and illustrated in Fig. 5-3, where each instruction is assumed to start at location 10. The figure shows the Op Code at location 10 and the following bytes. It explains the function of each byte and gives a sample instruction for each mode.

5-5.1
Immediate Addressing Instructions

All the *immediate instructions* in Table 5-2 require two bytes. The first byte is the OP code and the *second byte* contains the *operand* or *information to be used*. If, for example, the accumulator contains the number 2C and the following instruction occurs in a program:

ADD A #$23

The # indicates that the hex value, $23 is to be added to the A accumulator. The immediate mode of the instruction is indicated by the # sign. After the instruction is executed, A contains 4F (23 + 2C).

Location		Example of Code	Instruction and Effect

Location		Example of Code	Instruction and Effect
10	OP Code	8B	ADD A #$33
11	Immediate value	33	Adds $(33)_{16}$ to A.

(a) Immediate addressing

10	OP Code	9B	ADD A $33
11	Direct address	33	Adds the contents of location 0033 to A.

(b) Direct addressing

10	OP Code	BB	ADD A $0133
11	High address byte	01	Adds the contents of location 0133 to A.
12	Low address byte	33	

(c) Extended addressing

10	OP Code	AB	ADD A $06,X
11	Offset	06	Adds the contents of the location given by the sum of the index register +6 to A.

(d) Indexed addressing

10	OP Code	1B	ABA
			Adds the contents of A to B. The results go into A.

(e) Inherent

Figure 5-3 Examples of the various addressing modes of the 6800.

Example 5-2
What does the following instruction do?   LDA B #$FF

Solution
The action of this instruction is shown in Fig. 5-4, where the OP code for the instruction LOAD B IMMEDIATE (C6) is in 40 and the immediate operand (FF) is in 41. The instruction places or LOADs the operand into the B accumulator.

5-5.2
Direct Instructions   Immediate instructions are used if the variable or operand is *known* to the programmer when he is coding.

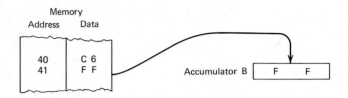

Figure 5-4 Action of a LOAD
IMMEDIATE instruction.

For example, if the programmer knows he wants to add 5 to a variable, it is more efficient to add it *immediately* than to store 5 in memory and do a direct or extended ADD. When one of the operands must reside in *memory,* however, *direct* or *extended* instructions are required.

Like immediate instructions, *direct instructions* require two bytes. The *second byte* contains the *address of the operand* used in the instruction. Since the OP code identifies this as a two-byte instruction, only 8 address bits are available. The μP contains 16 address lines, but for this instruction, the 8 MSBs of the address are effectively set to 0. The memory locations that can be addressed by a direct instruction are therefore restricted to 0000 to 00FF. It is often wise to place variable data in these memory locations because this data is usually referenced frequently throughout the program. The programmer can then make maximum use of direct instructions and reduce memory requirements by up to 25%.

Example 5-3
What happens when the instruction

LDA A $55

is encountered in a program? Assume that location 55 contains CA.

Solution
This is a direct instruction. The second byte of this two-byte instruction is the address (0055). The LDA A $55 instruction causes the μP to read location 0055 and load its contents into A. At the end of the instruction, the A accumulator contains CA.

The action of this instruction is shown in Fig. 5-5. The OP code for the LOAD A DIRECT (96) is again in memory location 40 and the operand (55) is in 41. Because this is a direct instruction, the operand is an address (0055) and the contents of that address (CA) are loaded into accumulator A.

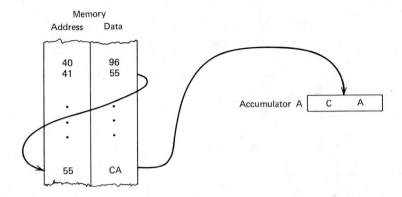

Memory

Address   Data

| 40 | 96 |
| 41 | 55 |

.	.
.	.
.	.

| 55 | CA |

Accumulator A   C   A

Figure 5-5 Action of a LOAD DIRECT instruction.

Example 5-4

If location 55 contains CA and the B accumulator contains 13, what does B contain after execution of the following instructions:

a. ADD B #$55
b. ADD B $55

Solution

a. The # indicates the IMMEDIATE mode. Thus, ADD B #$55 causes 55 to be added to 13 and the result is 55 + 13 = **68**.

b. Since the address of 55 is less than 100, this is a DIRECT mode instruction. It causes the contents of 55 to be added to B and the result stored in the B register. Since location 55 contains CA, the result stored is CA + 13 = **DD**.

5-5.3
Extended Instructions

Extended instructions are 3-byte instructions. The OP code is followed by two bytes that specify the address of the operand used by the instruction. The second byte contains the 8 high order bits of the address. Because 16 address bits are available, any one of the 65,536 memory locations in the **6800** μC can be selected. Thus, extended instructions have the advantage of being able to select *any* memory locations, but direct instructions only require two bytes in the program instead of three. Direct instructions also require one less cycle for execution so they are somewhat faster than the corresponding extended instructions.

Example 5-5

What occurs when the instruction

                            STA A $13C

appears in a program?

Solution

Since this operand is a hex address greater than 100, this is an EXTENDED
mode instruction. The instruction causes the contents of the A accumulator
to be *stored* or written into location 013C.

5-5.4
Indexed Instructions

As its name implies, an indexed instruction makes use of the *index
register* (X)[1] in the **6800** μP. *For any indexed instruction, the address referred to is the sum of the number* (called the OFFSET) *in
the second byte of the instruction, plus the contents of X.*

   Table 5-3 is a list of instructions that apply to the index register
and stack pointer. Notice the **6800** provides instructions to LOAD,
STORE, INCREMENT, and DECREMENT X as well as the stack
pointer (SP).

Example 5-6

What does the following program accomplish?

LDX #$0123
ADD A $A0,X

Solution

The first instruction is an immediate LOAD of the index register. It causes
the number 0123 to be loaded into X. The second instruction is an
INDEXED ADD. In executing this instruction, the μP adds the second
byte (A0) to the contents of X (0123) to get the data address. Thus, *the
contents of memory location 01C3 are added to the A accumulator.*

Index registers are useful when it is necessary to *relocate* a program. For example, if a program that originally occupied locations
0000 to 00CF must be moved or relocated to locations 0400 to 04CF,
all addresses used in the original program must be changed. In particular, direct instructions cannot be used because the program no
longer occupies lower memory. If X is loaded with the base address
of the program (400 in this example), then all direct instructions can

[1]Most manufacturers refer to the index register as the X register or simply X.

Table 5-3
Index Register and Stack Pointer Instructions

POINTER OPERATIONS	MNEMONIC	IMMED OP	~	#	DIRECT OP	~	#	INDEX OP	~	#	EXTND OP	~	#	IMPLIED OP	~	#	BOOLEAN/ARITHMETIC OPERATION	H (5)	I (4)	N (3)	Z (2)	V (1)	C (0)
Compare Index Reg	CPX	8C	3	3	9C	4	2	AC	6	2	BC	5	3				$X_H - M, X_L - (M+1)$	●	●	⑦	↕	⑧	●
Decrement Index Reg	DEX													09	4	1	$X - 1 \rightarrow X$	●	●	↕	↕	●	●
Decrement Stack Pntr	DES													34	4	1	$SP - 1 \rightarrow SP$	●	●	●	●	●	●
Increment Index Reg	INX													08	4	1	$X + 1 \rightarrow X$	●	●	↕	↕	●	●
Increment Stack Pntr	INS													31	4	1	$SP + 1 \rightarrow SP$	●	●	●	●	●	●
Load Index Reg	LDX	CE	3	3	DE	4	2	EE	6	2	FE	5	3				$M \rightarrow X_H, (M+1) \rightarrow X_L$	●	●	⑨	↕	R	●
Load Stack Pntr	LDS	8E	3	3	9E	4	2	AE	6	2	BE	5	3				$M \rightarrow SP_H, (M+1) \rightarrow SP_L$	●	●	⑨	↕	R	●
Store Index Reg	STX				DF	5	2	EF	7	2	FF	6	3				$X_H \rightarrow M, X_L \rightarrow (M+1)$	●	●	⑨	↕	R	●
Store Stack Pntr	STS				9F	5	2	AF	7	2	BF	6	3				$SP_H \rightarrow M, SP_L \rightarrow (M+1)$	●	●	⑨	↕	R	●
Indx Reg → Stack Pntr	TXS													35	4	1	$X - 1 \rightarrow SP$	●	●	●	●	●	●
Stack Pntr → Indx Reg	TSX													30	4	1	$SP + 1 \rightarrow X$	●	●	●	●	●	●

COND. CODE REG.

be changed to indexed instructions and the program will function as before.

Example 5-7

A data list that starts at memory location 1000 is to be moved or relocated to start at location 2000. Write a program to accomplish this.

Solution

In this program, it is necessary to read a byte from 1000, write it in 2000, read a byte from 1001, write it in 2001, etc. Before starting the program, two *pointers,* one for the read addresses and one for the write addresses, must be set up. Let us assume locations 80–83 are unused and set them aside for the pointers. Note that a pointer is an address and therefore requires two bytes to hold its 16 bits. The program can then proceed as follows.

Code		Mnemonics		Comments
CE 1000		LDX	#$1000	
DF 80		STX	$80	Store pointer 1
CE 2000		LDX	#$2000	
DF 82		STX	$82	Store pointer 2
DE 80	START	LDX	$80	Get pointer 1
A6 00		LDA	A 0,X	Get data at X into A
08		INX		Update pointer 1
DF 80		STX	$80	Store pointer 1
DE 82		LDX	$82	Get pointer 2
A7 00		STA	A 0,X	Store data in new table
08		INX		Update pointer 2
DF 82		STX	$82	Store pointer 2
20 F0		BRA	START	Loop back for next byte

The program proceeds by loading pointer 1 into X, doing an indexed LOAD, incrementing X, and restoring the incremented pointer. This leaves the data word in the accumulator. It then loads pointer 2 into X, stores the data in its new location, increments X, and restores pointer 2. It then branches back to get the second data word, etc. Of course this routine, as written, never ends. Methods used to terminate loops should be used and are discussed in Secs. 4-5.2 and 6-3.

The index register is often used by programs that are required to perform *code conversions.* Such programs might convert one code to another (ASCII to EBCDIC, for example), or might be used for trigonometric conversions where the sine or cosine of a given angle may be required.

Example 5-8

If the number in A represents an angle from 0 to 360° in 2° intervals [such that $(01)_{10} = 2°$, $(15)_{10} = (OF)_{16} = 30°$, up to $(179)_{10} = (B3)_{16} = 358°$],[2] write a program to obtain the sine of the angle to the nearest hundredth.

Solution

To solve this problem, a rudimentary sine table must first be written into memory. The base or beginning address is written into X. The sine of any angle can be obtained by going to that location whose address is the sum of the base address, plus the angle in A and loading that location with the sine of the corresponding angle. Since 8 bits are available, the values between $+127$ and -128 can be represented. The numbers $+100$ and -100 can represent 1.00 and -1.00 and the sine of each angle can be expressed to the nearest 0.01.

To illustrate the use of the table, note that the sine of $60° = 0.866 = 0.87$ to the nearest 0.01. If the base address of the table is 500, the 60° value occupies the 30th entry, or location 51E. Since the sine is scaled between $+100$ and -100, the number 0.87 becomes $(87)_{10} = (57)_{16}$. Therefore the contents of location 51E must be $(57)_{16}$. The table in memory is illustrated in Fig. 5-6.

Once the sine table is in memory, a program for taking an angle in A and producing its sine in B can be written as follows.

Addr	Code		Mnemonic	Comments
100	CE 04FF	LOOP	LDX #$4FF	Place pointer to table in X
103	08		INX	Increment index register
104	80 01		SUBA #1	Decrement angle in A
106	24 FC		BCC LOOP	Branch if carry clear, to LOOP
108	E6 00		LDA B 0,X	Load B from addr in X ($+0$)
...	...		...	etc.

This program uses a common technique of searching a table by incrementing X while simultaneously decrementing the value in A. Numbers larger than 128 in A will use bit 7 and thus we can not use a conditional branch decision that depends on the negative bit. We must use the carry bit (i.e., BRANCH IF CARRY CLEAR). In this type of program, DECA is usually used but it does not set the carry bit, and therefore our program must use a SUBA #1 instruction instead.

To illustrate further, if the sine of 210° is required, A must contain $(105)_{10} = (69)_{16}$. Location 0569 should contain $(-0.5) = -50$ (on our scale) $= (-32)_{16} = CE$. The program then loads the contents of 0569, or CE, into B.

Modifications and improvements to the above program are cer-

[2]Two degree intervals were used so that all angles from 0 to 360° could be represented within a single byte.

Memory address	Memory data	
500	00	sine of 0°
501	04	sine of 2°
502	07	sine of 4°
503	0A	sine of 6°
.	.	
.	.	
.	.	
50F	32	sine of 30° = 0.5 = 50 = $(32)_{16}$

Figure 5-6 The sine table in memory.

tainly possible. One obvious possibility is to limit the angle to 90° or less, which could improve the resolution. This example was presented primarily to show how tables can be constructed and used in a **6800** μP.

5-5.5
Implied Addressing

Implied instructions are used when *all* the information required for the instruction is already within the CPU and *no external operands* from memory or from the program (in the case of immediate instructions) are needed. Since no memory references are needed, implied instructions only require one byte for their OP code. Examples of implied instructions are CLEAR, INCREMENT and DECREMENT the accumulators, and SHIFT, ROTATE, ADD, or SUBTRACT accumulators.

Example 5-9

What does the following instruction do?

SBA

Solution

This is a one-byte instruction. SBA is the mnemonic for SUBTRACT AC-CUMULATORS. Table 5-2 shows that the operation is (A) − (B) → (A). Thus the number in the B accumulator is subtracted from the A accumulator and the results are stored in A. At the end of the instruction, A contains the result (difference), while B contains the original subtrahend and its value is unchanged.

5-6
Condition Codes

The **6800** uses 6 *condition codes,* labeled H, I, N, Z, V, and C. These codes reside in the condition code register (CCR). As shown in Fig. 5-1, the 1s in the two MSBs of the CCR are merely to fill it out to 8 bits.

The function of most of the condition codes is to retain information about the results of the last arithmetic or memory operation. The effect of an instruction on each condition code is shown in the six rightmost columns of Table 5-2. Two symbols dominate this part of the table; the dot (·) means that the instruction does not affect the condition codes, and the ↕ symbol indicates that the condition code is SET or CLEARED as a result of the instruction execution.

The I condition code is set or cleared to enable the μP to be *interrupted.* Its action is discussed in the chapter on interrupts (Chapter 10). None of the accumulator and memory instructions affect the I bit, but CLI and SEI will clear or set it.

5-6.1
The Z Bit

The Z (for zero) bit in the Condition Code Register is SET whenever an instruction results in a 0 being entered into the destination register or memory location. The Boolean algebra equation for the Z bit is:

$$Z = \bar{R_7}\,\bar{R_6}\,\bar{R_5}\,\bar{R_4}\,\bar{R_3}\,\bar{R_2}\,\bar{R_1}\,\bar{R_0}$$

which means that **Z is 1 only if all 8 bits of the result are 0.**

One function of the **compare instruction** *is simply to set the Z bit. Compare instructions internally subtract an operand from an accumulator, but* **do not** *change the contents of either. They simply change the bits of the CCR. A μP can determine if two operands are equal by comparing them. If the Z bit is SET after execution of the compare instruction, it indicates the two operands are indeed equal. This information is often used by branch instructions (see Sec. 6-3).*

5-6.2
The C Bit

The C or carry bit in the condition code register is mainly set in one of four ways.

1. It is SET during *add instructions* when the result of the addition produces a *carry* output.
2. For *subtraction and comparison instructions,* it is SET when the *absolute value of the subtrahend is larger than the absolute value of the minuend.* Generally this implies a *borrow.*
3. It is changed when executing SHIFT and ROTATE instructions. For

these instructions the bit shifted out of the accumulator becomes the carry bit and is not lost.

4. It is SET when an SEC instruction is executed.

Some other instructions, such as CLEAR and TEST, affect the carry bit. The careful programmer should consult the notes attached to Table 5-2 when there is any doubt about how an instruction affects the carry bit.

Two instructions, ADD WITH CARRY and SUBTRACT WITH CARRY, use the carry bit as part of the instruction. This simplifies the addition or subtraction of numbers that are longer than eight bits. If, for example, the least significant bytes are added and produce a carry output, an ADC (add with carry) instruction is used to add the more significant bytes and also adds 1 if the sum of the least significant bytes produced a carry output.

Example 5-10

The 16-bit number in memory locations F2 and F3 is to be subtracted from the 16-bit number in F0 and F1. The result is to be stored in F4 and F5. Assume F0 is the MS byte of the minuend and F2 is the MS byte of the subtrahend.

a. Write a program to subtract the numbers.

b. Show how the program operates if the minuend is $+4$ and the subtrahend is -5.

Solution

a. First the least significant bits (LSBs) of the minuend must be loaded into an accumulator, then the LSBs of the subtrahend is subtracted. *This may produce a borrow even if the final result is a positive number.* The result is stored and the MSBs of the minuend are loaded into an accumulator. The MSBs of the subtrahend are then subtracted from the accumulator, *with carry,* so that if a borrow had set the carry bit to 1, it is now subtracted from the more significant result. The program is shown in Fig. 5-7a.

b. To check this problem the machine language was written into the memory of a **6800** system equipped with a MINIBUG 3 monitor program (Chapter 11). This debugging program has the ability to step through the user's program one instruction at a time and to display the registers after each step. This is shown in Fig. 5-7b.

The contents of the Condition Code register are shown in Fig. 5-7b and Fig. 5-7c shows its interpretation. Note that the two MSBs of the CCR are always 1, and the status of each flag can be determined. For example, the

```
ADDR    OBJECT      MNEMONICS       COMMENTS

1000    96 F1       LDA A $F1       Load LS byte of minuend into A
1002    90 F3       SUB A $F3       Subtract [F3] from A
1004    97 F5       STA A $F5       Store A in F5
1006    96 F0       LDA A $F0       Load MS of minuend into A
1008    92 F2       SBC A $F2       Subtrct [F2] from A w/ borrow
100A    97 F4       STA A $F4       Store A in F4
```

a. Subtraction program listing

```
*M 00F0 12 00  1f
*  00F1 2B 04   1f
*  00F2 A3 FF   1f
*  00F3 44 FB   cr

   CC B  A   X     PC   SP                H I N Z V C
*D0 XX 01 XXXX 1000 A063             1 1 0 1 0 0 0 0
*D0 XX 04 XXXX 1002 A063             1 1 0 1 0 0 0 0
*D1 XX 09 XXXX 1004 A063             1 1 0 1 0 0 0 1
*D1 XX 09 XXXX 1006 A063             1 1 0 1 0 0 0 1
*D5 XX 00 XXXX 1008 A063             1 1 0 1 0 1 0 1
*D5 XX 00 XXXX 100A A063             1 1 0 1 0 1 0 1
*D5 XX 00 XXXX 100C A063             1 1 0 1 0 1 0 1

*M 00F4 00  1f                      c. Condition Code (CC)
*  00F5 09  cr                         binary equivalents
```

b. Minibug III debug program display (X = unimportant values)
       (Operator entries are underlined)

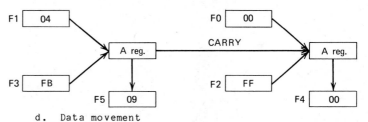

d. Data movement

Figure 5-7 Subtraction program for Example 5-10.

D0 in the first entry of the condition codes means that only 3 bits are set, the two MSBs, as always, and the I bit. All other condition codes are 0 at this point.

After the program has been entered in memory, starting at 1000, as shown at the top of Fig. 5-7a, the data is entered, starting at F0 as shown at the top of Fig. 5-7b. Note that −5 is entered in its 2s complement form (FFFB).

The first step of the program loads the Least Significant byte (04) from F1 into the A accumulator as shown in the second line of Fig. 5-7b, and increments the PC to 1002. The data movement is shown pictorially in Fig. 5-7d. The second step subtracts the contents of F3, which is the LS byte of the subtrahend. The result (09) is left in the A accumulator. This can produce a borrow, as in this case, and if the D1 is translated, as shown in Fig. 5-7c, the CARRY bit is SET. Step 3 stores the contents of A into location F5 (LS byte of the result). This is not seen unless the M command is used to display this memory location, as shown at the bottom of Fig. 5-7b. The Most Significant byte (MS byte) of the subtrahend is then subtracted in steps 4 and 5, but this time the carry is included. Step 5 subtracts FF from 00, which is the same as subtracting −1 from 0 and will give +1. This is a subtract with carry (borrow), however, and since the carry bit is SET, a 1 is subtracted from the result. Thus, the MS byte of the final result is 00 and the entire result is 0009, which is correct. Note that the carry bit is also SET at the end of the fifth instruction, but this has no effect on this problem. This program works because the carry bit that is SET in step 2 is not affected by the STA A and LDA A instructions (instructions 3 and 4), so it can be used in instruction 5.

As the program progresses it is instructive to follow the condition codes, especially the C and Z flags, which are important here. At the beginning the CCR contains D0, indicating both C and Z are 0. The subtractions SETs C and changes the CCR to D1. The load of F0, which contains 00, SETs Z and changes the CCR to D5.

5-6.3 The N Bit

The N (negative) bit of the CCR is SET whenever the results of an operation are negative. The N bit is SET whenever the MSB of the result is a 1 (an MSB of 1 indicates a negative number in 2s complement arithmetic). The Boolean equation for the N bit is $N = R_7$. Note that all accumulator and memory instructions, except PSH and PUL affect the N bit.

Example 5-11

The numbers 03A4 and 123F are in locations F0, F1, F2, and F3, respectively.

a. Write a program to add them and store the results in F4 and F5.
b. What instructions in the program set the N bit?

Solution

The program is shown in Fig. 5-8a. First the LS bytes are added and stored. Then the MS bytes are added (with carry) and stored.

The object program was loaded into memory using the MINIBUG 3 debug program and, as described in Example 5-10, was executed a step at a time, as shown in Fig. 5-8b. Figure 5-8d shows the binary equivalent of the hex values in column CC of Fig. 5-8b. The data movement is also shown in Fig. 5-8c. These three figures show the following.

1. The N bit is set by the first instruction because a negative number (A4) is loaded into A.

STEP	ADDR	OBJECT	MNEMONIC	COMMENTS
1	1000	96 F1	LDA A $F1	LOAD LS BYTE OF AUGEND
2	1002	9B F3	ADD A $F3	ADD LS BYTE OF ADDEND
3	1004	97 F5	STA A $F5	STORE RESULT IN F5
4	1006	96 F0	LDA A $F0	LOAD MS BYTE OF AUGEND IN A
5	1008	99 F2	ADC A $F2	ADD W/C MS BYTE OF ADDEND
6	100A	97 F4	STA A $F4	STORE MS BYTE

a. Program listing

```
*M 00F0 29 03   1f
*   00F1 46 A4   1f   augend
*   00F2 49 12   1f
*   00F3 57 3F   cr   addend
```

CC	B	A	X	PC	SP		H	I	N	Z	V	C
*D0	XX	01	XXXX	1000	A078		0	1	0	0	0	0
*D8	XX	A4	XXXX	1002	A078		0	1	1	0	0	0
*F8	XX	E3	XXXX	1004	A078		1	1	1	0	0	0
*F8	XX	E3	XXXX	1006	A078		1	1	1	0	0	0
*F0	XX	03	XXXX	1008	A078		1	1	0	0	0	0
*D0	XX	15	XXXX	100A	A078		0	1	0	0	0	0
*D0	XX	15	XXXX	100C	A078		0	1	0	0	0	0

d. Condition codes

```
*M 00F4 15   1f
*   00F5 E3   cr   answer
```

b. Execution by steps   (Operator entries underlined)

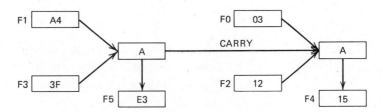

F1 [A4]   F0 [03]
            CARRY
   [A]   [A]

F3 [3F]   F2 [12]

        F5 [E3]   F4 [15]

Figure 5-8 Program analysis for
Example 5-11.

c. Data movement between memory and accumulator

2. The second step adds the 3F from F3. The result in A is seen to be E3, which also SETs the N bit because bit 7 of that byte is a 1.
3. The result is stored in step 3. The N bit remains SET.
4. The fourth step CLEARs the N bit because a positive number is loaded into A.
5. The N bit remains CLEAR during the fifth and sixth steps because the sum (in A) is a positive number.

Note that the N bit was SET by the first addition. Since this is an intermediate step in the summation, however, the N bit has no significance. At the end of the addition, the N bit is CLEAR, indicating a positive result. Note also that the carry bit was never SET by the numbers used in this program. If it was initially SET, it would have been cleared by the first addition (instruction 2).

5-6.4
The V Bit

The *V* or *overflow* bit is SET when an arithmetic operation results in a *2s complement overflow* or *underflow*. *Overflow occurs when the result of an arithmetic operation produces a number larger than the register can accommodate* (i.e., the sign bit is affected). *Underflow occurs when the result produces a number more negative than the register can accommodate* (less than 128). This also affects the *sign* bit.

The limitations on the numbers that can be handled by an *n*-bit register are $2^{n-1} - 1$ positive numbers, and 2^{n-1} negative numbers. A single 8-bit byte is thus restricted to numbers between $+127$ and -128.

To illustrate overflow, consider the number 100 expressed as an 8-bit number, 01100100. If an attempt is made to add 100 plus 100, the result is 200 (11001000). Unfortunately, considered as a 2s complement number, it equals -56. This ridiculous result occurred because the answer, $+200$, was *beyond the range* of numbers that could be handled by a single byte.

There are two criteria for overflow and underflow in the **6800**.

1. For *addition* instructions the basic Boolean equation for overflow is

$$V = \overline{A_7}\overline{B_7}R_7 + A_7 B_7 \overline{R}_7 \qquad (1)$$

where it is assumed that the operation is *A* plus $B \rightarrow R$ and A_7 is the MSB of *A* (the augend), B_7 is the MSB of *B* (the addend), and R_7 is the MSB of the result. The plus sign in the equation indicates the logical OR.

If the first term of the equation is 1, it indicates that two positive numbers have been added (because A_7 and B_7 are both 0) and the result is negative (because $R_7 = 1$). This possibility has been illustrated in the preceding paragraph.

The second term indicates that two negative numbers have been added and have produced a positive result.

Example 5-12
Show how the hex numbers 80 and C0 are added.

Solution
80 + C0 = 40 plus a carry (see Sec. 4-3.3). Note that 80 and C0 are both negative numbers, but their sum (as contained in a single byte) is positive. This corresponds to the second term of equation 1. Fortunately, this addition sets the V bit to warn the user that overflow (in this case underflow) has occurred.

2. For *subtraction* operations, the Boolean equation is

$$V = A_7\overline{B}_7\overline{R}_7 + \overline{A}_7B_7R_7 \quad (2)$$

The assumption here is that $A - B \rightarrow R$. The first term indicates that a negative number has been subtracted from a positive number and produced a negative result. The second term indicates that a positive number has been subtracted from a negative number and produced a positive result. In either case, the overflow bit is set to warn the user.

Example 5-13
If the numbers 23C4 and FDAB are added by the program of Example 5-11, what flags are set after the:

  a. LS bytes are added?
  b. MS bytes are added?

Solution
  a. First the μP adds the least significant bytes, C4 and AB, to obtain 6F. This addition sets the C and V bits. The V bit is set because two negative numbers were added and the result, 6F, is positive. This positive result also clears the N bit.
  b. The next part of the program adds the MS bytes, 23 and FD, and the 1 in the C bit. The result is 21. The C bit is SET, but both N and V are CLEAR. Because numbers of unlike sign were added, overflow is impossible and V is CLEAR.

The significance of the overflow bit depends on the program. In Example 5-13, the V bit was set after the first addition but, because this was an intermediate step, the V bit could be ignored. After the final addition the V bit was CLEAR, indicating that the result was correct.

5-6.5
Manipulations of the Condition
Code Register

Table 5-4 shows those instructions that affect the CCR.

1. Specific instructions exist to SET or CLEAR the C, V and I bits.
2. The CCR can be transferred to the A accumulator by a TPA instruction. This would be done if the program had to preserve the present contents of the CCR for future use. The CCR could be transferred to A and then saved in RAM by a STORE A or PUSH A instruction.
3. The contents of accumulator A can be transferred to the CCR by a TAP instruction. This would be done when the contents of the CCR are being restored from memory.

Table 5-4
Condition Code Register Instructions

| | | IMPLIED | | | | COND. CODE REG. | | | | | |
| | | | | | | 5 | 4 | 3 | 2 | 1 | 0 |
OPERATIONS	MNEMONIC	OP	~	#	BOOLEAN OPERATION	H	I	N	Z	V	C
Clear Carry	CLC	0C	2	1	$0 \rightarrow C$	•	•	•	•	•	R
Clear Interrupt Mask	CLI	0E	2	1	$0 \rightarrow I$	•	R	•	•	•	•
Clear Overflow	CLV	0A	2	1	$0 \rightarrow V$	•	•	•	•	R	•
Set Carry	SEC	0D	2	1	$1 \rightarrow C$	•	•	•	•	•	S
Set Interrupt Mask	SEI	0F	2	1	$1 \rightarrow I$	•	S	•	•	•	•
Set Overflow	SEV	0B	2	1	$1 \rightarrow V$	•	•	•	•	S	•
Acmltr A → CCR	TAP	06	2	1	$A \rightarrow CCR$	①—————					
CCR → Acmltr A	TPA	07	2	1	$CCR \rightarrow A$	•	•	•	•	•	•

R = Reset
S = Set
• = Not affected
① (ALL) Set according to the contents of Accumulator A.

Example 5-14

At a point in a program the H, I, and C bit of the CCR should be SET and
the N, V and Z bits should be CLEAR. Write a sequence of instructions
to set the bits accordingly.

Solution

According to Fig. 5-7c, the CCR should look like this:

11110001

It can be forced into this configuration by the following instructions.

OP code	Mnemonic	Comment
86 F1	LDA A #$F1	Load desired contents of CCR into A
06	TAP	Transfer A to CCR

5-7

BCD Addition and the H Bit

Although programmers and readers of this book can use hex fluently,
most people prefer to communicate with their computers using or-
dinary *decimal numbers*. Normal input devices, such as teletypes or
hand calculator keyboards, have only keys for the numbers 0 through
9, and their outputs, whether presented as a type-out by a teletype
or on a 7-segment display by a hand calculator, must be in decimal
form.

In applications that deal with money, such as cash registers, it is
preferable to keep the numbers in decimal form, rather than converting them to binary or hex. The use of the H bit of the CCR and

Decimal Digit	Binary Coded Decimal (BCD) representation
0	0000
1	0001
2	0010
3	0011
4	0100
5	0101
6	0110
7	0111
8	1000
9	1001
X	1010
X	1011
X	1100
X	1101
X	1110
X	1111

Figure 5-9 The BCD code conversion tables.

the DAA (decimal adjust accumulator) instruction makes decimal arithmetic possible.

5-7.1
Expressing Numbers in BCD[3]

Decimal numbers are usually entered into a computer in BCD (binary coded decimal) form. The BCD code uses four binary bits called a *decade* to represent a single decimal digit from 0 to 9. Since numbers greater than 9 are *not* used, the 4-bit representation of the numbers from 10 to 15 should *never* appear in a BCD output. The BCD code conversion table is shown in Fig. 5-9.

When a number consisting of several decimal digits is to be represented in BCD form, each digit is represented by its own group of 4 bits. Therefore, there are four times as many bits in the representation as there are decimal digits in the original number.

Example 5-15
Express the number 6309 in BCD form.

Solution
From the code conversion table, we find that:

$$6 = 0110$$
$$3 = 0011$$
$$0 = 0000$$
$$9 = 1001$$

[3]Readers familiar with BCD may omit this section.

The number 6309 is expressed by stringing these bits together:

$$(6309)_{10} = \underbrace{0110}\underbrace{0011}\underbrace{0000}\underbrace{1001}$$

$$\qquad\qquad\quad 6 \quad\; 3 \quad\; 0 \quad\; 9$$

Numbers given in BCD form can be converted into decimal numbers simply by dividing them into 4-bit decades, starting at the least significant bit, and assigning the correct decimal digit to each decade.

Example 5-16

Find the decimal equivalent of the BCD number

$$0001\,0101\,1000\,0111\,0100$$

Solution

The given number is divided into groups of 4 bits each and the decimal digit for each decade identified:

$$\underbrace{0001}\underbrace{0101}\underbrace{1000}\underbrace{0111}\underbrace{0100}$$

$$\quad 1 \qquad 5 \qquad 8 \qquad 7 \qquad 4$$

The decimal equivalent of the given BCD number is **15,874**.

5-7.2
Adding BCD Numbers

Since each **6800** memory location contains 8 bits and each BCD decade contains 4 bits, it is natural to store two BCD digits in a single memory location. This is sometimes called *packing,* or *packed BCD,* and is a function of the input-output routine.

Addition and subtraction of BCD numbers is possible, but since all addition and subtraction instructions in the **6800** assume *binary* numbers, the *binary results must be manipulated to convert them to BCD.* This is done by using the H bit and the DAA instruction.

Table 5-2 shows that the H bit is changed only by addition instructions. *It is SET when the addition produces a carry out of bit position 3 and into bit position 4.* For BCD numbers the *H* bit is SET whenever the sum of the two digits, plus carry, is equal to or greater than $(16)_{10}$. Because this carry occurs midway through the byte, the *H* bit is sometimes called the *half-carry* bit.

Example 5-17

The A and B accumulators contain the decimal numbers 48 and 79, respectively. They are added by an ADD accumulator (ABA) instruction. What is the result and what are the conditions of the C and H bits after the addition?

```
*M  1100  1B

    CC   B   A   X     PC    SP
*DO 79  48  XXXX  1100  XXXX
*FA 79  C1  XXXX  1101  XXXX
```

```
H I N Z V C
1 1 1 1 1 0 1 0
   F      A
```

Figure 5-10 Program execution for Example 5-17.

a. Results of one instruction step.

b. Condition Code reg

Solution

The **6800** adds 48 and 79 as though they were hex digits, placing the sum, **C1**, in the A accumulator. The results are shown in Fig. 5-10. At the end of the addition the H bit is SET (because the sum of 8 and 9 produces a carry), but the carry bit is CLEAR because the sum of the two most significant digits is less than 16.

5-7.3
The DAA Instruction

The result of Example 5-17 (48 + 79 = C1) is unsatisfactory if decimal arithmetic is being used. Addition instructions must be followed by a *decimal adjust accumulator* (DAA) instruction to convert the hex result to the correct BCD result.

The DAA instruction modifies an answer as shown in Table 5-5. It examines four parts of the result.

1. The lower half-byte
2. The upper half-byte
3. The H bit
4. The C bit

It then adds 00, 06, 60, or 66 to the answer. This transforms the result to BCD.

Example 5-18

What happens if a DAA instruction follows the result of Example 5-17?

Solution

In Example 5-17, the sum was C1. The DAA notes:
1. The lower half-byte is 0–3.
2. The H bit is SET.
3. The upper half-byte is A–F.
4. The C bit is CLEAR.

These conditions occur on line 6 of Table 5-5. The table shows that the DAA adds 66 to the result and SETs the C bit. After the DAA, A contains C1 + 66 = 27 and the carry bit is SET, which indicates a carry (a weight of 100 in decimal arithmetic). Therefore the BCD sum is 127, which is correct. The progress of the program is illustrated in Fig. 5-11.

ACCUMULATOR AND MEMORY REFERENCING INSTRUCTIONS

Table 5-5
Action of the DAA Instruction

State of C-bit before DAA (Col. 1)	Upper Half-byte (bits 4–7) (Col. 2)	Initial Half-carry H-bit (Col. 3)	Lower Half-byte (bits 0–3) (Col. 4)	Number Added after by DAA (Col. 5)	State of C-bit DAA (COl. 6)
0	0–9	0	0–9	00	0
0	0–8	0	A–F	06	0
0	0–9	1	0–3	06	0
0	A–F	0	0–9	60	1
0	9–F	0	A–F	66	1
0	A–F	1	0–3	66	1
1	0–2	0	0–9	60	1
1	0–2	0	A–F	66	1
1	0–3	1	0–3	66	1

Example 5-19

The decimal numbers 2946 and 4957 are in locations F0, F1 and F2, F3, respectively. Write a program to add them and store the BCD result in locations F4, F5.

Solution

The program and its analysis are shown in Fig. 5-12a. Figure 5-12b is the result of executing one instruction at a time with the debug program (MINIBUG III). Figure 5-12c shows the binary representation of the Condition Code Register for each step. The first addition SETS the N and V bits. These bits are both RESET and carry is SET by the DAA instruction. The last instruction shows how the two adjacent bytes containing the answer can be fetched as a 16-bit or 4 decimal digit number for further manipulation by the program. The result in the X register is the correct answer.

```
*M 1100 1B
   1101 19

   CC   B    A    X      PC     SP              H I N Z V C

*D0  79   48   XXXX   1100   XXXX            0 1 0 0 0 0

*FA  79   C1   XXXX   1101   XXXX            1 1 1 0 1 0

*F1  79   27   XXXX   1102   XXXX            1 1 0 0 0 1
```

Figure 5-11 Program execution for Example 5-18.

a. Results of instruction steps   b. Condition Code reg.

STEP	ADDR	OBJECT	MNEMONIC	COMMENTS
1	1000	96 F1	LDA A $F1	LOAD LS BYTE OF AUGEND
2	1002	9B F3	ADD A $F3	ADD LS BYTE OF ADDEND
3	1004	19	DAA	ADJUST FOR HALF CARRY, IF ANY
4	1005	97 F5	STA A $F5	STORE RESULT IN F5
5	1007	96 F0	LDA A $F0	LOAD MS BYTE OF AUGEND IN A
6	1009	99 F2	ADC A $F2	ADD W/C MS BYTE OF ADDEND
7	100B	19	DAA	ADJUST RESULT
8	100C	97 F4	STA A $F4	STORE MS BYTE
9	100E	DE F4	LDX $F4	LOAD 16 BIT ANSWER INTO X

a. Program listing

```
*M 00F0 29 lf
   00F1 46 lf
   00F2 49 lf
   00F3 57 cr
```

CC	B	A	X	PC	SP		H	I	N	Z	V	C
*D0	XX	01	XXXX	1000	A071		0	1	0	0	0	0
*D0	XX	46	XXXX	1002	A071		0	1	0	0	0	0
*DA	XX	9D	XXXX	1004	A071		0	1	1	0	1	0
*D1	XX	03	XXXX	1005	A071		0	1	0	0	0	1
*D1	XX	03	XXXX	1007	A071		0	1	0	0	0	1
*D1	XX	29	XXXX	1009	A071		0	1	0	0	0	1
*F0	XX	73	XXXX	100B	A071		1	1	0	0	0	0
*F0	XX	79	XXXX	100C	A071		1	1	0	0	0	0
*F0	XX	79	XXXX	100E	A071		1	1	0	0	0	0
*F0	XX	79	7903	1010	A071		1	1	0	0	0	0

b. Register changes   c. Condition codes

Figure 5-12 Program execution for Example 5-19.

5-7.4
Subtracting BCD Numbers

BCD subtraction in the **6800** μP can be accomplished by complementation. *Subtraction by complementation* is a method of performing subtraction by addition, and works well for decimal numbers. In subtraction by complementation, the subtrahend must be replaced by its 9s complement, which is obtained by taking each decimal digit and replacing it with the difference between itself and 9. The 9s complement of 2, for example, is 7, and the 9s complement of 0 is 9.

Example 5-20

Find the 9s complement of the decimal number 399704.

Solution

The 9s complement is obtained by replacing each digit with its 9s complement as shown:

$$
\begin{array}{ll}
399704 & \text{(original number)} \\
600295 & \text{(9s complement)}
\end{array}
$$

Note that each digit plus its 9s complement adds to 9.

Decimal subtraction can be performed by using the following procedure:

1. Take the 9s complement of the subtrahend and add it to the minuend.
2. Remove the most significant 1, and add it to the least significant digit.
This is known as an *end-around-carry*.

Example 5-21

Subtract 19,307 from 28,652.

Solution

The 9s complement of 19,307 is 80,692. Adding this to the minuend, we
obtain

$$
\begin{array}{lll}
\text{(minuend)} & 28,652 & \text{(original number)} \\
\text{(subtrahend)} & \underline{80,692} & \text{(9s complement)} \\
& 109,344
\end{array}
$$

Removing the most significant 1 and adding it to the least significant digit
yields

$$
\begin{array}{ll}
109,344 & \\
+ \qquad 1 & \text{(end-around-carry)} \\
\hline
\mathbf{9,345}
\end{array}
$$

This is the correct result.

In the **6800** the H bit is *not* set by subtraction instructions but BCD
subtraction can be accomplished by complementing and adding, because addition sets the H bit (if digit total exceeds 9). The **6800** can be
programmed for BCD subtraction as follows:

1. Load the A accumulator with 99.
2. Subtract the subtrahend (to obtain the 9s complement).

3. Add 1 (to make the 10s complement).

4. Add the minuend (BCD addition).

5. Decimal adjust the accumulator.

In this method, each digit can be subtracted from nine without "borrows" and thus binary subtraction instructions can be used.

Example 5-22

Subtract 35 from 82 using the method described above. Assume 82 is in F0 and 35 is in F2.

Solution

The program is shown in Fig. 5-13a and the status of the CCR is shown in Fig. 5-13c. The progress of the program is shown in Fig. 5-13b. The correct answer, 47, appears in A at the end of the program. Some adjustments are required in the program if multiple byte subtraction or the possibility of negative results are to be allowed.

```
ADDR    OBJECT      MNEMONICS        COMMENTS

1000    86 99       LDAA #$99        MAKE 9s COMPLEMENT
1002    90 F2       SUBA $F2         GET SUBTRAHEND
1004    4C          INCA             MAKE 10s COMPLEMENT
1005    9B F0       ADDA $F0         ADD OTHER NUMBER
1007    19          DAA              DECIMAL ADJUST
```

a. Program Listing

```
    *M 00F0 82 1f
       00F2 35 cr
```

	CC	B	A	X	PC	SP		H	I	N	Z	V	C
*XX		XX	XX	XXXX	1000	XXXX		1	1	X	X	X	X	X
*D8		XX	99	XXXX	1002	XXXX		1	1	0	1	1	0	0	0
*D2		XX	64	XXXX	1004	XXXX		1	1	0	1	0	0	1	0
*D0		XX	65	XXXX	1005	XXXX		1	1	0	1	0	0	0	0
*D8		XX	E7	XXXX	1007	XXXX		1	1	0	1	1	0	0	0
*D1		XX	47	XXXX	1008	XXXX		1	1	0	1	0	0	0	1

b. Register contents   c. Condition Code reg.

Figure 5-13 Program execution for Example 5-22.

5-8

Logic Instructions

The **6800** contains AND, OR, and EXCLUSIVE OR instructions. They allow the programmer to perform Boolean algebra manipulations on a variable, and to SET or CLEAR specific bits in a byte. They can also be used to test specific bits in a byte, but other logic instructions such as BIT, TEST, or COMPARE may be more useful for these tests.

Since logic operations are performed on a *bit-by-bit* basis, the C bit has no effect. It is unchanged by all logic operations. The V bit is cleared by logic operations. The N and Z bits are set in accordance with the result.

5-8.1

Setting and Clearing Specific Bits

AND and OR instructions can be used to SET or CLEAR a specific bit or bits in an accumulator or memory location. This is very useful in those systems where each bit has a specific meaning, rather than being part of a number. In the control and status registers of the PIA or ACIA, for example (see Chapters 9 and 10), each bit has a distinct meaning.

Example 5-23

Bit 3 of A must be SET, while all other bits remain unchanged. How can this be done?

Solution

If A is ORed with 08, which contains 1 in bit position 3, bit 3 of the result will be SET and all other bits will remain as they were. The instruction ORA A #08 (8A 08) accomplishes this.

Example 5-24

Bits 3, 5, and 6 of A are to be cleared while all other bits remain unchanged. How can this be done?

Solution

If A is ANDed with 97, which contains 0s in positions 3, 5, and 6, then these bits of the result are 0 and the rest are unchanged. The instruction 84 97 (AND A immediate with 97) accomplishes this.

5-8.2

Testing Bits

In addition to being able to SET or CLEAR specific bits in a register, it is also possible to *test* specific bits to determine if they are 1 or 0. In the Peripheral Interface Adapter (PIA), for example, a 1 in the MSB of the control register indicates some external event has occurred. The μP can test this bit and react appropriately. Typically the results of the test sets the Z or N bit. The program then executes a conditional branch (see Chapter 6) and takes one of two different paths depending on the results of the test.

Accumulator bits can be tested by the AND and OR instructions, but this modifies the contents of the accumulator. If the accumulator is to remain unchanged, the BIT TEST instruction is used. This ANDs memory (or an immediate operand) with the accumulator without changing either.

Example 5-25

Determine if bit 5 of accumulator B is a 1 or 0 without changing B.

Solution

The instruction BIT B #$20 (C5 20) is a BIT TEST immediate. It ANDs the contents of B with 20. Since 20 only contains a 1 in the bit 5 position, the result is 00 if bit 5 of B is 0 and 20 if bit 5 of B is 1. The Z bit is CLEARed or SET accordingly and retains the result of this test.

5-8.3
Compare Instructions

A COMPARE instruction essentially subtracts a memory or immediate operand from an accumulator, leaving the *contents of both memory and accumulator unchanged*. The actual results of the subtraction are discarded; the function of the COMPARE is to SET the condition code bits.

There are two types of COMPARE instructions; those that involve accumulators, and those that use the index register. Effectively, the two numbers that are being compared are subtracted, but neither value is changed. The subtraction serves to SET the condition codes. In the case of the CPX instruction, only the Z bit is significant, but for the COMPARE accumulator (CMP A or B) instruction, the carry, negative, zero and overflow bits are affected and allow us to determine which of the operands is greater.

The COMPARE INDEX REGISTER instructions compare the contents of the Index Register with a 16-bit operand. They are often used to terminate loops (Example 6-5). These instructions set the Z bit properly, but the N and V bits are often *set incorrectly* and the reader is warned *not* to use N or V after a COMPARE INDEX REGISTER instruction.

Example 5-26

Determine if the contents of location CB are equal to the number F2.

Solution

One program that does this is:

```
C6 F2        LDA  B   #$F2      (LOAD B IMMEDIATE)
D1 CB        CMP  B   $CB       (COMPARE B DIRECT)
```

The first instruction loads F2 into B. The second instruction compares the contents of B (F2) with the contents of CB. The Z bit is SET if they are equal, since the result of the subtraction is 0.

Example 5-27

Determine if the contents of 80C0 are greater than, equal to, or less than 2A.

Solution

A program that does this is

```
86 2A        LDA  A   #$2A      (LOAD A IMMEDIATE)
B1 80C0      CMP  A   $80C0     (COMPARE A EXTENDED)
```

Three possibilities exist:

1. 2A is greater than the contents of 80C0. In this case, N = Z = 0 after the compare, indicating the result is not 0 and not negative.
2. The contents of 80C0 equal 2A. In this case, the Z bit is SET.
3. The contents of 80C0 are greater than 2A. Here the subtraction gives a negative result and N is set.

5-8.4
The TEST Instruction

The TEST (TST) instruction subtracts 0 from an operand and therefore does not alter the operand. Its effect, like that of compares or bit tests, is to set the N and Z bits. It differs in that it always CLEARs the overflow and carry bits. It is used to set the condition codes in accordance with the contents of an accumulator or memory location.

Example 5-28

Determine if the contents of location F0 are positive, zero, or negative.

Solution

This problem is solved by using the TEST instruction. Since F0 is below FF it is generally addressed in direct mode, but this mode is not available with the test instruction (see Table 5-2). We can, however, use extended addressing. The instruction

```
                    TST $F0        7D 00F0
```

sets the N and Z bits and allows us to determine the sign of the number in F0.

5-9
Other 6800 Instructions

The remaining **6800** instructions listed in Table 5-2 are well described by their name and mnemonics.

5.9.1
CLEAR, INCREMENT, and DECREMENT Instructions

These allow the user to alter the contents of an accumulator or memory location as specified. Those instructions referring to memory locations can be executed in extended or indexed modes only. They are simple to write, but require 6 or 7 cycles for execution because the contents of a memory location must be brought to the CPU, modified, and rewritten to memory.

5.9.2
SHIFT and ROTATE Instructions

SHIFTs and ROTATEs have already been discussed in Sec. 3-6.1. The drawings in Table 5-2, which are the same as Figs. 3-4 and 3-5, show diagrammatically how they work. Note that they all use the carry bit, either for input, output, or both. Rotates are 9-bit rotates that combine the 8-bit accumulator and the carry bit.

5.9.3
Accumulator Transfer Instructions

The TAB and TBA instructions allow the transfer of data from A to B and B to A, respectively. These instructions help the user make use of both accumulators, which simplifies the programming of the **6800**.

5.9.4
COMPLEMENT and NEGATE Instructions

The COMPLEMENT instructions invert all bits of a memory location. They are useful as logic instructions and in programs requiring complementation, such as the BCD subtraction program.

The NEGATE instructions take the 2s complement of a number and therefore negates it. The negate instruction works by subtracting the operand from 00. Since the absolute value of the operand is always greater than the minuend, except when the operand itself is 00, the negate instruction SETs the carry flag for all cases, except when the operand is 00.

Example 5-29
There is a 16-bit number in F0 (MS byte) and F1. Write a program to negate the 16-bit number.

Solution
The general method of negating a number is to complement all the bits and add 1. Alternatively, it can be subtracted from zero as the NEGATE instruction does. The simple solution to this problem, negating both F0 and F1, fails because it effectively adds 1 to both bytes (i.e., if F0 and F1 contain C1D2 and both are negated, the result is 3F2E which is *not* −C1D2). Negating the LS byte and complementing the MS byte works in all cases *except* if the LS byte is 00.

A program that works for all cases is:

```
CLR   A
NEG   $F1
SBC   A $F0
STA   A $F0
```

The NEGATE instruction produces a carry for all cases except when F1 contains 00. Now the SBC subtracts out the carry, complementing the MS byte. If F1 contains 00, there is no carry and the SBC instruction negates the MS byte as required (see Problem 5-20).

5-10
Summary

In this chapter the accumulator and memory instructions available in the **6800** μP were introduced. Five modes of addressing were discussed and examples using each mode were given.

The function of each bit of the CCR was explained and the way in which instructions CLEAR and SET these bits was discussed. The addition and subtraction instructions were introduced, and examples of multibyte arithmetic using the carry bit were presented. Finally, logical instructions and miscellaneous instructions, such as transfers, compares, increments, and decrements, were discussed to complete this introduction to **6800** programming.

5-11
Glossary

BCD (binary coded decimal) The use of four bits to represent a single decimal digit (a number from 0 to 9).

Condition code register (CCR) The register that contains the flags or condition codes. In the **6800** the CCR contains six flags and two unused bits (always 1).

Decimal adjust accumulator (DAA) An instruction that adjusts a binary addition to make the results appear as BCD.

End-around-carry The process of adding the most significant 1 to the least significant digit during subtraction by complementation.

Flags Bits within a μP that retain information about the results of previous operations. Condition codes are also called flags.

Immediate operand An operand that is used directly by the program.

Index register A 16-bit register within a computer or μP. During indexed instructions an offset (sometimes zero) is added to the specified instruction address to obtain the memory address actually used.

Mnemonic An abbreviated form of a word designed to aid the reader's memory.

Overflow A result that is too large to be contained in a single word or byte.

Underflow A result that is too negative to be contained in a single word or byte.

5-12
References

Bishop, Ron, *Basic Microprocessors and the 6800,* Hayden Book Co., Rochelle Park, N.J., 1979.

Joseph Greenfield, *Practical Digital Design Using ICs,* John Wiley, New York, 1977.

Leventhal, Lance, *6800 Assembly Language Programming,* Osborn & Associates, Berkeley, California, 1978.

Motorola, *M6800 Programming Reference Manual,* Motorola, Phoenix, Arizona, 1976.

Motorola, *M6800 Microcomputer System Design Data,* Motorola, Phoenix, Arizona, 1976.

5-13
Problems

5-1 Why doesn't the instruction set include a STORE IMMEDIATE instruction?

5-2 If A contains 45 initially, what will it contain after the following instructions?

a.	8A 77	ORA A #$77	**f.**	4F	CLR A
b.	80 23	SUB A #$23	**g.**	43	COM A
c.	84 77	AND A #$77	**h.**	4A	DEC A
d.	8B 77	ADD A #$77	**i.**	40	NEG A
e.	88 77	EOR A #$77			

5-3 Assume each location in memory between 40 and 4F contains 3 more than its own address (i.e., 40 contains 43, 41 contains 44, etc.). If A contains 21 and the index register contains 20, what does A contain after executing each of the following instructions:
a. 88 42   EOR A #$42
b. 9B 42   ADD A $42
c. AB 23   ADD A $23,X

5-4 How many cycles and bytes do *subtract* instructions take in the:
a. Immediate mode
b. Direct mode
c. Indexed mode
d. Extended mode
e. Implied mode

5-5 Show that the instruction 88 FF is equivalent to the instruction 43.

5-6 Show how the program of Example 5-8 operates if the angle is:
a. 44°
b. 144°
c. 244°
d. 344°
What memory locations are accessed and what do they contain?

5-7 Write a program to add the 32 bit number in F3-F0 to the 24 bit number in F6-F4. Place the results in FF-FC.

5-8 If the two numbers in Problem 5-7 are
$$F35C2472 \quad \text{and} \quad CC8142$$
show the results in the accumulator and the state of the H, V, Z, N, and C bits after each step in your program.

5-9 Write a program to add the decimal numbers
$$4972 \quad \text{and} \quad 3729$$
Use BCD arithmetic. Show the status of the accumulator and H, V, N, Z, and C after each instruction.

5-10 Write a program to subtract 016359 from 242214. Use BCD arithmetic. Show the status of the accumulator and H, V, N, Z, and C after each instruction.

5-11 Write a program to SET bits 2, 4, 6, and 7 leaving all other bits unchanged.

5-12 Write a program to CLEAR bits 2, 4, 6, and 7, leaving all other bits unchanged.

5-13 Compare the bytes in F0 with F1 to determine if they are equal.
a. Use the compare instruction.
b. Use the Exclusive OR (XOR) instruction.

5-14 Test the contents of F3 to determine if bit 4 is a 1.
a. Use an AND instruction.
b. Use a bit test instruction.
How do the condition codes indicate whether the bit is a 1 or a 0?

5-15 **a.** What does each instruction of the following program do?

96 40	C9 00	97 42
D6 41	8B 05	98 43
48	C9 00	

b. If the numbers in 40 and 41 initially are 7E and 23, what numbers appear in 42 and 43 at the end of the program?

5-16 Suppose Y is an integer $(0 \leq Y \leq 10)$ in the A accumulator and we must calculate $20Y^3 - 10Y^2 + 5$. This is to be done by table lookup, rather than making the μP do the calculations. Construct the table and a program to write the correct result into locations D0 and D1.

5-17 When two numbers are added the result is positive when the N bit and V bit are both CLEAR or both SET. Explain. Give an example of each case using numbers.

5-18 Explain why the N and V bits are SET in Fig. 5-7.

5-19 A 16-bit number is in locations F0 (MS byte) and F1. Write a program to shift it two bits to the left. Bring 0s into the vacated positions. Ignore the two MSBs.

5-20 Consider the three programs:

NEG $F1	NEG $F1	CLR A
NEG $F0	COM $F0	NEG $F1
		SBC A $F0
		STA A $F0

What is the result of each program if F0, F1 contain

a. 1357

b. 1300

In which cases do each of these programs correctly negate the number?

After attempting to solve the problems, try to answer the self-evaluation questions in Sec. 5-2. If any of them still seem difficult, review the appropriate sections of the chapter to find the answers.

Chapter 6 Branch and Jump Instructions

6-1
Instructional Objectives

This chapter continues the presentation of the **6800** instruction set by introducing the BRANCH and JUMP instructions, the stack, and the instructions that allow the use of subroutines. After reading it, the student should be able to:

1. Use JUMP instructions in programs.
2. Calculate the effective address of a BRANCH instruction and use BRANCH instructions.
3. Write programs containing loops, including those where the exit from the loop depends upon a *conditional branch* instruction.
4. Use instructions involving stacks, such as PUSH, PULL, and JUMP TO SUBROUTINE.
6. Use indirect jumps.
7. Write programs using subroutines and preserve the contents of the main program's registers during subroutine execution.
8. Write multiply and divide routines.

6-2
Self-Evaluation Questions

Watch for the answers to the following questions as you read the chapter. They should help you to understand the material presented.

1. Explain why branch instructions are said to be in the *relative* mode. What are they relative to?
2. What is the difference between a jump and a branch?
3. Why must a JUMP instruction be used when the object of the jump is more than $+129$ or -126 locations away?
4. What is the difference between a BRANCH GREATER THAN OR EQUAL instruction and a BRANCH IF PLUS instruction?
5. What is the function of the stack pointer (SP) register? Why must it be initialized if it is going to be used?
6. Explain why instructions that write to the stack (i.e., PUSH) decrement the SP, while instructions that read from the stack (i.e., PULL) increment the SP.
7. In a jump or branch to subroutine, how and why are the program counter (PC) contents preserved?

6-3
Branch and Jump
Instructions

The programs of Chapter 5 were constrained because BRANCH and JUMP instructions were not introduced. Table 6-1 shows the BRANCH and JUMP instructions available in the **6800** μP. They complete the **6800** instruction set and allow programs requiring *decisions, branches,* and *subroutines* to be written.

6-3.1
Jump Instructions

One of the simplest instructions in Table 6-1 is the JUMP instruction. It loads the PC with a new value and thereby transfers or *jumps* the program to a *new location.*

The JUMP instruction can be specified in one of two modes, indexed or extended, as shown in Fig. 6-1. The JUMP INDEXED (JMP 0,X) is a two-byte instruction; its function is shown in Fig. 6-1a. The second byte or *offset* is added to the index register and the sum is loaded into the PC. One use of the INDEXED JUMP instruction is to enable interrupts in the MEK-6800-D2 system (see Sec. 11-7).

Table 6-1
Jump and Branch Instructions

OPERATIONS	MNEMONIC	RELATIVE			INDEX			EXTND			IMPLIED			BRANCH TEST	COND. CODE REG.					
		OP	~	#	OP	~	#	OP	~	#	OP	~	#		5 H	4 I	3 N	2 Z	1 V	0 C
Branch Always	BRA	20	4	2										None	•	•	•	•	•	•
Branch If Carry Clear	BCC	24	4	2										C = 0	•	•	•	•	•	•
Branch If Carry Set	BCS	25	4	2										C = 1	•	•	•	•	•	•
Branch If = Zero	BEQ	27	4	2										Z = 1	•	•	•	•	•	•
Branch If ≥ Zero	BGE	2C	4	2										N ⊕ V = 0	•	•	•	•	•	•
Branch If > Zero	BGT	2E	4	2										Z + (N ⊕ V) = 0	•	•	•	•	•	•
Branch If Higher	BHI	22	4	2										C + Z = 0	•	•	•	•	•	•
Branch If ≤ Zero	BLE	2F	4	2										Z + (N ⊕ V) = 1	•	•	•	•	•	•
Branch If Lower Or Same	BLS	23	4	2										C + Z = 1	•	•	•	•	•	•
Branch If < Zero	BLT	2D	4	2										N ⊕ V = 1	•	•	•	•	•	•
Branch If Minus	BMI	2B	4	2										N = 1	•	•	•	•	•	•
Branch If Not Equal Zero	BNE	26	4	2										Z = 0	•	•	•	•	•	•
Branch If Overflow Clear	BVC	28	4	2										V = 0	•	•	•	•	•	•
Branch If Overflow Set	BVS	29	4	2										V = 1	•	•	•	•	•	•
Branch If Plus	BPL	2A	4	2										N = 0	•	•	•	•	•	•
Branch To Subroutine	BSR	8D	8	2											•	•	•	•	•	•
Jump	JMP				6E	4	2	7E	3	3				See Special Operations	•	•	•	•	•	•
Jump To Subroutine	JSR				AD	8	2	BD	9	3					•	•	•	•	•	•
No Operation	NOP										01	2	1	Advances Prog. Cntr. Only	•	•	•	•	•	•
Return From Interrupt	RTI										3B	10	1		①					
Return From Subroutine	RTS										39	5	1		•	•	•	•	•	•
Software Interrupt	SWI										3F	12	1	See Special Operations	•	•	•	•	•	•
Wait for Interrupt *	WAI										3E	9	1		•	②	•	•	•	•

*WAI puts Address Bus, R/W, and Data Bus in the three-state mode while VMA is held low.

① (All)   Load Condition Code Register from Stack. (See Special Operations)
② (Bit 1) Set when interrupt occurs. If previously set, a Non-Maskable Interrupt
            is required to exit the wait state.

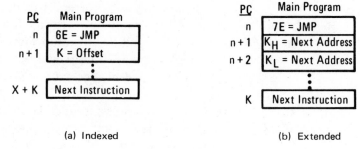

(a) Indexed   (b) Extended

Figure 6-1 Jump instructions in the **6800** μP.

Example 6-1
What does the following program accomplish?

    LDX #$5234 CE 5234
    JMP $2D,X   6E 2D

Solution
The first instruction, LDX #$5234 is an immediate load and loads 5234 into the index register (X). The second instruction is an indexed jump. It adds the second byte, 2D, to the contents of X and loads the sum, 5261, into the PC. Thus the next OP code to be executed is in location 5261.

Extended jumps are three-byte instructions, where the last two bytes are a 16-bit address. Their action is shown in Fig. 6-1b. Since a 16-bit address is available, they allow the program to jump to any location in memory. They are very easily understood because they require no calculations.

**6-3.2
Unconditional Branch Instructions**

Branch instructions are two-byte *relative address* instructions. The second byte contains a *displacement*. Normally, when a branch instruction is executed, the contents of the PC are incremented twice to point to the address of the next instruction. When the branch is taken, the PC is altered by the displacement, and the next OP code is found at *the address that equals the address of the branch instruction plus two, plus the displacement*. The displacement is treated as an 8-bit *signed* number that is added to the PC. Displacements with MSBs of 1 are negative numbers, which cause the program to *branch backward*. Since the maximum positive number that can be represented by an 8-bit signed byte is 127_{10} and the most negative number is -128, the program can branch to any location between PC $+129$ and PC -126, where PC is the address of the first byte of the BRANCH instruction.

The *unconditional branch,* BRA, causes the program to branch whenever it is encountered. It is equivalent to a JUMP instruction, but since it is only a two-byte instruction, it is used when the location being jumped to is within the range of $+129$ or -126 bytes relative to the current PC address.

Example 6-2
The instruction

$$\text{BRA} \quad *+\$2E \qquad (20\ 2C)$$

is found in location 213B. What happens when it is executed?

Solution
The operand $(*+\$2E)$ of this instruction will be explained in Chapter 7. The operation (OP) codes [20 2C] indicate that this instruction is an unconditional branch to location 213B + 2 + 2C = 2169. The next instruction that the program executes is in location 2169.

Example 6-3
When the previous program reaches 213B, assume it must branch back to 212E. What instruction is required in 213B?

Solution
In this problem the displacement must be calculated. When relative address mode instructions are specified in a source program, the assembler program (see Chapter 7) calculates the proper offset and inserts it in the second byte of the machine language program. It can be done manually by *subtracting the location of the branch instruction + 2 from the target address* and using the LS byte of the subtraction.

$$212E - (213B + 2) = 212E - 213D = F1$$

The correct displacement is F1 and the instruction (**20 F1**) transfers the program from 213B to 212E.

Backward branches, as in this program, result in negative displacements. For forward branches the target address is higher than the branch location and the displacement is positive. The above method works for both forward and backward branches. If the subtrahend is larger than the minuend, as in this problem, the negative result gives the correct offset for the backward branch.

Example 6-4

The instruction 20 FE (BRA *) is often used to halt the program. Explain how it works.

Solution

The displacement in this instruction is FE = −2. The instruction causes the program to branch to PC + 2 − 2 = PC, or back to its own location where it executes the instruction again. Thus, BRA * causes the program to continuously branch back to its own location and execute itself again, effectively halting the μP.

6-3.3
Out of Range Branches

If a program is to branch to a location further than +126 or −129 bytes away from the branch instruction, a jump instruction must be used. Conditional branches can still be taken by branching around the jump instruction, as Example 6-5 shows.

Example 6-5

Assume the instruction in location 20 is COMPARE A IMMEDIATE TO CB (CMP A #$CB). If the contents of A is CB, the program is to go to location 5000; otherwise it is to continue. Write this section of the program.

Solution

This problem can be solved by placing a jump to 5000 if the results of the comparison are 0, but now we must branch around the jump if the results are not 0. The portion of the program can look like this:

Add	Mnemonic	Codes
20	CMP A #$CB	81 CB
22	BNE $27	26 03
24	JMP 5000	7E 5000
27	Continue	

If the results are not 0, the conditional branch (BNE) causes the program to skip the jump instruction.

6-3.4
Conditional Branch Instructions

A *conditional branch instruction branches only* when a particular condition code or combination of condition codes are SET or CLEAR. Therefore the *results of instructions preceding the branch determine whether or not the branch is taken.* Conditional branches allow the user to write programs that make *decisions* and give the μP its ability to compute.

There are 14 conditional branches in the **6800** instruction set. Eight of them simply test the C, Z, N, and V bits and branch accordingly. They are listed below.

Instruction	Mnemonic	OP Code	Condition
Branch if carry SET	BCS	25	C = 1
Branch if carry CLEAR	BCC	24	C = 0
Branch if zero	BEQ	27	Z = 1
Branch if not zero	BNE	26	Z = 0
Branch if minus	BMI	2B	N = 1
Branch if plus	BPL	2A	N = 0
Branch if overflow SET	BVS	29	V = 1
Branch if overflow CLEAR	BVC	28	V = 0

Example 6-6

Assuming that all the bytes between 0100 and 01FF contain positive numbers, write a program to add them.

Solution

Because there are no negative numbers in this problem, the N and V bits can be ignored. For example, 01100100 + 01100100 = 11001000, which can be interpreted as $+200$ or -56. Here it is interpreted as the straight binary result, $+200$, because all numbers are positive. We must, however, make provision for overflow out of the byte. This is indicated by the C bit, not the V bit, because bit 7 is used for magnitude, not sign. Note that the above sum sets V, but not C, and there is no overflow if the byte is treated as an 8-bit binary number.

Using the foregoing approach, the least significant part of the result can be placed in A, and B can be incremented each time a carry out appears. The addresses are most conveniently incremented by using the Index Register (X). X can also be used to determine when to end the program.

Before writing the program, the flowchart of Fig. 6-2 was prepared. The program of Table 6-2 was then written and proceeds as follows.

1. The first three instructions are initializations; they clear the accumulators and load the first address into X.
2. The contents of the first location are then added to A.
3. The carry flag is checked. If C = 1, the branch is taken and B is incremented. If C = 0, the BCS instruction allows the PC to proceed to 29.
4. The index register is incremented and checked. If it equals 200, the program is complete and halts. If not, the program loops back and adds the contents of the next location to A.

Note that the program contains two conditional branches and two unconditional branches, one of which is the halt (20 FE). The branch locations were all calculated as in Sec. 6-3.2.

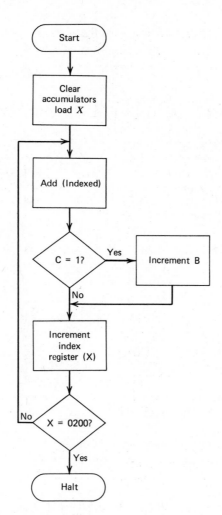

Figure 6-2 Flowchart for Example 6-5.

Table 6-2
Program for Example 6-6

Location	Code	Mnemonics	Comments
20	4F	CLR A	Clear A
21	5F	CLR B	Clear B
22	CE 0100	LDX #$100	Load X with $100
25	AB 00	ADD A 0,X	Add number in 1st location to A
27	25 08	BCS $31	Branch if carry set to increment B
29	08	INX	Increment X
2A	8C 0200	CPX #$200	Reached end yet ?
2D	26 F6	BNE $25	No, loop back to $25
2F	20 FE	BRA $2F	Halt program
31	5C	INC B	Increment B
32	20 F5	BRA $29	Branch back to $29

6-3.5
Other Conditional Branch
Instructions

The six additional BRANCH instructions listed below depend on the result of the last ALU operations.

1. **Branch if greater than or equal to zero (BGE).** We have already seen that it is possible to add two positive numbers and get a negative result if overflow occurs (Sec. 5-6.4). The BGE instruction takes the branch if the result of the last operation was positive or 0, *even if the N bit is 1*. It is often used after subtraction or compare instructions and branches only if the minuend is greater than or equal to the subtrahend. The logic equation is $N \oplus V = 0$.

2. **Branch if greater than zero (BGT).** This instruction is very much like BGE. It branches only if the result of the last operation was positive and not equal to 0. The logic equation is $Z + N \oplus V = 0$.

3. **Branch if higher (BHI).** This instruction is meant to be executed after a compare or subtract instruction (CBA, CMP, SBA, or SUB). It branches if the minuend, considered as an unsigned binary number, is greater than the subtrahend. The logic equation is $C + Z = 0$, so the instruction will not branch if C is 1 (indicating the results of the subtraction is negative; see Sec. 5-6.2) or, if Z is 1, indicating that the minuend and subtrahend are equal and the results of the subtraction are 0.

4. **Branch if less than or equal to zero (BLE).** This instruction branches if the result of the last operation is less than or equal to 0. It allows for the possibility that $N = 0$ due to overflow.

5. **Branch if less than zero (BLT).** Similar to the BLE, but no branch is taken if the last result is 0.

6. **Branch if lower or the same (BLS).** This instruction complements the BHI. It is also meant to be executed after a compare or subtract instruction and causes a branch if the subtrahend is greater than or equal to the minuend. Since the logic equation is $C + Z = 1$, the branch is taken if the result of the subtraction is negative ($C = 1$) or 0 ($Z = 1$).

Example 6-7

Assume the A accumulator contains 60 and B contains 90.

  a. Which number is higher?
  b. With which of the following programs will it branch?
1. CBA   2. CBA   3. CBA
    BHI   BGT   BPL

Solution

  a. Considered as unsigned numbers B > A, but if signed numbers are being used, the 60 is positive and 90 is negative, therefore A > B.

  b. CBA is the mnemonic for COMPARE accumulators. The result of the compare is 60 − 90 = D0, with the C, N, and V bits all SET. The contents of the A and B accumulators remain 60 and 90, however, because they are not affected by a COMPARE instruction.

Program 1 will not branch because 90 is higher (in absolute value) than 60, and the subtraction SETs the C bit so that $C + Z \neq 0$.

Program 2 will branch because the BGT considers signed numbers and $A > B$. Note that the logic equation $Z + N \oplus V = 0$ is satisfied because $Z = 0$ and both N and $V = 1$.

Program 3 will not branch because the result SETs the N bit and the **6800** considers the result as negative.

The results of this program show that the BHI instruction should be used when comparing *absolute* numbers but, when comparing 2s complement signed numbers, the BGE or BGT instructions are correct.

Example 6-8

If the following program is executed, what numbers must be in the B accumulator for the program to branch?

```
LDAA #$FD
CBA
BHI
```

Solution

The first instruction loads FD into A and the second instruction compares the accumulators. Unless B contains FF, FE, or FD, the minuend is higher than the subtrahend and the program will branch.

6-4
Stacks

In **6800** μPs and many larger computers, memory is divided into three distinct areas; the program and data areas that we have already considered, and the stack. *The stack is an area of memory used for the temporary storage of important information or data that is changed frequently.* Subroutines (see Sec. 6-5) and interrupts (see Chapter 10) make use of the stack. Since it must be written to, as well as read, the stack must be in RAM.

6-4.1
The Stack Pointer

The system designer must determine the area of memory allocated to the stack during initialization. The *stack pointer* (SP) is a register within the μP that contains the *address of the next location available for the stack*. Since SP decrements automatically when data or return addresses are stored, it must be initially set to the highest address in the stack area. This location is often called the *top of the stack,* and is pointed to when nothing is stored in the stack. The following instructions pertain to the stack pointer:

Mnemonic	Description
DES	Decrement stack pointer
INS	Increment stack pointer
LDS	Load stack pointer (This instruction can be executed in the immediate, direct, indexed or extended modes.)
STS	Store stack pointer (This instruction can be executed in the direct, indexed, or extended modes.)
TXS	Transfer the contents of the index register (minus 1) to the stack pointer register.
TSX	Transfer the contents of the stack pointer register (plus 1) to the index register. (see table B-2 in Appendix B)

Example 6-9

The stack is to occupy locations 0200 to 02FF. What instructions are required at the beginning of the program to initialize the SP?

Solution

The SP points to the highest vacant location in the stack. At the beginning of the program the entire stack is empty so the SP must point to 02FF. The single instruction

        LDS #$2FF   (8E 02FF)

is a LOAD IMMEDIATE that loads 02FF into the SP. This instruction initializes the stack so that it starts at 02FF. Whenever the stack is used the SP is decremented. The stack must not be allowed to become so large that it invades memory area set aside for programs or data, or it will overwrite them. One common programming mistake is to do something that causes the stack pointer to decrement and to fail to increment it later. This can cause the stack to overflow and destroy the program.

6-4.2
PUSH and PULL

Two memory instructions which were not discussed in Chapter 5 because they involve the SP are PUSH and PULL.[2] These are implied instructions that refer to the A or B accumulators.

A PUSH takes the contents of the accumulator and *writes* it in the stack at the SP location. It then *decrements* the SP because the original stack location is no longer vacant; it contains the *pushed byte*.

---

[2]The word POP is often used instead of PULL by other computer manufacturers.

Example 6-10
If A contains CB, what do the following instructions accomplish?

```
LDS #$2FF
PSH A
```

Solution
The first instruction loads 02FF into the SP, as in Example 6-9. The second instruction pushes A onto the stack. After execution, location 02FF contains CB and the SP contains 02FE, which points to the highest vacant location in the stack.

A PULL instruction first *increments* the SP, then *transfers* the contents of the stack at the new value of the SP to the accumulator. Note that once the contents of a stack location has been pulled, it is considered vacant although the byte is still there. It will be over-written by the next PUSH or other usage of the stack.

Example 6-11
If the SP contains 200, location 200 contains CB and 201 contains CC, what happens in response to a PUL B instruction?

Solution
The SP is incremented to 201 and the stack is read. At the end of the instruction, B contains CC and the SP contains 201. Now 200 and 201 are both considered to be vacant.

   Note that the stack acts as a LAST-IN-FIRST-OUT (LIFO) register. *A PULL retrieves the information that was last PUSHed onto the stack.*

**6-5
Subroutines**
A *subroutine* is a small program that is generally used more than once by the main program. Multiplications, 16-bit adds, and square roots are typical subroutines. In Sec. 5-5.4 a program to obtain the sine of an angle was given. If the sine had to be calculated more than once during the execution of the main program, the sine program would surely be a subroutine.

   Figure 6-3 illustrates the use of the same subroutine by two different parts of the main program. The subroutine located at 200 can be entered from either location 0011 or 00CC by placing a JUMP TO SUBROUTINE(AD, BD, or 8D, depending on the mode) in these addresses. The PC actions, as a result of the subroutine jump

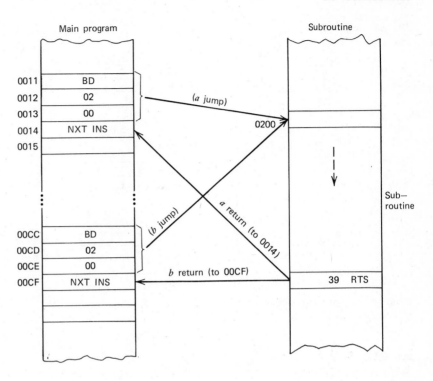

Figure 6-3 Use of a subroutine.

at 0011, are identified by the *a* in Fig. 6-3 and *b* identifies jumps from 00CC.

After the subroutine is complete, the program resumes from the instruction following the location where it called the subroutine. Because the subroutine must return to one of *several* locations, depending on which one caused it to be entered, the *original contents of the PC must be preserved* so the subroutine knows where to return.

6-5.1
Jumps to Subroutines

The JUMP TO SUBROUTINE (JSR) instruction remembers the address of the next main instruction by *writing it to the stack* before it takes the jump. The JSR can be executed in the indexed or extended mode. There is a BRANCH TO SUBROUTINE (BSR) that can be used if the starting address of the subroutine is within +129 to −126 locations of the program counter. The advantage of the BSR is that it requires one less byte in the main program.

The action of the subroutine instructions are illustrated in Fig. 6-4. In each case they store the address of the next main instruction on the stack before taking the jump.

SPECIAL OPERATIONS

JSR, JUMP TO SUBROUTINE:

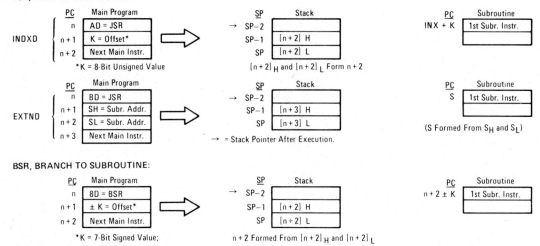

Figure 6-4 Jumps and branches to subroutines in the **6800** μP.

Example 6-12

If the SP and X registers both contain 0200, what happens when the instruction

$$\text{JSR } \$20,X$$

in location 30 is executed?

Solution

This is the indexed mode of the instruction JSR. Since the OP code for the JSR (AD) occupies location 30 and 20 (the offset) occupies location 31, the address of the next instruction, 0032, is written to the stack. Location 0200 then contains 32 and location 01FF contains 00. The SP has been decremented twice and contains 01FE. The program then jumps to 0220 (the sum of the contents of X and the offset), which should be the starting location of the subroutine.

6-5.2
Return from Subroutine The JSR instructions preserve the contents of the PC on the stack, but a *return from subroutine* (RTS) instruction is required to properly return. The RTS is the last instruction executed in a subroutine. Its action is shown in Fig. 6-5. It places the contents of the stack in the PC and causes the SP to be incremented twice. Because these bytes contain the address of the next main instruction in the program (put

RTS, RETURN FROM SUBROUTINE:

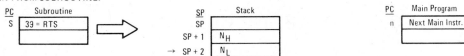

Figure 6-5 Action of the Return-From-Subroutine (RTS) instruction.

there by the JSR or BSR that initiated the subroutine), the program resumes at the place where it left off before it entered the subroutine.

Example 6-13

Many programmers make use of *indirect jumps* where the program must jump to an address that is the contents of a memory location, rather than the memory location itself. Assume the address to which we wish to jump is contained in locations 40 and 41. How can an indirect jump be performed in the **6800** μP?

Solution

First the two bytes are placed in the X register with a LDX direct instruction (LDX $40). Then the JMP 0,X indexed instruction is used, which transfers X to the PC, effectively completing the indirect jump while using only 4 bytes.

6-5.3
Nested Subroutines

In some sophisticated programs the main program may call a subroutine, which then calls on a second subroutine. The second subroutine is called a *nested subroutine* because it is used by and returns to the first subroutine.

The situation is shown graphically in Fig. 6-6. The main program does a JSR (JUMP-TO-SUBROUTINE) extended at address 40. This puts 0043 on the stack. The first subroutine does a JSR at 01C3, placing 01C6 on the stack and jumping to the second subroutine. When the second subroutine is complete, an RTS returns it to 01C6 and increments the SP twice. Now the first subroutine picks up where it left off. When the first subroutine finishes, it ends with an RTS that causes a return to the main program. By making use of the stack as shown, there can be any number of nested subroutines, limited only by the stack size.

6-5.4
Use of Registers During Subroutines

During the execution of a subroutine, the subroutine will use the accumulators; it may use X and it changes the contents of the CCR. When the main program is reentered, however, the contents of these

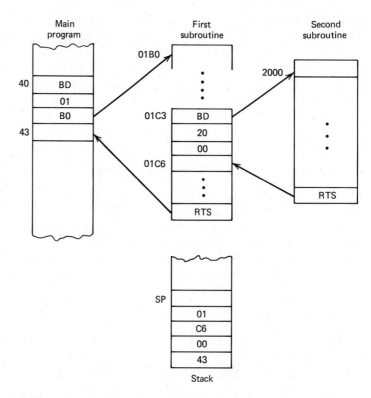

Figure 6-6 Nested subroutines.

registers must often be as they were before the jump to the subroutine.

The most commonly used method of preserving register contents during a subroutine is to write the subroutine so that it PUSHes those registers it must *preserve* onto the stack at the beginning of the subroutine and then PULLs them at the end of the subroutine, thus *restoring their contents* before returning to the main program.

Example 6-14
A subroutine uses the A and B accumulators and the CCR. How can the main program contents of these registers be preserved?

Solution
To preserve the contents of these registers for the main program, the first four instructions of the subroutine should be:

OP Code	Mnemonic
36	PSH A
37	PSH B
07	TPA
36	PSH A

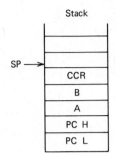

Stack

SP →

| CCR |
| B |
| A |
| PC H |
| PC L |

Figure 6-7 Contents of the stack after entering the subroutine of Example 6-14 and executing the first four instructions.

This puts the contents of A, B, and the CCR on the stack as shown in Fig. 6-7.

To restore these registers before returning to the main program, the instructions at the beginning must be executed in *reverse* order. The last five instructions of the subroutine must be:

OP Code	Mnemonic
32	PUL A
06	TAP
33	PUL B
32	PUL A
39	RTS

Note that the A register had to be preserved. It is also used by the TPA and TAP instructions. Thus its contents are overwritten and will be lost unless it is first pushed onto the stack.

6-6 Multiplication

In a μC multiplication and division are performed far less often than addition, subtraction, and logical operations. There are no multiply and divide instructions in the **6800** μP, and multiplication is done using a software subroutine. In this section a subroutine for multiplying two bytes is developed.

6-6.1 The Multiplication Algorithm

Multiplication starts with a multiplier, multiplicand, and PRODUCT REGISTER. The PRODUCT REGISTER, which is initially 0 and eventually contains the product, must be as long as the number of bits in the multiplier and multiplicand added together. In computers, the multiplier and multiplicand are typically one n-bit word each, and two n-bit words must be reserved for the product.

Multiplication can be performed in accordance with the following algorithm:

1. Examine the least significant bit of the multiplier. If it is 0, shift the PRODUCT REGISTER one bit to the right. If it is 1, add the multiplicand to the MSB of the PRODUCT REGISTER and then shift.

2. Repeat step 1 for each bit of the multiplier.

At the conclusion the product should be in the PRODUCT REGISTER.

It is common to shift the multiplicand one bit left for each multiplier bit and then add it to the PRODUCT REGISTER. This is analogous to multiplication as taught in grade school. The algorithm presented here, however, holds the position of the multiplicand constant but shifts the PRODUCT REGISTER right. This algorithm is more easily implemented in a μP.

Example 6-15
Multiply 22 × 26 using the above algorithm.
Note: All numbers are decimal.

Solution
The solution is shown in Fig. 6-8. The multiplier bits are listed in a column with the LSB on top. The multiplication proceeds in accordance with these bits as the leftmost column shows.

Consider line 5 as an example. Since the multiplier bit is 1, the 5-bit multiplicand (26) is added to the 5 MSBs of the PRODUCT REGISTER that appear on line 4 as 13. The result, 39, appears on line 5. The product moves steadily to the right. The final product appears on line 9 and is a 10-bit number in this case. Note that the MSB of the PRODUCT REGISTER is reserved for carries that may result from the additions.

**6-6.2
Multiplication Subroutine**
Multiplication can be performed in accordance with the above algorithm by using the **6800** μP. A routine for a one-byte by one-byte

```
Multiplier = 22 =  1  0  1  1  0

Multiplicand = 26 = | 1  1  0  1  0 |

Line Number                                              Multiplier
                                                            Bit

    1          | 0  0  0  0  0 |                                    Initial product
    2          | 0  0  0  0  0 | 0                         0        Shift product register
    3          | 1  1  0  1  0 | 0                         1        Add multiplicand
    4          | 0  1  1  0  1 | 0  0                                Shift product register
    5        1 | 0  0  1  1  1 | 0  0                       1        Add multiplicand
    6        1 | 0  0  1  1  | 1  0  0                               Shift product register
    7          | 0  1  0  0  1 | 1  1  0  0                 0        Shift product register
    8        1 | 0  0  0  1  1 | 1  1  0  0                 1        Add multiplicand
    9          | 1  0  0  0  1 | 1  1  1  0  0                       Shift — final product
```

Figure 6-8 Multiplying 22 × 26.

multiplication is shown in Table 6-3. Before the program starts, these assumptions are made:

1. The multiplicand is in location 80.
2. Locations 82 and 83 are reserved for the 16-bit product. Actually the partial products will be in the A accumulator and location 83. At the end of the program, A, which contains the MS byte of the product, is stored in 82.
3. Location 84 contains the multiplier.

The program starts by storing the required number of shifts into 81 and storing the multiplicand into B. It then shifts the multiplier right. If the bit of the multiplier that is shifted into the carry FF is a 1, the multiplicand is added to the product register (A). The reader may have noticed that a 1 is sometimes carried out of the product register in the illustrative example. Fortunately this 1 goes into the carry FF and is preserved.

The two ROR instructions then shift A and location 83. This is essentially a 16-bit shift of the product register. Location 81 keeps track of the number of shifts and the program halts when it decre-

Table 6-3
A One-Byte Multiply Routine

Location	Machine Code		Mnemonic			Comments
20	C6	08	LDA	B	#8	Put 8 in B register
22	D7	81	STA	B	$81	Save shift count in $81
24	D6	80	LDA	B	$80	Load multiplicand into B
26	4F		CLR	A		Clear A
27	74	0084	LSR		$84	Shift multiplier right
2A	24	01	BCC		$2D	Skip to $2D if carry clear
2C	1B		ABA			Add accumulators
2D	46		ROR	A		Shift product MS byte Rt.
2E	76	0083	ROR		$83	Shift product reg LS byte
31	7A	0081	DEC		$81	Decrement count
34	26	F1	BNE		$27	Branch back to 27 if not 0
36	97	82	STA	A	$82	Is 0. Done. Store MS byte
38	20	FE	BRA		$38	HALT program by looping
			END			
	Reserved locations					
80	Multiplicand					
81	Count					
82	Product Register (MS byte)					
83	Product Register (LS byte)					
84	Multiplier					

ments to 0. Multiplying larger numbers requires 16-bit adds and 32-bit shifts, but can proceed in accordance with the same general algorithm.

6-6.3
Parameter Passing in Subroutines

In order to use subroutines correctly, several conditions must be observed:

1. If any constants change during the execution of the subroutine, they must be *reinitialized* whenever the subroutine is used again. In the multiplication subroutine, location 81, the shift count, is an example. It is decremented to zero during the course of the subroutine. Therefore it must be reinitialized every time the subroutine is started. This is done by the first two instructions of the subroutine.
2. The calling routine must know where to put the parameters. In the multiplication subroutine the calling routine must place the multiplicand in location 80 and the multiplier in 84 before it can call the subroutine.
3. The calling routine must know where to find the result of the subroutine. In the multiplication subroutine the results are always stored in 82 and 83.

The last two conditions are called *parameter passing*. The calling routine must provide the subroutine with the proper input parameters (i.e., multiplier and multiplicand) and the subroutine must make its results available to the calling program (i.e., storing them in locations 82 and 83).

Example 6-16
There are numbers in A1, A2, B1, and B2. Describe a program to find the sum of the two products:

$$S = (A1)(B1) + (A2)(B2)$$

Store S in C1 and C2.

Solution
The first decision is to use the multiply routine of Sec. 6-6.2 as a subroutine to obtain both of the required products. Once this decision is made the program can start in 100 (for example) to keep it out of the way of the multiply subroutine and the data. The stack can start at 200 to keep it out of the way of everything else. The program then proceeds as follows:

1. Load the stack pointer. Whenever a program requires use of the stack (and subroutines use the stack) the SP must be initialized before it is used. Otherwise the SP may be pointing to a random location and the jump or branch to subroutine may overwrite the program or data.

2. Move A1 to 80 and B1 to 84. This sets up the multiplier and multiplicand for the subroutine. This is an example of parameter passing.
3. Jump to 20 to enter the multiply subroutine.
4. Move the product in 82 and 83 to C1 and C2.
5. Move A2 and B2 to 80 and 84, for the second product.
6. Jump to the multiply subroutine again.
7. Add the contents of 82 and 83 with C1 and C2 to get the sum of the two products. Store the results in C1 and C2. This completes the program.

6-7
Using Jumps for Program Patching and Debugging

The jump instruction can be very useful when making program patches and debugging. While a monitor system (see Chapter 11) offers the easiest way to make changes, monitor systems may not be available on some small μC systems. In this case, bytes can be changed or entered as described below.

6-7.1
Program Patching

Debugging a machine language program usually results in correcting inverted logic (BNE where BEQ is needed), replacing the value of an offset, or inserting forgotten statements. In the first two cases, a one byte code is simply replaced with another but in the last case, no room exists for the addition. This is done by a method known as patching. *Program patching is the addition or deletion of a group of instructions*. Patches are usually made during development when the programmer realizes that some instructions that are needed within the program have been omitted. The patch to add the instructions consists of a jump from the main program to a vacant area of memory. The additional instructions are written in this area, plus those instructions in the main program that were wiped out by inserting the jump. The patch is completed by jumping back to the main program.

Example 6-17
Assume that the stack pointer had to be initialized at the start of the multiplication routine (Table 6-3). How can this be done?

a. Assume the addresses before location 20 are available.

b. Assume the addresses before location 20 contain information that cannot be changed.

Solution
a. If the locations before 20 are available, we can write the three-byte LDS IMMEDIATE instruction into locations 1D, 1E, and 1F. Then the starting address of the program (the contents of FFFE and FFFF) can be changed to 1D and the program will operate correctly.

b. If locations 1D, 1E, and 1F are unavailable, a patch must be made. The contents of locations 20, 21, and 22 are replaced by a JMP $0040 (assuming 40 is a vacant memory area). At 40 we can write:

40	8E XXXX	LDS	#$XXXX	Load the stack pointer
43	C6 08	LDA	B #$8	Replace overwritten
45	D7 81	STA	B $81	instructions
47	7E 0024	JMP	$24	Return to main Program

This completes the patch, which includes the main program instructions that were overwritten by the jump to the patch, plus the necessary additional instruction.

If, after the program is written, an instruction is found to be unnecessary, it can be replaced by a NOP (or several NOPs). This removes the instruction without causing the entire program to be rewritten. If a group of instructions are found to be unnecessary, they can be replaced by a jump following the last useful instruction to the point where the program must resume.

All of the above changes are made only during program development. The program should be "cleaned up," eliminating useless NOPs and awkward jumps, before it is finalized and written to a ROM.

The example shows that it is unwise to start experimental programs at location 0000. If a program is started at 20 instead, and the need arises to add instructions at the beginning of the program, locations 0000 to 001F can be used for these instructions, instead of having to patch by jumping.

6-7.2
Using Jumps in Debugging

When long programs, such as the multiplication routine of Sec. 6-6 do not work (and they usually won't work on the first try), it is necessary to fix or debug them. The easiest way to isolate the faults is to use a development system, as described in Chapter 11, because the monitor programs make it possible to trace and print out the contents of the μC registers. They also include many other aids to the designer to find and correct programming errors as well as hardware faults.

It is possible, however, to find some of the difficulties by other means. If a test system incorporates hardware to HALT and STEP the μP, as described in Secs. 8-7.2 and 8-7.3, and lights and switches to control the address and data buses, as described in Sec. 11-3.1, several software tricks can be used to find problems. One is to use a branch-on-self instruction (BRA *) or 20 FE, as shown in Table 6-3. In this case, after the program is manually entered in memory with the switches, it is started and is then stopped by the RUN/HALT switch. The contents of the various storage locations in memory can then be examined by means of the address switches and data bus lights. If the program failed to get to the end, or did the wrong thing, the branch instruction is moved to occur sooner in the program and the routine retried. Another way is to insert a JMP to a convenient location where a routine stores the registers in memory and then executes a branch-on-self instruction so that the μP can be halted and memory examined as above. Of course these and many other useful routines are provided in the variety of monitor ROMs described in Chapter 11.

Example 6-18

Assume that an error occurred in Example 5-22 (the BCD subtraction problem of Chapter 5). The error can be traced by examining the contents of the accumulator and the CCR at each step in the program. How can this be done?

Solution

The easiest way is to use MINIBUG III or an equivalent monitor program. This displays the contents of the registers after each step, as shown in Fig. 5-13.

If a control program is not available, however, the contents of A and the CCR can still be preserved in memory. One way would be as follows:

1. Initialize the X and SP registers.
2. Place a JSR after each LOAD, ADD, or DAA instruction.
3. Write a subroutine as follows:

Instructions	Comments
STA A 0,X	Store the contents of A
INX	Increment X
TPA	Transfer CCR to A
STA A 0,X	Store A at X
DEX	Decrement X
LDA A 0,X	Reload the contents of A
INX	Increment X
INX	" "
RTS	Return from subroutine

This subroutine stores the contents of A and the CCR each time it is used, and leaves the result in memory starting at the initial value of X. Note that the contents of A are destroyed by the TPA instruction because it writes the CCR into A. Therefore the program "backs up" to reload A and then adjusts X to point to the next vacant location before exiting via the RTS instruction.

6-8
A BCD-to-Binary
Conversion Problem

As a final practical example that uses lists, indexed instructions, subroutines, and stacks, let us consider the problem of converting BCD information to binary. BCD (binary coded decimal) has been introduced in Sec. 5-7. BCD information can be entered into a μP system from the terminal keyboard. Each ASCII number must be ANDed with an $0F to remove the four MSBs. This leaves a BCD digit. Other peripherals may also supply BCD information.

BCD numbers must often be converted to binary before computations can be made using the number. One way to convert from BCD to binary[3] is to assign a weight to all the BCD bits and then add the weights for all bits that are 1 in the BCD representation of the number. The weights are assigned in accordance with the value represented by each BCD bit; that is, 1, 2, 4, 8, 10, 20, 40, 80, 100, 200, ... A table of the decimal numbers and binary weights corresponding to each BCD bit is given in Fig. 6-9.

Example 6-19
Convert the number 169 to binary using the add algorithm.

Solution
The number 169 is expressed in BCD form as:

$$\underbrace{0001}_{1}\underbrace{0110}_{6}\underbrace{1001}_{9}$$

where the LSB is on the right. There are 1s in positions 1, 4, 6, 7, and 9.
The weights corresponding to these numbers are (from Fig. 6-9)

$$
\begin{array}{r}
0001 \\
1000 \\
10100 \\
101000 \\
1100100
\end{array}
$$

The simple addition of these binary numbers yields 10101001, which is the binary equivalent of decimal 169.

Computers, which generally have binary adders, often use the add algorithm to convert from BCD to binary.

Now that the method of converting BCD to binary has been explained, a conversion program using the **6800** can be written.

[3]A thorough discussion of BCD to binary and binary to BCD conversion is given in Greenfield, *Practical Digital Design Using ICs*.

Bit Position	Decimal Number	Binary Number
1	1	1
2	2	1 0
3	4	1 0 0
4	8	1 0 0 0
5	1 0	1 0 1 0
6	2 0	1 0 1 0 0
7	4 0	1 0 1 0 0 0
8	8 0	1 0 1 0 0 0 0
9	1 0 0	1 1 0 0 1 0 0
1 0	2 0 0	1 1 0 0 1 0 0 0
1 1	4 0 0	1 1 0 0 1 0 0 0 0
1 2	8 0 0	1 1 0 0 1 0 0 0 0 0
1 3	1 0 0 0	1 1 1 1 1 0 1 0 0 0
1 4	2 0 0 0	1 1 1 1 1 0 1 0 0 0 0

Figure 6-9 Tables of weights for BCD-to-binary conversion.

Example 6-20

A four-digit BCD number is in location F0 and F1, with the least significant digit in F1, bits 3 – 0, and the most significant digit is F0, bits 7 – 4. Write a routine to convert this number to binary.

Solution

First we start with a vague general idea of how to perform the conversion; add the proper number wherever a 1 appears in the given BCD number. Each bit can be tested by performing a shift right and testing the carry bit.

We also realize now that the list of Fig. 6-9 must be placed in memory so that the proper number can be added to the sum. Figure 6-9 shows that smaller binary values can be included in one byte but the larger values need two bytes. For uniformity, it is wise to allocate two bytes for each binary entry. It will soon become clear that this simplifies the programming. The list is arbitrarily started at location 100, so 100 and 101 contain the binary equivalent of 1 (hex 0001); the list continues to 11F, where locations 11E and 11F contain the binary equivalent of 8000, 1F40, or

	1 F		4 0
11E	0001 1111	11F	0100 0000

The result can be no larger than $(9999)_{10}$, which means it can be represented by a 14-bit binary number. Let us reserve F2 and F3 for this number. We also assume that the addition is done by a subroutine so the stack pointer is arbitrarily initialized to 200. The flowchart can now be drawn and is shown in Fig. 6-10.

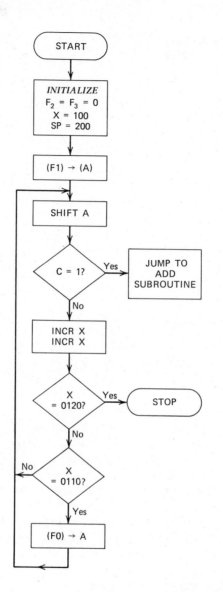

Figure 6-10 Flowchart for Example 6-20.

The flowchart assumes that the list and the numbers to be converted are already in memory. The program proceeds in the following way.

1. The sum is initialized to 0, the index register (X) to 100, and the SP to 200.
2. The first word (two least significant digits) are loaded into the A accumulator and shifted out. After each shift, the carry bit is tested.

3. The X register is then incremented twice to point to the next two-byte numbers in the list. It should now be apparent that if the list contained both one- and two-byte entries, additional programming would have been required to determine the starting address of the next item. This is why two bytes were allocated to each item in the list whether they were required or not.

4. X is tested for the HALT condition. The program should HALT after 16 shifts or when the list is exhausted. Since the list contains 16 two-byte numbers, it is exhausted when X equals $(120)_{16}$.

5. The second word to be converted must be loaded into A after 8 shifts or 16 increments of X. This occurs when the number in X = 0110. Note that in this program, the X register is performing the dual function of selecting the appropriate number in the list and determining whether or not branches are to be taken.

6. When C = 1 the add subroutine is entered. Since the A accumulator is used by both the main program and the subroutine, it is immediately pushed onto the stack to save it for the main program.

7. The proper number in the list (as determined by X) is added to the LSBs of the sum in F3.

8. The MSBs of the list are added (with carry) to F2. This completes a 16-bit addition.

9. The A accumulator is restored to its original value and the main program is reentered.

Using the detailed flowchart of Fig. 6-10, the coding is straightforward and is shown in Table 6-4. Before coding can begin, a starting address must be arbitrarily assigned to the main program (20) and the subroutine (80). The only caution is that these areas must not overlap each other, the data, the list, or the stack area.

The student may have observed that this program is not optimum. There is no real need for a subroutine (it could have been included in the main program) and some instructions could have been saved by using the B accumulator. The program was used because it demonstrates many of the features available in **6800** software.

6-9
Summary

This chapter introduced the BRANCH and JUMP instructions available in the **6800** μP. The conditions that caused the branches were explained, as were the methods of calculating the branch locations.

The stack was then introduced. Its use in conjunction with PUSH and PULL instructions and subroutines was explained. Finally a multiplication program and a BCD to binary conversion program were presented as examples that used many of the features of the **6800**.

Table 6-4
Program for Example 6-20

```
                        MAIN PROGRAM

ADDRESS   CODE        MNEMONICS        COMMENTS
   20     4F          CLR A            Clear A
   21     97 F2       STA A $F2        Clear F2
   23     97 F3       STA A $F3        Clear F3
   25     8E 0200     LDS #$200        Initialize Stack Pointer
   28     CE 0100     LDX #$100             "     Index Register
   2B     96 F1       LDA A $F1        Load LS BCD digit into A
   2D     47          ASR A            Shift A right
   2E     24 02       BCC $32          Skip to $32 if C = 0
   30     8D 4E       BSR $80          To Add subroutine if C = 1
   32     08          INX              Increment X twice to
   33     08          INX                  point to next entry
   34     8C 0120     CPX #$120        Reached end of list ?
   37     27 09       BEQ $42          Yes - branch to HALT at $42
   39     8C 0110     CPX #$110        Is word 1 finished ?
   3C     26 EF       BNE $2D          No, loop back & shift again
   3E     96 F0       LDA A $F0        Yes, load MS digits into A
   40     20 EB       BRA $2D          Loop to $2D & shift MS digit
   42     20 FE       BRA $42          Repeat and HALT prog.

              *  ADD SUBROUTINE

   80     36          PSH A            Save A on stack
   81     A6 01       LDA A 1,X        Load from list-LS byte
   83     9B F3       ADD A $F3        Add LS byte of sum
   85     97 F3       STA A $F3        Update LS byte of sum
   87     A6 00       LDA A 0,X        Load MS byte from list
   89     99 F2       ADC A $F2        Add MS byte w/ carry
   8B     97 F2       STA A $F2        Update MS byte of sum
   8D     32          PUL A            Restore A
   8E     39          RTS              Return to main prog.
```

**6-10
Glossary**

BRANCH A jump where the location jumped to is close to the current value of the PC.

Conditional branch instruction Instructions that cause branches only if certain conditions are met.

Displacement The number of locations between the PC + 2 and the object of a branch.

JUMP An instruction that causes the program to jump or fetch the next instruction from a location that is not in sequence.

PULL An instruction that copies the lowest occupied location in the stack into an accumulator.

PUSH An instruction that copies the contents of the accumulator onto the stack.

Relative mode An instruction mode where destination addresses are calculated relative to the current PC.

Stack An area of memory reserved for program parameters.

Stack pointer A register that contains the address of the highest vacant location in the stack.

Subroutine A subprogram called upon by the main program.

6-11 References

Bishop, Ron, *Basic Microprocessors and the 6800,* Hayden Book Co., Rochelle Park, N.J., 1979.

Greenfield, Joseph D., *Practical Digital Design Using ICs,* John Wiley, New York, 1977.

Leventhal, Lance, *6800 Assembly Language Programming,* Osborn & Associates, Berkeley, Ca., 1978.

Motorola *M6800 Microcomputer System Design Data,* Motorola, Phoenix, Arizona, 1976.

Motorola *M6800 Programming Reference Manual,* Motorola, Phoenix, Arizona, 1976.

6-12 Problems

6-1 Show that 20 00 is a NOP.

6-2 The instruction in locations 012D and 012E is BRA XX. Where will the program branch to if XX equals:
a. F2
b. E5
c. 26
d. 05

6-3 In the program of Example 6-5, the B register could have been incremented by a C9 00 instruction and the BCS routine omitted. Rewrite the program using this instruction.

6-4 Write a program to write the number C2 into all locations between 0250 and 02FF.

6-5 Write a program to transfer the contents of locations 0100 to 0120 to locations 0110 to 0130. Hint: Start by moving 120 to 130, then 11F to 12F, etc.

6-6 The Boolean equation for BGE is $(N \oplus V) = 0$. Explain what it implies.

6-7 If the SP contains 021C and X contains 022C, write the contents of the stack and the starting address of the subroutine if the instruction in location 40 is
a. JSR $30,X   AD 30
b. JSR $C2,X   AD C2
c. JSR $15F   BD 015F
d. BSR ∗+$25   8D 23
e. BSR ∗−6   8D F8

6-8 Write a program to convert a 13-bit binary number to BCD. The algorithm is to subtract the highest number in Fig. 6-9, which is less than the given number from it, and write 1s in all positions where these subtractions are performed.[4]

6-9 Your receivables are positive numbers in locations 0100 to 01FF. Your expenses are positive numbers in locations 0200 to 02FF. Write a program to determine your net worth.

6-10 Describe in words what the following program does.

Location	Machine Code	Mnemonic	
40	CE 0130	LDX	#$130
43	8E 01D0	LDS	#$1D0
46	A6 00	LDA	A 0,X
48	36	PSH	A
49	09	DEX	
4A	8C 0100	CPX	#$100
4D	26 F7	BNE	$46
4F	20 FE	BRA	$4F

6-11 Using the multiplication routine of Table 6-3, multiply 127 by 75. Show the contents of the accumulator after each step.

6-12 Write a divide routine. Reserve one byte for the quotient and one byte for the remainder.

6-13 Write the code for Example 6-16.

6-14 A business deals in a series of items. If the price of each item is listed in locations A0 to BF and the corresponding number of items sold is in locations C0 to DF, write a program to determine the gross receipts.

After attempting to solve the problems, try to answer the self-evaluation questions in Sec. 6-2. If any of them still seem difficult, review the appropriate sections of the chapter to find the answers.

---

[4]A more complete description is given in Greenfield, *Practical Digital Design Using ICs,* Chapter 10.

Chapter 7 Assembly Language for the 6800

7-1
Instructional Objectives

The purpose of this chapter is to acquaint the **6800** system designer with standard methods of writing and documenting software and to expand upon the use of mnemonics for ease of programming. The assembler and editor programs are presented to handle the mechanics of program development.

After studying this chapter, the student should be able to:

1. Translate flowcharts or other program concepts into the assembly language mnemonic statements of a source program.
2. Write the program and save it on tape or disk.
3. Specify the assembler directives needed to properly assemble the program.
4. Assemble and reedit the source program until it assembles without errors.
5. Obtain the program listing and object code output tapes or disk files needed to load the program into memory for testing.

7-2
Self-Evaluation Questions

Watch for the answers to the following questions as you read the chapter. They should help you understand the material presented.

1. How are mnemonics used to express addressing modes and addresses?
2. What is the difference between a source program and an object program?
3. What is an assembler program?
4. What is the function of the program comments?
5. What is the difference between an instruction and an assembler directive?
6. What steps are required to assemble a source program using a **6800** μP system and a tape terminal?
7. How much RAM is needed in the software development system for the tape version of the assembler and the editor program?

7-3
Assembly Language Programming

The use of mnemonics as the basis of assembly language programming was briefly described in Chapter 5. In this chapter we show how these expressions are used to write programs and how the *assembler* and *editor programs* are used.

The mnemonic Operator (OP) codes of the Motorola **6800** Assembly Language (shown in Table 5-1 of Chapter 5), all use three letters,

143

and are followed by an Operand (or Dual Operand), that modifies each OP code according to the addressing mode. The various addressing modes and some examples of how they apply to the LDA instruction are shown below.

Addressing Mode	Mnemonic	Machine Code
1. Extended addressing	LDA A $A0F3	B6 A0F3
2. Direct addressing	LDA A $F3	96 F3
3. Immediate addressing	LDA A #$F3	86 F3
4. Indexed addressing	LDAA 3,X	A6 03

The above instructions are in *assembly language format* (see Sec. 7-4). The $ sign denotes a hexadecimal value, and the # sign indicates an immediate operand.

In analyzing these listings the following points should be noted:

A. The **6800** μP assembler recognizes addresses below $100 $(256)_{10}$, as *direct* addresses. As shown in line 2 above, the assembler generates instructions that are two bytes in length (the OP code plus one 8-bit address byte). Three-byte *extended* addressing instructions, as shown in line 1, are used to reference addresses above 00FF.

B. The *immediate* instruction of line 3, loads the value F3 into the A accumulator, instead of loading the contents of location F3 as would be the case for the direct mode shown in line 2 above.

C. The 3 shown in the *indexed* instruction (line 4) is an example of an *offset* value that is added to the index register when this instruction is executed. The offset is limited to one byte, and is considered to be positive. It is expressed in machine language as the second byte of that instruction (03 in this case).

D. When referencing either accumulator, the space after the OP code is optional, as shown in line 4 above.

Below are several other addressing modes that were not shown because they are not applicable to the LDA instruction.

Addressing Mode	Mnemonic	Machine Code
5. Relative addressing	BPL *+5	2A 03
6. Inherent addressing	ABA	1B
7. Accumulator addressing	ASL A	48

Here, the * is interpreted as the value of the PC at the *beginning* of the instruction, and the second byte adjusts the PC *relative* to the value it would have, after this instruction is executed (i.e., the original PC + 2 + 3). A minus sign could have been used, and the second byte would be the 2's complement of the minus number, also adjusted by the two bytes of the instruction. The second byte therefore can represent a maximum offset of + 127 ($7F) or − 128 ($80) bytes relative to the address of the first byte of the *following* instruction.

The last two instructions are *inherent* instructions. They need only *one* byte to address them because all the information needed for their execution is already within the μP and no memory locations or immediate operands are required.

7-3.1
Use of Mnemonics to
Express Addresses

Mnemonics can be used to express *addresses* as well as OP codes. When used in this way they are called *labels*. For example a program to add three numbers and then branch back to itself might be:

```
BEGIN    LDA A FIRST
         ADD A SECOND
         ADD A THIRD
         STA A SUM
         BRA BEGIN
```

Here the operands that represent addresses were given the *symbolic* names of FIRST, SECOND, THIRD, BEGIN, and SUM. These are the names of the locations in memory from which the contents are fetched (in the case of the first 3 instructions), and to which the results (in A), are stored in the fourth. The *symbols* chosen are usually whatever pops into the programmer's mind and are therefore considered to be *mnemonic* because they usually give some clue to what they represent. Note that the program starts with a label called BEGIN and it is referenced in the operand of the branch instruction.

7-3.2
Source and Object Programs

When several mnemonic or assembly language statements are written to form a program as in the BEGIN routine above, it is known as a *source* or *assembly language* program. To make this program intelligible to a μC, it must be processed by an *assembler* program. This is a program that runs in a computer and converts the source program into machine language (also called the *object program*). The object program can be expressed in a number of ways, but the assembler being described here assigns *hexadecimal* digits to the OP codes and addresses. The assembler also produces a *program listing* that shows both the *object codes* and the *mnemonics*.

Most assembler programs are written in the language of the computer for which the program being assembled is intended. In some cases the user may want to use a minicomputer or Time-Sharing computer because printers or other facilities are already available. Assemblers that run in one computer and generate code for another type are called *cross-assemblers*. Chapter 11 includes descriptions of **6800** μP Development Systems that are generally used to do these assemblies in all but very large companies where multiple usage of the larger systems can economically justify them.

Example 7-1

If the program of Sec. 7-3.1 was assembled and the addresses were assigned to the labels as follows: FIRST = 40, SECOND = 41, THIRD = 42, SUM = 43, and BEGIN = 20, what would the assembler produce as an object program?

Solution

To illustrate, a simplified program listing is shown below:

Addr	Object	Label	Mnemonic	Comments
20	96 40	BEGIN	LDA A FIRST	LOAD A FROM LOC 40
22	9B 41		ADD A SECOND	ADD CONTENTS OF 41 TO A
24	9B 42		ADD A THIRD	ADD CONTENTS OF 42 TO A
26	97 43		STA A SUM	STORE CONTENTS OF A TO 43
28	20 F6		BRA BEGIN	BRANCH BACK TO BEGIN

Note that the assembler substitutes the appropriate machine code or address for each part of the mnemonic statement [i.e., 96 = LDA A (direct), and 40 = FIRST, etc.]. In the last statement the assembler program calculated the offset value for the branch (-10 = F6). This is not a practical program since it results in an endless loop, but could be used as a test program. When using assemblers, the programmer is not required to calculate the offset values for branch instructions. The assembler will do it for him.

7-4
Program Listings
A source program consists of a number of lines of *source statements,* and each line must be written in a *specific format* so that it can be interpreted by the assembler. These lines can have one or more mnemonics and possibly a comment, terminated by a carriage return. All must be printable ASCII characters (except line feed, carriage return, and spaces).

When the *source program* is processed by the assembler program, it produces two outputs: the *program listing,* and the machine language *object listing*. The program listing is normally printed on the operators terminal of the software development system, or on a line printer that is part of that system. The object program, or machine code output, is usually put on *tape* or in a *disk* file so that it can be loaded into the computer for which it is intended and tested. This process is described in detail in Chapter 11.

A program listing of a sample program is shown in Fig. 7-1. This is *not* a real program. It is *only* intended to demonstrate the many features of the assembler and to show the distinctions between the various mnemonic expressions. The comments on each line explain the feature involved. Examples of several useful programs are given later in this chapter. Figure 7-1 shows that the assembler formats the listing into seven *columns* or fields.

```
LINE   ADDR  CODE     LABEL  OP   OPERAND          COMMENTS
 1      2     3         4     5      6                 7

00001                         NAM  PGM
00002                 * REVISION 1
00003                         OPT  O,S            OBJECT + SYMBOLS OPTIO
00004  0100                   ORG  256
00005        000A     COUNT   EQU  @12            @ INDICATES OCTAL
00006  0100  8E 0132  START   LDS  #STACK         LOAD STACK POINTER
00007  0103  FE 0136          LDX  ADDR           LOAD X EXTENDED
00008  0106  C6 0A            LDA B #COUNT         IMMEDIATE ADDRESSING
00009  0108  96 0A    BACK    LDA A 10             DIRECT ADDRESSING
00010  010A  A1 02            CMP A 2,X            INDEXED ADDRESSING
00011  010C  27 05            BEQ  FOUND           RELATIVE ADDRESSING
00012  010E  09               DEX                  INHERENT ADDRESSING
00013  010F  5A               DEC B                ACCUMULATOR ONLY ADDR
00014  0110  26 F6            BNE  BACK            LABEL REFERENCE
00015  0112  3E               WAI                  WAIT FOR INTERRUPT

00017  0113  BD 0119  FOUND   JSR  SUBRTN          JUMP TO SUBROUTINE
00018  0116  7E 0100          JMP  START           EXTENDED ADDRESSING
00019                 * COMMENT STATEMENT NOTE TRUNCATION 012345678
00020  0119  16       SUBRTN TAB                   COMMENT FIELD TRUNCATI
00021  011A  BA 0133          ORA A BYTE           SET MST SGNIFICNT BYTE
00022  011D  39               RTS                  RETURN FROM SUBROUTINE

00024  011E  0014             RMB  20              AREA FOR STACK
00025  0132  0001     STACK   RMB  1               START OF STACK
00026  0133  80       BYTE    FCB  $80             FORM CONSTANT BYTE
00027  0134  10               FCB  $10,%10010111   % IS FOR BINARY
       0135  97
00028  0136  0138     ADDR    FDB  DATA            FORM DOUBLE BYTE
00029  0138  53       DATA    FCC  'SET' FORM CONSTANT CHARACTERS
       0139  45
       013A  54
00030                         END

COUNT  000A START   0100 BACK    0108 FOUND  0113 SUBRTN 0119
STACK  0132 BYTE    0133 ADDR    0136 DATA   0138

TOTAL ERRORS 00000
```

Figure 7-1 Sample program to show assembler features.

1. Line numbers
2. Addresses
3. Object codes
4. Labels
5. Operators
6. Operands
7. Comments

The mnemonic expressions in columns 5 and 6 are translated by the assembler into the machine code shown in Column 3. This code resides at the addresses in Column 2. Some of the lines (1, 3, 4, 5, 24, 26, 29, and 30) of Fig. 7-1 include statements that are not listed as instructions in Table 5-1. These mnemonic statements are *assembler directives* and are listed in Table 7-1 (see Sec. 7-5). Some of these directives produce object code (lines 26, 27, 28, and 29 of Fig. 7-1), but those that do not are used to control the assembler or to format the listing. Each column of Fig. 7-1 will now be described.

7-4.1
Line Numbers (Column 1)

Each line in the listing is numbered and the line numbers appear in Column 1. When the programmer writes source statements, *line numbering* is *optional*. If the source program has line numbers, they will be printed as each line is assembled. If numbers were not originally used, the assembler will provide them. Line numbers are decimal, and 65536 is maximum.

7-4.2
Addresses (Column 2)

The addresses correspond to the location in memory for each byte. Addresses are listed as four-digit hexadecimal numbers and are automatically incremented by the number of bytes required for each instruction by the assembler. The starting address is determined by the ORG statement (described in Sec. 7-5) specified by the programmer.

7-4.3
Object Codes (Column 3)

Each instruction is translated into machine language and the codes are printed on each line in hexadecimal format. These instructions can be one, two, or three bytes in length depending on the instruction and addressing mode involved. Section 7-9 gives details on the Object Code Output of the assembler.

7-4.4
Labels (Column 4)

In Sec. 7-3.1 we explained that mnemonics could be assigned to *addresses* as well as *OP Codes*. Mnemonics that apply to addresses are called *labels*. The labeled addresses can be operands, but they can also refer to the location of the program steps. When labels are program locations, they are listed in Column 4 of the assembled program.

Both types of labels are used on line 6 of Fig. 7-1. The label START in Column 4 refers to the starting address of the program. Column 2 shows that the starting address of the program is 0100 or that START = 0100.

Line 6 also contains the label STACK, whose address is loaded into the SP by the *immediate* instruction. Note that the second and third bytes of Column 3 are 0132, which is the value of STACK. STACK is used as a label on line 25 where it is further defined (Sec. 7-5.1).

Example 7-2

a. What is the address of the instruction on line 8?

b. How can it be expressed symbolically?

Solution

a. The location of the LOAD instruction in line 8 is at 0106 as given on the assembler printout (Column 2). It could have been calculated by realizing that this instruction occurs after 2 three-byte instructions from START (0100).

b. This location can be expressed symbolically as START+6, or the programmer can assign a mnemonic of his own choice.

Labels are generally used for program locations that are the objects of branch instructions. In Fig. 7-1, the labels FOUND and BACK are used this way. The branch instruction on line 14 (BNE BACK), for example, returns the program to BACK (location 0108) if the branch is taken. The use of labels here eliminates the problem of *calculating offsets*. The assembler calculates the proper value for the second byte of a branch instruction and inserts it into the offset (F6 in this case).

Specific rules apply when writing labels. The **6800** assembler has the following requirements.

1. A label consists of from 1 to 6 alphanumeric characters.

2. The first character of a label must be alphabetic.

3. A label must begin in the first character position of a statement.

4. All labels within a program must be unique.

5. A label must not consist of any one of the single characters A, B, or X. (These characters are reserved for special syntax and refer to accumulator A, accumulator B, and the index register X, respectively.)

The EQU directive is used to assign *values* to labels. Line 5, for example, reads COUNT EQU @12. This sets the value of COUNT to octal 12 (or hex 000A).

Here are some typical labels:

START START2 E3 W B120 SUBRTN

7-4.5
Operators (Column 5)

The operation codes (OP codes) appear in Column 5. Mnemonics that are not in Table 5-1 are assembler directives; these are discussed in Sec. 7-5.

7-4.6
Operands (Column 6)

The operand field of an instruction contains a *value,* an address, or a label that references one of them. Inherent instructions do not need an operand (see line 12). Operands can also reference a label. In line 8 of Fig. 7-1 the value (000A) (which has been given to COUNT by the EQU statement on line 5), is used by the assembler. The EQU assumes the number can be up to 16 bits long. Since the number involved is less than 256, it does not overflow when loaded into the 8-bit accumulator by the instruction in line 8 of Fig. 7-1. This instruction is an example where the label is preceded by the # sign to indicate the *immediate* mode of addressing. An operand can also contain an expression such as *+5, which will be evaluated algebraically by the assembler. (This operand is interpreted as the current value of the program counter plus 5.)

Examples of statements with various operands are:

LDA A #$F3   Immediate load of hex value F3
LDX SUZY,X   "X" indicates indexed instruction.
                Offset equals the *value* of SUZY
JMP $1200   Jump to 1200 (hex)
BRA EXIT   Branch to label called EXIT
BEQ *+5   Branch to address of this instruction plus 5.

Numbers can be expressed in several ways in all operands, but, except for decimal, must be preceded by a symbol as follows:

1. Hexadecimal $
2. Octal   @
3. Binary   %
4. Decimal   (none)

Example 7-3
What do the instructions on lines 9 and 10 of Fig. 7-1 do?

Solution

Line 9 contains LDA A 10. It loads the contents of location 10 ($A in hex) (not defined in this printout), into the A register.

Line 10 compares the contents of A with the contents of the address in the index register + 2. Since X contains 138 (see line 7 and 28), A is compared with the contents of 013A, which are seen to be 54 (see line 29). Thus the instruction in line 10 compares the contents of A with 54 and sets the flags.

7-4.7
Comments (Column 7)

Comments are used to explain what each line or each section of the program is doing. They can be added to any statement by separating it from the operand (or operator if no operand is used), with one or more spaces. A comment can also be used on a line by itself, if preceded by an * in the first character position of the line. Comments do not generate machine code but are simply copied from the source to the program listing (verbatim). *Comprehension* of the program is aided immeasurably when proper comments are used. Comments are *required* if the program is to be understood by someone other than the programmer.

Good comments should indicate the function of the instruction in the program. For example, the comment, ''JUMP TO SUB-ROUTINE AT LOC 20'', or ''STORED EXTENDED'', are poor comments because they do not tell what the instruction is doing in the *context* of the program. The program flow can be more readily understood if these comments are replaced by comments such as ''JUMP TO MULTIPLICATION SUBROUTINE'', or ''STORE ADDEND''.

The comments in Fig. 7-1 are poor because this is not a normal program that does something. They can be contrasted with Fig. 7-3, which contains good comments.

7-5
Assembler Directives

When writing a program, options are available to enable the programmer to reserve memory bytes for data, specify the starting address of the program, and select the format of the assembler output. These options are called *assembler directives* and are listed in Table 7-1.

Assembler directives are all three-letter mnemonics (with the exception of PAGE), and are written into the source program and interpreted during the assembly process. Three of the directives generate object code in the form of data, but others only control the assembler. Table 7-1 shows that the *assembler directives* are divided into three major catagories.

Table 7-1
Assembly Directives

Directive	Function
Assembly control	
NAM XXXXXXXX[a]	Program name (8 letters maximum)
ORG nnnn[b]	Origin (any number base)
END	Program end
Listing control	
PAGE	Top of page
SPC n	Skip "n" lines
OPT NOO	No object tape
OPT O	The Assembler will generate an object tape (selected by default).
OPT M	The Assembler will write machine code to memory.
OPT NOM	No memory (selected by default).
OPT S	The Assembler will print the symbols at the end of Pass 2.
OPT NOS	No printing of symbols (selected by default).
OPT NOL	The Assembler will not print a listing of the assembler data.
OPT L	The listing of assembled data will be printed (selected by default).
OPT NOP	The Assembler will inhibit format paging of the assembly listing.
OPT P	The listing will be paged (selected by default).
OPT NOG	Causes only 1 line of data to be listed from the assembler directions FCC, FCB, and FDB.
OPT G	All data generated by the FCC, FCB, and FDB directions will be printed (selected by default).
Data definition storage allocation	
FCC "MESSAGE"	Character string data ⎫ Generates
FCB XX, YY, ZZ, etc.	One-byte data ⎬ data
FDB XXXX, YYYY, ZZZZ, etc.	Double-byte data ⎭
RMB nnnn	Reserve n memory bytes ⎫ No data
Symbol definition	⎬ generated
EQU nnnn	Assign permanent value ⎭

[a]X's indicate alphanumeric characters.
[b]n's refer to any number base: 65420, $F100, @7756. We usually show 4 n's since the number we use is often a 4-digit hex number.

1. **Assembly control**, which names the program, defines its starting address, and tells the assembler when to stop processing the source program.
2. **Listing control**, which specifies the output format of the assembly, and which options are to be used.
3. **Data definition**, which specifies the type of data and where it will be stored in memory.

Reference to the program listing of Fig. 7-1 shows how the directives are used. The NAM statement must be the first line of the program and the name used (up to 8 characters) is printed at the top of each page along with the page number during assembly. Other directives, such as OPT and ORG, are also used. Certain options are selected by the assembler by default and are identified in Table 7-1. (These differ with various versions of the assembler.)

7-5.1
The RMB Directive

The RMB (Reserve Memory Byte) directive reserves a location in memory or a group of locations where data is to be stored. If several areas are required for different types of data, several RMBs can be used.

Example 7-4

In Fig. 7-1 where is the stack located and how is it specified by the assembler?

Solution

The RMB directive on line 24 specifies that 20 decimal or 14 hex locations are to be reserved. The RMB on line 25 specifies the top or start of the stack (since it decrements when used). The programmer merely writes RMB 20 and RMB 1 for the start of the stack. The assembler then reserves 14 hex locations for the stack, plus 1 location for the start of the stack. In this example the assembler has thus assigned 21 locations from 011E to 0132 inclusive, for the stack.

7-5.2
The FCB, FDB, and FCC Directives

The FCB (Form Constant Byte) and FDB (Form Double Byte) directives are used to define data used by the program. These mnemonics must be followed by a decimal, hex, octal, or binary number, or a label. The byte on line 26 is labeled BYTE and used by the instruction on line 21. The FCB is used on lines 26 and 27 of Fig. 7-1. Note that on line 27 two operands are defined, one written in hex and one written in binary. They occupy locations 134 and 135 in memory. Many bytes can be defined by a single FCB or FDB provided that the data values are separated by commas, and they don't overflow the line.

A two-byte constant, labeled ADDR, is defined by the FDB (Form Double Byte) directive on line 28. The operand of the FDB is the label DATA. The assembler assigned an address to DATA and thereby defined 0138 as the FCB reference.

The FCC (Form Constant Characters) directive (used on line 29) is useful for formating ASCII expressions or messages that are to be printed by a program. This directive generates the machine language equivalents for the ASCII characters included between the delimiters (apostrophes in this case). Here the word SET is translated to its hex equivalent of 53, 45, and 54, respectively.

If a large number of operands, or a longer message are used, the directives FCB, FDB, and FCC take a lot of room to print. For this reason the OPT NOG directive is generally used to inhibit all but the first line of each of these statements. The object tape or floppy disk file is not affected, however, and contains all the data bytes.

7-5.3
The Symbol Table

When OPT S is specified, the assembler will print a *symbol table* at the end of the program listing. The symbol table lists each symbol used by the program and the address or value of that symbol. In a large program this can be very helpful in locating a particular symbol (or label) location. The symbols are listed across the page in the order of their occurrence.

In Fig. 7-1, nine symbols are used. They are listed in the symbol table immediately below the END statement.

Example 7-5
In the assembly of Fig. 7-1, what is the starting address of the subroutine?

Solution
We find the label for the subroutine is SUBRTN. Its address can be found by examining the code but, in a long program, it can be found more easily by going directly to the symbol table which, in this case, shows that SUBRTN equals 0119.

7-6
Writing a Program

Several assembler programs have been written for the **6800**. All those written by Motorola have the same mnemonics but do have slightly different directives. Before writing a source program the user should consult the manual for his particular assembler. Section 7-13 contains references to several such manuals. The user must understand the directives and rules that apply to the assembler actually being used or else errors will occur.

As an example of assembly language programming, let us write the source program for the BCD-to-binary program of Sec. 6-8. It starts with the NAM directive that provides the name at the top of each page. Comment lines can be used at any time after the NAM statement but must be preceded by an * in the first character position. When typing the source program, an Editor program is used because its features help place the lines in the proper format. After each carriage return for example, it inserts a line feed and four nulls. The nulls provide a delay to allow time for the carriage to return (see Chapter 11 for more detail). When writing and correcting long programs, the *search* and *change* features of this editor are very useful. Figure 7-2 shows the source program as it appears when finished. The instructions are the same as the program for Example 6-20. Notice that all labels and the asterisks are in the first character position of each line. If a statement is an instruction or directive without a label, it must have one or more spaces at the start of the line. One space between each field is sufficient. Blank lines are not allowed, but if one or more are desired in the assembly printout, either an * followed by a CR, or the SPC directive can be used. To provide multiple blank lines, the SPC is followed by a number to indicate the number of blank lines desired. SPC 5 is an example. The required space between the C and the 5 illustrates the need for proper formatting. Line 23 of Fig. 7-1 is an SPC 2.

The programmer must also specify where every block of code will start so that it coincides with the hardware locations of memory. To do this, the ORG statement is used, and is followed by the desired address. Labels are assigned for all data locations and destinations of jumps or branches that will not be known until the assembly is done. This is a convenience since it eliminates any requirement for calculations on the part of the programmer. Section 7-7 describes how the assembler determines the location of the labels.

For the data locations, let us specify:

a. WORD1 and WORD2 (the BCD to be converted to binary).
b. SUM1 and SUM2 (the locations holding the binary equivalent of the BCD word).

The RMB directive is generally used to provide a place to store data such as this but, by using the FCB directive, it is possible to

```
            NAM BCDBIN
         *PROGRAM TO CONVERT BCD NUMBERS TO BINARY
         *WORD1 & WORD2 CONTAIN THE BCD WORDS
         *SUM1 &SUM2 CONTAIN THE BINARY EQUIVALENT
         *WRITTEN BY J. D. GREENFIELD 1/24/78
          OPT O OUTPUT OBJECT PGM
          OPT S OUTPUT SYMBOL TABLE
         *
          ORG $20
         WORD1 FCB 1 MSB BCD NUMBER
         WORD2 FCB $69 LSB  PACKED BCD NUMBER
         SUM1 FCB 0 BINARY RESULT
         SUM2 FCB 0 2ND BINARY BYTE
          SPC 1
         START1 LDS #$200 SET STACK
          LDX #LIST
          LDA A WORD2 GET LSB WORD TO BE CONVERTED
         SHIFT2 ASR A SHIFT RIGHT
          BCC INCR
          BSR START2 GO TO ADD SUBROUTINE
         INCR INX
          INX
          CPX #$120 LIST COMPLETED?
          BEQ HALT YES-GO INTO LOOP ON SELF
          CPX #$110 TEST FOR WORD1
          BNE SHIFT2 LOOP FOR NEXT BIT
          SPC 1
          LDA A WORD1 LOAD MSB BCD WORD
          BRA SHIFT2
          SPC 1
         HALT BRA * LOOP BACK 2 BYTES
          SPC 1
         * ADD ALGORITHM SUBROUTINE
          SPC 1
         START2 PSH A
          LDA A 1,X LOAD LSB FROM LIST
          ADD A SUM2 ADD LSB OF SUM
          STA A SUM2 UPDATE SUM
          LDA A 0,X LOAD MSB FROM LIST
          ADC A SUM1 ADD MSB OF SUM
          STA A SUM1 UPDATE SUM
          PUL A
          RTS RETURN TO MAIN PROGRAM
          SPC 2
          ORG $100
         LIST FDB 1
          FDB 2
          FDB 4
          FDB 8
          FDB 10
          FDB 20
          FDB 40
          FDB 80
          FDB 100
          FDB 200
          FDB 400
          FDB 800
          FDB 1000
          FDB 2000
          FDB 4000
          FDB 8000
          SPC 1
          END
```

Figure 7-2 Source program for Example 6-20.

create a location and to *preset it to a prescribed value* at the same time. This avoids the necessity of writing an initialization routine. (The value of 169 for the BCD digits to be converted was arbitrarily chosen in this example.) Here, the FCB 0 takes the place of the first three instructions of Example 6-17, whose purpose was to initialize the SUM to zero.

Next, the program locations that are to be referenced can be labeled. The program entry is called START1 and the first statement of the subroutine is called START2. Other labels are added as required. For example, the program loops back to the address labeled SHIFT2. The SPC directive is used to format the listing for easy reading. Skipping a line after each branch or jump instruction usually clarifies the flow of the program. The ORG statement, or options such as OPT NOL and OPT L, can be repeated as often as necessary, and ORG is used again in this program to locate the lookup table at $100. An END statement must be used to tell the assembler when to stop inputting data and to terminate the processing. It then returns program control to the system monitor or disk executive (see Chapter 11).

An absolute address for the location of the stack is specified in the START1 line. This is usually done as shown in Fig. 7-1 to be sure that the stack is separate from the program and data areas, and does not overwrite them. Remember the stack decrements when used. Also note that the X register is initialized in effect, by referencing it to the immediate value (#) of the LIST label (i.e., its address). The value of LIST is assigned by the assembler.

To summarize, the program of Sec. 6-8 is shown in Fig. 7-2 as written in the assembly format using the following steps.

1. The name BCDBIN was assigned to the program on the top line by the NAM directive.
2. Four lines of comments were added. Comments should be used for every program.
3. The options desired (those not selected by default) were added by using OPT O and OPT S directives.
4. The program was set to start at address $20 by the ORG statement, and initialization of the data locations was accomplished by using the FCB directive to set initially the BCD words to 169 and the sum to 0.
5. The program continues until the HALT label is encountered. This "branch-on-self" instruction will lock up the PC in a loop.

   Note the use of labels such as SHIFT2 for all instructions that are the object of branches or jumps. Note also that blank lines were used after each branch by means of the SPC directive.

6. The subroutine is located outside the main program flow but is referenced by the START2 label.
7. The list table was written as a string of FDB directives because each one should be a 16-bit number. Decimal numbers are used for convenience and the assembler converts them to hex.
8. The END statement completes the source program.

The assembled program is shown in Fig. 7-3. It should be carefully compared with the source listing of Fig. 7-2. Note the formatting into fields and blank lines. One can also see how the decimal values and offset address were calculated by the assembler. The blank lines are created by the SPC directive.

7-7
The Two-Pass Assembler

To convert a source program to an object program, this Motorola assembler reads the source program twice. It is known as a *two-pass* assembler. When it reads through the program the first time (called the first pass or pass 1), the number of bytes required for each instruction is determined and the PC is incremented accordingly. As each label or symbol is encountered, its address is stored away in the symbol table but nothing is printed (except errors if they occur). During the second reading (pass 2), the values of these labels are inserted in the object code and the offsets are calculated by the assembler for each branch instruction. It then prints the assembly listing as shown in Fig. 7-3. It also produces the object code in a form that allows it to be entered into the μC (see Sec. 7-9).

7-8
Error Indication

If the source program is not written in accordance with the rules specified for each type of statement, error lines will be printed. A list of these errors are found in Table 7-2. Note that each error has a number. The manual provides an explanation of each type of error as an aid to debugging. The most common causes of errors are improper spacing or the use of illegal characters.

Most of the errors are printed during pass 1 and allow the operator to abort the assembly to make corrections. If there are only a few errors and they are not serious, he or she may elect to let the assembler complete the listing anyway, so an object machine code file can be obtained and tested. Usually, other revisions are also required. In addition to the printing of an error number, which identifies the type of error, the original line is reprinted (unformatted) so the programmer can find any mistake. Many times the error is not obvious, and

```
00001                                    NAM     BCDBIN
00002                          *PROGRAM TO CONVERT BCD NUMBERS TO BINARY
00003                          *WORD1 & WORD2 CONTAIN THE BCD WORDS
00004                          *SUM1 &SUM2 CONTAIN THE BINARY EQUIVALENT
00005                          *WRITTEN BY J. D. GREENFIELD 1/24/78
00006                                    OPT     O        OUTPUT OBJECT PGM
00007                                    OPT     S        OUTPUT SYMBOL TABLE
00008                          *
00009 0020                               ORG     $20
00010 0020 01                  WORD1     FCB     1        MSB BCD NUMBER
00011 0021 69                  WORD2     FCB     $69      LSB  PACKED BCD NUMBER
00012 0022 00                  SUM1      FCB     0        BINARY RESULT
00013 0023 00                  SUM2      FCB     0        2ND BINARY BYTE

00015 0024 8E 0200             START1    LDS     #$200    SET STACK
00016 0027 CE 0100                       LDX     #LIST
00017 002A 96 21                         LDA A   WORD2    GET LSB WORD TO BE CONVERTED
00018 002C 47                  SHIFT2    ASR A            SHIFT RIGHT
00019 002D 24 02                         BCC     INCR
00020 002F 8D 12                         BSR     START2   GO TO ADD SUBROUTINE
00021 0031 08                  INCR      INX
00022 0032 08                            INX
00023 0033 8C 0120                       CPX     #$120    LIST COMPLETED?
00024 0036 27 09                         BEQ     HALT     YES-GO INTO LOOP ON SELF
00025 0038 8C 0110                       CPX     #$110    TEST FOR WORD1
00026 003B 26 EF                         BNE     SHIFT2   LOOP FOR NEXT BIT

00028 003D 96 20                         LDA A   WORD1    LOAD MSB BCD WORD
00029 003F 20 EB                         BRA     SHIFT2

00031 0041 20 FE               HALT      BRA     *        LOOP BACK 2 BYTES

00033                          * ADD ALGORITHM SUBROUTINE

00035 0043 36                  START2    PSH A
00036 0044 A6 01                         LDA A   1,X      LOAD LSB FROM LIST
00037 0046 9B 23                         ADD A   SUM2     ADD LSB OF SUM
00038 0048 97 23                         STA A   SUM2     UPDATE SUM
00039 004A A6 00                         LDA A   0,X      LOAD MSB FROM LIST
00040 004C 99 22                         ADC A   SUM1     ADD MSB OF SUM
00041 004E 97 22                         STA A   SUM1     UPDATE SUM
00042 0050 32                            PUL A
00043 0051 39                            RTS              RETURN TO MAIN PROGRAM

00045 0100                               ORG     $100
00046 0100 0001                LIST      FDB     1
00047 0102 0002                          FDB     2
00048 0104 0004                          FDB     4
00049 0106 0008                          FDB     8
00050 0108 000A                          FDB     10
00051 010A 0014                          FDB     20
00052 010C 0028                          FDB     40
00053 010E 0050                          FDB     80
00054 0110 0064                          FDB     100
00055 0112 00C8                          FDB     200
00056 0114 0190                          FDB     400
00057 0116 0320                          FDB     800
00058 0118 03E8                          FDB     1000
00059 011A 07D0                          FDB     2000
00060 011C 0FA0                          FDB     4000
00061 011E 1F40                          FDB     8000

00063         0000              END
WORD1   0020 WORD2   0021 SUM1     0022 SUM2    0023 START1 0024
SHIFT2  002C INCR    0031 HALT     0041 START2  0043 LIST    0100
```

Figure 7-3 Assembly listing for BCDBIN program.

```
TOTAL ERRORS 00000
```

Table 7-2
Assembler Error Messages

---

201 NAM DIRECTIVE ERROR
MEANING: The NAM directive is not the first source statement, or it occurs more than once in the same source program (Applies only to version 1.2)

202 EQU DIRECTIVE SYNTAX ERROR
MEANING: The EQU directive requires a label (Applies only to version 1.2)

204 STATEMENT SYNTACTICALLY INCORRECT
MEANING: The source statement is syntactically incorrect.

205 LABEL ERROR
MEANING: The statement may not have a label or the label is syntactically incorrect.

206 REDEFINED SYMBOL
MEANING: The symbol has been previously defined.

207 UNDEFINED OPCODE
MEANING: the symbol in the operation code field is not a valid operation code mnemonic or directive.

208 BRANCH ERROR
MEANING: The branch count is beyond the relative byte's range. The allowance is
$(*+2) - 128 \leq D \leq (*+2) + 127$
where D = address of the destination of the branch
where D = instruction.
* = address of the first byte of the branch instruction.

209 ILLEGAL ADDRESS MODE
MEANING: The mode of addressing is not allowed with the operation code type.

210 BYTE OVERFLOW
MEANING: A one-byte expression has been converted to a value greater than 255_{10} or less than -128_{10}.

211 UNDEFINED SYMBOL
MEANING: The symbol does not appear in the label field.

213* EQU DIRECTIVE SYNTAX ERROR
MEANING: The EQU directive requires a label.

216 DIRECTIVE OPERAND ERROR
MEANING: The directive operand field is in error.

218 MEMORY ERROR
MEANING: The memory option was used and the object code was directed to overwrite the assembler/editor or into nonexistent memory.

220   REDEFINED LABEL ERROR
       MEANING: The symbol in the label field has been redefined and
                has a different value on pass 2 than on pass 1.

221   SYMBOL TABLE OVERFLOW
       MEANING: The symbol table has overflowed. See assembler and
                editor memory requirements in Sec. 7-11 for extending
                the symbol table.

---

*In version 1.2 ERROR 213 is a redefined symbol error.

the rules may have to be reviewed before the reason is found. Some errors are not encountered until pass 2 is in progress, such as error 208 (out-of-range). This occurs in pass 2 because the relative addressing offsets cannot be calculated by the assembler until the label table is completed during pass 1. An error total is printed at the end of each assembly.

The assembler listing of a program to provide communication through an Asynchronous Communications Interface Adapter (ACIA) is shown in Fig. 7-4a. This device is described in Chapter 9.

Errors were discovered on line 15 during assembly of the program. This resulted in two errors being printed during pass 1 (Fig. 7-4b), and 3 during pass 2 (in the listing of Fig. 7-4a). Table 7-2 indicates that a 216 is an operand error. A study of line 13 shows a similar instruction and it appears the errors were caused by an omitted space following the binary number in the operand. This is obviously also a syntax (204) error. The 211 error was listed because the assembler thought it found a new undefined label. Note also that the machine code was incorrectly calculated (10 instead of 11). The total error count is the total for both passes. Figure 7-4c is explained in Sec. 7-9. Other errors, not related to spacing or improper syntax, frequently occur in new programs, because of label conflicts. If a label is forgotten, a 211 error (undefined symbol) is printed, and the label, followed by FFFF, is printed during pass 1. If a label is used twice, a 206 error (redefined label) is printed, and all references to the label are printed during pass 1. In each case a line number is also printed, which makes it easy to find.

**7-9
Object Code Output**

All Motorola assembler programs, whether on time-sharing or resident in the μP Development System, produce object tapes (or files) in an ASCII-Hex format, as shown in Table 7-3. This format includes three types of lines; the S0, or *name* line, the S1, or *data* line, and

(a)

```
00001                         NAM    ACIA1
00002              *PROGRAM FOR AN ACIA IN SYSTEM NOT REQUIRNG
00003              *ERROR CHECKING OR WIRED INTERRUPTS

00005      8008    ACIACS EQU   $8008    CONTROL/STATUS REG ADDR
00006      8009    ACIAD  EQU   $8009    DATA REGISTERS ADDR
00007                     OPT   O,S      SELECT OBJECT & SYMBOLS

00009 0100                ORG   $100

00011              *INITIALIZATION

00013 0100 86 03   INIT   LDA A #%00000011 =HEX 3
00014 0102 B7 8008        STA A ACIACS  MASTER RESET
****ERROR  216
****ERROR  204
****ERROR  211
00015 0105 86 10         LDA A #%00010001= 8 BITS+2 STOP+DVD BY 16
00016 0107 B7 8008        STA A ACIACS  PROGRAM THE ACIA
00017 010A 39             RTS           RETURN TO OTHER SYSTEM INIT.

00019 010B B6 8008 INPUT  LDA A ACIACS  GET STATUS WORD
00020 010E 47             ASR A         SHIFT RDRF INTO CARRY
00021 010F 24 FA          BCC   INPUT   LOOP TIL BIT SET
00022 0111 B6 8009        LDA A ACIAD   BRING IN CHARACTER

00024 0114 F6 8008 OUTPUT LDA B ACIACS  GET STATUS
00025 0117 C5 02          BIT B #2      TX BIT SET?
00026 0119 27 F9          BEQ   OUTPUT  NO LOOP TIL READY
00027 011B B7 8009        STA A ACIAD   PRINT CHARACTER
00028 011E 39             RTS
00029                     END
ACIACS 8008
ACIAD  8009
INIT   0100
INPUT  010B
OUTPUT 0114

TOTAL ERRORS 00005
```

(b)

```
****ERROR  216
****ERROR  204
0015 0105 86 10      LDA A #%00010001= 8 BITS+2 STOP+DVD BY 16

          FFFF
```

(c)

```
                  A C I A 1
S00B00004143494131202020 55
T B   A                   C

                                                    data
S11E01008603B780088610B7800839B680084724FAB68009F68008C50227F9C3
T B   A                                                        C
      data
S107011BB780093963
T B   A         C

S903F564A3
T B   A C
```

Figure 7-4 Assembler output showing an error.
(a) Program listing (pass 2)
(b) Printout for pass 1
(c) Printout of object code output

T = Type of line
B = Byte count
C = Checksum
A = Address

the S9, or *terminating* line. Figure 7-4c shows the object output for the ACIA1 program.

Each line starts with either S0, S1, or S9, which identifies the type of line. This is followed by a *byte count* (two hexadecimal characters) that define the number of bytes in the remainder of the line. The *address* where the data will go is then listed, followed by the data bytes themselves. The line ends with a checksum byte. The checksum is used by the loader routine, to verify that no errors were made. As Table 7-3 shows, *the checksum is the one's complement of the summation of all of the data, byte-count, and address bytes.* It is calculated by the assembler, and is punched (or recorded) into the tape, as the last byte of each line. The loading function of the monitor program used in the development system (see Chapter 11), recalculates the sum as it loads the program and prints an error message if it's wrong. This avoids wasting time with a faulty program.

7-9.1
The S0 Line

The three types of lines produced by the assembler for the ACIA1 program are shown in Fig. 7-4c. The top line is the S0 line. S0 is followed by the byte count (0B), indicating that there are 11 bytes following. The next two bytes are not used and are set to 0000 for the S0 line. The remaining bytes are the ASCII codes for each letter of the program name. The 20s are ASCII spaces and indicate that the assembler will accept up to eight characters in the name. If the bytes following the 0B are added it will be found they total AA. The 1s complement is 55, as shown in the checksum.

7-9.2
The S1 Line

The S1 lines contains the object codes of the program. There may be many S1 lines since the largest number of data bytes for each line is 27. This varies with different assemblers or monitors, which also generate this format. Some programs provide 16 bytes of data per line. The last line can be anything less, even only one byte of data.

Figure 7-4c shows two S1 lines. Note the address of the first line is 0100, which corresponds to the ORG statement as the starting address. The bytes of data then follow (i.e., 86 03 37 . . . . . etc.) The address in the second line is 011B, which is the address of the 28th byte of data.

7-9.3
The S9 Line

The S9 line signifies the end of the object code. The bytecount and checksum for this terminating line are calculated in the same way as for the other type lines. The address is shown as 0000 in most as-

Table 7-3
Object Code ASCII-Hex Format

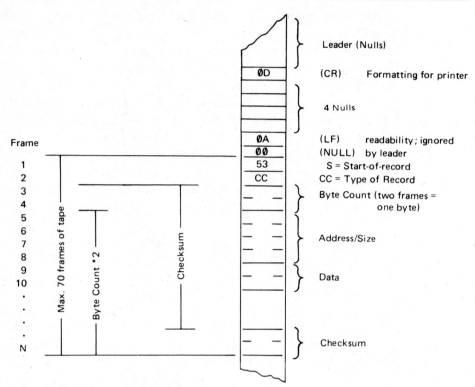

	Leader (Nulls)
ØD	(CR) Formatting for printer
	4 Nulls
ØA	(LF) readability; ignored
ØØ	(NULL) by leader
53	S = Start-of-record
CC	CC = Type of Record
— —	Byte Count (two frames = one byte)
— —	Address/Size
— —	Data
— —	Checksum

Frames 3 through N are hexadecimal digits represented by a 7-bit ASCII character.
Two hexadecimal digits are combined to make one 8-bit byte.

The checksum is the one's complement of the summation of 8-bit bytes.

Frame	CC = 30 Header Record		CC = 31 Data Record		CC = 39 End-of-File Record	
1. Start-of-Record	53	S	53	S	53	S
2. Type of Record	30	Ø	31	1	39	9
3. Byte Count	31	12	31	16	30	03
4.	32		36		33	
5.	30		31		30	
6. Address/Size	30	0000	31	1100	30	0000
7.	30		30		30	
8.	30		30		30	
9. Data	34	48-H	39	98	46	FC
10.	38		38		43	
.	34	44-D	30	32		(Checksum)
.	34		32			
.	35	52-R				
.	32		41	A8 (Checksum)		
.			48			
.	39	9E				
N. Checksum	45					

semblers, but later versions have an option to include the starting address for the program in the S9 line as shown in Figure 7-4c.

**7-10
Assembler Operation**

Various assembler programs are provided by Motorola and other companies to generate **6800** system software. All are designed to be used with one of the standard µP Development Systems (see Chapter 11). These systems are specialized **6800** systems and have *monitor control* programs in IC ROMs. They contain the I/O routines to work with terminals that use paper tape or cassettes and that respond to the ASCII control codes (e.g., DC1). One of the functions of these systems is to serve as a software development station to write, edit, assemble, and debug **6800** programs. Various versions of these monitor programs are in use under the names of EXBUG, MIKBUG, MINIBUG, MICROBUG, or JBUG. Each one requires a different version of the assembler/editor programs, primarily because of the different addresses for the I/O routines. Disk versions are available only for EXBUG.

**7-10.1
Assembler Operation Using a
Tape Equipped Terminal**

One of the most common ways of storing and loading programs has been to use punched paper tapes, where each character is determined by the hole pattern punched into the tape. Figure 7-5 shows such a tape and the hole pattern for each ASCII character (a hole is equivalent to a "1"). The most commonly used device for punching or reading these tapes is the ASR33 (Automatic Send-Receive) teletypewriter. This terminal has been very popular because it combines these features:

1. Keyboard entry
2. Hard copy (printed paper) output
3. Tape punch (to save programs)
4. Tape reader (to load programs)

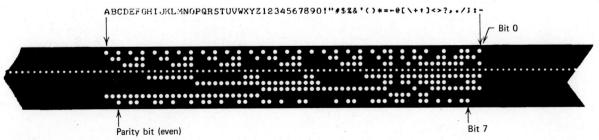

Figure 7-5 Hole patterns for TTY paper tape showing all printable characters.

The TTY is being replaced in most laboratories by newer devices because it is noisy and slow. The equivalent functions can be had in the newer, quieter, and faster ASR733 made by TI. The ASR733 uses magnetic cassettes in place of paper tape. Since both the ASR33 and ASR733 tape terminals respond to the standard ASCII control characters (DC1, DC2, DC3, and DC4) to start and stop the tapes [i.e., to read or record (punch) the tapes], the same version of the assembler (and editor) can be used. It must be selected to match the monitor ROM in use, however.

Here are the steps in the development of software using tape.

1. The assembler/editor programs are loaded into memory from tape using the LOAD routine of the system monitor program (e.g., EXBUG, MIKBUG, MINIBUG).
2. Once loaded, the editor program is entered (at $103) and prints the editor heading.
3. If the terminal uses cassettes, a blank tape is placed in the record side of the terminal. (With a TTY, it is only necessary to see that paper tape is in the punch.)
4. The source statements are then typed on the terminal and are transferred to tape by the editor. (See the editor manual referenced in Sec. 7-13 for full instructions.)
5. After the source tape has been run through edit until it is fully corrected and complete, it is rewound and set up in the reader. Another blank cassette is installed if an object tape is desired.
6. The assembler program is entered (at $100) and prints the assembler heading.
7. The pass number is entered on the terminal keyboard. Enter 1P, or 1S, for pass 1, (with or without clearing the symbol table), or 2L, 2T, or 2P, for pass 2 to request a listing, an object tape, or both.
8. The assembler outputs a reader ON command (ASCII DC1) to start the tape.
9. The characters of each line are stored in the assemblers buffer until the CR is detected.
10. After the carriage return and line feed characters are sent, the reader OFF character (DC3) is transmitted and the reader stops.
11. The assembler scans its buffer and processes each instruction. OP codes are looked up in a table, and stored temporarily. The line number and PC counters are incremented as required. If pass 1 is in progress the labels and their address are stored away in the symbol table. Nothing is printed unless an error is detected. When the END statement is encountered, the assembler heading is printed again. The tape is then rewound and step 7 is repeated.
12. When pass 2 is executed, steps 8 through 11 are repeated. After the

OP codes are processed, the PRINT routine of the assembler is entered. This routine prints the line number, program counter, and machine codes previously stored. It looks up all references in the symbol table and inserts the proper values for each label. It formats these properly (inserting the necessary spaces or lines) and then prints the contents of the line buffer, which was read from the source tape, exactly as the programmer wrote it, (except for added spaces). Any comments that follow on the same line are also printed but are limited to 29 characters since the assemblers are set for a maximum of 72 characters on a line.

13. When the assembler begins pass 2, it will read the first source statement, which is the NAM line, and will print the page number and program name at the top of a page. It will then output a line of code to the output tape. This line will be formatted as described in Sec. 7-9. After about five source lines are read, processed, and printed, enough bytes will have been saved to output another object code line.

14. The succeeding lines are then read and processed as described until the END statement is reached. The remaining object codes are then put on the tape as shown in line three of Fig. 7-4c. The tape is terminated by an end of file record (or line) which begins with an S9 (last line of Fig. 7-4c).

15. The program prints the assembler header message again as described in step 2 and waits for another command. If an ''X'' is typed at this point, the program control is returned to the system monitor program (e.g., EXBUG or MIKBUG).

7-10.2
Assembler Operation Using
Floppy Disk Storage

The assembler program for use with floppy disk systems is nearly identical to that described for tape. The I/O routines are different, however, because the source program must be read from a file on the disk instead of from a tape, and the object code is written into another disk file. The assembly operation is also similar except that both passes are performed when only one command is typed. The program control returns to the disk executive when assembly is completed. The command line includes the names of the input and output files and any option, to specify whether an object file, or program listing, or both is wanted. (Refer to disk operating system manuals available with the product.)

7-10.3
Macroassembler with Relocatable
Object Output

A more sophisticated assembler program is also available from Motorola that allows the use of macro statements in the source program and will produce relocatable object modules that can later be linked into a continuous program similar to that produced by the standard assembler. The more advanced student is referred to the macroassembler manual in the references (Sec. 7-13).

7-11
Assembler and Editor
Memory Requirements

When using the tape assembler in a μP Development System a minimum of 8K of RAM is required. The assembler occupies memory from 300 to 1610, as shown in the memory map of Fig. 7-6. The area from 100 to 300 is used for I/O routines, and the symbol (label) table extends above 1D00. The area of memory below 100 is used for scratch (RMBs). It will also be seen that the Editor program (which is used to write the source program) can be in memory simultaneously between 1610 and 1D05. This *co-residency* is a desirable feature since, in the case of paper tape terminals, the time required to load the assembler is about 25 minutes.

In the course of program development, it is not uncommon to reedit a source program and reassemble it several times before all errors are eliminated. The editor uses the same I/O routines and scratch memory area. It also uses the memory between the top of the editor (1D05), and the end of an 8K RAM module (1FFF), for the edit buffer (755 bytes). The assembler uses the same area for a symbol table. This provides for 93 symbols. If a larger symbol table is required, this area can be extended at either end. Selecting the Editor-overwrite feature, increases the area to accommodate up to 312 symbols, since the area will then start at 1610; however, it will be necessary to reload the editor to use it again. The assembler overwrite flag can be used to extend the edit buffer but, if more than 8K of RAM is available in the software development system, the table can be extended to the end of available memory by modifying the end-of-memory vector without overwriting either program.

7-12
Summary

Because of its mnemonic nature, assembly language is used for programs far more often than machine language. This chapter explained how to write an assembly language source program and how to translate it to machine language. Detailed printouts of assembler programs were shown and their features presented in detail. Directives, symbol tables, and error messages were demonstrated to help the user write and debug programs. Finally, we presented a method of translating source programs to assembly language programs using the **6800** μP.

7-13
References

Motorola Assembler Manual M68CRA(D), November, 1976. Motorola, Inc., Integrated Circuits Division, Microsystems, 3102 N. 56th Street, Phoenix, Arizona.

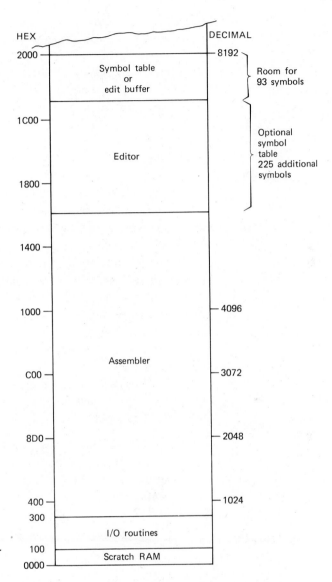

Figure 7-6 Coresident Assembler/Editor memory map (tape version).

Resident Software Supplement, Third Edition, 1975. Motorola, Inc., Integrated Circuits Division, Microsystems, 3102 N. 56th Street, Phoenix, Arizona.

M6800 Macro Assembler Reference Manual M68ASM(D), February, 1977. Motorola, Inc., Integrated Circuits Division, Microsystems, 3102 N. 56th Street, Phoenix, Arizona.

M6800 Programming Reference Manual M68PRM(D), November, 1976. Motorola, Inc., Integrated Circuits Division, Microsystems, 3102 N. 56th Street, Phoenix, Arizona.

M6800 Co-resident Editor Reference Manual M68CRE(D), January, 1977. Motorola, Inc., Integrated Circuits Division, Microsystems, 3102 N. 56th Street, Phoenix, Arizona.

7-14
Glossary

ASSEMBLER A program used to translate the programmer's mnemonics to the computer's machine language object codes.

Checksum A byte calculated by the assembler and appended to each line of the object program. It is checked by the loader.

Editor A program used to write or edit source programs and save them on tape or disk.

Label A mnemonic word used to reference an address or value.

Macro Instructions An OP code (instruction) that the macro-assembler replaces with a sequence of assembly language statements.

Mnemonics The words used to specify each instruction. Because the spelling of the words resembles English.

Monitor A control program, usually in ROM, that provides routines to load or dump programs and to test them.

OBJECT PROGRAM The machine language program produced by the assembler from the source program.

SOURCE PROGRAM The assembly language statements written by the programmer.

7-15
Problems

7-1 In Fig. 7-3, what is the location of:
 a. SUM1
 b. START2
 c. LIST
 d. SHIFT2

7-2 In Fig. 7-3, why aren't lines 27, 30, 32, and 34 printed?

7-3 Which of the following labels are satisfactory.
 SAM
 SUZY Q
 SUZYQ
 2SUZY
 SUZY2
 BILLANDJOE
 X
 Y
 Z

7-4 Verify the relative offset value in location 30 of Fig. 7-3 by adding it to the location of the PC.

7-5 Write an assembly language source program for the program of Table 6-2.

7-6 Write an assembly language source program for the program of Table 6-3.

7-7 What would have happened to the listing of Fig. 7-3 if line 7 (the options) had been omitted?

7-8 Explain how each byte of the second S1 line in Fig. 7-4c was obtained.

After attempting to solve the problems, try to answer the self-evaluation questions in Sec. 7-2. If any of them still seem unclear, review the appropriate sections of the chapter to find the answers.

Chapter 8

The Hardware Configuration of the 6800 System

This chapter introduces the student to the hardware components of the **6800** system and examines some of the problems encountered when interconnecting them. After reading the chapter the student should be able to:

1. List each component of the **6800** system and explain its function.
2. Explain the functions of the address and data buses and each line of the **6800** control bus.
3. Determine the number of clock cycles and the number of data bytes required by each instruction.
4. Determine the exact data that appears on the address and data buses at the end of each instruction.
5. Allocate memory space to the various components of a system.

Watch for the answers to the following questions as you read the chapter. They should help you understand the material presented.

1. What are the three states of a 3-state driver?
2. Why do memories need 3-state driver/receivers on their data lines but only receivers on their address lines?
3. What is the purpose of the "memory ready" circuit in the clock module?
4. Are the μP data bus drivers enabled when the R/W line is in READ or WRITE mode? Explain.
5. Explain why BA does not go HIGH as soon as HALT goes LOW.
6. What is the relationship between the access time of the memory used and the clock frequency? Why is it important?
7. Why is it advantageous to have many CS lines on a component?

The basic **6800** family of microcomputer components consists of five parts:

1. The **MC6800** microprocessor (μP).

2. **MC6830** masked programmable Read Only Memory (ROM) (1024 bytes of 8 bits each).
3. **MC6810** Static Random Access Memory (RAM) (128 bytes of 8 bits each).
4. **MC6820** Peripheral Interface Adapter (PIA) (for parallel data Input/Output).
5. **MC6850** Asynchronous Communications Interface Adapter (ACIA) (for serial data Input/Output).

As shown in Fig. 8-1, a complete μC can be built using the components listed above, plus a clock, which is needed to control the timing of the system. Several clock devices, such as the **MC6871A** and the **MC6875** are available. These are *crystal controlled oscil-*

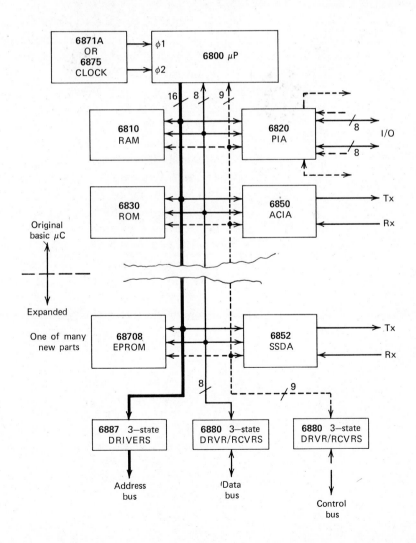

Figure 8-1 The **6800** family components.

lators that provide the necessary two-phase nonoverlapping timing pulses and are equipped with output circuits suitable for driving MOS circuitry.

Figure 8-1 also shows that other components are being added to this basic family periodically, mostly to interface various peripheral devices to the **6800** bus. The basic units also have been redesigned to incorporate depletion loads and other technological improvements, but they are functionally equivalent and physically interchangeable with the older parts. Faster (up to 2 MHz) and wider temperature range units are now available as a result.

8-4
6800 **System Hardware** Features

The suitability of the **6800** family of components as elements of a μC system depends on several factors. First, is the requirement that *all elements of a computer be present* and, second, that they be partitioned into the various packages so that they are *modular* and a variety of configurations can be easily assembled. Finally, there is a need for a simple way to interconnect them.

In the system of Fig. 8-1, the program instructions for the system would typically be stored in the **6830** ROM or **68708** EROM, and all variable data would be written into or read from the **6810** RAM. The Input/Output (I/O) of data for the system would be done via the PIA, ACIA or SSDA.

To understand the ways these units work together, it is necessary to know the hardware features of each part. Figure 8-1 also shows that the system components are interconnected via a 16-wire address bus, an 8-wire data bus, and a 9-wire control bus. For a component to be member of the **6800** μC family and to insure compatibility, it must meet specific system *standards*. The standards must also make it convenient for external devices to interface (or communicate) with the **6800** μP. These standards, which apply to all **6800** components, are as follows:

1. 8-bit bidirectional data bus
2. 16-bit address bus
3. 3-state bus switching techniques
4. TTL/DTL level compatible signals
5. 5 volt N channel MOS silicon gate technology
6. 24 and 40 pin packages
7. Clock rate 100 KHz to 1 MHz (**MC6800B**)
8. Temperature range of 0° to 70°C

8-4.1
The Data Bus

Since the basic word length of the **6800** is 8-bits (one byte) it communicates with other components via an 8-bit data bus. The data bus is *bidirectional,* and data is transferred into or out of the **6800** over the same bus. A read/write line (one of the control lines) is provided to allow the μP to control the direction of data transfer.

An 8-bit data bus can also accommodate ASCII (American Standard Code for Information Interchange) characters and packed BCD (two BCD numbers in one byte).

8-4.2
The Address Bus

A 16-bit address bus was chosen for these reasons.

1. For programming ease, the addresses should be multiples of 8 bits.
2. An 8-bit address bus would only provide 256 addresses but a 16-bit bus provides 65,536 distinct addresses, which is adequate for most applications.

8-4.3
Three-State Bus Concepts

A typical digital line is normally either HIGH (at a "1" level), or LOW (at a "0" level). A technique to use 3-state output devices to interface a number of components has been developed which is advantageous when they must communicate with each other (as in a μC) on a common bus. The concept depends on the ability of all of the interconnected components to be switched to a third state that presents a very *high impedance* to the bus. In this way *one, and only one, component is selected* to drive the bus at one time. The selected **6800** system component causes a 1 or 0 to be placed on each line of the bus in accordance with the data word being transmitted. *All unselected components* must place their bus drivers in the *high-impedance state.* Simultaneously, one of the other components on the bus is enabled to read the data, thus transferring or transmitting it in one direction. This 3-state switching (or selection) is controlled by the μPs Read/Write (R/W), and Valid Memory Address lines (VMA), along with the address bus. The transfer of information via the data bus can therefore be *bidirectional* over the same 8-line bus. All components of the **6800** family include this 3-state capability in their data output circuits.

External devices, not part of the family, can be connected to the bus via 3-state driver/receivers that are available in DIP packages. The **MC6880/MC8T26** is a 3-state bus driver/receiver whose pin configuration is shown in Fig. 8-2a. The driver/receiver is a quad IC with four lines connected to the bus, four receiver outputs from the bus, and four driver inputs to the bus. A typical bus application for the **MC6880** is shown in Fig. 8-2b.

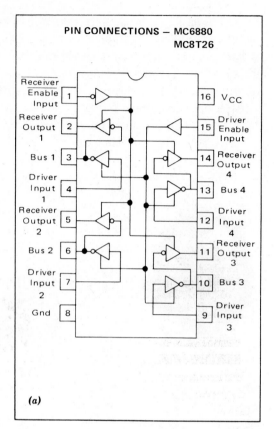

(a)

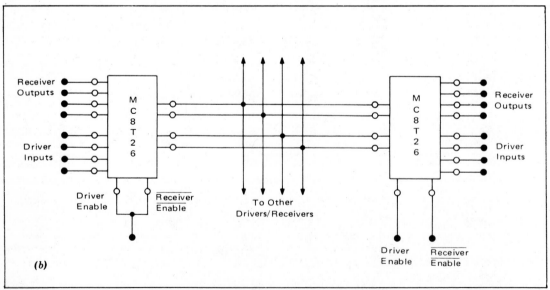

(b)

The receiver gates are enabled by a LOW (ground) signal on the $\overline{\text{Receiver}}$ $\overline{\text{Enable}}$ (Pin 1). These gates invert the data and transfer the information on the bus to the TTL devices connected to the receiver outputs. When $\overline{\text{Receiver}}$ $\overline{\text{Enable}}$ is HIGH, the four receiver outputs are in the high impedance state, and are effectively disconnected from the bus. The **6880** drives the bus whenever its Driver Enable input (pin 15) is HIGH. The state of the four driver inputs determines the state of the four bus lines, and the data is again inverted. If Driver Enable is LOW, the bus outputs of the **6880** are in the high impedance state, allowing another device to drive the bus.

An inverted data bus presents no problem since the data is reinverted by the following receiver. The **8T28** is a similar device for use where a noninverted bidirectional data bus is desired. It has greater propagation delay, however.

Each of the **6800** components has outputs capable of driving 10 MOS inputs or 1 TTL load. In a small system, directional switching is very simple since it is determined by internal logic in both the μP and the RAMs. The R/W line controls the RAM so that either the μP or the RAM output circuits are ON, depending on whether the μP is writing or reading.

When the system is larger, however, driver/receivers such as the **6880** are used. Care must be taken in this case, to provide external logic for proper operation. (That is, in addition to selecting the RAM for a read or write, the data path must be switched for the direction needed.)

(c)

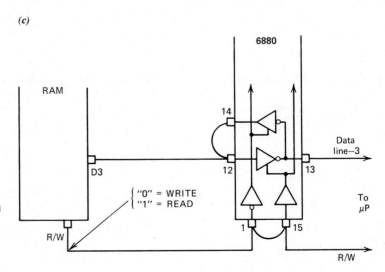

Figure 8-2 The **6800** family 3-state bus driver/receiver.
(a) Pin configuration
(b) Typical bidirectional bus application
(c) Signal flow diagram

If the **6880** is arranged as shown in Fig. 8-2c, with a jumper from pin 12 to pin 14, the drivers and receivers are connected so that the direction of transmission is determined by the R/W line. This line is connected to the Driver Enable and Receiver Enable inputs (pins 1 and 15). The Driver Enable input is enabled when the μP is reading memory (R/W = 1), and the $\overline{\text{Receiver Enable}}$ input is enabled when the μP is writing to memory (R/W = 0).

Example 8-1

Which component drives the bus when:

a. The μP is reading memory?
b. The μP is writing to memory?

Solution

a. When the μP is *reading* memory it must receive information that is in memory. The memory must drive the data bus with that information so that the μP can read it. All other devices must be in their *high-impedance state*.

b. When *writing* the μP is sending information to the memory. Therefore the μP bus drivers are active. The memory receivers must be ON and all other bus drivers (including the receiving memory), must be in the *high-impedance state*.

8-4.4
TTL Signal Compatibility

The **6800** components are designed to be compatible with available digital circuitry. At present, the **7400** TTL series dominates the field of digital ICs. Consequently the design standard chosen for the **6800** series of components requires that each output will drive one standard TTL load (defined as 1.6 mA at 0.4 V) plus a capacitive load of 130 pF (at 1 MHz).

8-4.5
5 Volt N Channel MOS Silicon Metal Gate Technology

The **6800** requires only +5 volts for its operation. The use of a single standard voltage gives it a significant advantage over other μPs and MOS devices that require several different voltages for their operation.

8-4.6
24- and 40-Pin Packages

The **6800** μP uses a 40-pin DIP package. This allows for 38 input/output connections (plus power and ground) so that it can simultaneously present the information on its 16 address lines, 8 data lines, and the various control lines. Other components in the **6800** series (the ACIA and memories) do not require full 16-bit addressing and use a smaller 24-pin DIP package.

8-4.7
Clock Rate

The clock rate determines the speed at which the μP executes instructions. The **6800B** can be driven by a clock up to 1 MHz but the newer **MC68B00** works up to 2 MHz (see Sec. 8-7).

8-4.8
Temperature Range

Since most μPs operate in a controlled environment, (comfortable rooms or laboratories) they are not subjected to extreme temperature variations. The temperature range chosen for the **MC6800B**, (0 to 70°C), is adequate for almost all industrial and commercial applications. This temperature range is also the same as the standard TTL temperature range. The **MC6800C** has a wider range of −40°C to +85°C. Military versions are also available for operation from −55°C to +125°C.

It should be recognized that all operating temperatures are measured at the device location in the housing. The system must not generate so much heat that it causes the temperature in the vicinity of any of the components to exceed specifications. If necessary, cooling fans can be placed in a system housing to dissipate excessive heat.

8-5
The 6800 Microprocessor Unit

Figure 8-3 shows the block diagram of a **6800** microprocessor (μP). An 8-bit internal bus interconnects the various registers with the instruction decode and control logic. The nine control lines that communicate with the external devices can be seen on the left, with the address bus at the top and the data bus at the bottom of the figure.

These are the features of the **6800** μP that will be discussed in the following chapters.

Vectored interrupts
Nonmaskable interrupt
Software interrupt
I/O treated like memory (addressable)
16-bit index register
16-bit program counter register
16-bit stack pointer register
Two 8-bit accumulators
DMA and multiprocessing capability
Halt/Go and single step capability
Dynamic logic and 2-phase clock
Wait instruction

8-5.1
Hardware Aspects of the 6800 ALU and Registers

The Arithmetic Logic Unit included in the **6800** is an 8-bit, parallel processing, 2s complement device. It includes the Condition Code (or processor status) Register. The functions of the Arithmetic/Logic

Unit (ALU) and the various registers have been described in Secs. 5-3.1 and 5-3.2. The clock hardware is described later in this chapter (Sec. 8-7). Interrupt functions, Direct Memory Access (DMA), and various hardware design features are described in later chapters.

8-5.2 Registers and Accumulators

As explained in Sec. 5-3.2 the **6800** system has a 16-bit address bus, but as seen in Fig. 8-3, the internal bus is 8-bits wide, and the index and stack pointer registers (and the address buffers) are implemented with a high (H) and low (L) byte. The two 8-bit accumulators, A and B, speed up program execution by allowing two operands to remain in the μP. Instructions that can be performed using both accumulators (e.g., ABA and SBA) are very fast because they do not require additional cycles to fetch the second operand.

8-5.3 Other Features of the 6800

Five of the six condition codes (H, N, Z, V, and C) have been described in Sec. 5-6. The action of the sixth condition code register bit (I) or interrupt mask, and DMAs (Direct Memory Accesses) are discussed in Chapter 10. The clock hardware and HALT modes are discussed in Sec. 8-7.

8-5.4 Vectored Interrupts

An interrupt is a signal to the μP that causes it to stop execution of the normal program and to branch (or jump) to another location that is the beginning address of an interrupt service routine. These routines are written to provide whatever action is necessary to respond to the interrupt. Four types of interrupts are provided in the **6800**, and each has its unique software service routine and vector. Three of them also are implemented by pins on the **6800**. The four types are:

> RESTART (RST)
> NONMASKABLE INTERRUPT (NMI)
> SOFTWARE INTERRUPT (SWI)
> INTERRUPT REQUEST (IRQ)

In order for the program to be branched to the appropriate routine, the top eight locations of the ROM or PROM that is highest in memory, are reserved for these interrupt vectors. The contents of these locations contain the 16-bit addresses where the service routines begin. When activated, the program is "vectored" or pointed to the appropriate address by the μP logic. This is called a "vectored interrupt." The details of these interrupts are discussed in Chapter 10.

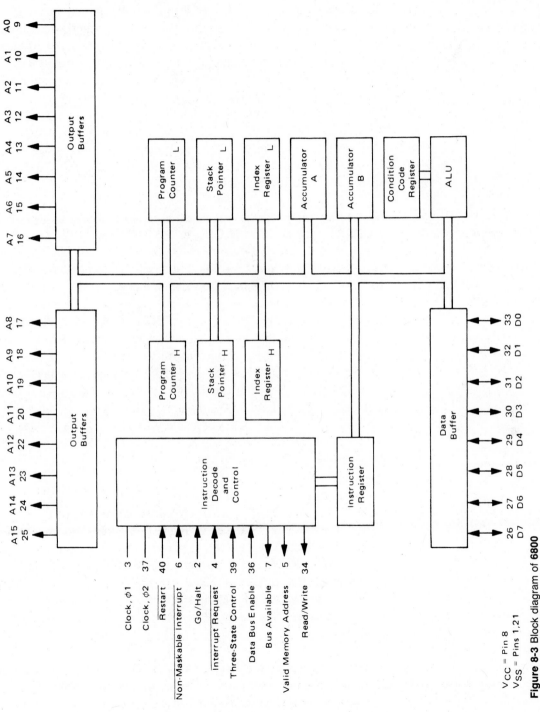

V_{CC} = Pin 8
V_{SS} = Pins 1, 21

Figure 8-3 Block diagram of **6800** microprocessor.

8-6
6800 Control Lines and Their Functions

The hardware aspects of system design involve interconnecting the components of the system so that the data is properly transferred between them and to any external hardware that is being utilized. In addition to the obvious requirement for power and ground to each component, the address bus, and the bidirectional data bus, numerous control signal lines are required. These control lines are in effect a third bus called the control bus. The lines are shown in Fig. 8-1 and are identified in Fig. 8-3, which also shows their pin numbers.

To design a system that performs properly, it is necessary to understand each signal's characteristics and function. These are described in the following paragraphs:

8-6.1
Read/Write (R/W)

This output line is used to signal all external devices that the μP is in a READ state (R/W = HIGH), or a WRITE state (R/W = LOW). The normal standby state of this line, is HIGH. This line is three-state. When Three State Control (TSC) (see Sec. 8-6.8) goes HIGH, the R/W line enters the high impedance mode.

8-6.2
Valid Memory Address (VMA)

The VMA output line (when in the HIGH state) tells all devices external to the μP that there is a valid address on the address bus. During the execution of certain instructions, the address bus may assume a random address because of internal calculations. VMA goes LOW to avoid enabling any device under those conditions. Note also that VMA is held LOW during HALT, TSC, or during the execution of a WAIT (WAI) instruction. VMA is not a 3-state line and therefore Direct Memory Access (DMA) cannot be performed unless VMA is externally opened (or gated).

8-6.3
Data Bus Enable (DBE)

The DBE signal enables the data bus drivers of the μP when in the HIGH state. This input is normally connected to the phase 2 (Ø2) clock but is sometimes delayed to assure proper operation with some memory devices. When HIGH, it permits data to be placed on the bus during a WRITE cycle. During a μP READ cycle, the data bus drivers within the μP are disabled internally. If an external signal holds DBE LOW, the μP data bus drivers are forced into their high impedance state. This allows other devices to control the I/O bus (as in DMA).

8-6.4
Interrupt Request, Nonmaskable Interrupt, and Reset

An active signal on the IRQ, NMI, or RESET lines initiates an interrupt sequence. The action of these lines is discussed in Chapter 10 where interrupts are considered in detail.

8-6.5
Phase One (Ø1)and Phase Two (Ø2)
of the Clock

These two pins are used for a two-phase, nonoverlapping clock. This clock runs at a frequency up to 1 MHz for the **M6800B** and up to 2 MHz for the depletion load versions of the **6800 (MC68B00)**.

8-6.6
HALT and RUN Modes

When the HALT input to the **6800** is HIGH, the μP is in the RUN mode and is continually executing instructions. When the HALT line goes LOW, the μP halts after completing its present instruction. At that time the μP is in the HALT mode. Bus Available (BA) goes HIGH, VMA (Sec. 8-6.2) becomes a 0, and all 3-state lines enter their high impedance state. Note that the μP does not enter the HALT mode as soon as HALT goes LOW, but does so only when the μP has finished execution of its current instruction. It is possible to stop the μP while it is in the process of executing an instruction by stopping or ''stretching the clock,'' as described in Sec. 8-7.

8-6.7
Bus Available (BA)

The bus available (BA) signal is a normally LOW signal generated by the μP. In the HIGH state it indicates that the μP has stopped and that the address bus is available. This occurs if the μP is in the HALT mode or in a WAIT state as the result of the WAI instruction.

8-6.8
Three-State Control (TSC)

TSC is an externally generated signal that effectively causes the μP to disconnect itself from the address and control buses. This allows an external device to assume control of the system. When TSC is HIGH, it causes the address lines and the READ/WRITE line to go to the high impedance state. The VMA and BA signals are forced LOW. The data bus is not affected by TSC and has its own enable (DBE). TSC is used in DMA applications discussed in Chapter 10.

The μP is a dynamic IC that must be periodically refreshed by its own clocks. Because TSC stops the clocking of the internal logic of the μP, it should not be HIGH longer than 3 clock pulses, or the dynamic registers in the μP may lose some of their internal data. (Up to 19 cycles at 2 MHz for the new **68B00**.)

8-7
Clock Operation

The **6800** utilizes a *two-phase clock* to control its operation. The waveforms and timing of the clock are critical for the proper operation of the μP and the other components of the family. The timing requirements are shown in the waveforms and table of Fig. 8-4. The clocks must be nonoverlapping and conform to the timing table (Fig. 8-4b).

The clock synchronizes the internal operations of the μP, as well as all external devices on the bus. The program counter, for example, is advanced on the falling edge of Ø1 and data is latched into the μP

FIGURE 7 – MICROPROCESSOR ϕ1 AND ϕ2 CLOCKS

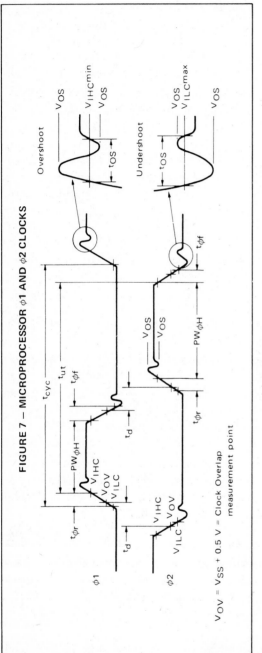

$V_{OV} = V_{SS} + 0.5$ V = Clock Overlap measurement point

(a) Waveforms

Frequency of Operation		f	0.1		1.0		MHz
Clock Timing (ϕ1 and ϕ2)							
Cycle Time		t_{cyc}	1.0		10		μs
Clock Pulse Width		PW$_{\phi H}$					
(Measured at V_{CC} - 0.3 V)	ϕ1		430		4500		ns
	ϕ2		450		4500		ns
Clock Up Time		t_{ut}	940		—		ns
Rise and Fall Times ϕ1, ϕ2		$t_{\phi r}, t_{\phi f}$	5.0		50		ns
(Measured between V_{SS} + 0.3 V and V_{CC} - 0.3 V)							
Delay Time or Clock Separation		t_d	0		9100		ns
(Measured at V_{SS} + 0.5 V)							
Overshoot Duration		t_{OS}	0		40		ns

(b) Timing table

Figure 8-4 6800 clock timing.
(a) Waveforms
(b) Timing table

on the falling edge of Ø2. All operations necessary for the execution of each instruction are synchronized with the clock.

Certain components and functions of the system affect the clock requirements. If dynamic memories are used, slow memories are involved, or Direct Memory Access (DMA) is required, the clock may have to be stopped momentarily, (that is, stretched). If the memory is slow, for example, phase 2 has to be long enough to allow the memory to complete its READ or WRITE operation. Since a memory that is too slow to operate with a 1 MHz clock (such as an Intel **1702A** EPROM), may only be addressed periodically, there is no need to slow the clock for the entire system, provided that a "memory ready" feature can be included in the clock.

The **MC6875** shown in Fig. 8-5 is a 16-pin IC that includes all

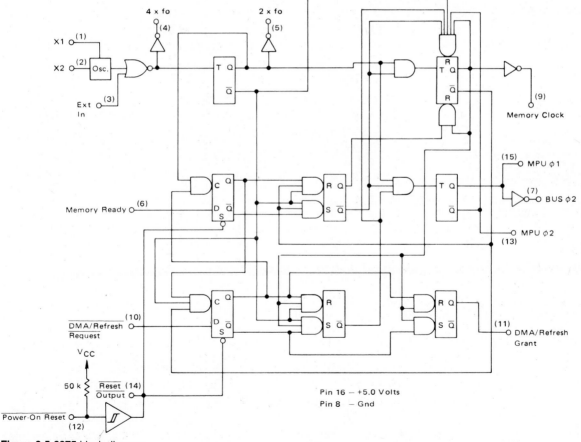

Figure 8-5 6875 block diagram.

the features necessary to control the timing of a **6800** system. It includes an internal oscillator whose frequency can be determined by an external crystal or RC network connected to pins X1 and X2. (An inexpensive 3.59 MHz crystal made for color TVs can be used.) Alternately, an external timing signal can be connected to the Ext. In pin. The oscillator frequency is divided by four and shaped to provide Ø1 and Ø2, the two-phase nonoverlapping clock required by the **6800** μP. If the system contains slow memories, the clock can be stretched with Ø2 high by holding Memory Ready low until the data is transferred. The **6875** also contains a Schmitt trigger input that controls $\overline{\text{Reset}}$. A capacitor to ground (power ON reset) and/or a reset switch may be used. DMA or dynamic memory refresh can also be accommodated. These will be discussed in Chapter 10.

8-7.1
Instruction Bytes and Clock Cycles

In the **6800** instruction table (Appendix B), the number of bytes and clock cycles are listed for each instruction. The number of bytes for each instruction determines the size of the memory, and the number of cycles determines the time required to execute the program. LDA A $1234 (which is the extended addressing mode), for example, requires three bytes, one to specify the operation (OP) code and two to specify the address, but requires four cycles to execute. Often an instruction requires the processor to perform internal operations in addition to the fetch cycles. Consequently, for any instruction the number of cycles is generally larger than the number of bytes.

Example 8-2

How long does it take to execute a **LDAA 0,X** (indexed) instruction if a 1 MHz oscillator is used as the system clock?

Solution

From Appendix B, we find that a **LDAA 0,X** instruction requires 2 bytes and 5 cycles. The 2 bytes are the OP code and the offset address. The μP must add the offset to the contents of its index register. This accounts for the large number of clock cycles required for this instruction. Since the instruction takes 5 cycles, it takes 5 μs to execute at a clock rate of 1 MHz.

Note that Chapter 13 describes the **6801** μC with an augmented instruction set (22 additional OP codes) that uses one less cycle for most instructions and yet they are compatible with the **6800**.

8-7.2
Single-Step Operation

In order to follow and understand a computer as it executes a program a step at a time, it is necessary to know the status of many things, both before and after each instruction is performed. The information required includes:

1. The address on the bus
2. The data on the bus
3. The state of each line of the control bus (i.e., HALT, BA, TSC, VMA, NMI, IRQ, and R/W)
4. The values in the μP registers, (i.e., PC, X, A, B, SP, and CC)
5. Contents of any memory location

Most large computers and minicomputers allow *single step* operation. In this mode the clock is stopped and the computer is stepped through a program one instruction at a time by a momentary contact switch. These computers usually have front panel displays and switches, so the address bus, data bus, and contents of the CPU registers can be examined and/or changed while the processor is halted. This method of analysis is slow and tedious but is frequently used when a program fails to perform as expected. A μP, however, is a dynamic device and the clock cannot be stopped for more than 4.5 μsec (9.5 μsec for 68B00) without losing data. Many μPs have no display whatever. For these reasons, several different debugging methods have evolved, which are described in Chapter 11.

The **6800** can be halted for an indefinite time with the clock still running and the internal registers will retain their information, but it is not possible to examine or change them with the processor halted. To examine and/or change memory locations while the processor is halted, switches and lights for the address and data buses are necessary.

The timing requirements for single-stepping a **6800** system are complex and are shown in Fig. 8-6.

The instruction illustrated is a 1-byte, 2-cycle instruction such as CLR A. When $\overline{\text{HALT}}$ goes LOW, the μP will halt after completing execution of the current instruction. The transition of $\overline{\text{HALT}}$ must occur at least 200 ns (tPCS) before the positive edge of Ø2 in the last cycle of that instruction (point A of Fig. 8-6). If $\overline{\text{HALT}}$ is HIGH at point A but goes LOW during Ø2 of that cycle, the μP halts after the completion of the next instruction. BA goes HIGH by tBA (bus available delay time) after Ø1 of the next cycle. At this time, VMA is LOW and R/W, the Address Bus, and the Data Bus are in the high impedance state. To step through programs instruction-by-instruction, $\overline{\text{HALT}}$ must be brought HIGH and then returned LOW as shown, at some point between C and D of Fig. 8-6. Again, the transition of $\overline{\text{HALT}}$ must occur tPCS before the positive edge of Ø2.

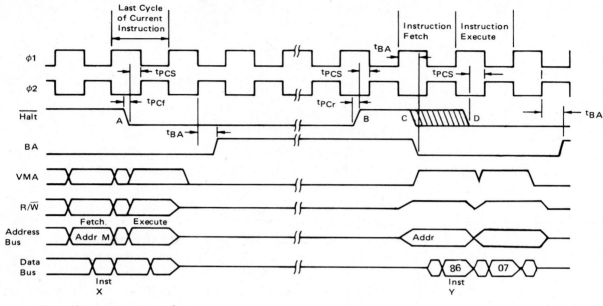

Figure 8-6 HALT and single-step operation.

BA will go LOW at tBA after the positive edge of the next Ø1, indicating that the Address Bus, Data Bus, VMA, and R/W lines are active again. During the first cycle of this instruction (LDA A #7), the OP code (86) is fetched and even though the $\overline{\text{HALT}}$ line has been taken LOW again, the second byte (07) is also fetched. Since the $\overline{\text{HALT}}$ line was taken LOW, more than 200 ns prior to the positive edge of Ø2, the processor halts after the end of the cycle and the data and address lines all go to their high impedance state. BA returns HIGH at tBA during the next cycle of the clock, indicating the µP is off the bus. If this instruction had used three cycles the length of the BA LOW time would have been increased by one cycle.

Example 8-3

Design a circuit to control a **6800** µP. Provide two momentary contact switches for RESET, and STEP, and one toggle switch for RUN/HALT.

Solution

One solution is shown in Fig. 8-7. The switches at the left are each followed by cross-coupled **7404** gates to provide debouncing.

If the RUN/HALT toggle switch is in the HALT position when the system is first turned ON, the D input of flip-flop 2 (FF2) is LOW. Therefore, on the first positive-going edge of the Ø1 clock, FF2 RESETS. This in turn causes the Q output of FF2 and the D input of FF1 to be LOW. On the next leading edge, FF1 will RESET and its Q output will hold the HALT line LOW, preventing program execution by the μP.

In the RUN position, the D input of flip-flop 2 (FF2) is HIGH. When the Ø1 clock input sees the next positive-going edge, it SETS FF2. FF1 SETS on the next positive-going edge of the Ø1 clock, and its Q output, that is connected to the HALT line of the μP, will be HIGH, allowing the system to RUN.

With the limitations described in Sec. 8-7.2 in mind, we can use the circuit of Fig. 8-7 to step through a program.

When the RUN/HALT switch is in the HALT position, the STEP switch can be used to advance the μP, one instruction at a time as follows: Normally, the output of A1 is LOW, and the output of A5 is therefore HIGH. Gate B1 (**7400**) sees one HIGH input and one LOW. B1's output will be HIGH and the SET input to FF2 will be disabled. When the step switch is depressed, the output of A1 goes HIGH instantly, and B1s output goes LOW, setting FF2. When the A1 output goes HIGH, A4 attempts to go HIGH but is held down until the capacitor can be charged. This takes approximately 100 ns with the part shown. When A5s input reaches its threshold it switches and removes one HIGH input from B1, thus allowing the SET input of FF2 to return HIGH. The circuit just described assures that a single 100 ns pulse will be provided to SET FF2 regardless of how fast the STEP switch is operated, or released. (A typical minimum time for the manual operation of this switch would be 25 ms.) When FF2 is SET by this pulse, it will remain SET until the next positive edge of Ø1. While FF2 is SET, it holds the D input of FF1 HIGH and, therefore, when the next positive edge of Ø1 occurs, it simultaneously SETS FF1 and RESETS FF2. Since it is not possible, with the time constants of the STEP circuits as they are, for FF2 to be SET again for many milliseconds, FF1 will be RESET by the next positive edge of Ø1. Thus, the HALT line of the μP is HIGH for exactly one clock cycle. Reference to Fig. 8-6 shows that this is the ideal way to single step the μP.

The RESET switch of Fig. 8-7 is connected directly to the μP (via the debounce circuit) and must be used initially to get the μP system started at the correct address. The details of the RESET function are described in Chapter 10.

8-7.3
Step-by-Step Program Tracing

Appendix C shows a table of cycle-by-cycle operation for each instruction in the **6800** repertoire. It gives the information that appears on the address and data buses during each cycle of each instruction.

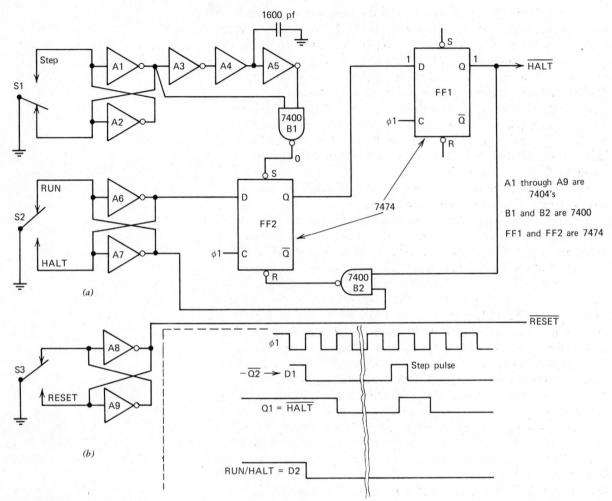

Figure 8-7 Single-step circuit.
(a) Circuit
(b) Timing

This information can be very helpful when examining a program in single step mode. Note, however, that the program is only halted after each instruction, not after each cycle of an instruction. Therefore, the user can only examine the address and data buses at the *end of each instruction,* but this information is sometimes enough to indicate the status of the program. Methods of determining the cycle-by-cycle operation of the instruction and other advanced debugging aids are discussed in Chapter 11.

When the μP is halted, the address and data buses are in their high impedance state and cannot be examined. Therefore, systems that use single cycle operation often gate the address and data buses into registers on each Ø2 clock when VMA is high. These registers drive displays. Thus the information in the displays, while the μP is halted, shows the status of the address and data buses during the last instruction cycle when the μP was running.

Example 8-4

What information appears on the address and data buses at the end of each instruction in the program shown in Table 8-1, and what can we deduce about the operation of the program?

Solution

If a chart is kept of the information displayed and the calculated effect of the A accumulator, it is possible to follow this program. A chart for this example is shown in Table 8-2. The operation performed during each instruction is explained on the right. If this problem involved the B accumulator, or index register, the chart would have to be more complex.

The first instruction (LDA A #$7B) is a 2-byte, 2-cycle immediate (#) mode instruction. From Appendix C it is seen that 7B is LOADED into the A accumulator during these two cycles. The displayed values, as latched at the end of the second cycle, are as shown on the step 1 line of Table 8-2.

Appendix C shows that on the last cycle of a LDA A or B instruction, the operand address, and operand data appear on the address and data buses. Therefore, we expect to see 21 and 7B on the buses.

Table 8-1
Program for Example 8-4

Addr	Data	Mnemonic	
20	86	LDA A #$7B	LOAD A accumulator with "immediate" value
21	7B		of Hex 7B.
22	48	ASL A	SHIFT A left.
23	8B	ADD A #3	ADD (to A) the "immediate" value of 3.
24	03		
25	2B	BMI *−2[a]	BRANCH (if number in A is negative) back
26	FC		to previous instruction (−4 bytes).
27	20	BRA *	BRANCH back 2 bytes unconditionally
28	FE		(repeats same instruction).

[a]The asterisk is used to denote the current location of the PC counter at the beginning of this instruction.

Table 8-2
Results of Single Stepping Program of Example 8-4

Step	Address Bus (Displayed)	Data Bus	"A" ACC (Calculated)	Operation (Performed)
STRT	20	XX	XX	
1	21	7B	7B	7B LOADed in A.
2	23	8B	F6	A SHIFTed left.
3	24	03	F9	3 ADDed to A.
4	23	8B[a]	F9	Result NEGATIVE-BRANCHed back.
5	24	03	FC	3 ADDed again.
6	23	8B[a]	FC	BRANCHed back.
7	24	03	FF	3 ADDed again.
8	23	8B[a]	FF	STILL NEG-BRANCH.
9	24	03	02	3 ADDed
10	26	FC	02	POSITIVE did not branch
11	28	FE	02	BRANCH always back 2 bytes.
12	28	FE	02	Again.

[a]Data may vary depending on bus capacitance.

The next instruction is an ASLA, an inherent instruction, since memory references are not required. The chart shows that the Operand address + 1 (23) and the OP code of the next instruction (8B) are on the address and data buses. This is an example of the *look-ahead* feature of the **6800**. The A register value of 7B becomes F6 when shifted left, but this cannot be seen when the μP is halted in this step mode. The calculated values are shown in Table 8-2, however, and are necessary to understand the progress of the program. (Chapter 11 describes the preferred methods for debugging with ways to display the registers.)

The add 3 immediate (ADD A #3) results in an address bus value of 24 and a data bus value of 03 (the OP code address + 1 and the operand data). The A accumulator becomes F9.

Step 4 executes the conditional branch on minus (BMI ∗ − 2) instruction. Since the result of the last instruction was negative, the program branches back four bytes (FC = −4) and displays the branch address (23) at the end of its fourth cycle. The data bus value may vary. Since no operation other than a change in the PC has taken place, the A accumulator remains the same.

Step 5 adds 3 again and A is now equal to FC. The following steps are identical as the program loops back and adds 3 until step 9. At this point, our calculations show that A will equal 02, which is a positive number, and as seen in step 10, the address bus has gone forward (did not branch) to a displayed value of 26. The last instruction (BRA ∗) branches to itself and thus halts further execution.

8-8
The 6810 **Random Access**
Memory (RAM)

Figure 8-8 shows the **6810**. It is a 1024-bit (128 words by 8 bits/ word) memory in a 24-pin package. It provides 128 bytes of read/ write memory and is designed for use in the **6800** system. The 8-bit word organization makes it uniquely applicable for small μP systems since many such systems only need 128 or 256 bytes of RAM.

The **6810** bus interface of Fig. 8-9 shows how a typical IC would be connected to the three buses. The pins include:

1. Eight data lines (D0-D7): These are 3-state bidirectional lines for compatibility with the **6800** data bus.
2. Seven address lines.
3. Six chip select lines.
4. A R/W line.

The **6810** is a static RAM, which requires only one power supply (+5 volts). It has four LOW level and two HIGH level chip select pins. These pins can be directly connected to address lines or voltage levels as shown in Fig. 8-9 to select the chip without additional decoders. When selected and R/W is HIGH, the output buffers are turned ON to drive the data bus (see Sec. 8-14 for details). The use of E and VMA connected to the CS lines is discussed in Sec. 8-14.

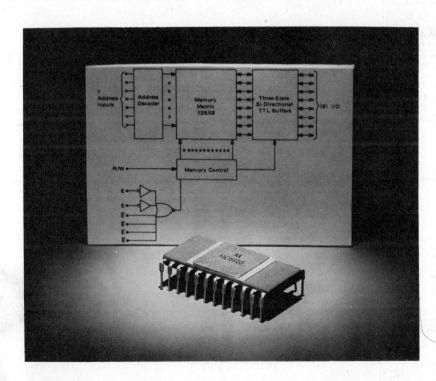

Figure 8-8 The **6810** random access memory (128 8-bit words).

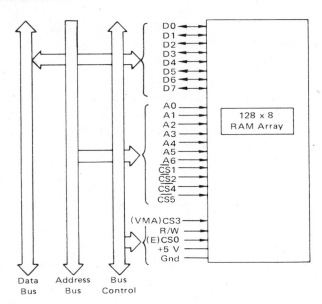

Figure 8-9 6810 RAM bus interface.

Six versions of **6810s** have been manufactured since the device was introduced in 1974. The current choices (see Table 8-3), depend on the desired clock rate, or environmental requirements.

Example 8-5

What is the maximum memory access time that a **6810** type component may have when used in a **6800** system with a 1 MHz clock.

Solution

Reference to the **6810** data sheet (see Sec. 8-17, References) indicates that the time from the point in the cycle where the *address* lines become stable (all 1s are above 2.0 V, and all 0s are less than 0.8 V), until the *data* becomes stable, is defined as the *memory read access time* (Tacc) and that the data will remain stable a minimum of 10 ns after the end of the cycle.

The **6800** data sheet READ timing figure shows that the time from the beginning of the cycle until all address, R/W, and VMA lines are stable is a maximum of 300 ns, and the minimum length of time that the data must be available (on the bus) is 100 ns. The clock timing waveform shows that at 1 MHz, the total time from where Ø1 starts setting the address until Ø2 cuts off the data (Tut) is 940 ns. Therefore, the access time for the memory is

$$\text{Tacc} = 940 - (300 + 100) = 540 \text{ ns}$$

This shows that all the newer **6810s** meet the requirements.

These calculations assume that a miminum configuration system is involved and therefore no additional delays are incurred in bus drivers or TTL decoders.

Table 8-3
Types of **6810** RAMS

Type	Access Time
MCM6810AL	450 ns
MCM68A10 (P or L)	360 ns
MCM68B10 (P or L)	250 ns

The A and B in the middle of the number denotes the 1.5 and 2 MHz depletion load versions. The L denotes ceramic and the P is for a plastic package. The ceramic versions of the last two types are also available in commercial and military temperature ranges ($-40°$ to $+85°C$) and ($-55°$ to $+125°C$), respectively.

8-9
The 6830 **Read Only Memory (ROM)**

The **6830** is the ROM designed originally for use in the **6800** system. Like the **6810** it comes in a 24-pin DIP package and features 3-state outputs capable of driving the data bus. The access time of the **6830A** is 500 ns, and is fast enough for any **6800** system running at 1 MHz. A **MCM68A30** version is available for 1.5 MHz systems.

The **6830** contains 1024 bytes of ROM. Its bus organization is shown in Fig. 8-10. Note that there are 10 address lines, 8 data lines, and 4 chip select lines. Because this is a ROM, no read/write line is needed. If this IC is selected, the byte at the addressed location will appear on the data bus. When the IC is not selected, its output drivers are in the high impedance state, allowing another device to drive the I/O bus.

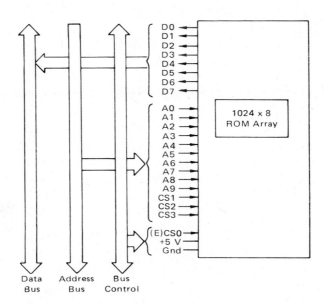

Data   Address   Bus
Bus   Bus   Control

Figure 8-10 6830 ROM bus interface.

8-9.1
Programming the 6830

To program the **6830**, the customer must generate a paper tape or a set of punched cards, giving the contents of each ROM location. The manufacturers specification sheets give instruction on how to prepare the cards or tape. They are used to create a *mask* that is then used to manufacture the customized **6830**. The user should be very sure of his program before he orders a custom ROM, because the **6830** is not reprogrammable and one erroneous bit generally makes a program useless.

Four pins on the **6830** are available for chip selects. These are defined to be 1 level or 0 level enables by the customer when the mask for the ROM is specified.

8-10
PROMs and EPROMs

It is often convenient for the μP designer to install the program for his ROM in his own laboratory. This can be accomplished by using a *programmable read only memory* (PROM) and eliminates the turn around time and expense of mask programmed ROMs.

Fusible-link PROMs are often used in μCs. One type of these come from the manufacturer with a fusible link in each bit of each word, and thus present an output pattern of all 0s. The user then puts them into a programmer, an electronic device that allows him to overdrive the bits corresponding to the 1s in his program, blowing the fuses to open each bit. Since the manufacturer of PROMs is not required to program them individually, they are produced in large quantities and are inexpensive. Several manufacturers produce 1024 × 8 or 2048 × 8 bit fusible link PROMs that can be used directly in **6800** systems.

Another type of PROM, an EPROM (erasable programmable read only memory) is also available. EPROMs can be erased by ultraviolet light and reprogrammed any number of times. They therefore are extremely valuable for program and system development.

Custom maskable programmable ROMs, which are pin compatible with these EPROMs, are available. This makes it possible for the designer to build his hardware in final form (with sockets for memories) so that the testing and program revisions can continue using EPROMs even after the first models of the product are shipped. Ultimately, a mask programmable ROM can be installed, either in the field or in future production. This would be done in high volume production systems because the mask programmable ROMs are approximately one half to one third of the price of EPROMs.

**8-11
6820 or 6821 Peripheral
Interface Adapters (PIAs)**

The **6820** Peripheral Interface Adapter (PIA), shown in Fig. 8-11, provides a simple means of interfacing peripheral equipment on a parallel or byte-wide basis to the **6800** μC system. This device is compatible with the **6800** bus interface on the μP side, and provides up to 16 I/O lines and 4 control lines on the peripheral side, for connection to external units. The **6820** outputs are TTL or CMOS compatible.

In April 1977, an augmented version of the **6820** was introduced (called the **MC6821**). It is identical to the **6820** except that it can drive 2 TTL loads on all A and B side buffers, and is capable of static operation (no clocking required). The PIA is discussed in detail in Chapter 9.

**8-12
The Asynchronous
Communications Interface
Adapter (ACIA)**

The **6850** ACIA is a 24-pin IC similar to all the others in the **6800** family and provides the circuitry to connect serial asynchronous data communications devices (such as a teletypewriter terminal TTY) to bus organized systems such as the **6800** μC system.

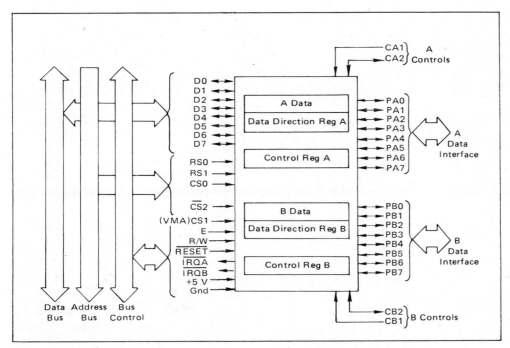

Figure 8-11 PIA bus interface and registers.

The bus interface includes select, enable, read/write, and interrupt signal pins in addition to the 8-bit bidirectional data bus lines. The parallel data of the **6800** system is serially transmitted and received (simultaneously) with proper ASCII formatting and error checking. The Control Register of the ACIA is programmed via the data bus during system initialization. It determines word length, parity, stop bits, and interrupt control of the transmit or receive functions. The operation of the **6850** is discussed in detail in Sec. 9-10.

The PIA and ACIA are the most used I/O components in the **6800** family. Other I/O devices are available however, and include.

6852 Synchronous Serial Data Adapter (SSDA).
6854 Advanced Data Link Controller (ADLC)
68488 General Purpose Interface Adapter (IEEE 488-1975 bus)
6845 CRT Controller (CRTC)
6843 Floppy Disk Controller
6844 Direct Memory Access Controller (DMAC)

The reader should consult the manufacturers literature for information on these Peripheral Controller Products.

8-13
Memory Space Allocation

The I/O devices in the **6800** system (e.g., the PIA, ACIA, and SSDA) all have internal registers that contain the I/O data or control the operation of the device. Each of these registers must be allocated a unique address on the address bus and is communicated with just as if it were memory. This technique is called *memory-mapped* I/O and, in addition to allowing the use of all memory referencing instructions for the I/O functions, it eliminates the need for special I/O instructions.

The process of addressing a particular memory location, includes not only selecting a cell in a chip, but also selecting that chip from among all those on the same bus. *The low order address lines are generally used to address registers within the chips, and the high order lines are available to single out the desired chip.* These high order lines could be connected to a decoder circuit with one output line used to enable each chip but, since most of the **6800** family devices have several chip select pins available, these are frequently connected directly to the high order address lines (A15, A14, A13, . . . , etc.) and separate decoders are not needed, particularly in simple systems.

Table 8-4 shows the number of addresses required and the number

Table 8-4
Addresses Required and Chip Select Pins Needed

Component	Addresses Required	Positive CS Pins	Negative CS Pins
6810 RAM	128	2	4
6830 ROM	1024	*	*
6820 PIA	4	2	1
6850 ACIA	2	2	1
6852 SSDA	2	0	1

*Four programmable enables are defined as positive or negative when the mask is made.

of chip select (CS) pins available for typical **6800** family components.

A component is selected only if all its CS lines are satisfied. The **6810**, for example, is enabled only if it sees a HIGH level on two of its select lines (CS0, pin 10 and CS3, pin 13), and a LOW level on its four negative select pins ($\overline{CS1}$, $\overline{CS2}$, $\overline{CS4}$, and $\overline{CS5}$). When unselected, a component places its outputs in a high impedance state and is effectively disconnected from the data bus.

When setting up a **6800** system, each component must be allocated as much memory space as it needs and must be given a *unique* address so that *no address selects more than one component*. In addition, one component (usually a ROM), must contain the vector interrupt addresses (see Chapter 10).

8-14
Addressing Techniques

Most systems do not use all 64K of available memory space. Therefore, not all of the address lines need to be used, and *redundant addresses* will occur (i.e., components will respond to two or more addresses). It is important, however, to choose the lines used so that no two components can be selected by the same address. Since the chip selects serve to turn ON the bus drivers (for a μP READ), only *one* component should be on at any time or something may be damaged.

For proper system operation, most memory and peripheral devices should only transfer data when Ø2 and VMA are HIGH. Consequently one CS line on each component is usually connected to each of these signals or a derivative of these signals. The **6820** PIA, for example, must have its E pin connected to Ø2 or it will not respond to an interrupt and can lock up the system following the receipt of a WAI instruction (the **6821** does not need Ø2).

When allocating memory, it is wise to place the "scratch pad" RAMs at the bottom of the memory map, since it is then possible to use the direct address mode instructions throughout the program when referencing these RAM locations. Because two-byte instead of three-byte instructions are used, a savings of up to 25% in total memory requirements is possible.

In summary, the following rules should govern the assignment of address bus lines to the various chip select pins.

1. Not all address bus lines need to be used for chip selection. Partial decoding is acceptable provided that precautions are taken to avoid two or more chips responding to the same address.
2. Ø2 must be included in the selection so that the bus drivers in each chip are only ON at the proper time.
3. VMA must be included to avoid chip selection by the chance state of the address bus during nonmemory referencing cycles.
4. When an address line is used as a positive enable on one chip, the same line should go to negative enables on all other chips, if possible. This prevents any two chips from being selected at the same time regardless of the state of the address bus.
5. One ROM (or PROM) should contain the interrupt vector addresses and should respond to FFF8 thru FFFF either directly or redundantly. (It also can respond to other redundant addresses.)
6. RAMs should respond to addresses 0000 through 00FF (256 bytes) to permit Direct Addressing Mode instructions to be used. (Only one **6810** is needed in small systems.)
7. PIAs and ACIAs must have Ø2 connected directly to E (the enable pin), in order to respond properly to interrupts. **6821s** do not require this since they are static parts.

Example 8-6
How many address lines are available to select

    a. A **6810**?
    b. A **6830**?

Solution
    a. A **6810** is a 128 word RAM that requires 7 bits to select a specific address, ($2^7 = 128$). Thus the 7 LSB address lines are connected to the **6810** address pins for word selection, leaving 9 bits available for chip selection.

    b. A **6830** is a 1024 word ROM. It requires 10 bits ($2^{10} = 1024$) to select a word, which leaves 6 bits available to select the chip.

Example 8-6 shows that there are more address lines for chip selection than there are CS pins on each component. For large systems where most of the available 64K of memory is used, it may be necessary to use all of the lines and some address decoding to provide a unique location in the memory map for each block. Most systems, however, use only a fraction of the available memory space. For these smaller systems, a judicious choice of memory locations to avoid interference between redundancies reduces the need for added TTL decoding.

A memory map, shown in Fig. 8-12, helps keep track of memory space allocations. For convenience the space is shown divided into 64 blocks of 1K (1024) each. A **6830** occupies an entire block but eight **6810s** can fit into one block. If, for example, we assign a **6830** ROM to address C4XX, the required binary states of the 6 most significant address line are as shown in the lower right of Fig. 8-12. This corresponds to position 50 in the map. The 10 LSBs of the

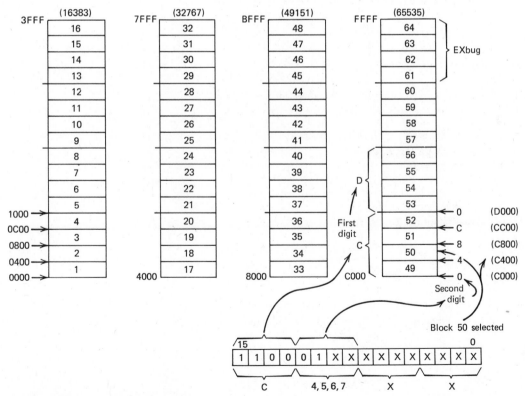

Figure 8-12 Sixteen-bit memory map showing address selection.

address are shown as "X", since they may take on a value of either 1 or 0 when a word in the block is selected.

Example 8-7

a. Which address does each component in the system configuration of Fig. 8-13 respond to?

b. Which component must contain the restart and the other vector addresses?

Solution

a. Figure 8-13 shows a small system where only address bits 13 and 14 are used for the decoding. In addition to address lines A14 and A13, VMA and Ø2 are also tied to all of the components being addressed. These signals are HIGH when a "Valid Memory Address" is present and when the data is to be transferred (during Ø2). They therefore contribute to the selection of the component that has the right combination of A14 and A13. It can be seen that ROM-1 contains 3 positive and 1 negative CS inputs. Since one of its positive CS inputs (CS2) is tied to Ø2 and another (CS3) is connected to VMA, it responds to any address that satisfies its other two CS inputs. The positive input (CS0) is connected to A14 and the negative input ($\overline{CS1}$) is connected to A13. Therefore, ROM-1 responds to any address of the binary form X10X XXXX XXXX XXXX, (X means either 1 or 0) or, any address whose most significant hex digit is 4, 5, C, or D. ROM-2 has all its inputs programmed for active HIGH, and responds to X11X XXXX XXXX XXXX, or any address whose most significant hex digit is 6, 7, E, or F.

The RAM has two of its negative $\overline{CS}$ bits connected to A13 and A14. It therefore responds to X00X XXXX XXXX XXXX, or any address whose most significant digit is 0, 1, 8, or 9.

The PIA inputs requires A13 (CS1) to be a 1 and A14 ($\overline{CS2}$) to be a 0. It responds to any address of the form X01X XXXX XXXX XXXX, or any address that has a most significant digit of 2, 3, A, or B.

Note. Each component in this system has a set of addresses that pertain uniquely to itself, since each responds to a different set of most signficant digits of the address.

b. ROM-2 must contain the restart and other interrupt vector addresses since this is the only component that responds to addresses whose most significant digit is F.

Example 8-8

A **6800** system consists of the μP, 2 ROMS (**6830s**), 8 RAMs (**6810s**), an ACIA, (**6850**) and a PIA (**6821**). Allocate memory space to each component. Use TTL logic gates as required.

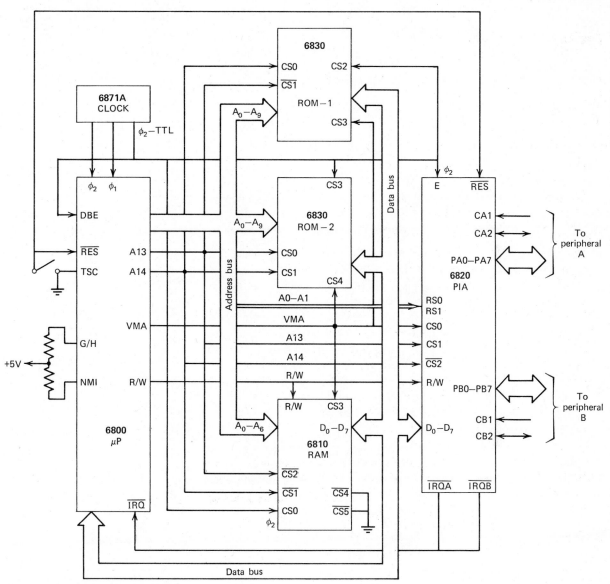

Figure 8-13 System configuration for Example 8-7.

Solution

In this problem, the number of elements that can be accommodated with the chip selects available is exceeded. By combining some of the signals that are common to a number of components with simple TTL gates, each component can be uniquely addressed.

First, to discriminate between the types of components the assignments of Table 8-5 are made.

Table 8-5
Chip Select Assignments for Example 8-8

	A15	A14	VMA	Ø2
ROM1	CS	CS	CS	CS
ROM2	CS	$\overline{CS}$	CS	CS
RAMX	$\overline{CS1}$	$\overline{CS2}$	CS0	CS3
ACIA	$\overline{CS2}$	CS0	CS1	E
PIA	$\overline{CS2}$	CS0	CS1	E

They satisfy all requirements for the ROMs but do not separate the RAMs from each other or distinguish the ACIA from the PIA.

There are several ways to select a particular RAM. There are two unused CS lines on the RAMs ($\overline{CS4}$ and $\overline{CS5}$) and these can be selected by IC decoders. For an alternate selection method however, proceed as follows.

1. VMA can be combined with $\overline{A15}$ to provide a negative chip select that is common to all RAMs and I/O. The ROMs do not need this since they already have VMA included. This takes two **7400** gates, as shown in Fig. 8-14.
2. We can then use A9, A8, and A7 to represent the binary numbers 0 through 7. Unfortunately, this doesn't work well because 000 requires three negative inputs and 111 requires three positive inputs. In both cases, only two are available. In addition, we need a positive input for Ø2.
3. If, however, Ø2 and A7 are put through inverters, as in Fig. 8-14, so that their complements are also available, then pin assignments can be made as shown in Table 8-6.

Table 8-7 summarizes the selections and shows the range of addresses in hexadecimal notation. The Xs indicate address lines that are not connected and are referred to as "don't care" bits. The Ys indicate bits that select the various locations in the chip. The upper range of addresses is the range covered by Y if we assume all Xs are 1s. The lower line is the range of Y if we assume all Xs are 0s.

If the Xs are assumed to be 0s, the top ROM is addressed at C000 to

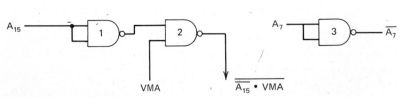
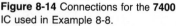
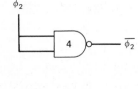

Figure 8-14 Connections for the **7400**
IC used in Example 8-8.

Table 8-6
Chip Select Assignments

	$\overline{A15}$·VMA	A14	A9	A8	A7	$\overline{A7}$	Ø2	$\overline{Ø2}$
RAM0	$\overline{CS1}$	$\overline{CS2}$	$\overline{CS4}$	$\overline{CS5}$		CS0	CS3	
RAM1	$\overline{CS1}$	$\overline{CS2}$	$\overline{CS4}$	$\overline{CS5}$	CS0		CS3	
RAM2	$\overline{CS1}$	$\overline{CS2}$	$\overline{CS4}$	CS0	$\overline{CS5}$		CS3	
RAM3	$\overline{CS1}$	$\overline{CS2}$	$\overline{CS4}$	CS0	CS3			$\overline{CS5}$
RAM4	$\overline{CS1}$	$\overline{CS2}$	CS0	$\overline{CS4}$	$\overline{CS5}$		CS3	
RAM5	$\overline{CS1}$	$\overline{CS2}$	CS0	$\overline{CS4}$	CS3			$\overline{CS5}$
RAM6	$\overline{CS1}$	$\overline{CS2}$	CS0	CS3	$\overline{CS4}$			$\overline{CS5}$
RAM7	$\overline{CS1}$	$\overline{CS2}$	CS0	CS3		$\overline{CS4}$		$\overline{CS5}$
ACIA	$\overline{CS2}$	CS1			CS0		E	
PIA	$\overline{CS2}$	CS1				CS0	E	

C3FF for programming purposes, but will respond to FC00 through FFFF when the interrupt or restart vectors are fetched (see Chapter 10).

The RAM is contiguous from 0000 to 03FF. This system therefore meets all the requirements of the rules and only requires the addition of one **7400** TTL IC.

Table 8-7
Final Address Line and Chip Select Assignments

	MS digit	3rd digit	2nd digit	LS digit	
ROM1	11XX	XXYY	YYYY	YYYY	FC00-FFFF C000-C3FF
ROM2	10XX	XXYY	YYYY	YYYY	BC00-BFFF 8000-83FF
RAM0	00XX	XX00	0YYY	YYYY	3C00-3C7F 0000-007F
RAM1	00XX	XX00	1YYY	YYYY	3C80-3CFF 0080-00FF
RAM2	00XX	XX01	0YYY	YYYY	3D00-3D7F 0100-017F
RAM3	00XX	XX01	1YYY	YYYY	3D80-3DFF 0180-01FF
RAM4	00XX	XX10	0YYY	YYYY	3E00-3E7F 0200-027F
RAM5	00XX	XX10	1YYY	YYYY	3E80-3EFF 0280-02FF
RAM6	00XX	XX11	0YYY	YYYY	3F00-3F7F 0300-037F
RAM7	00XX	XX11	1YYY	YYYY	3F80-3FFF 0380-03FF
ACIA	01XX	XXXX	1XXX	XXXY	7FFE-7FFF 4080-4081
PIA	01XX	XXXX	0XXX	XXYY	7F70-7F73 4000-4003

8-15
Summary

This chapter introduced the hardware components of the **6800** system. The μP, clock, and memory were discussed in detail. The function of each signal on the I/O bus was explained; methods of running, halting, and single stepping the μP were described. Finally, we explained methods of allocating memory space among the system components and gave an example.

8-16
Glossary

BA (bus available) A signal generated by the μP to tell an external device when the μP is halted.

Bus Driver/Receiver An IC capable of driving and receiving information from a bidirectional I/O bus.

DBE (Data Bus Enable) A signal to the μP allowing it to activate its data bus drivers.

DMA (Direct Memory Access) The ability to communicate directly with memory with the μP disabled.

HALT mode The mode in which the processor has stopped executing instructions.

Interrupt A signal from an external device that causes the processor to stop executing its program and branch to a service routine.

Reset An interrupt that vectors the program to the restart address.

RUN mode The mode where the processor is continually and normally executing instructions.

Trap To jump to an address where service routines or special instructions are located.

TSC (three-state control) A signal to the processor that, when HIGH, causes it to disconnect the address bus and R/W line drivers.

Vectored interrupt An interrupt that also provides an address of the appropriate service routine.

VMA (Valid Memory Address) A signal generated by the processor that indicates there is a valid address on the address bus.

8-17
References

Greenfield, Joseph D., *Practical Digital Design Using ICs,* John Wiley, New York, 1977.

Motorola Programming Manual M68 PRM (D), or *Motorola Programming Manual,* Second Edition, 9780, printed March 1975.

Motorola Training Manual.

Motorola Monitor, Vol. 9, No. 2, October, 1971.

M6800 Microcomputer System Design Data, 9701-5, February, 1976.

8-18
Problems

8-1 How many bytes and how many cycles are required for each of the following instructions:

AND IMMEDIATE
LOAD EXTENDED
STORE DIRECT
STORE INDEXED
ROTATE LEFT EXTENDED
JSR EXTENDED

8-2 What information appears on the address and data buses at the conclusion of each instruction of the following program: Make a table as shown for Example 8-4.

Address	Program
20	86
21	C2
22	8B
23	AB
24	97
25	C3
26	20
27	FA

8-3 How long does it take to execute each loop in the program of Problem 8-2?

8-4 A system using several **6830s** should only have one that responds to positive levels on all its CS lines. Explain why this is so.

8-5 A **6800** system has its components connected to the address bus as given by the following table.

Address Bits	ROM1	ROM2	RAM1	RAM2	PIA1
A15	CS1	CS1	$\overline{CS1}$	$\overline{CS1}$	CS1
A14	CS2	CS2	$\overline{CS2}$	$\overline{CS2}$	$\overline{CS2}$
A13	CS3	$\overline{CS3}$	$\overline{CS4}$	$\overline{CS4}$	CS0
A7			$\overline{CS0}$	$\overline{CS5}$	

Which addresses does each component respond to? Which component contains the vector addresses?

8-6 A **6800** consists of 4 ROMs, 8 RAMs, 2 PIAs, and an ACIA. Allocate the memory space for each IC. Give the addresses that affect each component. Use **7400** series ICs as required as in Example 8-10.

8-7 If a **6800** system's memory space is to be filled entirely with **6810s**, how many **6810s** can be accommodated?

After attempting to solve the problems, try to answer the self-evaluation questions in Sec. 8-2. If any of them still seem difficult, review the appropriate sections of the chapter to find the answers.

Chapter 9 Input/Output

9-1
Instructional Objectives

The object of this chapter is to introduce those components that control the input/output (I/O) operations of the **6800** system. After reading it, the student should be able to:

1. Explain how a μC can control an external device using PIAs, Digital/Analog (D/A), and Analog/Digital (A/D) converters.
2. Explain the function of each signal connected to the PIA.
3. Explain the function of each bit in the PIA's Control and Direction Registers.
4. Utilize the PIA to transmit data.
5. Utilize the PIA to communicate with a peripheral, by using CB1 and CB2 to control the data flow.
6. Explain the function of each register and I/O line in the ACIA.
7. Write a program to transmit asynchronous serial data using the ACIA.
8. Connect an ACIA to a TTY or MODEM.

9-2
Self-Evaluation Questions

Watch for the answer to the following questions as you read the chapter. They should help you to understand the material presented.

1. What are the two basic methods of I/O?
2. Explain the difference between control words and status words.
3. What is the function of A/D and D/A converters?
4. What is initialization?
5. What is the difference between the control lines and the other I/O lines on the PIA?
6. Why is the B side of the PIA better suited for outputting data and the A side better suited for receiving data?
7. What is the function of START and STOP bits?
8. Explain the interaction between the Transmit Data Register and the Transmit Shift Register, and the interaction between the Receive Shift Register and the Receive Data Register.

9-3
Introduction to Input/Output

The bus-structured organization of the **6800** system discussed in Chapter 8 is an efficient method for the components of the computer to communicate with each other. The *purpose of a μC, however, is to control an external device* such as a line printer or a drill press. The μC exercises this control by sending commands to the device.

Usually these commands are based on comparisons between desired and actual conditions existing in the external system. It may be necessary, for example, to stop the drill press if its motor temperature or speed exceed a certain predetermined limit. The system must monitor these crucial conditions and send this information to the μP. *The communications that allow the μC to receive information from an external system* (INPUT) *and present data and commands to it* (OUTPUT) *is referred to as INPUT/OUTPUT.*

9-3.1
Methods of Input/Output (I/O)

Two basic methods are used to perform I/O functions between the bidirectional internal bus of the μC and the lines associated with the external devices. The fastest and most popular is the *parallel interface,* where many lines can be used to transfer data simultaneously in one step. A second method is to use *serial transmission* of the bits of each byte over one signal path (for each direction). This is done either asynchronously or synchronously. (Synchronous means in step with a clock or timing signal.) The need for only two transmission paths makes the serial method attractive where the device being controlled is some distance away. These methods are implemented in the **6800** system by several unique parts.

1. The **6820** (or **6821**) Peripheral Interface Adapter (PIA), or **68488** General Purpose Interface Adapter (GPIA) for *parallel* transfer.
2. The **6850** Asynchronous Interface Adapter (ACIA), the **6852** Synchronous Serial Data Adapter (SSDA), or the **6854** Advanced Data Link Controller (ADLC), for *serial* transfer.

All of these MOS LSI ICs include *control, status,* and *data* registers that are accessible from the μC buses because they are *addressable.* The mode of operation of each IC is determined by storing one or more control words in the ICs *Control* Registers. The *status* registers are accessed by the μC to sense the condition of the external device as determined by signals from it.

9-3.2
Control Words and Data Words

The **6800** communicates with external devices via the PIA, ACIA, SSDA, ADLC, or GPIA. The μP can send out either *data words* or *control words* and receive either *data words* or *status words.*

The *control* word selects the mode of operation of the interface component, and determines whether the I/O lines are to operate as inputs or outputs. It also selects the polarity sensed by the control lines. Once the interface is properly programmed, the data registers can then be used to transmit commands or data to the external device.

Command words are commands to the external device. They tell it what to do (or control it).

If command words are used, the external hardware is often designed so that each bit controls a different function. For example, bit 0 could control a solid-state relay, bit 1 could be connected to a solenoid, and bit 2 could drive an indicator light for the operator.

Data words are used to represent either a *code* or a *magnitude*. As a code, for example, one byte could tell a teletypewriter which alphanumeric character to print. As a magnitude, it might tell a drill press how fast to rotate or determine the cutting depth of a lathe.

The **6800** can receive either *data* words or *status* words. Data words typically represent system parameters such as the position of a tool or the temperature of a motor. *Status* words give the μC the state of the system (e.g., is a relay ON or is a tape rewinding).

9-3.3
Digital-to-Analog (D/A)
Conversion 1[1]

If the μC is sending out a word designed to control something like the cutting depth of a lathe, the bits in the output word must, in many systems, be converted to an analog quantity, typically, a voltage. The magnitude of this voltage is determined by bits of the output word.

To convert the output bits of a μC to a voltage, a *digital-to-analog* (D/A) converter is used. Thus, to control the lathe's cutting depth, the following steps are necessary.

1. The μC must determine the desired cutting depth and present this as a digital word to the interface IC. (The PIA is assumed in this case.)
2. The digital output of the PIA must be connected to the input of a D/A converter.
3. The voltage output of the D/A converter then drives a mechanical converter, which sets the cutting depth of the lathe.

A block diagram of this system is shown in the upper part of Fig. 9-1. The wide arrow represents 8 or more digital input lines to the A/D converter, depending on the resolution required, and the single output line carries the output voltage of the converter.

Example 9-1

The cutting depth of the lathe can vary from 0 to 16 cm. If the D/A converter has an 8-bit input, how close can the cutting depth be set?

---

[1]D/A and A/D converters are discussed further in Sec. 13-6.

Solution

Since an 8-bit input allows for 256 (2^8) different numbers, each digital increment corresponds to 16 cm/256 = **0.0625 cm.** This is the *resolution* of the converter. If greater resolution is required, more than eight lines must be used in the converter. This requires a somewhat more sophisticated hardware system.

9-3.4

Analog-to-Digital (A/D) Conversion

In order to control an external system, a μC must be able to monitor it. This monitoring is usually accomplished by using *sensors, transducers,* and *analog-to-digital* (A/D) converters.

Sensors and *transducers* convert physical quantities to voltages. *Sensors* are generally used to sense relatively static quantities, such as the temperature at a particular point or the weight of the liquid in a fuel tank. *Transducers* generally convert more dynamic physical quantities, such as pressures or velocities, to voltages.

The output voltages of the sensors or transducers must be in digital form before being sent to the μC. An A/D converter accomplishes this.[2] It accepts a voltage as its input and produces a corresponding digital output. A/D converters with 8, 10, and 12 bit outputs are readily available. The more bits provided, the higher the resolution of the converter, as shown in Example 9-1 above. Any size digital

[2]Many transducers and sensors have direct digital outputs and do not need A/D conversion.

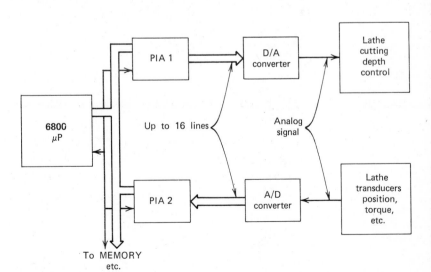

Figure 9-1 A typical microprocessor Analog INPUT/OUTPUT system.

word can be accommodated by multiplexing it (dividing it in 8-bit bytes that are brought in sequentially), but if the resolution is adequate, it is simplest to use a byte size converter. A block diagram of the μC input system is shown in the lower part of Fig. 9-1.

Thus, the functions of computer controlled systems generally are as follows.

1. The operation of the system is monitored by sensors and transducers.
2. Their outputs are converted to digital quantities by an A/D converter, if not already in digital form.
3. The ouputs are sent to the μC via the PIA.
4. The computer program examines the inputs to determine if the system is operating properly.
5. If the μC determines that adjustments are required, it sends commands out via the PIA.
6. The outputs are converted by a D/A converter to voltages that adjust the system and restore optimal operation.

**9-4
The PIA in Detail**

The Peripheral Interface Adapter (PIA) is a 40 pin LSI IC designed to control *parallel* data transfers between the **6800** system and external devices. PIAs are used to transfer data or commands when the equipment to be controlled is nearby, and the many lines are easily accommodated. Sections 9-9 to 9-14 describe the uses of the serial interfaces, which are more often used for distant control.

A block diagram of the **6820** (or **6821**) PIA that is used for parallel data transfer in **6800** systems, is shown in Fig. 9-2. It shows the registers within the PIA, the interface to the **6800** data, address, and control buses on the left, and the interface connections to external devices on the right.

**9-4.1
The PIA Registers**

Figure 9-2 shows that the PIA is a dual I/O port unit (a port is defined as an 8-bit parallel interface) with two similar sides labeled *A* and *B*. Each side contains three registers.

1. **The Control/Status Register.** This controls the operation of its side of the PIA.
2. **The Direction Register.** This register determines the direction of data flow (input or output) on each I/O line.
3. **The Data Register.** This holds the I/O data going between the external system and the PIA.

The action of these registers is discussed in detail in Secs. 9-5 and 9-6.

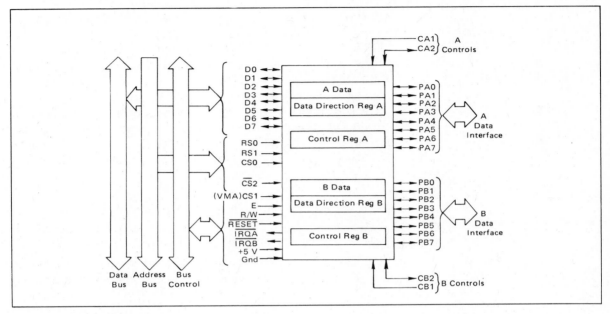

Figure 9-2 6820 PIA bus interface.

9-4.2
The PIA/6800 Interface

The PIA registers are treated as a *set of memory locations* by the **6800** system. It reads and writes these registers as it would any memory location. The user must assign these PIA addresses as he would other memory addresses, as described in Chapter 8.

The lines connecting the PIA to the **6800** I/O bus are shown on the left side of Fig. 9-2. This interface consists of:

1. **Inputs D0–D7.** The 8-bit data bus.
2. **Inputs RS0, RS1 and CS0, CS1, and $\overline{CS2}$.** These lines are normally connected to the **6800** address bus. RS0 and RS1 are usually connected to A0 and A1, and determine, along with a bit in the Control Register, which of the six registers within the PIA, is selected. The chip select lines CS0, CS1, and CS2 are used to select the particular PIA (see Sec. 8-14).
3. **Enable (E).** The Enable (E) pin of the **6820** PIA must be clocked continuously, since it is a dynamic part. The E pin is generally connected to a signal that is derived from the Ø2 clock. The **6821** is a static part that allows pin E to be used as another Chip Select.
4. **PIA READ/WRITE.** This signal is generated by the μP to control the direction of data transfers on the data bus. A LOW state on the PIA READ/WRITE line enables the input buffers. Data is transferred from the μP to the PIA on the E signal if the device has been selected. A HIGH on the READ/WRITE line sets up the PIA for a transfer of data

to the μP via the bus. The PIA output buffers are enabled when the proper address and the E pulse are present.

5. **RESET.** This active low Reset line is used to reset all register bits in the PIA to a logical 0 (LOW). This pin of the PIA is normally connected to the RESET line of the μC system, and is usually activated by a momentary switch or automatic restart circuit during POWER ON.

6. **IRQA and IRQB.** These are the PIA interrupt lines. They are designed for wire-OR operation and are generally tied together and wired to the interrupt input on the **6800**. A LOW signal on either of these lines causes the **6800** to be interrupted. Details of this operation are described in Sec. 10-5.

9-4.3
The Interface Between the PIA and External Devices

The connections between the PIA and external devices are shown on the right side of Fig. 9-2. There are two groups of eight bidirectional data lines (PA0–PA7, and PB0–PB7) and two control lines (CA1, and CA2, or CB1, and CB2) for each side. The control lines are used to regulate communication between the PIA and the external devices.

9-5
Data Transfers Between the PIA and External Devices

Before any data transfers can take place via the PIA, its Control Registers and Data Direction Registers have to be set up to determine the mode of operation and the direction of the data transfer (in or out of the PIA). This is known as *initialization*. Once initialized, these registers generally remain unchanged, although one of the PIA's outstanding capabilities is its programmable nature and ability to change system function during the operation of a program. This permits many unique features to be implemented in special programs with a minimum of external hardware, and also permits the same PIA to be used in many applications.

9-5.1
The Direction Register

The Direction Register determines the direction of each bit of data being transferred on the PIA's bidirectional data lines. The Direction Register is eight bits long, so there is a one-to-one correspondence between the bits of the Direction Register and the PA0–PA7 or PB0–PB7 lines. A 1 in any bit of the Direction Register causes the corresponding PA or PB line to act as an output, whereas a 0 causes it to become an input. Typically Direction Registers contain 00 or FF so that an entire byte is transferred in or out, but some bits of either side of a PIA can act as inputs and some as outputs, as shown in Example 9-3.

9-5.2
The Data Register

The Data Register contains the data being transferred in or out of the PIA. The Data and Direction Registers have the same address, but whether a word to that address reaches the Data Register or the Direction Register depends on bit 2 of the Control Register.

Table 9-1a shows the addressing scheme for the PIA registers. When RS1 is a 0, the A registers are addressed and, when it is a 1, the B side is accessed. Since RS0 is generally connected to A0 and RS1 to A1, the Control/Status Registers for both sides are located at an odd address, and the Data/Direction Registers are at the prior even address. Although there are six registers, only four addresses are used, as shown in Table 9-1b. If bit 2 of the Control Register (CRA2 or CRB2) is a 1, the Data Register is accessible, whereas if bit 2 is a 0, only the Direction Register can be accessed.

9-5.3
Initializing the PIA

The PIA must always be initialized by a system reset. When the RESET line of the PIA is taken LOW, it clears (or 0s) all registers. This sets up the PA0–PA7, PB0–PB7, CA2 and CB2 lines as inputs and disables all interrupts. Since bit 2 is also 0, the Direction Registers are set to be accessed. The RESET line is normally connected to the μP RESET, and therefore a RESTART program routine is automatically accessed whenever RESET is activated. The desired

Table 9-1
PIA Addressing

(a) Internal Addressing				
RS1	**RS0**	**CRA2**	**CRB2**	**Registers**
0	0	1	X	Data Register A
0	0	0	X	Direction Register A
0	1	X	X	Control/Status Reg. A
1	0	X	1	Data Register B
1	0	X	0	Direction Register B
1	1	X	X	Control Register B

(b) Memory Location	
Address	**Registers**
XXX11	B Control/Status (1 register)
XXX10	B Data/Direction (2 registers)
XXX01	A Control/Status (1 register)
XXX00	A Data/Direction (2 registers)

PIA configuration is selected during the execution of this RESTART program routine.

If the PIA needs to be reconfigured without using the RESET line, it must be done in the following sequence.

1. Clear the Control/Status Register (including bit 2).
2. Rewrite the Direction Register.
3. Rewrite the Control Word with bit 2 SET to select the Data Register.
4. Write or read data.

Example 9-2

Write a program to send the contents of locations 40 and 41 to a peripheral device. Assume the Control Register is at address 8009, and the Direction Register and Data Register are both at address 8008.

Note that because bit 1 of the address is 0, the A side of the PIA is being used.

Solution

The steps of the solution are listed below. The coding has been omitted to save space.

1. Accumulator A is cleared and stored in 8009. This clears all the bits of the Control Registers; in particular, it clears bit 2.
2. Accumulator A is loaded (Immediate) with FF and stored in 8008. Because bit 2 of the Control/Status Register is now a 0, when FF is written to address 8008, it enters the Direction Register and causes all the data lines to act as outputs.
3. An 04 is now loaded (LDA A Immediate) into the accumulator and stored in 8009. This changes bit 2 of the Control Register to a 1, which latches the Direction Register and allows the Data Register to be accessed.
4. The contents of location 40 are loaded into the accumulator and stored at 8008. Because bit 2 of the Control/Status Register is now a 1, these bits go to the Data Register and are output on the I/O lines.
5. After the first word has been read by the peripheral, and sensed by reading the status bits (usually signaled by one of the control lines, as described later), the contents of location 41 are loaded in A and stored at 8008. This places that data on the I/O lines.

Note that once the Control and Direction Registers have been set up, data can be sent out repeatedly without reinitializing those registers.

Example 9-3

Write a program to read the state of four switches and send the data out to a hexadecimal display.

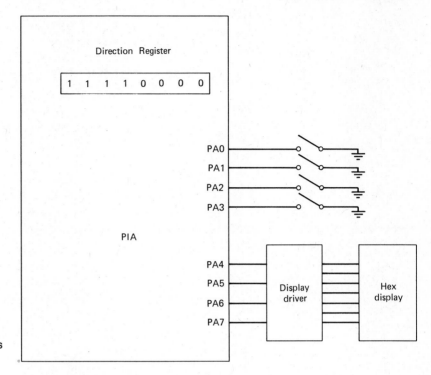

Figure 9-3 The PIA and its connections for Example 9-3.

Solution

One solution is shown in the circuit of Fig. 9-3 where the four switches are connected to lines PA0 through PA3, and the display inputs are connected to peripheral lines PA4 to PA7. The program for the solution proceeds.

1. During initialization, F0 is written into the Direction Register. This configures the 4 LSBs as inputs and the four MSBs as outputs.
2. The Control Register is then rewritten to make bit 2 a 1. The instruction LOAD A (from) 8008 reads the switch contents into the four LSBs of the accumulator.
3. Four LEFT SHIFT instructions shift the switch settings into the MSBs of the accumulator.
4. Now a STORE A at 8008 places the switch settings on the output lines (PA4–PA7) where they can drive the display.

**9-6
Handshaking with the PIA**

When an external device has information for the μC, it must send the PIA a signal (often called DATA READY). When the byte is read by the PIA, it typically acknowledges receipt of the information by sending an ACK (for acknowledge) signal to the device. A similar situation exists when the PIA is transmitting information to the device. The protocol and signals that control the exchange of information is called *handshaking*.

In Sec. 9-5 we concentrated on the data lines and ignored the CA1 and CA2 (or CB1 and CB2) lines, which control the interchange of information. The operating mode of these control lines is determined by the bits in the A and B Control/Status Registers. The control lines, in turn, affect the contents of bits 6 and 7 of the Control/Status Registers as will be explained.

The configuration of the Control/Status Register is shown in Table 9-2. The upper register (CRA) is for the "A" side of the PIA, and the lower one (CRB) is an identical register used to control the "B" side. The function of bit 2 (Direction Register access) has been described in Sec. 9-5. Status bits 6 and 7 are SET by the transitions of the CA1 and CA2 (CB1–CB2) lines. The rest of the bits in the Control/Status Register are used to select the functions of the control lines. Bits 6 and 7 cannot be changed from the μP bus but are RESET indirectly by a READ data or WRITE data operation, as explained later.

9-6.1
Control Lines CA1 and CB1

Control lines CA1 and CB1 are input only lines that function identically. As shown in Table 9-2, they are controlled by bits 0 and 1 of the Control/Status Register, and their action can be determined from Table 9-3. Table 9-3 shows the following.

1. If CRA1 (CRB1) is a 0, status bit 7 of the Control/Status Register is set HIGH whenever there is a negative transition ($\downarrow$) on the CA1 (CB1) line. These lines are typically connected to an external device that causes a transition whenever it requires attention. If CRA1 (CRB1) is a 1, a positive transition ($\uparrow$) on CA1 (CB1), SETs status bit 7 of the corresponding Control/Status Register.

2. If CRA0 of the Control/Status Register is a 0, the interrupt line IRQA is disabled and IRQA remains HIGH, even when status bit 7 goes HIGH

Table 9-2
PIA Control Word format

	7	6	5	4	3	2	1	0
CRA	IRQA1	IRQA2	CA2 Control			DDRA Access	CA1 Control	

	7	6	5	4	3	2	1	0
CRB	IRQB1	IRQB2	CB2 Control			DDRB Access	CB1 Control	

Table 9-3
Control of Interrupt Inputs CA1 and CB1

CRA-1 (CRB-1)	CRA-0 (CRB-0)	Interrupt Input CA1 (CB1)	Interrupt Flag CRA-7 (CRB-7)	MPU Interrupt Request $\overline{IRQA}$ ($\overline{IRQB}$)
0	0	↓ Active	Set high on ↓ of CA1 (CB1)	Disabled — $\overline{IRQ}$ remains high
0	1	↓ Active	Set high on ↓ of CA1 (CB1)	Goes low when the interrupt flag bit CRA-7 (CRB-7) goes high
1	0	↑ Active	Set high on ↑ of CA1 (CB1)	Disabled — $\overline{IRQ}$ remains high
1	1	↑ Active	Set high on ↑ of CA1 (CB1)	Goes low when the interrupt flag bit CRA-7 (CRB-7) goes high

Notes:
1. ↑ indicates positive transition (low to high)
2. ↓ indicates negative transition (high to low)
3. The Interrupt flag bit CRA-7 is cleared by an MPU Read of the A Data Register, and CRB-7 is cleared by an MPU Read of the B Data Register.
4. If CRA-0 (CRB-0) is low when an interrupt occurs (Interrupt disabled) and is later brought high, $\overline{IRQA}$ ($\overline{IRQB}$) occurs after CRA-0 (CRB-0) is written to a "one".

as a result of the CA1 line transitions. If CRA0 is a 1, the IRQA line goes LOW when bit 7 goes HIGH and interrupts the μP, provided that IRQA is connected to the μP IRQ line, and the interrupt is not masked in the μP (see Chapter 10).

Example 9-4

What happens if 06 is written into Control/Status Register A?

Solution

A control word of 06 results in the conditions specified on line 3 of Table 9-3. Bit 7 is SET by a positive transition of the CA1 line. IRQA is disabled. The Direction Register is unaffected because Bit 2 is also SET. If 06 is written to the Control/Status Register and read back before a positive transition on CA1 occurs, the μP reads it back as 06, but if a transition occurs between the writing and reading, the μP reads it back as an 86, because CRA7 is now SET. Once SET, CRA7 can only be cleared by reading Data Register A, as stated in the footnotes to Table 9-3.

9-6.2
Interrupts and Line Monitoring

The **6800** system has three ways of responding to line transitions, that indicate an external device is requesting attention.

1. By continuously polling status bits.
2. By electronically responding to the hardware interrupt request lines and then polling the status bits to find the responsible device.

3. By using a hardware device such as the **6828** Priority Interrupt Controller (PIC), which generates the interrupt service routines address without a need for polling. The PIC is described in Chapter 10.

If CRA0 (CRB0) is set to 0, the hardware interrupt is disabled, but the presence of a 1 in Bit 7 of the register can be sensed by a *polling routine*. Polling means that the system program periodically reads the Control/Status Registers of all I/O devices to determine if the flag bit of one of them has been SET.

A CRA0 (CRB0) bit that has been set to 1 will cause the μP to be interrupted whenever CA1 (CB1) sees a transition, if the IRQA and IRQB pins are connected to the μP IRQ line and the μP is not masked (Condition Code register bit 4 is SET). If it allows interrupts (Bit 4 = 0), the **6800** μP branches to a polling routine and thence to a service routine as soon as an interrupt occurs. This routine allows the system to respond properly to the request initiated by the external device. During the course of this routine, the PIAs Data Register is normally read to get the information and, in doing so, the CRA7 (CRB7) bit is RESET. See Chapter 10 for details of interrupt operation.

Example 9-5
A **6800** system has several PIAs. The IRQAs and IRQBs are all tied to the μP IRQ line. How can the system determine which one is interrupting?

Solution
This cannot be done electrically because of the common IRQ line. However, when this line is pulled LOW the interrupt vector points to a polling routine that must read each PIAs Control/Status registers until it finds one where CRA7 (or CRB7) is SET. It then branches to the service routine for that particular PIA. This allows the user to establish priorities among PIAs by causing the program to examine the most important PIA first.

Example 9-6
Write a program to monitor constantly the CA1 line and to take action when a transition occurs. Assume the Control/Status Register's address is 8009 (hex).

Solution
First the Control/Status Register must be initialized to select the proper transition (↓ or ↑) and disable interrupts. Then the program can proceed as shown in Table 9-4.

Table 9-4
Program for Example 9-6

Addr	Data	Mnemonic	Comment
1000	B6 8009	LDA A $8009	Get status
1003	2A FB	BPL *−3	If plus, branch back to 1000 and repeat.
1005	B6 8008	LDA A $8008	Get data.
Etc.	. . . .	. . . .	

The instruction at location 1000 loads the contents of the status register into the A accumulator and it is tested by the following instruction (at 1003), to see if Bit 7 (the interrupt flag bit) is SET. If not, the contents are positive and the instruction branches back to 1000 and fetches the status again. It continues to loop in this fashion until Bit 7 goes HIGH. Since the resulting byte is then negative, the program falls through to the following instruction. The PIAs Data Register at 8008 is then read to reset CRA7 and get the data.

Note that this is a very tight loop; that is, the computer did nothing but monitor the PIA. If the PIAs interrupt line for the A side (IRQA), is connected to the µPs IRQ, and the interrupt is enabled by a proper control word, the µP can be running a main program and doing useful work while waiting for this interrupt.

Example 9-7

A PIA is located at 8004–8007. A debounced switch is connected to CA1 and the outputs PA0–PA6 drive a 7-segment display, as shown in Figure 9-4. Write a program to increment the number in the 7-segment display every time the switch is thrown. When the number reaches 9 the display must return to 0 after the next switch throw.

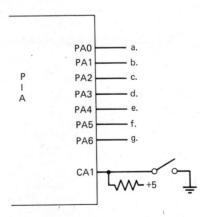

Figure 9-4 Control of a 7-segment display using the PIA.

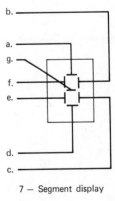

7 — Segment display

Solution

The program is shown in Table 9-5. It starts by initializing the A port for outputs. It then monitors Control/Status register A. A switch throw causes a transition on CA1 and causes CRA7 to go HIGH. When this occurs, the program falls through to location 35 where it:

1. Reads the A Data Register to reset CRA7.
2. Increments X and resets it to 0 if X has gone beyond 9.
3. Jumps to a table to get the proper codes to drive the 7-segment display.

In this program the table starts at location A0. To show a 0 on the display, the data must cause all segments except g to light. The code in A0 must therefore be 3F. If A1 is accessed, a 1 should appear by lighting segments B and C, so that A1 should contain 06. (Figure 9-4 shows the segments with their PIA interconnections.)

Many μP kits such as the **MEK-6800-D2** (see Sec. 11-7) drive their displays directly by using similar tables. Note that this program provides a way for the μP to count and display external events as they occur.

Table 9-5
Program and Data Table for Example 9-7

a. Program

ADDR	CODE		MNEMONIC	COMMENTS
20	CE 0000		LDX #0	CLEAR X
23	7F 8005		CLR $8005	CLR BIT 2 TO SELECT DIR REG
26	86 FF		LDA A #$FF	SET TO ALL 1s
28	B7 8004		STA A $8004	SET DIRECTION FOR OUTPUTS
2B	86 04		LDA A #$4	GET WORD FOR NEG GOING CA1 &
2D	B7 8005		STA A $8005	SET CRA2 TO SELECT DATA REG
30	B6 8005	LOOP	LDA A $8005	GET STATUS
33	2A FB		BPL LOOP	WAIT FOR CRA7 TO BECOME 1
35	B6 8004		LDA A $8004	CLEAR BIT 7
38	08		INX	INCREMENT X
39	8C 000A		CPX #$A	IS IT > 9 ?
3C	26 03		BNE *+5	NO- SKIP NEXT INSTRUCTION
3E	CE 0000		LDX #0	YES-CLEAR X
41	A6 A0		LDA A $A0,X	GET THE 7-SEGMENT CODE
43	B7 8004		STA A $8004	OUTPUT IT TO DISPLAY
46	20 E8		BRA LOOP	RTN TO 30 AGAIN

b. Data table

Location	Contents	Decimal number to be displayed
A0	3F	0
A1	06	1
A2	5B	2
A3	4F	3
A4	66	4
A5	6D	5
A6	7D	6
A7	07	7
A8	7F	8
A9	6F	9

9-6.3 Control Lines CA2 and CB2

Lines CA2 and CB2 can be used either as input or output control lines, and are controlled by bits 3, 4, and 5 of the Control/Status Register. If bit 5 of the Control/Status Register is a 0, the lines function as interrupt inputs as shown in Table 9-6. Table 9-6 reveals that these lines function exactly as CA1 and CB1 do except that transitions caused by the external devices set bit 6 instead of bit 7 of the Control/Status Register.

Example 9-8

Assume a tape drive is connected to a **6800** system, and it must send the **6800** either data or status information on the same I/O lines. The data would be the words read from the tape, and the status information tells the system what the tape is doing (e.g., running forward, rewinding, at end-of-tape). How can the system distinguish between data and status information?

Solution

One solution is to connect both CA1 and CA2 to the tape drive. If the tape drive is sending data, it raises CA1 every time it has a byte to send, while if it is sending status information, it raises CA2. The μP system can distinguish between status and data requests by examining bits 6 and 7 of the PIAs Control and Status Register.

Table 9-6

Control of CA2 and CB2 as Interrupt Inputs. CRA5 (CRB5) is LOW

CRA-5 (CRB-5)	CRA-4 (CRB-4)	CRA-3 (CRB-3)	Interrupt Input CA2 (CB2)	Interrupt Flag CRA-6 (CRB-6)	MPU Interrupt Request IRQA (IRQB)
0	0	0	↓ Active	Set high on ↓ of CA2 (CB2)	Disabled — IRQ remains high
0	0	1	↓ Active	Set high on ↓ of CA2 (CB2)	Goes low when the interrupt flag bit CRA-6 (CRB-6) goes high
0	1	0	↑ Active	Set high on ↑ of CA2 (CB2)	Disabled — IRQ remains high
0	1	1	↑ Active	Set high on ↑ of CA2 (CB2)	Goes low when the interrupt flag bit CRA-6 (CRB-6) goes high

Notes: 1. ↑ indicates positive transition (low to high)

2. ↓ indicates negative transition (high to low)

3. The Interrupt flag bit CRA-6 is cleared by an MPU Read of the A Data Register and CRB-6 is cleared by an MPU Read of the B Data Register.

4. If CRA-3 (CRB-3) is low when an interrupt occurs (Interrupt disabled) and is later brought high, IRQA (IRQB) occurs after CRA-3 (CRB-3) is written to a "one".

Table 9-7
Control of CB2 as an Output. CRB5 is HIGH.

CRB-5	CRB-4	CRB-3	CB2	
			Cleared	**Set**
1	0	0	Low on the positive transition of the first E pulse following an MPU Write "B" Data Register operation.	High when the interrupt flag bit CRB-7 is set by an active transition of the CB1 signal.
1	0	1	Low on the positive transition of the first E pulse after an MPU Write "B" Data Register operation.	High on the positive edge of the first "E" pulse following an "E" pulse which occurred while the part was deselected.
1	1	0	Low when CRB-3 goes low as a result of an MPU Write in Control Register "B".	Always low as long as CRB-3 is low. Will go high on an MPU Write in Control Register "B" that changes CRB-3 to "one".
1	1	1	Always high as long as CRB-3 is high. Will be cleared when an MPU Write Control Register "B" results in clearing CRB-3 to "zero".	High when CRB-3 goes high as a result of an MPU Write into Control Register "B".

9-6.4
Use of CB2 as an Output in the Handshake Mode

The action of the CB2 line as an output is described in Table 9-7. Note that the CB2 line goes LOW after a WRITE to the Data Register. This simplifies the programming and therefore makes it preferable for the B section of the PIA to be used to send data to external devices (output).

The top line of Table 9-7 illustrates a mode of operation commonly called the handshaking mode. This case is illustrated in Fig. 9-5 and the sequence of events is as follows:

1. The control word to the B side is written as shown. Note that CRB 5, 4, and 3 are 100, respectively.
2. When the system must send data out it writes the data to Data Register B. This causes CB2 to go LOW.
3. The peripheral device acknowledges receipt of the data by placing an acknowledge pulse on CB1. The negative transition of this pulse causes CB2 to return HIGH and raises the CRB7 flag.
4. The **6800** system responds to a HIGH on CRB7 as an indication that the data has been accepted by the peripheral, and the next byte can be written to the PIA.
5. Before the next output byte can be written to the PIA, Data Register B must be read to reset CRB7.

Example 9-9
The data between memory locations 1000 and 104F must be sent to a peripheral using the system of Fig. 9-5. Draw a flowchart to show how this is accomplished.

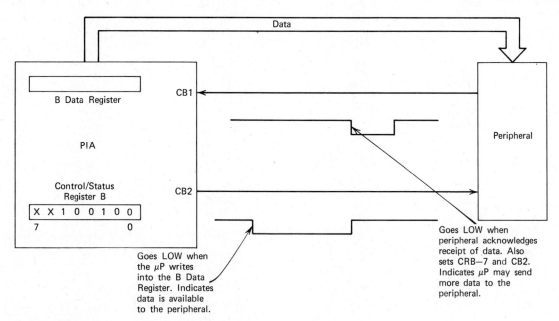

Figure 9-5 Handshaking with the "B" side of the PIA.

Solution

The solution is shown in Fig. 9-6 and proceeds in the following way.

1. The Control/Status Register is set to 00 (or the PIA is RESET).

2. Direction Register B is initialized to FF (all bits to be outputs) and then the Control/Status Register is set to 24 (hex) to initialize the handshaking procedure described above.

3. The index register is set equal to 1000 and the first memory word to be transmitted is loaded from that location into the accumulator and stored in Data Register B. This causes CB2 to go LOW.

4. The program goes into a loop until the peripheral accepts the data and causes a negative transition (↓) on CB1. This SETS CRB7 and CB2. Before the transition, the result is positive (MSB = 0) and the program continues to loop. After the transition the result is negative and the program exits from the loop.

5. The program reads the B data register to reset CRB7. It then tests to determine if it has exhausted its data area by comparing the index register with 1050, each time after it has been incremented. If it has, it stops; if it has not, it loads the next data word causing CB2 to go LOW again and repeats the above steps.

9-6.5
Use of CB2 in the Pulse Mode

If a peripheral device is connected to a PIA as shown in Fig. 9-7, and bits 5, 4, and 3 of the Control/Status Register are 101 as also shown, the CB2 line will be pulsed LOW as data is written into the "B" data register. This line can be used to inform the peripheral

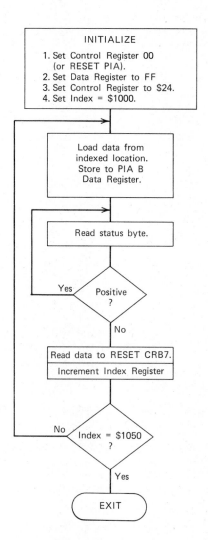

INITIALIZE

1. Set Control Register 00 (or RESET PIA).
2. Set Data Register to FF
3. Set Control Register to $24.
4. Set Index = $1000.

Load data from indexed location. Store to PIA B Data Register.

Read status byte.

Positive ? — Yes

No

Read data to RESET CRB7.
Increment Index Register

Index = $1050 ? — No

Yes

EXIT

Figure 9-6 Flowchart for Example 9-9.

that new data is available on the PIA output lines. If the peripheral can accept the data without fail, in the few microseconds it takes before the program can output the next byte, there is no need for an acknowledgment. The pulse mode of the PIA is outstanding for its simplicity of programming. Every WRITE into the B Data Register causes CB2 to be pulsed. This mode is capable of very fast operation and is best used for high speed peripherals like a floppy disk system.

Example 9-10

Show how the pulse mode can be used on the B side to output data to a high speed device like a floppy disk system. Give an example of a program. Assume the base address of the PIA is 8004, and the PIA has been initialized with a Control Word of 2D.

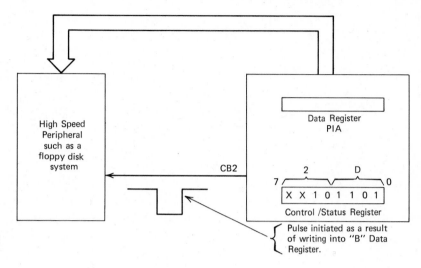

Figure 9-7 Pulse Mode of the PIA used with "B" side.

Solution

Refer once more to Fig. 9-7 and to the program shown in Table 9-8. Again, this pulse mode assumes that data can be accepted as fast as it is put out by the program. The CB2 line can be used to strobe a data latch, or to increment an address counter so that the data can be stored in memory in the peripheral, for example. The program shown in Table 9-8 is written to reside at 1000 and assumes that the data to be transmitted is in memory at 2000 to 20FF (256 bytes).

The first instruction sets the Index Register to the starting address of the data. The instruction at 1003 loads the A accumulator from the location specified by the Index Register. This byte is then stored in the PIA Data Register (or output), which informs the peripheral by pulsing the CB2 line. The program then increments the Index Register to the address of the next byte. The compare Index (immediate) instruction is used to determine if all of the data has been sent out. This is done by the instruction at location 1009 to see if the Index Register has gone past the end address of the data and, if not, looping back for the next byte.

Table 9-8
Program for Example 9-10

Addr	Data	Label	Mnemonics	Comments
1000	CE 2000		LDX #$2000	Get pointer to data.
1003	A6 00	LOOP	LDA A 0,X	Get data.
1005	B7 8006		STA A $8006	Store to B data register.
1008	08		INX	Increment pointer.
1009	8C 2100		CPX #$2100	End of data ?
100C	26 F5		BNE LOOP	No. Get next byte.
100E	. . . .		etc.	

Table 9-9
Control of CA2 as an Output. CRA-5 is HIGH.

| CRA-5 | CRA-4 | CRA-3 | CA2 | |
			Cleared	Set
1	0	0	Low on negative transition of E after an MPU Read "A" Data operation.	High when the interrupt flag bit CRA-7 is set by an active transition of the CA1 signal.
1	0	1	Low on negative transition of E after an MPU Read "A" Data operation.	High on the negative edge of the first "E" pulse which occurs during a deselect.
1	1	0	Low when CRA-3 goes low as a result of an MPU Write to Control Register "A".	Always low as long as CRA-3 is low. Will go high on an MPU Write to Control Register "A" that changes CRA-3 to "one".
1	1	1	Always high as long as CRA-3 is high. Will be cleared on an MPU Write to Control Register "A" that clears CRA-3 to a "zero".	High when CRA-3 goes high as a result of an MPU Write to Control Register "A".

at end of Read instruction

9-6.6
ON-OFF Control of CB2

The last two lines of Table 9-7 specify a mode of operation in which the level of CB2 can be directly programmed. If CRB5 and CRB4 are both 1s, the CB2 line assumes the same level as CRB3. This allows the program to control the length of time CB2 is LOW or HIGH (See Example 9-16).

9-6.7
Control of CA2 as an Output
(Handshaking Mode)

CA2 can be used as an output line to regulate the flow of data from the peripheral to the PIA in the same way that CB2 does (see Ex. 9-9), except that the CA2 line is taken LOW on the negative transition of E instead of on the positive, and after a READ of the A Data Register, instead of a WRITE of B (See Table 9-9). Use of CA2 is therefore to be preferred when data input is involved.

Example 9-11

A **6800** system must read several words from a disk. To do so, it must first send the disk controller several bytes of information that tell it, for example, the disk address and the number of words to be read. Describe how the transfer can be accomplished.

Solution

1. The Direction Register (B side) is set up for output (FF), and the A side Direction Register is set for input (00).
2. The **6800** sends commands to the disk controller via the data lines PB0 through PB7, using the handshaking procedure discussed in Sec. 9-6.4. CB2 controls the flow of commands as shown in Fig. 9-5.

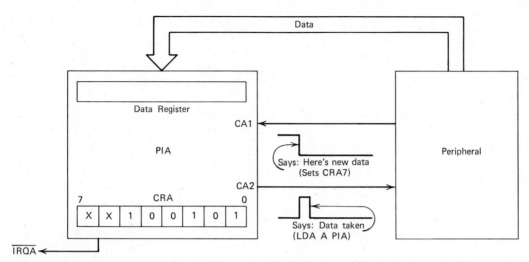

Figure 9-8 Handshaking with a Peripheral on the "A" side.

3. When the first word is ready, the controller causes a transition on CA1, which SETS CRA7 and CA2 (See Fig. 9-8).
4. The **6800** system now reads the first word from the PIA and places it in memory. This RESETS CA2, which requests new data from the disk. The read also RESETS CRA-7.
5. This procedure continues until the required number of bytes have been transferred from the disk to the μCs memory.

9-6.8
Pulse Mode for CA2

If CRA5, 4 and 3 are 101, respectively, the A side of the PIA operates in a pulse mode identical to that described for the B side, but it is triggered by a READ instead of a WRITE data operation.

9-6.9
ON-OFF Mode for CA2

When CRA5 and CRA6 are both 1s, the state of CA2 will be the same as that of bit CRA3 and, therefore, CA2 can be set HIGH or LOW as desired. This gives the program total control of CA2.

Example 9-12

A PIA is to be used to interface a High-Speed Paper Tape Reader to a **6800** system. The reader has 8 TTL output lines (one for each bit) and a sprocket hole output for a *ready* signal. The tape is advanced a character at a time by a stepper motor that requires a negative-going pulse. What are the Control Words for the ON/OFF mode of the PIA? Give an example of a program. Assume a base address of 8004.

Solution

As shown in Fig. 9-9, the 8 data lines from the reader's photocell outputs are connected to PA0–PA7 of the PIA, and the sprocket hole output is

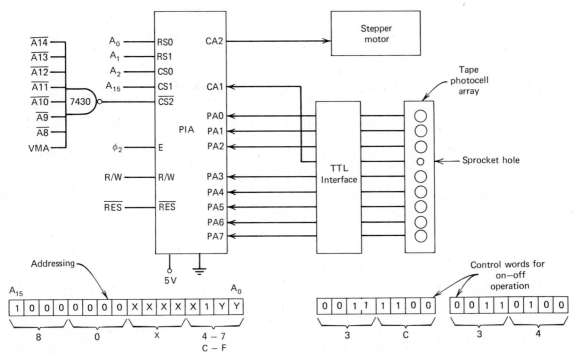

Figure 9-9 PIA circuit for a high speed tape reader (for Example 9-12).

connected to CA1. CA2 is connected to the stepper motor pulse circuit in such a way that a negative going pulse will step the tape. Reference to Table 9-9 shows that the Control Word should be 3C initially, and is changed to a 34 in order to strobe the stepper motor. The program to control this circuit is shown in Table 9-10.

The first instruction is a dummy READ operation to clear CRA7. The A accumulator is loaded with the value in the next (IMMEDIATE) byte (34) and it is output to the PIA Control Register. This causes CA2 to go LOW, thus starting the strobe pulse. The next two instructions repeat this action except the Control Word is 3C and bit CRA3 is now brought HIGH, which causes CA2 to return HIGH terminating the strobe pulse to the stepper motor. The mechanical design is such that one pulse moves the tape one frame (to the next character). The next step is to watch for the sprocket hole signal to SET the interrupt flag status bit CRA7. This is determined by testing the word loaded into A to see if it is positive. (Bit 7 is a 0.) If it is positive, the program is branched back to input the word again and test it. This loop is repeated until the status goes negative.

Since this program is controlling a mechanical tape reader that reads about 100 characters per second, it takes 10 milliseconds to move the tape to the next character. The μP will loop back about 1250 times before the

Table 9-10
Program for Example 9-12

Addr	Data	Mnemonic	Comment
1000	B6 8004	LDA A #$8004	Read A Data Register to clear interrupt (CRA7).
1003	86 34	LDA A #$34	Load A with 34.
1005	B7 8005	STA A $8005	Store Control Word to turn on pulse.
1008	86 3C	LDA A #$3C	Load A with 3C.
100A	B7 8005	STA A $8005	Store Control Word to end pulse.
100D	B6 8005	LDA A $8005	Load A with Status Register contents.
1010	2A FB	BPL *−3	If plus, branch back 5 bytes to 100D.
1012	B6 8004	LDA A $8004	Load A from Data Register.
1015	39	RTS	Return to the main program.

tape *arrives* at the new position as sensed by the sprocket hole photocell. In a real system it would be advisable to include a time-out loop at this point to generate an error message if the tape doesn't advance in a reasonable time. Once the tape has reached the sprocket hole, as indicated by the CA1 line going LOW, the program *falls through* the decision point and LOADS the data into the A accumulator. The RTS instruction causes the main program to be resumed and it stores or prints the data (in A) before it returns for the next character.

9-7
Timing Loops

It is often necessary for μPs to send timing signals at precise intervals to devices they control. These intervals can be anything from a few microseconds to minutes or even hours. Timing sequences and intervals can be controlled very precisely by a μP because it, in turn, is controlled by the highly accurate crystal clock that generates its Ø1 and Ø2 signals.

9-7.1
Construction of a Basic Timing Loop

The basis for μP timing control is the *timing loop,* which is simply a program loop that requires a specific time for completion.

Since the number of cycles required by each instruction and the clock frequency are known, the time to traverse the loop can be calculated. Timing loops are generally constructed by loading the Index Register (X), an accumulator, or a memory location with the numbers of times the loop is to be traversed, decrementing it each time around the loop, and leaving the loop when it equals 0. A memory location or the accumulator both allow up to 256 counts, but since X is a 16-bit register, it will handle up to 65536 loops. Still longer times can be generated using a combination of the two.

Example 9-13
Set up a program for a 0.1 second delay. Assume the basic μP clock is 1 MHz.

Solution
The program for a 0.1 second delay is:

Code	Mnemonic	Cycles	
CE 2710	LDX #10000		
09	DEX	4	
01	NOP	2	timing loop
26 FC	BNE *−2	4	

This timing program was constructed by realizing that the DEX and BNE had to be in the loop. Each of these requires 4 cycles. The NOP (2 cycles) was added simply to pad the loop so it contains a convenient number of cycles. This loop takes 10 cycles or 10^{-5} seconds if a 1 MHz clock is used. Since the required delay is 10^{-1} seconds, the loop must be traversed 10,000 times. Therefore the number $(2710)_{16}$ which is the hex equivalent of the decimal 10,000 is loaded into X at the start of the program. The program branches back to the DEX instruction 10,000 times before reducing X to 0 and falling through. Note that the timing can easily be changed by changing the number loaded into X.

Example 9-14
In Example 9-13, can the stack pointer be used instead of X?

Solution
The SP cannot be used instead of X because Table 5-3 shows that decrementing the SP does not set the Z bit. Again, one must carefully determine which instructions set the flags for correct operation.

9-7.2 Longer Delays Longer delays can be obtained by combining several loops. This can be done by using one timing loop as a subroutine and having a second timing loop jump to it during its execution. It is very convenient to have the subroutine take exactly one second, because this is often used as a timing base.

Example 9-15
Write a one second timing loop subroutine.

Solution
If the timing loop only takes 10 cycles as in Example 9-13, a one second delay is impossible because the largest number that can be loaded into X is 65,535. If, however, the timing loop is increased to 20 cycles, a one second delay is possible and the subroutine can be written as follows:

Code		Mnemonic	Cycles	
DF FO		STX $ FO	5	
CE C34F		LDX #49999	3	
08	LOOP	INX	4	
09		DEX	4	
09		DEX	4	20 cycle
01		NOP	2	timing loop
01		NOP	2	
26 F9		BNE LOOP	4	
FE 0200		LDX $200	5	
01		NOP	2	
39		RTS	5	

The first step in the subroutine is to store X, in case the index register is used by both the main program and the subroutine. Next X is loaded with the proper timing value and the main loop is entered. This loop has been padded so that it takes exactly 20 cycles, and effectively decrements X once. When X becomes 0, the subroutine restores the original value of X and exits. For a one second delay the 20 cycle loop should be traversed 50,000 times, minus provision for overhead.

The cycles in the subroutine that are not in the main loop are *overhead*. The overhead cycles have also been padded so that they also take exactly 20 cycles. These 20 cycles of overhead are compensated for by reducing the original X value by one, or from $(50,000)_{10}$ to $(49,999)_{10}$ or $(C350)_{16}$ to $(C34F)_{16}$.

Example 9-16
Set up a circuit to turn a light on for one hour and off for half an hour cyclically.

Solution
One way to do this is to use the CA2 or CB2 line as an output to control the light. The program proceeds as follows.

1. Set CA2 HIGH turning on the light.
2. Delay for one hour.
3. Set CA2 LOW turning off the light.
4. Delay for one half hour.
5. Return to step one.

Table 9-11 shows the program. It starts at location 10 and the PIA is at 8000.

The one second timing routine is as described in Example 9-15. By loading $(3600)_{10}$ into X we achieve a one hour delay and by loading $(1800)_{10}$ into X we achieve a half hour delay. Note that far more complex timing patterns can be generated by this method, and the timing can be changed in response to input signals to the μP by modifying the program.

Table 9-11
Program for Example 9-16

Location	Code	Label	Mnemonic	Comments
10	86 3C	START	LDA A #3C	Store Control Word
12	B7 8001		STA A $8001	to make CA2 go HIGH
15	CE 0E10		LDX #3600	Set hour delay
18	BD XXXX	LOOP1	JSR DLY 1	JSR to 1 sec delay
1B	09		DEX	Decrement X.
1C	26 FA		BNE LOOP1	Loop back to addr 18
1E	86 34		LDA A #34	Store Control Word
20	B7 8001		STA A #8001	to make CA2 go LOW.
23	CE 0708		LDX #1800	Set half hour delay
26	BD XXXX	LOOP2	JSR DLY 1	JSR to 1 sec delay
29	09		DEX	Decrement X.
2A	26 FA		BNE LOOP2	Rtn to location 26
2C	20 E2		BRA START	Rtn to location 10

9-7.3 Traffic Light Controllers

The program of Sec. 9-7.2 can obviously be adjusted to control traffic lights at road intersections where the lights must be alternately red and green. If the traffic lights merely cycle repetitively, electromechanical devices can do as well as μPs. Traffic flow, however, can be optimized using algorithms that consider the volume and speed of the traffic on the intersecting roads, the time of day, and other factors. Traffic control algorithms are becoming more complex and require the computational ability of the μP. Therefore, when traffic control goes beyond just switching the lights on and off, and attempts to adjust the lights for optimum control, the intelligence and programmability of the μP are indispensable.

9-8 Real Time Clocks

In many applications it is necessary for the μC to keep track of the time certain events occurred, or to cause external events to occur at specific times. This timing can be generated internally using software, by an external real time clock, or by a timer IC such as the **6840** (discussed in Sec. 10-10).

9-8.1 Hardware Real Time Clocks

Hardware real time clocks can be fabricated in many ways, and they must be interfaced to the μC so that the time information is available as needed. One way is to use an electric clock motor, which closes a mechanical contact every minute. This obviously can be connected to CA1 of a PIA and used to increment a software routine. In these days of solid-state electronics, a more reliable method would be to use some digital counter ICs that are driven by the 60 Hz power line. A variety of circuits are possible using divide-by-60 counters, one of which is shown in Fig. 9-10, but even here the resulting pulses must

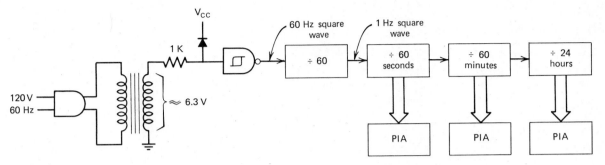

Figure 9-10 A real time clock.

be brought into the μC system and processed with some type of program. Another way, however, which is more appropriate for μC designers, is to use one of the many Timer LSI circuits that are proliferating in the industry. These devices are simple to use because they are self-contained and connect directly to the μC bus. Outside of the LSI IC itself, a quartz crystal is all that is needed. One such device is the **MC146819** real time clock/RAM. It is a programmable device that generates seconds, minutes, hours, days, date, month, and year as well as alarms or periodic rates. It can also be battery powered to keep time in the event of power failures, since it uses low-power CMOS technology. A 64 × 8 RAM is included with 12 bytes for the clock and 52 bytes for the users' data. The time data is simply picked up in byte form on the data bus by a suitable program. This timer is thus very much like any peripheral chip in the **6800** family and therefore is easily incorporated in a system.

9-8.2
Software Generated Clocks

To generate a real-time clock using software, a timing loop (see Sec. 9-7) should be set up with the time interval set to a value appropriate to the particular problem. One second and one minute are typical time values. Each time the timing loop expires, it increments a memory location or pair of memory locations. The number in the memory location therefore represents the elapsed time.

Example 9-17

It is necessary to record the time whenever a person passes through a gate, such as at an airport, during the course of an hour. The time of each entry is to be recorded in memory, starting at A0. Two memory locations are used for each event. The 8 bits of the upper location are divided into 2 BCD digits that represent the minutes of the hour and the lower location has 2 BCD digits that represent the seconds. Describe how to implement this system.

Solution

The following steps are necessary.

1. A photo cell and light beam detector can be used to determine when a person enters the gate. Every time the light beam is interrupted, the photo cell puts a pulse on the CA1 or CB1 line of the PIA, which sets bit 7 of the PIA Control/Status register.

2. The X and SP registers and the PIA control register must be initialized before the program can start.

3. Since the time storage is 16 bits long, a pair of memory locations must be reserved for the clock.

4. A one-second subroutine must be written (see Example 9-15). Each time it expires, it increments the clock. Note that the clock must be set up so that each time the Least Significant Digit (LSD) of the seconds reaches 10, it must return to 0 and increment the MSD of the seconds and, when the MSD of the seconds reaches 6, it must increment the LSD of the minutes, etc.

5. Bit 7 of the PIA Control Register can now be monitored or polled. This can be done within the one-second timing loop.

6. Each time bit 7 goes HIGH the contents of the clock can be transferred to memory starting at A0.

7. At the end of the hour memory will contain a list of the times people entered the gate.

   The code for this program is too long to be presented here, but the student should be capable of writing it.

9-9
Serial Data Transmission

When digital data is being transmitted or transferred between components in a **6800** μC system, it is moved a byte at a time by means of the 8-bit data bus. This is *parallel transmission,* and is synchronized by the system clock. When signals are sent to equipment not located in the same cabinet, the separate ground points create problems of noise or interfering signals. Extraneous current pulses and alternating currents (AC) are carried by the same ground wires and can induce unwanted pulses or glitches into the digital signals. To alleviate these problems, parallel digital signals are often converted to *serial* form on a single line, and transmitted *a bit at a time.*

When the distance is more than 50 or 100 feet, as in a system involving a main computer and several satellite terminals, this serial digital signal is frequently changed to audio tones by means of a MODEM (MODulator-DEModulator) and transmitted over telephone circuits. Some MODEMs provide for duplex operation (one serial path in each direction) over one telephone circuit. Obviously, serial transmission with only one pair of wires is simpler and cheaper to implement than parallel transmission with 8 or more lines, particularly since the grounding problems are eliminated. The operation of a full duplex data transmission system that transmits serial data in both directions simultaneously is shown in Fig. 9-11.

In the transmit part of the MODEM, the digital information modulates an audio tone that is then transmitted to the distant device, usually over telephone circuits. The receive part of the remote MODEM demodulates the audio signals and sends them to the local equipment as digital data.

9-9.1
Asynchronous Transmission

Most serial systems use asynchronous (unclocked) data transmission. The characters are sent in a standard format or code so that equipment made by different manufacturers can be used together in a system. The most common code for asynchronous data transmission is the ASCII (American Standard Code for Information Interchange). As used in the Model 33 and 35 Teletypewriters (TTYs), it is an 11-bit START-STOP code. The basic pattern for this code is shown in Fig. 9-12. When the line is quiescent (transmitting no data), it is constantly in the MARK or 1 state. The start of a character is signaled by the START bit that drives the line to the 0 or SPACE state for 1-bit time. The 8 bits immediately following the START bit are the data bits of the character. The bits are sent with the least significant bit (LSB) first. In most systems the ASCII code is used. The ASCII code (see Appendix E) uses 7 bits to generate 128 unique codes. These include upper and lower case letters A to Z, the numbers 0 to 9, plus many punctuation and mathematical symbols. Many nonprintable control characters are also provided. The character consists of 7 data bits and a parity bit.

Normally, *even* parity is used in the incoming direction because most TTY keyboards are connected to generate *even* parity characters (the number of 1s in each character are *even*). The TTY does not check parity on data to be printed, but many high speed data terminals do.

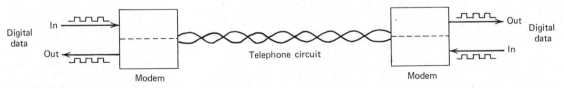

Figure 9-11 A full-duplex data transmission system.

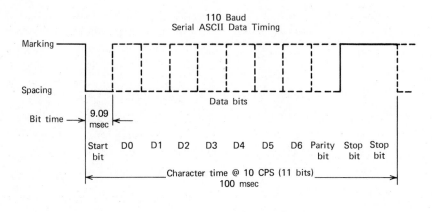

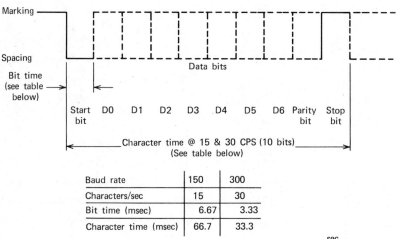

Baud rate	150	300
Characters/sec	15	30
Bit time (msec)	6.67	3.33
Character time (msec)	66.7	33.3

$$\text{Bit time} = \frac{\text{sec}}{\text{Baud rate}}$$

Figure 9-12 ASCII character bit timing.

150 & 300 Baud Serial ASCII Data Timing

After the last data bit, the transmission line must go HIGH for either 1- or 2-bit times. These are the STOP bits. TTYs use 2 STOP bits, but terminals operating at the higher baud rates use only one. If no further data is to be transmitted, the line simply stays HIGH (marking) until the next START bit occurs. This data pattern thus uses 10 or 11 bits as follows:

a. One START bit (always a space or 0).
b. Eight data bits (including parity).
c. One or two STOP bits (always a mark or 1).

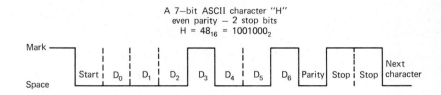

Figure 9-13 Character pattern for Example 9-18.

Example 9-18

a. What is the bit pattern of the character shown in Fig. 9-13?

b. Is the parity odd or even?

Solution

a. As shown in Fig. 9-13, the waveform bits are 00001001011. The first 0 is the START bit and the next 8 are the character. Since the LSBs are transmitted first, they must be reversed to correspond to the convention used in most μP literature and in this book. Therefore the character is 01001000 (48 hex, or ASCII "H"). The two 1s following the last data bit are STOP bits. Any additional 1s following the STOP bit merely indicate that the line is idle.

b. Since the character contains an even number of 1s, this is an even parity character.

9-10
The ACIA

In the **6800** system, serial data transmission is implemented by the **6850** asynchronous communications interface adapter (ACIA). The ACIA is designed to accept parallel data from the μC system data bus, a byte at a time, and to send the bits serially to an asynchronous serial data device such as a TTY, CRT terminal, line printer, or MODEM. At the same time, other circuits in the ACIA can accept serial data characters from a keyboard, a MODEM, or a tape reader, and place them on the μC bus as parallel bytes. Figure 9-14 shows the block diagram of the ACIA.

The left side of the diagram shows the lines that connect to the data, address, and control bus lines of the μP. The right side shows the lines used for the serial interface with external hardware.

The ACIA appends start, stop, and parity bits to the 7 or 8 data bits used for each character. The data could be a standard 7-bit ASCII character or any other 7- or 8-bit code such as EBCDIC, or even binary. The resulting character is either 10 or 11 bits long, depending on whether the character has one or two stop bits. Since the characters can be sent asynchronously, the time between each character can be from zero up. The ACIA is programmed during initialization via the μP data bus for the desired data configuration. It thus provides the following functions.

1. Parallel-to-serial and serial-to-parallel conversion of data (simultaneously).

2. Asynchronous transmission by means of start and stop bits.

3. Error control by means of parity, framing, or overrun error detection.

9-10.1
Parallel-to-Serial and
Serial-to-Parallel Conversion

The ACIA block diagram shown in Fig. 9-14 includes TRANSMIT and RECEIVE shift registers. The transmit shift register is loaded in parallel from the data bus and then shifted right to send the bits

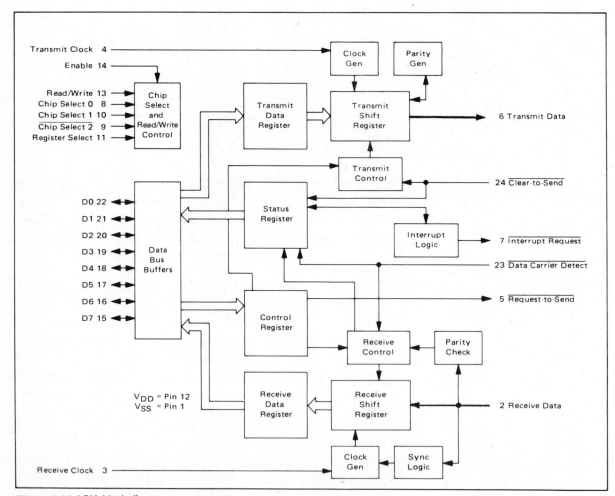

Figure 9-14 ACIA block diagram.

MC6850 ACIA

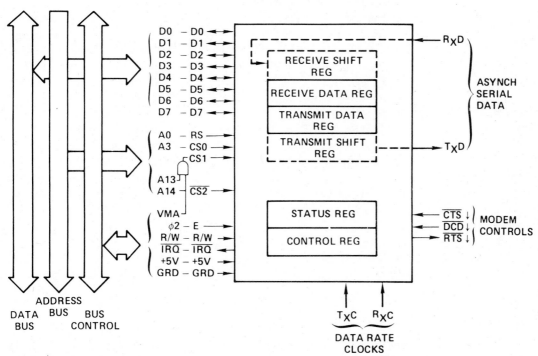

Figure 9-15 ACIA bus interface and register configuration.

out serially on one line. The receive shift register accepts serial data as input and sends it to the data bus in 8-bit bytes. The wide arrows in Fig. 9-14 indicate the parallel side of the device (8 lines). The receive and transmit bit rate clocks are used to shift these registers at the appropriate standard serial data rate (e.g., 110, 300, 2400, etc., bits per second). Note that these serial clock inputs are completely independent and can be used simultaneously at different rates if desired.

9-10.2
ACIA Registers

Figure 9-15 is a programmer's model of the ACIA. It shows the μP bus connections and the internal registers. Here is a list of the registers.

1. Transmit data register. The byte to be transmitted is written to the Transmit Data Register by the μP. It is transferred to the Transmit Shift Register, if it is empty. The byte is then shifted out serially. While one byte is being shifted out, a second byte can be loaded into the Transmit

Data Register. It is automatically loaded into the Transmit Shift Register when transmission of the first byte is completed.

2. **Receive Data Register.** Information from external devices enters the ACIA serially via the Receive Shift Register, which strips off the START and STOP bits and sends the byte in a parallel transfer to the Receive Data Register. The μP must read the Receive Data Register while the second byte is being received. If it is not read in time, the ACIA loses data, and causes the RECEIVE OVERRUN bit in the status register to be set (Sec. 9-10.6).

3. **The Control Register.** This register controls the format of both the transmitted and received data. It is discussed in detail in Sec. 9-10.4.

4. **The Status Register.** The Status Register monitors the progress of data transmission and reception and sends it to the μP. It is discussed in detail in Sec. 9-10.6.

Example 9-19

A standard 110 bits per second TTY is sending 11-bit characters continuously to the ACIA. How much time does the μP have to read each character?

Solution

Since each character consists of 11 bits, the data rate is 10 characters per second. This allows the μP 0.1 second to read each character before the next character is assembled in the Receive Data Register.

9-10.3 ACIA Signal Lines

The lines connected to the ACIA are shown in Fig. 9-14. The IC pin number for each line is also shown. The lines and their functions are as follows.

1. **Eight bidirectional data lines.** These are connected to the **6800** data bus.

2. **Three Chip Select lines.** Like the PIA, the ACIA occupies specific locations in the address map. The Chip Select lines and Register Select line are connected to the address bus to select the ACIA. (See Secs. 8-13 and 8-14.)

3. **READ/WRITE and Register Select.** The combination of these two inputs selects one of the four major registers. The Transmit Data Register and Control Register are write only; the μP cannot read them. If R/W is HIGH (for read), the Receive Data or Status Register is read (depending on whether the REGISTER SELECT pin is HIGH or LOW, respectively). If R/W is LOW, a word is written to either the Transmit Data Register or to the Control Register (depending on whether REGISTER SELECT is HIGH or LOW, respectively).

9-10.4
The ACIA Control Register

Table 9-12 shows the contents of the ACIA registers. The Boolean statements at the top of the table are the signals required to address each register. The Control Register, for example, has the equation $\overline{RS} \cdot \overline{R/W}$. This means the Control Register is addressed only if both the RS and R/W inputs to the ACIA are 0.

The Transmit and Receive Data Registers hold the data to be transmitted or received. A word to be transmitted is written to the Transmit Data Register, where it remains until the Transmit Shift Register is empty. Received words remain in the Receive Data Register until displaced by the next data word that is received. They must be read while they are available (see Example 9-19) or they will be lost.

The Transmit Control Register is more complex and is explained below in greater detail.

The function of the counter divide bits (CR0 and CR1) is shown in Table 9-13 and allows three choices;

Table 9-12
Definition of ACIA Register Contents

Data Bus Line Number	Buffer Address			
	$RS \cdot \overline{R/W}$ Transmit Data Register	$RS \cdot R/W$ Receive Data Register	$\overline{RS} \cdot \overline{R/W}$ Control Register	$\overline{RS} \cdot R/W$ Status Register
	(Write Only)	(Read Only)	(Write Only)	(Read Only)
0	Data Bit 0*	Data Bit 0	Counter Divide Select 1 (CR0)	Receive Data Register Full (RDRF)
1	Data Bit 1	Data Bit 1	Counter Divide Select 2 (CR1)	Transmit Data Register Empty (TDRE)
2	Data Bit 2	Data Bit 2	Word Select 1 (CR2)	Data Carrier Detect ($\overline{DCD}$)
3	Data Bit 3	Data Bit 3	Word Select 2 (CR3)	Clear-to-Send ($\overline{CTS}$)
4	Data Bit 4	Data Bit 4	Word Select 3 (CR4)	Framing Error (FE)
5	Data Bit 5	Data Bit 5	Transmit Control 1 (CR5)	Receiver Overrun (OVRN)
6	Data Bit 6	Data Bit 6	Transmit Control 2 (CR6)	Parity Error (PE)
7	Data Bit 7***	Data Bit 7**	Receive Interrupt Enable (CR7)	Interrupt Request (IRQ)

* Leading bit = LSB = Bit 0
** Data bit will be zero in 7-bit plus parity modes.
*** Data bit is "don't care" in 7-bit plus parity modes.

Table 9-13
Counter Divide Select Bits

CR1	CR0	Function
0	0	÷ 1
0	1	÷ 16
1	0	÷ 64
1	1	Master Reset

It divides the incoming clock by either 1, 16, or 64, depending on CR1 and CR0.

The ÷ 1 mode can only be used if the Receive Clock is synchronized with the data being received and a bit is available at every positive transition of the Receive Clock. Most systems using an ACIA are asynchronous, however, and the arrival of a byte is signaled by a START bit that can occur at any time. For these cases, the ÷ 16 or ÷ 64 options must be used.

Example 9-20

An ACIA operates using the ÷ 16 mode.

a. If the bit frequency is 100 bps, what receive clock frequency is required?

b. At what point after the START bit begins should the data be sampled?

Solution

a. Since the clock is divided by 16, the receive clock frequency must be 1600 bps to accept data at a 100 bps rate.

b. The START bit can be thought of as occupying counts 1 to 16, the first data bit counts 17 to 32, etc. For maximum accuracy, each bit should be sampled, or clocked into the receive shift register in the middle of its time slot or at counts 8, 24, 40, etc. This is automatically accomplished by the internal logic of the ACIA. (See Fig. 9-16).

Bit synchronization in the ÷ 16 and ÷ 64 modes is initiated by the leading mark-to-space transition of the START bit. The START bit on the receiver data input sampled during the positive transitions of the external clock is shown in Fig. 9-16b. If the input remains at a LOW level for a total of 8 separate samplings in the ÷ 16 mode or 32 samplings in the ÷ 64 mode, which is equivalent to 50% of a bit time, the bit is assumed to be a valid START bit. This START bit is shifted into the ACIA circuitry on the negative edge of the

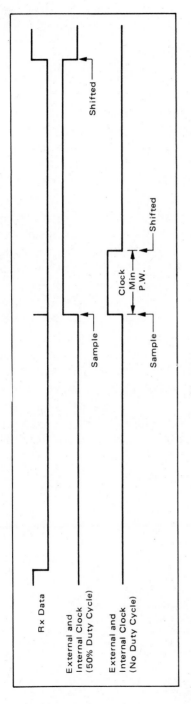

(a) Divide – by – 1

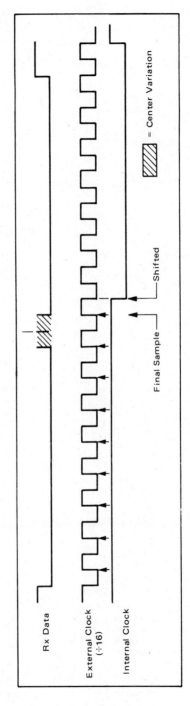

(b) Divide – by 16

Figure 9-16 Relation of the data and sampling clock in an ACIA.

internal clock. Once a valid START bit has been detected, the remaining bits are shifted into the Shift Register at their approximate midpoints.

If the receiver input returns to a mark state during the START bit sampling period, this false START bit is ignored and the receiver resumes looking for the mark-to-space transition or a valid start bit; this technique is called *false bit detection*.

Divide-by-1 mode selection will not provide internal bit synchronization within the receiver. Therefore, the external receive clock must be synchronized to the data under the following considerations. The sampling of the START bit occurs on the positive edge of the external clock, and the START bit is shifted into the shift register on the negative edge of the external clock, as shown in Fig. 9-16a. For higher reliability of sampling the positive transition of the external clock (sampling point) should occur at the approximate midpoint of the bit interval. There is no requirement on the duty cycle of the external receive clock except that the clock must meet the minimum pulse width requirement, as noted on the ACIA data sheet.

Bits CR2, CR3, and CR4 of the control word are written to the ACIA during initialization and determine the configuration of the words being transmitted and received. The user can choose the number of data bits transmitted in each character (7 or 8), the parity (odd, even, or no parity), and the number of stop bits (1 or 2). The options are given in Table 9-14. Note that when transmitting with parity, the user need not concern himself with the parity of the data he sends to the ACIA. It calculates the correct parity and inserts the proper bit.

Bits CR5 and CR6 provide Transmit Interrupt Control, as well as control of RTS, as shown in Table 9-15. (RTS is the Request-To-

Table 9-14
Word Select Bits

CR4	CR3	CR2	Function
0	0	0	7 Bits + Even Parity + 2 Stop Bits
0	0	1	7 Bits + Odd Parity + 2 Stop Bits
0	1	0	7 Bits + Even Parity + 1 Stop Bit
0	1	1	7 Bits + Odd Parity + 1 Stop Bit
1	0	0	8 Bits + 2 Stop Bits
1	0	1	8 Bits + 1 Stop Bit
1	1	0	8 Bits + Even Parity + 1 Stop Bit
1	1	1	8 Bits + Odd Parity + 1 Stop Bit

Table 9-15
Transmitter Control Bits

CR6	CR5	Function
0	0	$\overline{RTS}$ = low, Transmitting Interrupt Disabled.
0	1	$\overline{RTS}$ = low, Transmitting Interrupt Enabled.
1	0	$\overline{RTS}$ = high, Transmitting Interrupt Disabled.
1	1	$\overline{RTS}$ = low, Transmits a Break level on the Transmit Data Output. Transmitting Interrupt Disabled.

Send signal used with MODEMs.) If CR6 and CR5 are 0 and 1, respectively, the ACIA interrupts the μP if IRQ is connected to the μP whenever the Transmit Data buffer is empty. This maximizes the data transmission rate since it causes the system to send the ACIA an output character as soon as it can accept one. If CR5 and CR6 are both 1s, the ACIA transmits a constant 0 level, called a *break*. A break is used as a control signal in some communications systems.

Bit CR7 is the Receive Side Interrupt Enable. If CR7 is a 1, the ACIA interrupts whenever the receive data register is full, or the Overrun or Data Carrier Detect conditions occur.

Example 9-21
What are the characteristics of a transmission system if the control register contains C2?

Solution
CR7 is a 1, so Receive Interrupts are enabled, but Transmit Interrupts are disabled because CR6 and CR5 are 1 and 0, respectively. Bits CR4, 3, and 2 are all 0s so the data word consists of 7 bits + even parity + 2 stop bits. Finally, because CR1 is a 1 and CR0 is a 0, the frequency of the input clock must be 64 times the bit rate of the data.

9-10.5
ACIA Power-ON Reset

The ACIA contains an internal Power ON reset circuit to detect the 5-V turn-on transition and to hold the ACIA in a RESET state until initialization by the μP is complete. This prevents any erroneous output transitions from occurring. In addition to initializing the transmitter and receiver sections, the Power-ON-RESET circuit holds the CR5 and CR6 bits of the Control Register at a logic 0 and logic 1, respectively, so that the Request-to-Send (RTS) output is held HIGH and any interrupt from the transmitter is disabled. The Power-ON-RESET logic is sensitive to the shape of the V_{DD} power supply turn-on transition. To insure correct operation of the reset function, the power turn-on transition must have a positive slope throughout its transition. The conditions of the status register and other ouputs during power-on reset or software master reset are shown in Table 9-16.

The internal ACIA POWER-ON RESET logic must be released prior to the transmission of data by performing a software Master Reset, followed by a second control word. During Master Reset, Control Register bits CR0 and CR1 are set to 1s, which releases the latched condition of bits CR5 and CR6, allowing them to be programmed in the following control word. In recent production the processes have produced faster parts and this release may occur during master reset. To guard against the possibility of RTS going LOW, it is advisable to use a master reset word of 43. This retains the preset conditions of bits CR5 and CR6. The final condition can then be determined in the second control word without any false or momentary shifts in the RTS level. This also applies to Receiver Interrupt Enable (RIE) which is controlled by bit CR7. The 43 will assure that the interrupt is inhibited until its state is specified in the second control word.

After Master Reset of the ACIA, the programmable Control Register must be set to select the desired options such as the clock divider ratios, word length, one or two stop bits, and parity (even, odd, or none). Bits CR5 and CR6 of the Control Register are no longer inhibited and can now be programmed for the options defined in Table 9-15.

9-10.6
The ACIA Status Register

The status of the ACIA, and what has happened to the data being handled, is determined by examining the Status Register at the proper time in the program. The function of each bit is given in Table 9-12.

Bit 0—Receive Data Register Full (RDRF). This bit is SET when a character has been received by the ACIA and should be read by the CPU.

Bit 1—Transmit Data Register Empty (TDRE). This bit indicates that a character to be transmitted can be sent to the ACIA.

Bits 2 and 3—Data-Carrier-Detected (DCD) and Clear-to-Send (CTS). These bits will only be HIGH if an RS232C MODEM is connected to the ACIA and not ready for transmission or operating improperly. They must be tied LOW if a terminal rather than a MODEM is being used.

Table 9-16
ACIA Initialization Sequence

	POWER-ON RESET	MASTER RESET (Release Power-On Reset)	MASTER RESET (General)	
Status Register	b7 b6 b5 b4 b3 b2 b1 b0 0 0 0 0 X X 0 0	b7 b6 b5 b4 b3 b2 b1 b0 0 0 0 0 X X 0 0	b7 b6 b5 b4 b3 b2 b1 b0 0 0 0 0 X X 0 0	
IRQ Output	1	1	1	
RTS Output	1	1	X	
Transmit Break Capability	Inhibit	Inhibit	Optional	
Internal: RIE	0	X	X	
TIE	0	0	X	

Held by Power-On Reset ——   Defined by Control Register——

(X-Independent of Reset function)

Bit 4—Framing Error (FE). A framing error indicates the loss of character synchronization, faulty transmission, or a break (all spaces) condition. If one of the above conditions is present, the internal receiver transfer signal will cause the FE bit to go HIGH. The next internal transfer signal will cause the FE status bit to be updated for the error status of the next character. A HIGH on the $\overline{DCD}$ input or a Master Reset will disable and reset the FE status bit.

Bit 5—Overrun Error (OVRN). A HIGH state on the OVRN status bit indicates that a character was received but not read from the Receiver Data Register, resulting in the loss of one or more characters. The OVRN status bit is SET when the last character prior to the overrun condition has been read. The read data command forces the RDRF and OVRN status bits to go HIGH if an overrun condition exists. The next read data command causes the RDRF and OVRN status bits to return to a LOW level. During an overrun condition, the last character in the Receive Data Register that was not read subsequent to the overrun condition is retained since the internal transfer signal is disabled. A HIGH state on the $\overline{DCD}$ input or a Master Reset disables and resets the OVRN status bit.

Bit 6—Parity Error (PE). If the parity check function is enabled, the internal transfer signal causes the PE status bit to go HIGH if a parity error condition exists. The parity error status bit is updated by the next internal transfer signal. A HIGH state on the $\overline{DCD}$ input or a Master Reset disables and resets the PE status bit.

Bit 7—Interrupt Request (IRQ). A HIGH level on the IRQ status bit may be generated from three sources:

a) Transmitter. If the Transmitter Data Register is empty (TDRE = 1), and TIE is SET.

b) Receiver. If the Receive Data register is full (RDRF = 1), and RIE is SET.

c) Data Carrier Loss. A loss of carrier (a HIGH level) on the $\overline{DCD}$ input, generates an interrupt, as indicated by the IRQ bit, if the RIE bit is SET.

Example 9-22

The status register of an ACIA reads A3. What is the status of the ACIA?

Solution

The data indicates that bits 0, 1, 5, and 7 are SET. Table 9-12 shows that:

a. The Receive Data Register is full.
b. The Transmit Data Register is empty.
c. A Receive Overrun Error has occurred.
d. An Interrupt Request is pending.

The Receive Data Register has overrun, indicating the μP did not fetch the last character during the time available. In addition, there is another character in the Receive Data Register waiting to be read, and the ACIA is trying to interrupt. The Transmit Data Register is available to accept any data for transmission. Essentially these conditions mean that the μP is not paying attention to the ACIA. They probably indicate that a timing problem (either hardware or software) has caused the system to malfunction.

9-11
Hardware Interfaces
to the ACIA

The ACIA serial inputs and outputs are TTL level signals. Two standard interfaces have evolved, and each requires additional hardware to make the signals compatible with the external device. Both interfaces are often included in General Purpose computers.

9-11.1
The TTY Interface

A standard teletypewriter has several interface options. The most popular is the 20 mA current loop. This is characterized by a steady 20 mA of direct current flowing in the keyboard and printer circuits, when no data is being transmitted. This is called the *mark* signal and coincides with the logic 1 TTL level of the ACIA. The current flow is interrupted (called a *space* signal), when a Logic 0 TTL level is sent, such as the start bit. Many higher speed data terminals including CRTs include a 20 mA option. Figure 9-17 shows the TTY interface and the way 20 mA current loops can be generated using the optical coupler.

Optical couplers are suggested for electrical signal isolation because the contacts in the TTY frequently produce serious noise spikes, and if the wire or cable to the terminal is very long, it can be exposed to interference from AC power lines, other TTYs, or

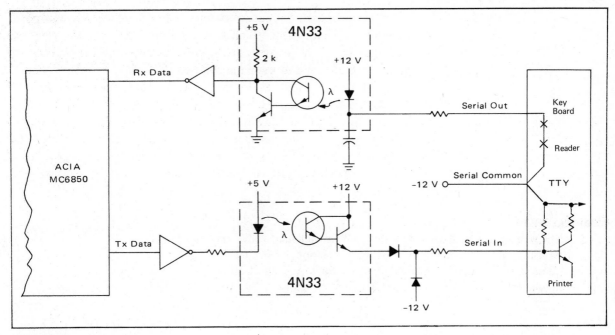

Figure 9-17 Teletypewriter 20 mA interface circuit.

radio signals. When such an isolation circuit is built, it is important to keep the wires associated with the digital side separated or shielded from those carrying the 20 mA currents to avoid electrostatic coupling of the noise spikes, which can defeat the purpose of the optical coupling. Common ground returns are to be avoided also, since extraneous current flowing can produce noise voltage differences that are effectively in series with the digital signals (see Sec. 13-4.1).

The path of the signal transmitted from the ACIA to the TTY is shown in the lower half of Fig. 9-17. The transmitted data output of the ACIA is coupled to a light-emitting diode (LED) within the optical isolator via a TTL inverter. In the *mark* state the diode is lit and turns on the photosensitive Darlington pair of transistors. This drives 20 mA into the printer. When a character is being shifted out of the ACIA, the 0s of the character turn off the LED, interrupting the current path. These 1s and 0s are mechanically latched in the TTY, and when all bits are received, the TTY printer types the character.

Note the use of the plus and minus 12 V in the TTY circuits. These voltages are desirable because it puts a total of 24 V across the TTY keyboard or reader contacts. These contacts are designed to work with up to 130 V and will not work reliably with very low voltages (like 0.7 or even 5 V), since insulating oxides or even particles of dirt will form on the contacts in time. The higher voltages will break through the oxides and provide reliable performance.

When a key is depressed on the keyboard, the TTY transmits its code to the ACIA, as shown in the upper half of Fig. 9-17. Here the bits of each character selected by the keys cause the receive LED to be turned ON and OFF, as they are sent. The photo-transistor detects the light changes and transmits it to the data input via a TTL inverter.

Example 9-23

An ACIA is to transmit and receive data from a TTY simultaneously. The data to be transmitted is in memory starting at location 1000, and the received data is to be stored in consecutive locations starting at 2000. Explain how to set up the ACIA and what the program must do.

Solution

First the timing must be set up, then the program must be written. A 1760 Hz clock would typically be used in the ÷ 16 mode to produce a 110 BPS signal compatible with a TTY.

If polling is to be used, the Control Register must be initialized to 01. This does the following:

a. Bits CR1 and CR0 are 01, selecting the ÷ 16 mode.

b. Bits CR2, CR3, and CR4 are each 0, selecting a word format of 7 bits + even parity + 2 stop bits. This is the format used by standard TTYs.

c. Bits CR5 and CR6 are each 0, disabling transmit interrupts.

d. Bit CR7 is 0, disabling receive interrupts.

Before the program can start, four memory locations must be reserved for the two pointers: two locations for the transmit data area starting at 1000; two locations for the receive data area starting at 2000.

The program can then proceed as follows:

1. Read the ACIA status register.
2. Test bit 0. If it is 0, skip step 3.
3. If bit 0 equals 1, the receive data register is full. Place the receive pointer in X, read the Receive Data Register, store the contents (indexed) into the Receive Data area, increment X (incrementing the receive pointer), and store X back into the receive pointer location.
4. Test bit 1. If it is 0, skip step 5.

5. If bit 1 equals 1, the transmit data register is empty. Place the transmit pointer in X, load the byte to be transmitted into A (indexed), store it in the Transmit Data Register, increment X, and rewrite X into the transmit pointer.

6. Return to step 1 and repeat.

This program does not check for errors, but could easily be expanded to do so. A similar program is shown in Chapter 7 (Fig. 7-4).

9-11.2
The RS232C Interface

For data transmission to remote terminals, MODEMs and telephone lines are used. The ACIA is connected to MODEMs in accordance with EIA (Electronic Industry Associates) specification RS232C. For asynchronous transmission, the following five signals go between the ACIA and the MODEM.

1. TRANSMITTED DATA—From the digital device to the MODEM. This is the data to be transmitted.

2. RECEIVED DATA—From the MODEM to the digital device. This is the data received from the remote MODEM.

3. REQUEST TO SEND—From the digital device to the MODEM. This signal should be a 0 whenever data is to be transmitted. It is important in half duplex transmission where it is switched to a 1 to tell the distant end that it should send data. In full duplex operation, it remains in the 0 state, as long as it desired to send data.

4. CLEAR TO SEND—From the MODEM to the digital device. This signal is a response to REQUEST TO SEND and indicates that the MODEM can accept data for transmission. In full duplex operation, it is normally always active and presents a 0 level to the digital device.

5. DATA CARRIER DETECTED (DCD)—From the MODEM to the digital device. A 1 on this line indicates that the data carrier is lost, usually because of an abnormal condition. This line must be in the 0 state for transmission or reception.

All RS232C signals must be between $+3$ and $+15$ V for a 0 or *space,* or between -3 and -15 V for a 1 or *mark*. Consequently, level translators are required between the TTL levels or the ACIA and the MODEMs. Two popular level translators are the **MC1488** and the **MC1489**, both manufactured by Motorola, Inc. The **MC1488** is a quad TTL-to-RS232C level translator for data going *to* the MODEM and the **MC1489** is a quad RS232C-to-TTL level translator for data coming *from* the MODEM to the digital ICs. Unfortunately, level translators require additional power supplies (typically, -12 V and $+12$ V) to generate the required signal voltages.

The connections between the ACIA and a MODEM are shown in Fig. 9-18.

The RS232C interface can also be used to connect to a local TTY or other terminal if it is equipped with an RS232C interface.

9-12
Uses of the ACIA

Typical applications using an ACIA are illustrated in Fig. 9-19.

System 1 shows how a terminal is connected to a μC. The interface box between the ACIA and the terminal is required to match the ACIA output voltages and the terminals input voltage or current requirements. The most common interfaces are the 20 mA current loop described in Sec. 9-11.1 and the RS232C interface discussed in Sec. 9-11.2. Most terminals are available with either or both of these.

System 2 shows a remotely located terminal, which can be in the next building or thousands of miles away. Here data transmission takes place via MODEMs. A number of standard MODEMs are available for various speeds of operation up to 9600 bits/second. Any MODEM that is faster than 300 bps usually requires two phone circuits (one for each direction). They usually cannot transmit over dial-up telephone lines and require special dedicated lines that must be rented from the telephone company at considerable expense.

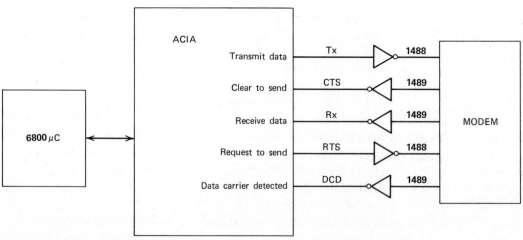

Figure 9-18 An RS-232C interface between the ACIA and a MODEM.

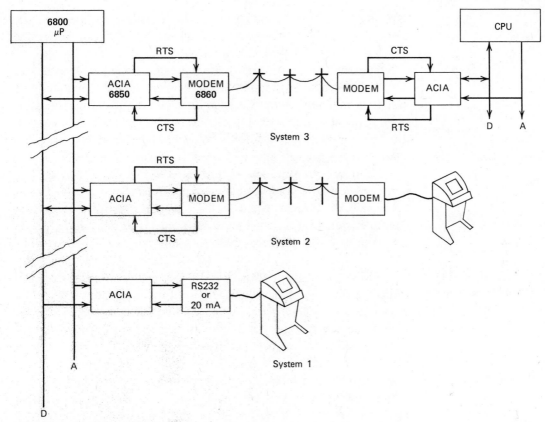

Figure 9-19 System applications of the ACIA.

System 3 shows a possible way for μCs to exchange data using MODEMs. The degree of automation depends on the ingenuity and capability of the designer.

**9-13
Synchronous
Communications**

Asynchronous communications via the ACIA are used primarily with slow speed terminals where information is generated on a keyboard (manually) and where the communication is not necessarily continuous. Synchronous communications are usually encountered where high speed continuous transmission is required. This information is frequently read to MODEMs, disk or tape systems at 1200 BPS or faster. Synchronous systems transmit a steady stream of bits even when no characters are available (a *sync* character is substituted). Because there are no start and stop bits to separate the characters, care must be taken to synchronize the receiving device with the transmitted signal so that the receiver end of the circuit can determine which bit is bit 1 of the character.

Synchronous systems usually use a preamble (all 1s, for example) to establish synchronization between the receiver and transmitter and will then maintain sync by transmitting a sync pattern until interrupted. Because start and stop bits are not needed, the efficiency of transmission is 20% better for 8-bit words (8 instead of 10 bits per character).

Synchronous transmission is illustrated in Fig. 9-20. The top line is the clock that is used in most systems to control the data. In this figure, all data changes occur on the positive edge of the clock. For maximum reliability, data should be sampled in the middle of the bit. Note that after the preamble, the data flows continuously.

9-13.1
The 6852 Synchronous Serial
Data Adapter (SSDA)

The SSDA is a 24-pin MOS LSI IC that provides a bidirectional serial interface for synchronous data information interchange with bus organized systems such as the **6800** μP. It is a complex device containing seven registers. Although primarily designed for synchronous data communications using a "Bi-sync" format, several of the **6852s** features and, in particular, the First-In, First-Out (FIFO) buffers, make it useful in other applications where data is to be transferred between devices that are not being clocked at precisely the same speed, such as tape cassettes, tape cartridges, or floppy disk systems. Because the SSDA is so complex, space does not permit a detailed discussion of it. The reader is referred to the manufacturers literature. (See the references in Sec. 9-16.)

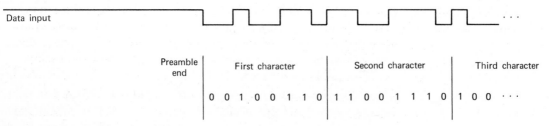

Figure 9-20 Synchronous transmission.

**9-14
Summary**

This chapter dealt with interfacing and communications between the **6800** μP and peripheral devices. The two most popular interfacing ICs, the PIA and the ACIA, were discussed in detail. The operation of their internal registers and the programs necessary to make them function properly were explained. The differences between parallel, serial synchronous, and serial asynchronous transmission were explained, so the designer could use the proper interface ICs for his particular system.

Other **6800** family devices generally known as peripheral controllers, such as the **6854** Advanced Data Link Controller and the **6844** Direct Memory Access Controller (DMAC), are manufactured to perform specific functions in μC systems (see Sec. 10-9.4). They are like the PIA because they are bus compatible and addressable, they have programmable Control Registers, Data Registers, and Status Registers. These devices are very complex and cannot be explained thoroughly in this book, but if readers have absorbed the principles of the PIA and ACIA operation, they should be able to understand these special purpose ICs after consulting the manufacturer's literature.

**9-15
Glossary**

ACIA (6850) 6800 family Asynchronous Communications Interface Adapter component.

A/D converter Analog-to-digital converter. It converts analog signals to digital signals for use by digital devices such as computers.

ASCII USA Standard Code for Information Interchange.

Asynchronous Data independent of a clock, (i.e., random).

Command words Words sent to a peripheral device to tell it how to act.

Control Register A register that contains a control word.

Control word Bits written to a PIA or ACIA register that controls the mode of operation.

D/A converter Digital-to-analog converter. It converts digital information to analog for use by external devices.

Direction Register A register within the PIA that controls the direction of data flow on each of the I/O lines.

EBCDIC Extended Binary Coded Decimal Interchange Code (IBM).

Handshaking An interchange of signals between devices to acknowledge or authorize communication.

Interrupts A signal that informs the μP that a peripheral device is requesting service. It generally causes the μP to jump to a service routine for the requesting device.

PIA (6820 **or** 6821) **6800** family Peripheral Interface Adapter component.

Polling Interrogating the status register of each peripheral device in turn to determine if it has data for the μP.

Resolution The voltage or quantity represented by the smallest change in the output.

Sensor A device that senses an analog quantity and typically converts it into a voltage that is proportional to the magnitude of the quantity.

SSDA (6852) **6800** family Synchronous Serial Data Adapter component.

START bit A bit that signals the start of a character in an asynchronous communication system.

Status Register A register that contains a status word.

Status word Bits in a PIA or ACIA register that indicate what is currently happening in that device.

STOP bits(s) One or two bits (always 1s) that indicate the end of an asynchronous character.

Subroutine nesting The incorporation of subroutines within subroutines.

Synchronous Data that is kept in step with a clock signal.

Transducer A device that converts a dynamic quantity, such as velocity, into a voltage.

9-16 References

Engineering Note 100 MIKBUG/MINIBUG ROM, Motorola SPD, Inc.

IBM File No. TP-09, Form GA-27-3004-1, Binary Synchronous Communications (Bi-sync).

Microprocessor Interfacing Techniques, Austin Lesea and Rodney Zaks SYBEX, Inc., 2020 Milvia St., Berkeley, California 94704.

M6800 Microcomputer System Design Data, Motorola SPD, Inc.

Motorola Data Sheets for **MC68488, MC6854, MC6852.**

USA Standard Character Structure and Character Parity Sense for Serial-by-bit Data Communication in the USA Standard Code for Information Interchange (ASCII), USAS X3.4, 1968, American National Standard Institute, Inc.

9-17 Problems

9-1 A D/A converter has 8 input bits. If its output ranges from 0 to 5 V, how much voltage does each digital step require?

9-2 Repeat Problem 9-1 if the output range is from -7 to $+7$ V.

9-3 A A/D converter is required to have an output range of 0 to $+20$ V. It must have an input resolution of 0.01 V or more. How many bits are required on the digital input?

9-4 Write a program to configure the A Direction Register of a PIA so that lines 6 and 7 are inputs and to configure the B Direction Register so that lines 1 and 2 are inputs. All other lines should be outputs.

9-5 Write the coding for Example 9-2.

9-6 Write the instructions for the program of Example 9-9 if the data between locations 100 to 150 is to be sent to the peripheral controller.

9-7 If a PIA Control Register reads 3F, what is the PIA doing?

9-8 A peripheral has two control lines, A and B. If it SETs A, it wants to read the data in location 100. If it SETs B, it wants to read the data in location 200. Write a program to initialize the PIA to allow this to happen. Assume that both control lines are not SET simultaneously.

9-9 Write a program so that a peripheral can write data into memory sequentially, starting at location 100.

9-10 In response to a switch closure, a signal line should be on for 300 μs, off for 100 μs, on for 200 μs, off for 100 μs, on for 500 μs, and then off. Using the PIA, write a program to accomplish this.

9-11 The status register of an ACIA reads 81. What action should the program take?

9-12 Write a program to transmit the contents of locations 100 to 1FF to a peripheral using an ACIA.

9-13 If a peripheral is transmitting serial data to a μP via an ACIA, write a program to store that data in sequential locations, starting at 100.

9-14 A TTY is sending data. The μP must "echo" by transmitting the same data it is receiving so the TTY operator sees the data he is sending. Write the ACIA program to accomplish this.

9-15 Every time a person enters a room a TTY is to type the word "hello." Describe the equipment and the program required to make this happen.

9-16 The following program uses a PIA at location 8020-8023:

Addr	Mnemonic
20	LDX #$100
23	CLR $8021
26	CLR $8020
28	LDA A #$24
2B	STA A $8021
2E	LDA A $8021
31	BPL *−2
33	LDA A $8020
36	STA A 20,X
38	INX
39	CMP X #$200
3B	BNE QQ
3D	BRA *

    a. Is the data flow in or out of the μP? Which side of the PIA is being used?

    b. What area of memory is reserved for data? How many bytes?

    c. Is CA1 or CB1 being used? If so, how?

    d. Is CA2 or CB2 being used? If so, how?

    e. What is QQ?

    f. Explain what the program is doing.

9-17 Modify Example 9-7 so that the 7-segment display shows the hex digits (0-9. A-F).

    After attempting to solve the problems, try to answer the self-evaluation questions in Sec. 9-2. If any of them still seem difficult, review the appropriate sections of the chapter to find the answers.

Chapter 10 Interrupts and Direct Memory Accesses

10-1
Instructional Objectives

This chapter introduces two methods whereby a peripheral device can communicate with a computer: *Interrupts* and *direct memory accesses*. After reading it, the student should be able to:

1. Write a *restart* routine to initialize a **6800** μP system.
2. Write an interrupt service routine for a device that uses the IRQ or NMI interrupt.
3. Utilize the SWI and WAI instructions.
4. Use the **6828** Peripheral Interrupt Controller.
5. Design controllers that can utilize DMA.

10-2
Self-Evaluation Questions

Watch for the answers to the following questions as you read the chapter. They should help you understand the material presented.

1. What is an *interrupt*? What advantages does it give a μP system?
2. How is the interrupt mask set and cleared?
3. In a system that allows several devices to interrupt on the same line, how is the interrupting device identified?
4. Why is the NMI a higher priority interrupt than the IRQ?
5. What is the difference between a WAI and an SWI?
6. What does the RTI instruction do? Why is it important?
7. In making a DMA, why can TSC not be held LOW longer than 9.5 μs?

10-3
Introduction to Interrupts

One of the most important features of a μP is its ability to control and act on feedback from peripheral devices such as line printers or machinery controllers. It must be able to sense the operation of the system under its control and respond quickly with corrective commands when necessary.

When conditions that require fast response arise, the system is wired so as to send a signal called an *interrupt* to the μP. *An interrupt causes the μP to stop execution of its main program and jump to a special program, an interrupt service routine, that responds to the needs of the external device.* The main program resumes when the interrupt service routine is finished.

Although a computer can perform many useful tasks without using or responding to an interrupt, the ability to do so is a necessary function for many system designs. The **6800** includes a powerful interrupt structure. Important aspects of this are the stack concept, the use of vectored interrupts, and the interrupt priority scheme provided by the μP logic.

10-3.1
The Stack Concept

As described in Chapter 6, the *stack* is an area in memory pointed to by the Stack Pointer (SP) register. The stack has three basic uses.

1. To save return addresses for subroutine calls.
2. To move or save data.
3. To save register contents during an interrupt.

Use of the stack during interrupts is discussed in this chapter.

10-3.2
Vectored Interrupts

The **6800** uses four different types of interrupts: *Reset* (RST), *Non-Maskable* (NMI), *Software* (SWI), and *Hardware Interrupt Request* (IRQ). Unique interrupt servicing routines must be written by the system designer for each type of interrupt used, and they can be located anywhere in memory. Access to the routines is provided by the μP that outputs a pair of addresses for the appropriate interrupt. The two locations addressed must contain the address of the required interrupt service routine. The eight addresses put out by the μP for the four interrupt types are:

1. Reset (RST)   FFFE – FFFF
2. Non-Maskable Interrupt (NMI)   FFFC–FFFD
3. Software Interrupt (SWI)   FFFA–FFFB
4. Interrupt Request (IRQ)   FFF8 – FFF9

These are shown in the memory map of Fig. 10-1.

It should be noted (as explained in Secs. 8-14, 15, and 16), that the actual ROM (or PROM) accessed may appear to be at some lower address as long as it also responds to the addresses shown above. When one of the four types of interrupts occurs, the μP logic fetches the contents of the appropriate two bytes and loads them into the program counter. This causes the program to jump to the proper interrupt routine. The fetched addresses are commonly called *vectors* or *vector addresses* since they *point to* the software routine used to service the interrupt.

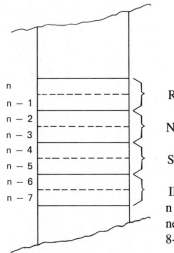

RST — Reset vector

NMI — Non-Maskable Interrupt vector

SWI — Software Interrupt vector

IRQ — Interrupt Request vector

n = memory location accessed when all address lines are 1s (not necessarily FFFF but the highest location in installed memory). See Sec. 8-15 and Table 8-7.

Figure 10-1 Memory map showing Restart and Interrupt vector locations.

Three of the interrupts (RST, NMI, and IRQ) are activated by signals on the pins of the μP, and the fourth (SWI) is initiated by an instruction. Each of these interrupts have similar, but different sequences of operation and each will be described.

10-4
Reset (RST)

A *reset* is used to start the program. A LOW pulse on the RESET pin of the μP causes the logic in the μP to be reset and also causes the starting location of the program to be fetched from the *reset vector* locations by the FFFE and FFFF that is put on the address bus by the μP and transferred to the PC.

10-4.1
Reset Timing

The μP's response is similar to its response to an interrupt. When the RESET line is pulled down and held, the following conditions exist.

1. The interrupt mask (the I bit in the condition code register) is SET.
2. VMA is LOW.
3. The Data Bus is high-impedance.
4. BA is LOW.
5. R/W is HIGH.
6. The address bus contains FFFE.

Figure 10-2 illustrates the system responses to the RESET line. When the voltage reaches 4.75 V, after the power is turned ON, and the

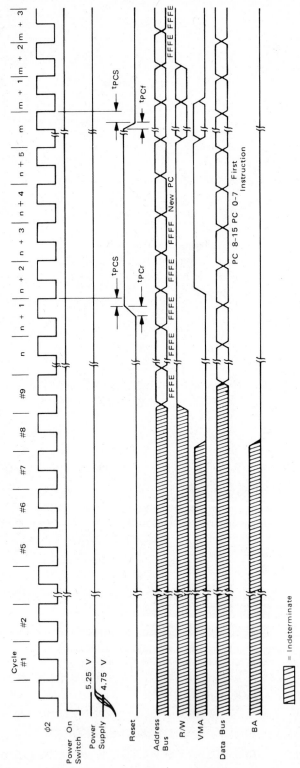

Figure 10-2 Reset timing.

clock oscillator stabilizes, it is necessary to wait at least eight cycles for the μP logic to clear before the program can be started.

During these eight cycles, $\overline{\text{RESET}}$ should be held LOW since VMA can be indeterminate. Any device such as a battery-backed RAM should also be inhibited by $\overline{\text{RESET}}$ since it could experience a false write.

$\overline{\text{RESET}}$ can go high asynchronously with the system clock anytime after the eighth cycle. When the $\overline{\text{RESET}}$ line is allowed to go HIGH, it will fetch the $\overline{\text{RESET}}$ vector and jump to it, as shown in Fig. 10-2.

The $\overline{\text{RESET}}$ line is also connected to any hardware devices that have a hardware reset and need to be initialized, such as the PIA (see Chapter 9). Grounding of the $\overline{\text{RESET}}$ line clears all registers in the PIA, and the restart service routine reprograms the Control and Direction registers before allowing the main program to start. The ACIA has no RESET pin and depends entirely on software initialization. All software flags, or constants in RAM, must also be preset. If the system, includes power-failure sensors and associated service routines, additional steps will be needed in the $\overline{\text{RESET}}$ service routine to provide the automatic restart function.

Example 10-1

The program starts at location 123 (hex). What must be done to assure a proper start?

Solution

Before a program can be started automatically, the $\overline{\text{RESET}}$ vector must be in place. In this case a 01 must be stored in a location that is accessed when FFFE is on the address bus and a 23 must be in the following location.

When a restart is caused (perhaps by a restart timer or by a pushbutton switch), the **6800** fetches the vector in two steps by outputting FFFE and then FFFF. When each byte appears on the data bus (01, followed by 23), they are loaded into the Program Counter, and the program starts in the proper place.

This automatic start is only possible if the vector, as well as the main program are in ROM (or EPROM). If a small test program is loaded in RAM, perhaps by hardware switches, it can also be started by entering the restart vector and operating the reset switch. Preferably a μP development system (Chapter 11) will be used and the program can be loaded and entered directly by routines in the ROM monitor program.

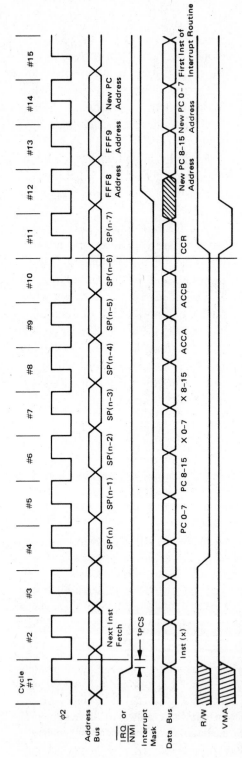

Figure 10-3 Interrupt timing.

10-5
The IRQ Interrupt

The IRQ interrupt is typically used when peripheral devices must communicate with the μP. It is activated by a LOW signal on the $\overline{IRQ}$ pin (pin 4) of the μP. Both the ACIA and PIA have $\overline{IRQ}$ pins that can be connected to the μP when desired. Even though this line is pulled LOW the $\overline{IRQ}$ interrupt does not occur if the I bit of the Condition Code (CC) register is SET. This is known as masking the interrupt. The I bit is SET in one of three ways.

1. By the hardware logic of the μP as a part of the restart procedure.
2. Whenever the μP is interrupted.
3. By an SEI (set interrupt mask) instruction.

Once SET, the I bit can be cleared only by a CLI (clear interrupt mask) instruction. Therefore, if a program is to allow interrupts, it must have a CLI instruction near its beginning.

Example 10-2
What conditions must be satisfied in order for an ACIA or PIA to interrupt the processor?

Solution
All of the following are required.

1. The $\overline{IRQ}$ output of the PIA or ACIA must be connected to the $\overline{IRQ}$ input of the μP.
2. The I flag of the μP must be CLEAR.
3. The control register in the ACIA or PIA must be programmed to enable interrupts.
4. A transition on one of the control lines (CA1 or CA2, for example), of the PIA, or the entry of a word into the ACIA shift register.

10-5.1
Interrupt Action

When an interrupt is initiated, *the instruction in progress is completed before the μP begins its interrupt sequence.* The first step in this sequence is to save the program status by storing the PC, X, A, B, and CC registers on the stack in the order shown in Fig. 10-4. These seven bytes are written into memory starting at the location in the stack pointer (SP) register, which is decremented on each write. When completed, the SP is pointing to the next empty memory location. The condition of the stack before and after accepting an interrupt is shown in Fig. 10-4. The μP next sets the interrupt mask bit (I), which allows the service program to run without being interrupted. After setting the interrupt mask, the μP fetches the address of the interrupt service routine from the IRQ vector location by plac-

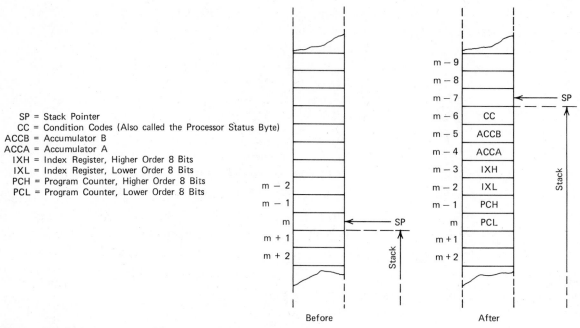

SP = Stack Pointer
CC = Condition Codes (Also called the Processor Status Byte)
ACCB = Accumulator B
ACCA = Accumulator A
IXH = Index Register, Higher Order 8 Bits
IXL = Index Register, Lower Order 8 Bits
PCH = Program Counter, Higher Order 8 Bits
PCL = Program Counter, Lower Order 8 Bits

Figure 10-4 Saving the status of the μP in the stack.

ing FFF8 and FFF9 on the address bus, and inserts it into the PC. The μP then fetches the first instruction of the service routine from the location now designated by the PC.

10-5.2
Nested Interrupts

Normally an interrupt service routine proceeds until it is complete without being interrupted itself, because the I flag is SET. If it is desirable to recognize another IRQ interrupt (or higher priority, for example), before the servicing of the first one is completed, the interrupt mask can be cleared by a CLI instruction at the beginning of the current service routine. This allows "an interrupt of an interrupt," or *nested interrupts*. It is handled in the **6800** by storing another sequence of registers on the stack. Because of the automatic decrementing of the stack pointer by each interrupt, and subsequent incrementing by the RTI instruction when an interrupt is completed (see Sec. 10-5.3), they are serviced in the proper order. Interrupts can be nested to any depth, limited only by the amount of memory available for the stack.

10-5.3
Return from Interrupt (RTI)

The interrupt service routine must end with an RTI (return from interrupt) instruction. The action of the RTI is shown in Fig. 10-5.

RTI, RETURN FROM INTERRUPT:

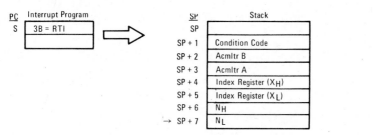

Figure 10-5 Operation of RTI—the return from interrupt instruction.

It reloads all the μP registers with the values they had before the interrupt and, in the process, moves the stack pointer to $SP + 7$, where it was before the interrupt. The RTI essentially consists of seven steps that write the contents of the stack into the μP registers and an additional one that allows the program to resume at the address restored to the PC (which is the same place it was before the interrupt occurred). Note that the RTI restores the CC register as it was previously, and interrupts will or will not be allowed as determined by the I bit.

**10-5.4
Interrupt Initialization**
For successful interrupt handling, the interfaces that communicate with peripheral devices, such as the PIA or ACIA, must be properly initialized at the start of the main program.

Example 10-3

Show how to program a system to use the A side of the PIA for inputs (from a keyboard, for example) and the B side for outputs (to a printer, perhaps). Use the IRQ line to interrupt the processor and indicate how the proper interrupt service routine is selected to input or output a character.

Solution

This program is an initialization or restart routine. It is executed whenever the RESET signal is activated either by the RESTART hardware, which automatically pulls down and releases the RST pin of the μP when power is applied to the system, or by a start pushbutton. Assuming that the PIA RESET pin is connected to the RESET line also (as it should be), all I/O lines are initialized as inputs and interrupts are disabled because all registers are cleared. The initialization program shown in Fig. 10-6, sets the registers, as required. Note that the PIA Control Word is the same for both sides. Bit 2 of Control Register A (CRA2), when set, latches the A side

INTERRUPTS AND DIRECT MEMORY ACCESSES

```
          ADDR  DATA   LABEL    MNEMONIC           COMMENTS

          1000  86 27  RESET  LDA A #%00100111   GET THE CONTROL WORD
          1002  B7 2001       STA A $2001        STORE CW IN CRA
          1005  70 2002       COM   $2002        SET B SIDE FOR OUTPUT
          1008  B7 2003       STA A $2003        STORE CW IN CRB
                              ETC
```

Figure 10-6 Initialization part of RESET service routine for Example 10-3.

Direction Register with the I/O lines selected as inputs, and bit 2 of CRB latches the B side lines as outputs. This latter occurs because the COM instruction inverted the 00 it found in the B Direction Register to FF (all 1s), before bit 2 was SET.

In the Control Register, the CA1 and CB1 lines are programmed to interrupt on positive-going transitions (bits 1 and 0 are 11), and are connected to external circuitry such that the keyboard produces a positive pulse whenever a key is pressed, and the printer provides a similar pulse when it has finished outputting a character. With control registers CRA and CRB set as shown, these actions cause the PIA to interrupt the μP.

Bits 5, 4, and 3 are 100 and, as described in Sec. 9-6, this programs the PIA to use the CA2 and CB2 lines to control the external device by taking the line LOW whenever the software READs or WRITEs the Data Registers. The WRITE to the B Data register takes CB2 LOW, which informs the printer that the PIA has new data for it. (The CA2 line is not needed since the character goes away when the key is released.) The READ or WRITE also clears the associated interrupt request.

10-5.5
Polling

In a system that allows several devices to interrupt, interrupt handling can be implemented by using *software polling*. In response to an interrupt, the polling routine starts by querying each device's interrupt status bit to determine which one interrupted the μP. A flowchart of the polling sequence for Example 10-3 is shown in Fig. 10-7, and the corresponding program is shown in Fig. 10-8. With this interrupt routine, the contents of the PIA's A side Control/Status Register are loaded into the A accumulator by the first instruction of the program shown in Fig. 10-8 and tested by the following BPL (branch-if-plus) instruction, to see if status bit 7 of CRA is SET. If it is, an interrupt has occurred and, since the resulting word is a negative number, the program falls through to the *input character* handling routine. If bit 7 is not SET, the word is positive and the BPL instruction branches to the POLL2 routine at address 120. If bit 7 of CRB (address 2003) is SET, the *output* interrupt has occurred, the BPL (2A) instruction at location 123 does not branch, and the *output character* handling routine is entered. Each of these character handling routines ends with an RTI instruction. They serve to return the program from the interrupt sequence and the main program resumes.

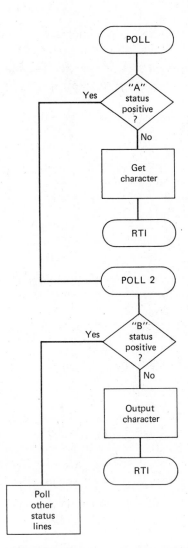

Figure 10-7 Polling sequence flowchart.

ADDR	DATA	LABEL	MNEMONICS	COMMENTS
100	B6 2001	POLL	LDA A $2001	GET "A" STATUS
103	2A 1D		BPL POLL2	BRANCH IF + TO POLL2
		*	INPUT CHARACTER ROUTINE	
...	B6 2000		LDA A $2000	GET DATA
...	XX		ETC	
11F	3B		RTI	RETURN FROM INTERRUPT
		*		
120	B6 2003	POLL2	LDA A $2003	GET "B" STATUS
123	2A 1D		BPL POLL3	BRANCH IF + TO OTHERS
		*	OUTPUT CHARACTER ROUTINE (PRINT)	
...	B7 2002		STA A $2002	OUTPUT DATA
...	XX		ETC	
...	3B		RTI	
			END	RETURN FROM INTERRUPT

Figure 10-8 Polling program for
Example 10-3

10-5.6
Writing Interrupt Service Routines

In response to an interrupt, a routine must be written to service the interrupt. The polling sequence of Sec. 10-5.5 could be part of the *interrupt service routine*. The main program must also be written to allow or prevent interrupts at the proper time, as Example 10-4b shows.

Example 10-4

Each time an event occurs (a switch being thrown or a person entering a room, for example) the time of this event must be recorded in three consecutive locations in memory in the following format:

HH   MM   SS

Where HH are two decimal digits (in one memory location) that represent the hour of the event, MM represents the time of the event in minutes, and SS represents the time of the event in seconds.

Assume the event interrupts the μP. Describe the routine required to service this event:

a. If a real-time clock, such as shown in Fig. 9-10 is available.
b. If a time clock is not available.

Solution[1]

For either case, an area in memory must be set aside to hold the time data, and a pointer to this area should also be stored at a given location in memory. The starting address of the interrupt routine is written into FFF8 and FFF9 and the program branches to it when the interrupt occurs.

a. With a real time clock available, the interrupt routine does the following:

1. Loads the pointer into X.
2. Reads the PIAs and stores seconds, minutes, and hours in memory (incrementing the pointer each time).
3. Stores the incremented pointer back in memory to await the next interrupt.
4. Returns from interrupt.

Note that we are not concerned about the fact that X has been used by the interrupt routine. It is restored to the value it had before the interrupt by the RTI instruction.

---

[1]Part b of this example was run as a laboratory exercise at R.I.T. A debounced switch was connected to a PIA, and each switch throw became an event.

b. If a real-time hardware clock is not available, the main program can generate a one second timing loop (see Example 9-15). This timing loop must control three locations in memory that contain the real time equivalent of seconds, minutes, and hours. When the timing loop expires, the program must:

1. Increment the seconds location.
2. DAA (to keep it in BCD)
3. If seconds = 60, clear seconds and increment minutes location.
4. DAA
5. If minutes = 60, clear minutes and increment hours.
6. DAA
7. If hours = 24, clear hours.

The main program is shown in the flowchart of Fig. 10-9. When an interrupt occurs the main program stops and the interrupt routine loads the real time from memory and stores it in the list area. The list pointer is incremented and the interrupt routine terminates with an RTI. (See Sec. 10-10.3 for a similar program.)

One subtle point remains. If the main program is interrupted while it is incrementing the time, it may be interrupted when it has just finished incrementing the seconds but has not yet incremented the minutes. If the interrupt routine stores the time, the minutes and seconds will not match. Note that numbers like 4A could also be stored in the list if the interrupt occurs between the increment and the DAA instructions.

To prevent these possibilities, one can use an SEI to mask interrupts before the incrementing part of the routine and then clear the interrupt flag to permit interrupts when returning to the timing loop, as shown in Fig. 10-9.

10-6
Nonmaskable Interrupt

A nonmaskable interrupt (NMI) is initiated by placing a LOW level on the NMI pin (pin 6) of the **6800**. When an NMI occurs, the program counter is loaded with the vector accessed by FFFC and FFFD. This causes the μP to jump to the start of the NMI service routine.

As its name implies, the NMI is not affected by the I bit of the CCR and an interrupt occurs whenever the NMI pin is pulled LOW. Consequently, NMI functions as a *very high priority interrupt*. It is usually reserved for events like a power failure in' the μP, or in a peripheral, which could be catastrophic if the μP did not recognize them and take immediate action.

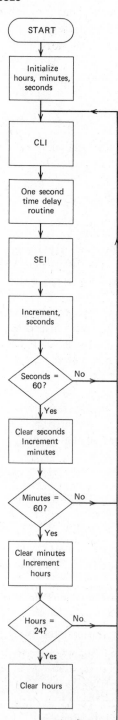

Figure 10-9 Flowchart for the timing routine for Example 10-4b.

Example 10-5

Assume a system like Fig. 10-10 is being used as a part of a financial terminal where transactions involving customer bank accounts are being handled, and the information must be preserved in the event of a power failure. Describe the interrupt service routines required.

Solution

Since it is necessary in this type of system to save all calculations and status, a nonvolatile RAM is needed with a *Powerfail* detector, as shown in Fig. 10-10.

The function of the battery is to act as an auxilliary source of energy for the RAM, so the RAM will not lose information when the main power fails.

When a power failure occurs, the NMI line is pulled down by the powerfail logic, the main program is interrupted at the end of the current instruction, and the registers are stored in the stack. (The power supply will take many milliseconds before the voltage is too LOW to operate the system, and this routine only takes microseconds.) The vector for the powerfail routine is fetched and the processor starts its execution. This routine's main function is to save, in nonvolatile memory, all relevant information such as the contents of PIA and ACIA registers. The stack should also be

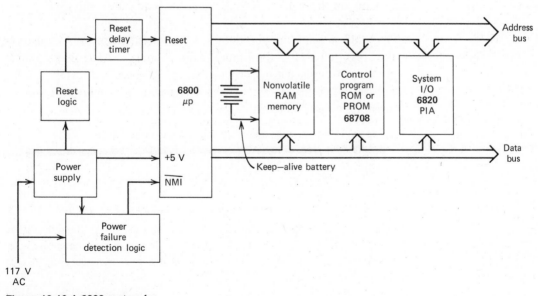

Figure 10-10 A **6800** system for automatic recovery from a power failure.

in nonvolatile memory. The program should then use a PIA to pull down the HALT line and wait until the power fails.

Figure 10-10 also includes the circuitry necessary to resume operation when the power comes on again. The box labeled ''Reset Logic'' must decide when the voltage is normal and it then initiates a RESET pulse. The RESET routine fetched by the RESET vector must not only reconfigure the PIAs and the ACIAs, for example, but must reload all interim products or data into the appropriate registers (the RTI restores the μP registers). The program then resumes from the address restored to the PC register without loss of any vital data.

10-7
The Software Interrupt (SWI)

An interrupt activated by an instruction is available in the **6800** and serves several interesting purposes. One use is as an aid in debugging systems, but it can be used for error indications or other uses. The SWI instruction, when encountered in a program, causes the registers to be put away on the stack and a vector to be fetched, just as for other interrupts. The vector for SWI is located at the address that responds to FFFA and FFFB. Monitor programs such as found in the MEK-6800-D2 kit (see Sec. 11-7) use an SWI to store the register contents on the stack where they can be read out to the user.

10-7.1
The WAI Instruction

The **6800** μP also incorporates a Wait-for-Interrupt (WAI) instruction. Figure 10-11 is the timing diagram for a WAI. It is similar to an interrupt sequence but provides a way to speed the response to an interrupt. In Fig. 10-11, a WAI instruction has been executed in preparation for an interrupt.

1. The WAI instruction initiates the interrupt sequence one cycle after it is decoded. It stores the seven bytes of μP register contents in the stack.
2. After cycle 9, the μP goes into a metamorphic state by placing the address, data, and R/W lines in their high-impedance mode with VMA held LOW and BA HIGH.
3. It remains this way until an interrupt (IRQ or NMI) occurs.
4. In the fourth cycle following the interrupt line transition, the appropriate vector is fetched and the service routine is started during the sixth cycle.
5. The interrupt mask bit (I) of the CC register must be clear if an IRQ is expected; otherwise the system will hang up indefinitely.
6. When the interrupt does occur, it is processed more quickly since the registers have already been moved to the stack (6 cycles are required until the service routine starts instead of 14).

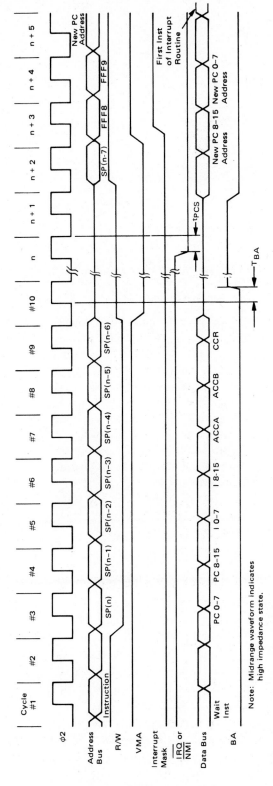

Figure 10-11 WAI (wait) instruction timing.

Example 10-6

What does the following program accomplish?

(a) Main Program

Addr	Label	Mnemonic	Comments
0FFE		. . .	
0FFF		. . .	
1000		SWI	Go to SWI service routine.
1001		LDA B #3	Resume program by loading B with 3, etc.
		. . .	

(b) SWI service routine

Addr	Label	Mnemonics	Comments
2000	SWISRV	INS	Increment stack pointer.
2001		LDA A $40	Load A direct.
2003		PSH A	Put A on stack.
2004		RTI	Return to main program.

The main program encounters a SWI instruction that places the contents of the registers in the stack and then branches to the SWI service routine. The INS instruction increments the stack pointer so that it points to the Condition Code byte rather than the highest vacant stack location. The A accumulator is then loaded and pushed on the stack, causing the contents of memory location 40 to overwrite the contents of the CCR, as stored in the stack. The PSH A instruction also restores the stack pointer to the value it had after the SWI. The RTI now causes the seven bytes following the stack pointer to be restored to the μP registers. At the end of the program, everything is exactly as it was when the program started, except that the CCR has been replaced by the contents of location 40.

There are easier ways to change the contents of the CCR, such as using the TAP instruction, but this program has been presented to demonstrate the operation of the SWI and RTI instructions.

10-8 The 6828 Priority Interrupt Controller (PIC)

In Sec. 9-5 we stated that all normal interrupts are frequently connected together to the one IRQ pin, and a polling routine is used to identify the interrupting device. For a system requiring higher speeds, the **6828** *priority interrupt controller* (PIC) is available. It generates a *modified address vector to point to the correct service routine* in response to prioritized interrupt lines. This hardware device is faster than the software polling routines it replaces. The block diagram and function table for the PIC are shown in Figs. 10-12a and 10-12b. Eight devices that are capable of interrupting can be connected to the designated lines ($\overline{IN0}$ through $\overline{IN7}$). When any device interrupts, by pulling one of these lines LOW, the IRQ line goes

LOW and the vector addresses are translated by the PIC as explained in Example 10-7, to fetch the start location of the proper interrupt service routine.

The use of the PIC in a system is shown in Fig. 10-13. The PIC is enabled by NANDing together the address lines required to address the top memory chip in the system and connecting the NAND gate output to $\overline{CS0}$ of the PIC. Note that the A1 through A4 lines of the highest memory are connected to the Z outputs of the PIC, rather than directly to the address bus. When the PIC is enabled, it transforms the address as shown in the truth table of Fig. 10-12b. This effectively creates *eight new vector addresses* (located from FFE8 to FFF6). *Each vector address points to the start of the service routine for one of the interrupting devices.*

If several devices interrupt at once, the PIC determines their priority. The device having the highest priority is connected to $\overline{IN7}$. The interrupt lines from the various external devices are connected in the order of importance. Priority is usually determined by how much time is available to respond to an interrupt before any data is lost. For example, A floppy disk that puts out data at 32 kilobytes/second needs to be serviced much more quickly than a TTY that takes 100 ms per character.

The user can also set a mask in the PIC. If SET, devices with lower priority than the mask cannot interrupt until the mask is cleared. This allows the user to determine which devices may interrupt at any point in the program.

Example 10-7

A device's interrupt line is connected to $\overline{IN5}$ (pin 9) of the PIC. What happens when the device interrupts?

Solution

If the PIC mask allows this device to interrupt, it brings $\overline{IRQ}$ LOW. If the I bit of the CC register is cleared (unmasked), the μP system responds by placing FFF8 on the address bus. This enables the PIC that translates bits A4, A3, A2, and A1 from 1100 to 1001, respectively, since $\overline{IN5}$ is LOW, as shown in Fig. 10-12c. The Z outputs place an address of FFF2 on the lines of the highest ROM. (Note that bit 0 is not changed by the PIC and thus selects the odd or even byte of the vectors.) On the next cycle, FFF9 is converted to FFF3 by the PIC. Thus the interrupt vector is fetched from FFF2 and FFF3 to initiate the service routine for this device.

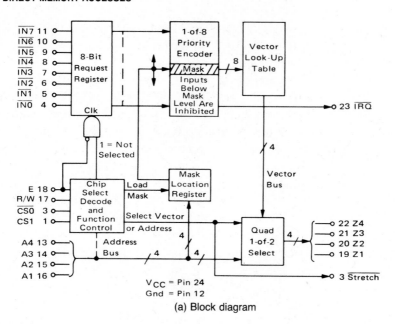

(a) Block diagram

		Output When Selected				Equivalent to Bits 1-4 of B0, B1 . . . , B15	Address ROM Bytes
Active Input		**Z4**	**Z3**	**Z2**	**Z1**	**Hex Address**	**Contain Address of:**
Highest	IN7	1	0	1	1	F F F 6 or 7	Priority 7 Routine
	IN6	1	0	1	0	F F F 4 or 5	Priority 6 Routine
	IN5	1	0	0	1	F F F 2 or 3	Priority 5 Routine
	IN4	1	0	0	0	F F F 0 or 1	Priority 4 Routine
	IN3	0	1	1	1	F F E E or F	Priority 3 Routine
	IN2	0	1	1	0	F F E C or D	Priority 2 Routine
	IN1	0	1	0	1	F F E A or B	Priority 1 Routine
Lowest	IN0	0	1	0	0	F F E 8 or 9	Priority 0 Routine
	None	1	1	0	0	F F F 8 or 9	Default Routine*

*Default routine is the response to interrupt requests not generated by a prioritized input. The default routine may contain polling routines or may be an address in a loop for an interrupt driven system.

(b) Address vector for each interrupt line

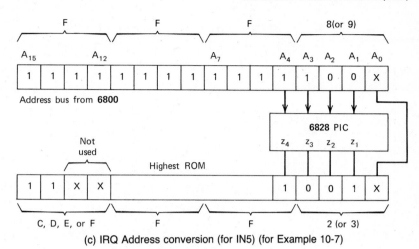

Figure 10-12 The **6828** Priority Interrupt Controller (PIC).

(c) IRQ Address conversion (for IN5) (for Example 10-7)

| 10-9 Direct Memory Access (DMA) | We have previously discussed input/output techniques using the PIA, ACIA, or SSDA LSI packages. These functional components, when properly programmed, make data communications between the μP data bus and the outside world possible. Using them results in a maximum transfer rate of approximately 40,000 bytes/second. |

Another method of I/O, commonly used in all computers, is Direct Memory Access (DMA); this is a way to connect an input or output device directly to the memory of a μC via the address and data buses. It allows the transfer of data without using the **6800**. To cause a DMA, an external device must be capable of taking over the bus and supplying the proper memory address and R/W signal. It must also have a data register to receive data on a READ memory cycle and provide data on a WRITE cycle. DMA is made possible in the **6800** system by the availability of internal logic, which is associated with several pins on the μP itself. These pins are TSC, DBE, HALT, and BA.

There are two basic methods of DMA in a **6800** system (see Fig. 10-14 and 10-16). One way involves stopping the clock, activating the TSC and DBE lines (to disconnect the bus lines), and using external logic to communicate with the system memories or I/O. The other method utilizes the $\overline{\text{HALT}}$ line to stop the processor.

10-9.1 DMA Using the $\overline{\text{HALT}}$ Line

The simplest way to execute a DMA is to have the peripheral device place a LOW on the $\overline{\text{HALT}}$ line, and wait for the μP to respond by setting Bus Available (BA) HIGH. At this time the address bus, data

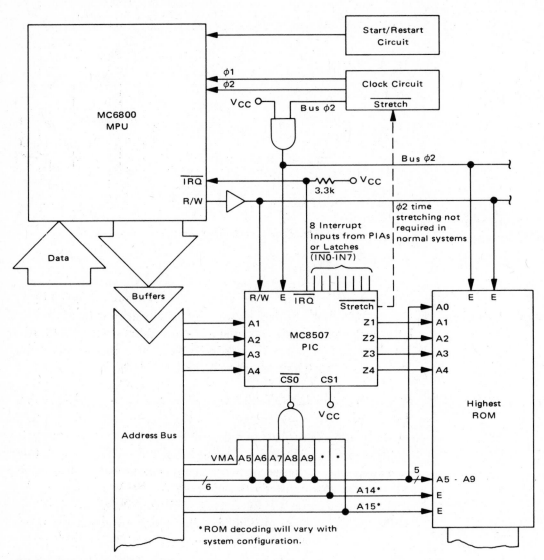

Figure 10-13 Typical **6800** system configuration (with **6828**).

bus, and R/W line from the μP are in their HIGH impedance state and VMA is forced LOW. The peripheral device can now access memory (VMA must be gated). When it completes its memory cycle, it releases the $\overline{\text{HALT}}$ line and the μP resumes normal operation.

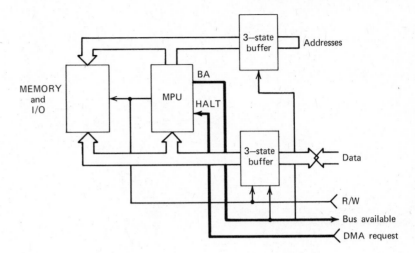

Figure 10-14 Direct Memory Access
(DMA) using HALT line.

Example 10-8

Design a circuit to allow DMA via the $\overline{\text{HALT}}$ line. Assume VMA is used
along with the addresses to enable the systems memories.

Solution

One solution is shown in Fig. 10-15. The peripheral makes a memory
request by setting the DMA REQUEST FF. This causes the $\overline{\text{HALT}}$ line to
go LOW via the NOR gate. When BA is received, the DMA one-shot fires,
which does four things:

1. It clears the DMA REQUEST FF.
2. It enables the 3-state drivers from the peripheral to control the address
   and data buses and the R/W line.
3. It holds the $\overline{\text{HALT}}$ line LOW.
4. It forces VMA HIGH, enabling the memory.

The pulse time of the one-shot should be equal to the cycle time of the
memory, plus any gate delays. When the one-shot pulse expires, the
$\overline{\text{HALT}}$ line returns HIGH and the μP resumes normal operation.

VMA is controlled by the VMA OR gate. In normal operation the DMA
one-shot is CLEAR, effectively connecting the μP's VMA to the memory.
During DMA, VMA is LOW, but the DMA one-shot forces VMA to the
memory HIGH so that a valid memory request can be made.

**10-9.2
DMA Using TSC and DBE**
When using the $\overline{\text{HALT}}$ line, the DMA must await the completion of
the current instruction, as signaled by a 1 on BA, before it can take
control. This could mean a delay of 2 to 13 μs. When high-speed

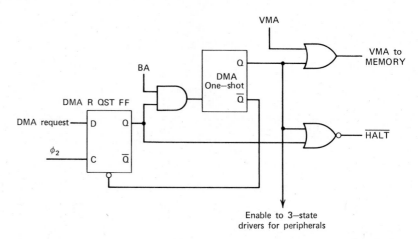

Figure 10-15 Making a DMA Request using the HALT line.

data transfers are required where the data must be handled instantly (within one or two microseconds), the TSC method of Fig. 10-16 is required. In order to appreciate the timing problems involved, the TSC signal characteristics must be carefully analyzed. Figure 10-17 shows the three-state control (TSC) timing requirements.

When the Three-State Control (TSC) line is HIGH, the address Bus and the R/W line are placed in a high impedance state by the **6800**. VMA and BA are forced LOW whenever TSC is HIGH to prevent false reads or writes on any device enabled by VMA. While TSC is held HIGH, the Ø1 and Ø2 clocks must be held HIGH and LOW, respectively, in order to delay program execution. Figure 10-17 shows that the transitions of TSC must occur within 40 ns after the positive-going edge of Ø1. VMA is forced LOW and the address and R/W line will reach the high impedance state after a delay of 700 ns (max) for the **MC6800B**, or 270 ns for the **MC68A00**. This is identified as t_{TSD}. (See data sheets on **MC68A00** and **MC68B00** in Reference Sec. 10-13. In this example, the Data Bus is also in the high impedance state while Ø2 is being held low since DBE is connected to Ø2. A DMA transfer can now occur on cycles #3 and #4. When TSC is returned low, the μPs address and R/W line drivers are reconnected to the bus. Because it is too late in cycle #5 to access memory, this cycle is dead and used for synchronization. Program execution resumes in cycle #6.

The **6800** uses dynamic logic and must be clocked periodically. Since TSC stops the clocks, it must not hold up the μP for more than 9.5 μs, or data may be lost. This is PW_{OHmax} in Fig. 10-17. (9.5 μs is allowed for **MC68A00** and **MC68B00** μPs.)

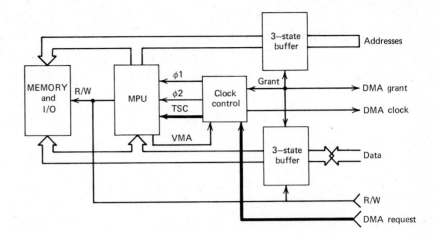

Figure 10-16 Direct Memory Access
(DMA) using TSC line.

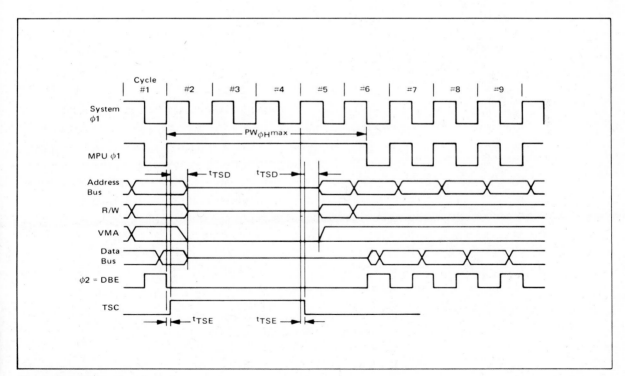

Figure 10-17 Three-State Control
(TSC) timing.

10-9.3
DMA by Cycle Stealing

A very nice way to perform DMAs is to use the **MC6875** as the clock generator (see Sec. 8-7). This IC provides nonoverlapping Ø1 and Ø2 clock signals and internal logic allows for stretching these clocks with Ø2 HIGH for slow memories, or with Ø1 HIGH for DMA or dynamic memory refresh. If properly interconnected with the μPs TSC as shown in Fig. 10-16, a DMA cycle stealing circuit can be built.

10-9.4
The 6844 Direct Memory Access
Controller (DMAC)

When DMA is used in a system, it usually requires the addition of considerable hardware to keep track of memory addresses and byte counts, as well as other logic requirements during a DMA transfer. A new **6800** family component was introduced in October, 1977 called the **MC6844**, Direct Memory Access Controller (DMAC). It contains all the registers and logic to provide for 4 DMA channels. It is intended to be used with a clock generator such as the **6875** and eliminates the need for most, if not all, additional TTL ICs. This device uses either the μP HALT and/or TSC function of the μP to provide three modes of operation:

1. HALT burst
2. HALT steal
3. TSC steal

The HALT burst mode uses the HALT line to stop the μP and then performs a data transfer of any number of bytes. In the HALT steal mode, the μP is restarted after each byte of data is transferred.

In the TSC steal mode, the TSC line is used to control the system buses, hence, only one byte can be transferred in 1 DMA cycle because of the limitation on the stretching of Ø1 (4.5 μsec maximum for the **MC6800B**). Maximum data transfer rates are 1 megabyte for the HALT burst mode, 70 K byte for the HALT steal mode and 250 K byte for the TSC steal mode (with a 1 MHz clock). This component is a 40-pin device with 16 registers that are accessible to the user. They are divided as follows:

4-Status Registers (8 bits each)
4-Channel Control Registers (8 bits)
4-Byte-count Registers (16 bits)
4-Address Registers (16 bits)

Bit 3 of the Channel Control Register determines whether the address registers are incremented or decremented after each DMA transfer.

**10-10
Interrupts and Timing—
the 6840 Programmable
Timer Module**

Many programs that interface the μP to external devices require precise timing for their information interchange. Software timing loops and hardware real-time clocks have been discussed in Chapter 9 and an interrupt and timing problem has been presented in Sec. 10-5.6.

The difficulty with software timing loops (used, for example, in Example 10-4) is that they completely tie up the computer program and do not allow the computer to do useful work. One simple solution to this problem is to construct a clock that interrupts the computer periodically (once a second, for example). The computer can respond to this interrupt by incrementing a set of memory locations that maintain clock time, as in Example 10-4, and then return to its main program. In this way, the main program has real time always available, but does not have the task of updating the clock. Another solution is to use a special *counter-timer* IC to keep track of time intervals and interrupt the μC periodically. Most μC manufacturers also produce such an IC.

**10-10.1
The 6840 Programmable Timer
Module (PTM)**

The **6800** family of components includes the **MC6840** NMOS programmable 28-pin IC timer. It consists of three independent software controllable 16-bit timing counters. They can be used to cause system interrupts or produce output signals based on internal (Ø2) or external clock signals. Figure 10-18 is the block diagram of the **MC6840** programmable timer module (PTM). The following tasks are possible:

1. Interval and frequency measurement
2. Event counting
3. Square wave generation
4. Delay signals
5. Single pulse of controlled duration
6. Pulse width modulation.

Figure 10-18 shows that each section has an external clock input ($\overline{C}$), a gate input ($\overline{G}$), and an output ($\overline{O}$). Each section can be used alone or cascaded (by connecting the output of one section to the input of the next) for longer time delays. When used for timing (or delays), the cascading produces longer intervals, which can be measured in days, or even years.

The three counter/timers are essentially identical except for a divide-by-8 prescaler that is part of timer 3 and a minor difference in the function of bit 0 of the control words.

Each timer has three 8-bit registers associated with it, a control register, and two 8-bit counter/latches. The PTM has a total of 15

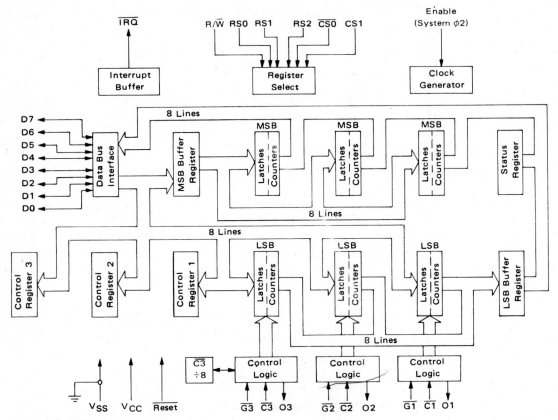

Figure 10-18 6840 Programmable
Timer Module (PTM) block diagram.

registers including a common STATUS register. These are addressed
as shown in Table 10-1.

Table 10-1
The 6840 PTM Register Selection

Register Select Inputs			Operations	
RS2	RS1	RS0	R/$\overline{\text{W}}$ = 0	R/$\overline{\text{W}}$ = 1
0	0	0	CR20 = 0 Write Control Register #3	No Operation
			CR20 = 1 Write Control Register #1	
0	0	1	Write Control Register #2	Read Status Register
0	1	0	Write MSB Buffer Register	Read Timer #1 Counter
0	1	1	Write Timer #1 Latches	Read LSB Buffer Register
1	0	0	Write MSB Buffer Register	Read Timer #2 Counter
1	0	1	Write Timer #2 Latches	Read LSB Buffer Register
1	1	0	Write MSB Buffer Register	Read Timer #3 Counter
1	1	1	Write Timer #3 Latches	Read LSB Buffer Register

The bits of the control register select the following:

1. Modes
2. Choices of internal (Ø2) or external clock
3. IRQ (masked or unmasked)
4. Output (enabled or not)
5. Square wave or variable duty cycle

Because of all these options, many applications for this device are possible.

10-10.2
Application of the 6840 PTM

The **6840** programmable timer module (PTM) can be used to provide delays and while the clock is counting, thousands or even millions of other instructions can be executed. The interrupt features of the **6840** and **6800** family (e.g., **6801** and **6809**) make this possible since the time-out function can be serviced at precisely the right time while only briefly interrupting other tasks.

Example 10-9

Provide a real-time clock function for use in a control system to display the time each second, or to provide scheduling for industrial processes. Use the **6840** PTM and show its connections as well as programs to provide these functions.

Solution

Figure 10-19 shows a block diagram of the **6840** with two counter sections connected in cascade to provide an interrupt (IRQ) every second. The assembly language routine needed to initialize the timers for this application is shown in Fig. 10-20. Since counter 2 is programmed to use the internal phase 2 (Ø2) enable signal, generated by the system crystal clock, the only connection required is to its output (O2—pin 3). This output is connected to the clock input (C1—pin 28) of counter 1. Counter 1 is programmed for external clocking to use that signal and provides the interrupt when it times out.

Note that 32 bits are available (two 16-bit sections) for this application. The one-second time delay is provided by writing the proper counts into the counters. The product of these is equal to the frequency of the Ø2 clocks.

Selecting the control words for the **6840** is very complex and no attempt will be made to cover all possible uses. This and the following example will help the reader to understand several of the continuous mode timing functions, however. The purpose of each bit in the control registers can be determined from a study of Fig. 10-21. The formatting of the two control words used in this example is

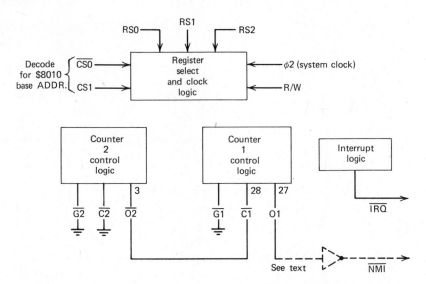

Figure 10-19 Connections for **6840** PTM as a 1 second timer.

shown in Fig. 10-22. As explained in the **6840** Data Sheet (see References in Sec. 10-13), the control registers and latches must be written in the prescribed sequence, as shown in the routine of Fig. 10-20. Register 2 bit 0 must be set to 1 so that Control Register 1 is addressable (at 8010). Register 1 bit 0 when reset to 0 *enables* all counters. The counters are initialized in some cases by writing to the latches as determined by bit 4. It is interesting to note how the values in the MSB and LSB registers determine the timers count. When a number is entered and decrementing starts, it will count down to 0 (called timeout) and, in the continuous mode, will reinitialize (reload the latches) and continue. This requires 1 cycle, so the number used must be 1 less than required. Another factor in this application is that the clock input (C1) of counter 1 only decrements after it sees a negative-going edge of the output signal from counter 2. This means that counter 2 must timeout twice before each counter 1 decrement occurs. It does not matter which value is placed in the first counter, but in the program of Fig. 10-20, the larger number was

```
00042                   *
00043 F039 86 83   INIT  LDA A  #$83      SET OUTPUT,INT CLK, SLCT REG
00044 F03B B7 8011       STA A  $8011     WRITE TO REG 2
00045 F03E CE 270F       LDX    #10000-1
00046 F041 FF 8014       STX    $8014     SET COUNT FOR CTR 2
00047 F044 CE 0031 INIT1 LDX    #50-1     "    "    "    "  1
00048 F047 FF 8012       STX    $8012
00049 F04A 86 40         LDA A  #$40
00050 F04C B7 8010       STA A  $8010     UNMASK IRQ AND ENABLE CTRS
00051 F04F 39            RTS
00052                   *
```

Figure 10-20 Initialization routine for PTM in example 10-9.

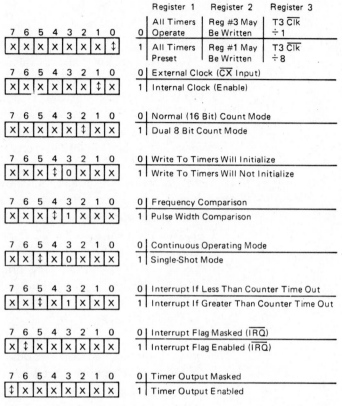

	Register 1	Register 2	Register 3
0	All Timers Operate	Reg #3 May Be Written	T3 C̄l̄k̄ ÷ 1
1	All Timers Preset	Reg #1 May Be Written	T3 C̄l̄k̄ ÷ 8

7 6 5 4 3 2 1 0
X X X X X X X ↕

0	External Clock (C̄X̄ Input)
1	Internal Clock (Enable)

7 6 5 4 3 2 1 0
X X X X X X ↕ X

0	Normal (16 Bit) Count Mode
1	Dual 8 Bit Count Mode

7 6 5 4 3 2 1 0
X X X X X ↕ X X

0	Write To Timers Will Initialize
1	Write To Timers Will Not Initialize

7 6 5 4 3 2 1 0
X X X ↕ 0 X X X

0	Frequency Comparison
1	Pulse Width Comparison

7 6 5 4 3 2 1 0
X X X ↕ 1 X X X

0	Continuous Operating Mode
1	Single-Shot Mode

7 6 5 4 3 2 1 0
X X ↕ X 0 X X X

0	Interrupt If Less Than Counter Time Out
1	Interrupt If Greater Than Counter Time Out

7 6 5 4 3 2 1 0
X X ↕ X 1 X X X

0	Interrupt Flag Masked (I̅R̅Q̅)
1	Interrupt Flag Enabled (I̅R̅Q̅)

7 6 5 4 3 2 1 0
X ↕ X X X X X X

0	Timer Output Masked
1	Timer Output Enabled

7 6 5 4 3 2 1 0
↕ X X X X X X X

Figure 10-21 6840 control register programming.

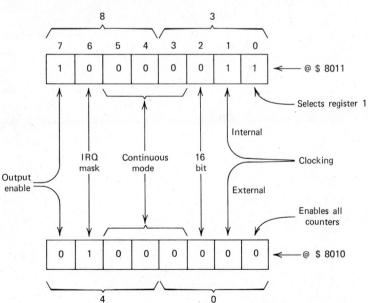

Figure 10-22 Control word formats.

used in counter 2. Since a "divide by" 1,000,000 is required with a 1 MHz crystal clock, it was elected to divide by 10,000 and then by 100. Hex 2710 is equal to 10,000. This was decreased by 1 to 270F. As explained above, this actually requires two timeouts and results in a negative-going signal on C1 every 20 milliseconds (Fig. 10-23). Therefore, instead of dividing by 100 ($64) in counter 1, a ratio of 50 (− 1) is used, which the assembler converts to $31. This results in an interrupt every second and has crystal-controlled accuracy just as is available in "quartz" watches.

10-10.3
Real-Time-Display

In the previous example, we showed how an interrupt is generated every second and it is now necessary to show how to use it. One way is shown in the complete program of Fig. 10-24.

This program includes an *Interrupt Service Routine* that updates and *prints* the time every second. The program is started at the "SET" Routine, which first prints "HH:MM:SS AM", and then provides for the correct time to be entered. It then initializes the timer. Note also that the IRQ vector is written into location FFF8 and 9. This was done in this case since the program was debugged in a development system that used RAM for the **6800** vectors. In a typical system, the vector would be in ROM and the initialization might be a subroutine called by the main initialization routine.

Another typical application might not require a continuous display and the updated time values would be used to schedule events. The time would be kept in memory and updated every second or sooner if desired. This scheduler program would scan a table each update time and implement scheduled tasks.

It will be found in using the continuous mode to generate maskable interrupts (IRQs) that two problems exist. First, it is necessary to reinitialize counter 1 each timeout to clear the $\overline{IRQ}$ signal, (see line 53 in Fig. 10-24). Second, it may not be possible to use other interrupts or to mask the IRQ without destroying the accuracy of the time (i.e., interrupts will be missed).

It therefore is advisable to use the NMI instead of IRQ for this

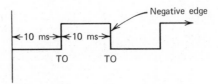

Figure 10-23 Output of counter 2.

```
PAGE  001   TIMER

00001                         NAM    TIMER
00002                *  PROGRAM TO DISPLAY TIME ON CRT
00003                *  4/16/79 WCWRAY
00004                *  USES 6840 PTM TO DIVIDE DOWN THE 1 MHZ CLK
00005                *  INTERRUPT (IRQ) USED ON COUNTER 1
00006                *  O2 CONNECTED TO C1
00007                *  DIVIDES BY 1,000,000
00008                *
00009        E14B    PDATA1 EQU   $E14B    MINIBUG 3 OUTPUT STRING
00010        E126    OUTCH  EQU   $E126    MINIBUG 3 OUTPUT CHAR
00011        E133    INCH   EQU   $E133    INPUT CHARACTER ROUTINE
00012                *
00013 F000            ORG   $F000
00014                 OPT   O
00015                *
00016 F000 OD    MSG1  FCB   $D
00017 F001 48          FCC   /HH:MM:SS AM/
      F002 48
      F003 3A
      F004 4D
      F005 4D
      F006 3A
      F007 53
      F008 53
      F009 20
      F00A 41
      F00B 4D
00018 F00C 04          FCB   4
00019                *
00020                *  PROGRAM TO DISPLAY TIME
00021                *
00022 F00D 8E A07F SET  LDS   #$A07F    SET STACK
00023 F010 CE F000      LDX   #MSG1     GET MSG1 POINTER
00024 F013 BD E14B      JSR   PDATA1    PRINT PROMPT
00025 F016 CE F001      LDX   #MSG1+1   GET MSG POINTER
00026 F019 86 OD        LDA A #$D       GET CR
00027 F01B BD E126      JSR   OUTCH     PRINT IT
00028 F01E BD E133 LOOP1 JSR  INCH      GET TIME TO SET
00029 F021 A7 00        STA A 0,X       PUT IN LINE
00030 F023 8C F00A      CPX   #MSG1+$A  DONE?
00031 F026 27 03        BEQ   CONF      YES- START COUNTING
00032 F028 08           INX             NO- GET NEXT NUMBER
00033 F029 20 F3        BRA   LOOP1
00034                *
00035 F02B CE F050 CONF  LDX  #IRQ      GET SUBROUTINE ADDR
00036 F02E FF FFF8      STX   $FFF8     PUT VECTOR IN RAM
00037 F031 BD F039      JSR   INIT      INITIALIZE PTM
00038 F034 01           NOP
00039 F035 OE           CLI             ALLOW INTERRUPT
00040 F036 01    LOOP2  NOP
00041 F037 20 FD        BRA   LOOP2     LOCK UP TIL INTRRUPT
00042                *
00043 F039 86 83  INIT  LDA A #$83      SET OUTPUT,INT CLK, SLCT REG
00044 F03B B7 8011      STA A $8011     WRITE TO REG 2
```

Figure 10-24 Display time program for **6840** PTM.

timer function. Since the NMI is not normally connected to the **6840**, and the output goes HIGH instead of LOW, it is necessary to install an inverter and connect it to the counter 1 output pin (O1–pin 27) as shown in the dotted circuitry of Fig. 10-19. This requires only minor revisions to the program. One is a change to the control word

---

```
PAGE  002   TIMER


00045 F03E CE 270F       LDX    #10000-1
00046 F041 FF 8014       STX    $8014       SET COUNT FOR CTR 2
00047 F044 CE 0031 INIT1 LDX    #50-1        "    "    "    "  1
00048 F047 FF 8012       STX    $8012
00049 F04A 86 40         LDA A  #$40
00050 F04C B7 8010       STA A  $8010       UNMASK IRQ AND ENABLE CTRS
00051 F04F 39            RTS
0X52                   *
00053 F050 8D F2   IRQ   BSR    INIT1       RELEASE IRQ LINE
00054 F052 CE F000       LDX    #MSG1       GET POINTER TO TIME STORAGE
00055 F055 86 39         LDA A  #$39        SETUP UPDATE INFO
00056 F057 C6 30         LDA B  #$30
00057 F059 A1 08         CMP A  8,X         REACHED 9 ?
00058 F05B 27 04         BEQ    SKIP2       YES - UPDATE
00059 F05D 6C 08         INC    8,X         NO - INCREMENT SECONDS
00060 F05F 20 5E         BRA    DISPLY      PRINT EVERYTHING
00061 F061 E7 08   SKIP2 STA B  8,X         CLR LSB
00062 F063 86 35         LDA A  #$35        GET MAX 10S DIGIT
00063 F065 A1 07         CMP A  7,X         REACHED 59 YET ?
00064 F067 27 04         BEQ    SKIP3       YES- UPDATE
00065 F069 6C 07         INC    7,X         NO - INCREMENT AGAIN
00066 F06B 20 52         BRA    DISPLY      PRINT RESULTS
00067 F06D E7 07   SKIP3 STA B  7,X         CLR MSB SECONDS
00068 F06F 86 39         LDA A  #$39        LAST NO. ?
00069 F071 A1 05         CMP A  5,X         REACHED 9 ?
00070 F073 27 04         BEQ    SKIP4       YES - UPDATE
00071 F075 6C 05         INC    5,X         NO - INCR LSB MIN.
00072 F077 20 46         BRA    DISPLY      PRINT RESULTS
00073 F079 E7 05   SKIP4 STA B  5,X         CLR LSB MINUITS
00074 F07B 86 35         LDA A  #$35        59 MINUITS ?
00075 F07D A1 04         CMP A  4,X
00076 F07F 27 04         BEQ    SKIP5       YES - UPDATE
00077 F081 6C 04         INC    4,X         NO - INCR
00078 F083 20 3A         BRA    DISPLY      PRINT IT
00079 F085 E7 04   SKIP5 STA B  4,X         CLR DIGIT
00080 F087 86 32         LDA A  #$32        LOOK FOR 2 OF 12
00081 F089 C6 39         LDA B  #$39
00082 F08B A1 02         CMP A  2,X         12 ?
00083 F08D 27 08         BEQ    SKIP6       YES - POSSIBLY
00084 F08F E1 02         CMP B  2,X         NO - 9 YET ?
00085 F091 27 24         BEQ    SKIP8       YES - UPDATE
00086 F093 6C 02         INC    2,X         NO - INCR
00087 F095 20 28         BRA    DISPLY      PRINT IT
00088 F097 86 31   SKIP6 LDA A  #$31
00089 F099 A1 01         CMP A  1,X         LOOK FOR 1 OF 12
00090 F09B 27 04         BEQ    SKIP7       YES - UPDATE
00091 F09D 6C 02         INC    2,X         NO - INCR
00092 F09F 20 1E         BRA    DISPLY      PRINT IT
00093 F0A1 A7 02   SKIP7 STA A  2,X         CHNG 11 TO 12
00094 F0A3 86 20         LDA A  #$20        GET SPACE
00095 F0A5 A7 01         STA A  1,X         CLR MSB HOUR
00096 F0A7 A6 0A         LDA A  $A,X
00097 F0A9 81 41         CMP A  #'A         IS IT AM?
00098 F0AB 26 04         BNE    AM          YES- PRINT IT
```

Fig. 10-24 (cont.)

of counter 1 ($80 instead of $40). It is not necessary to reinitialize the counter in this case since it just generates a 1 cycle per second square wave. This means that the NMI remains LOW for ½ second. Since it is an edge-sensitive signal instead of level-sensitive however, as in the case of IRQ, it will not interfere with other interrupts. Since NMI is "nonmaskable" and has highest priority, nothing will inter-

```
---
```

```
PAGE   003   TIMER


00099 FOAD 86 50        LDA A  #'P      NO- SWITCH TO PM
00100 FOAF 20 02        BRA    AM1
00101 FOB1 86 41   AM   LDA A  #'A
00102 FOB3 A7 OA   AM1  STA A  $A,X     UPDATE DISPLAY
00103 FOB5 20 08        BRA    DISPLY   PRINT IT
00104 FOB7 86 30  SKIP8 LDA A  #$30
00105 FOB9 C6 31        LDA B  #$31
00106 FOBB A7 02        STA A  2,X      9 TO 10
00107 FOBD E7 01        STA B  1,X      "
00108 FOBF CE FOOO DISPLY LDX  #MSG1
00109 FOC2 BD E14B      JSR    PDATA1   PRINT NEW DISPLAY
00110 FOC5 3B           RTI             RETURN FROM INTERRUPT
00111              *
00112                   END
```

Fig. 10-24 (cont.)   TOTAL ERRORS 00000

fere with the accuracy of the time. When IRQ is used, an interrupt occurs after each timeout while NMI will only respond on negative-going edges. Therefore the count value of one of the latches must be cut in half as compared to the interrupt (IRQ) implementation in order to get the 1 second update.

10-11 Multiprocessing

In some computer systems, the amount of work required exceeds the capabilities of a single μP. Since μPs are small and inexpensive, it is often feasible to add a second μP to share the load. The use of two or more processors, working semi-independently on parts of the same task, is called *multiprocessing*. If the two (or more) μPs can be connected so that they can perform separate tasks at the same time, then a real increase in throughput can occur. In such a system, it is necessary to transfer data between subsystems, but this may take only a small percentage of the time.

One of the most time-consuming tasks in μC systems is in the input or output of data. If the data is being printed by a teletypewriter, for example, it takes 100 ms for each character. A processor can run 100,000 cycles (30000 to 50000 instructions) during that time. Consequently, if the external printer device requires any degree of intelligence to perform its task, it could be practical to provide a dedicated μP for that purpose.

10-11.1 Master-Slave Systems

In many multiprocessing systems, one μP is designated as the *master*. It controls the operation of the system and apportions tasks between itself and the other μPs, which are called *slaves*. In the system described above, for example, the master μP might sense that there is data for the printer located in a certain area of memory. It can then inform the slave μP that controls the printer, and it becomes the slave's task to send this information to the printer while the master μP does other things. Typically, master and slave μPs share common memory. Because of coordination problems, programming master-slave or other multiprocessor systems is often complex.

One clever method that allows the computers to share memory is shown in Fig. 10-25. The two μPs run on opposite clocks (Ø1 of μP1 is Ø2 of μP2). Since each μP only enables memory on its own Ø2, they never access memory at the same time. This system requires fast memory. Normal speed memories require a priority circuit to avoid conflicts when both μPs need to access the same memory location.

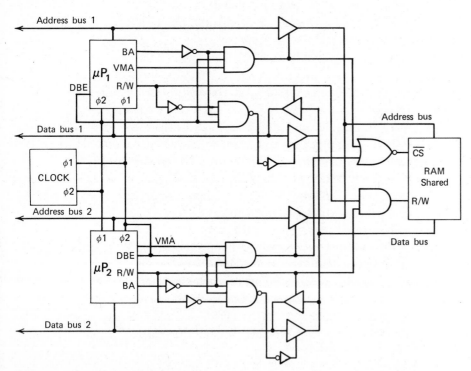

Figure 10-25 Multiprocessing using transposed clock phases and shared memory.

**10-12
Summary**

In this chapter we described the response of the μP system to an interrupt (storing the registers on the stack, executing the interrupt service routine, restoring the registers, and resuming the main program). Each type of interrupt that occurs in the **6800** system and the events associated with it are discussed and, in addition, I/O transfers using DMA and multiprocessing are explained. These features facilitate communication between the **6800** system and its peripherals.

**10-13
References**

Ferguson, Bob, *The 6800 Handles Clock Stealing, Digital Design,* October, 1978. M6800 Microcomputer System Design Data. Motorola Semiconductor Products, Inc., Box 20912, Phoenix, Arizona 85036.

Greenfield, Joseph D., *Practical Digital Design Using ICs,* Wiley, New York, 1977.

Motorola, *M6800 Microprocessor Applications Manual,* Motorola Semiconductor Products, Inc., (9703) March, 1975. Box 20912, Phoenix, Arizona 85036.

Motorola, *M6800 Microcomputer System Design Data,* Motorola Semiconductor Products, Inc., (9701-9) November, 1976. Box 20912, Phoenix, Arizona 85036.

**10-14
Glossary**

ACIA, PIA, SSDA 6800 family interface components. They are Asynchronous Communications Interface Adapter, Peripheral Interface Adapter, and Serial Synchronous Data Adapter.

DMA Direct Memory Access. Communication between memory and a device without using the processor.

Interrupt A signal to the μP that causes it to halt execution of its normal program and branch to a service routine for the interrupting device.

IRQ, NMI, RST, TSC, DBE Pins (or signals) on the **6800** μP. They are Interrupt Request, Non-Maskable Interrupt, Reset, Three-State-Control, and Data Bus Enable.

Multiprocessing Using two or more processors to work on related but separate tasks simultaneously.

Nesting An interrupt within an interrupt, or a subroutine within a subroutine.

PC Program Counter (register) of the μP. Controls the sequencing of the program.

PIC Priority Interrupt Controller (**6828**). An IC that controls the priority of interrupting devices.

Polling The act of querying each peripheral device to determine if it interrupted the μP's program in process.

RTI, SWI, WAI, SEI, CLI Mnemonics for **6800** instructions that involve interrupts. They are Return-from-Interrupt, Software Interrupt, Wait-for-Interrupt, Set-Interrupt Mask, and Clear-Interrupt-Mask.

Volatile Memory Memory that loses its contents when power is removed.

10-15 Problems

10-1 If a system responds to both high and low priority interrupts, why must each low priority service routine have a CLI instruction near its beginning?

10-2 If a system uses a 1 μs clock, what is the minimum time that reset may be held low?

10-3 A program consists of a main program and an interrupt routine. In addition, a portion of the main program must not be interrupted. Describe where each SEI and CLI instruction should go in the program.

10-4 A low priority device interrupts the program and is then interrupted by a high priority device. With reference to the original stack pointer, what are the contents of SP-3? Of SP-12?

10-5 A μP system stores an equivalent of real time as a 16-bit number in locations 100 and 101. The μP is interrupted once a second by a one second clock, and must increment the 16-bit number in those locations. Assume it is interrupted by a positive transition on a line.
   a. Bring the line in via the PIA and write the initialization routine for the PIA.
   b. Write the interrupt service routine.
   c. Design the hardware to cause the interrupt. Assume the 1 second pulse is achieved by counting down the 60 cycle from the AC power lines.

10-6 A μP uses an ACIA. Whenever the Transmit Data Register is empty, it interrupts. If the address of the Transmit Data Register is 8011, write an interrupt routine to transfer the contents of location 40 to the ACIA.

10-7 An ACIA whose data register is at 8011 interrupts each time it receives a character. The first character received should go into location 0100, the second into 0101, etc. When location 01FF is used, the program should execute an SWI and go to 0500. Write the interrupt routine.

10-8 A device is connected to IN2 of the PIC. Where are its interrupt vectors?

10-9 List the parts a controller must have if it is to make DMAs using the TSC line. Describe the function of each part.

10-10 Explain the following statement: "Whenever the flags are stored by an IRQ interrupt, the I flag is always 0.'' Is this statement true for NMI and SWI interrupts?

10-11 An ACIA is to communicate with a TTY as in Example 9-23. If the system is to use interrupts rather than polling, write the interrupt service routine.

After attempting to solve the problems, try to answer the self-evaluation questions in Sec. 10-2. If any of them seem unclear, review the appropriate sections of the chapter to find the answers.

Chapter 11   Monitor Systems

11.1
Instructional Objectives

This chapter describes the use of monitor systems and μP development systems to help the user debug his hardware and software. It starts with very simple debugging tools and progresses to the EXORcisor, a powerful testing system developed specifically for the **6800**.

After reading this chapter, the reader should be able to:

1. Display and change memory locations using a monitor system.
2. Display and change registers using a monitor system.
3. Insert breakpoints into a program.
4. Punch a paper tape and load it using a monitor program.
5. Determine trade-offs of time saved and ease of use to cost of Microcomputer Development Systems (MDS).
6. List the steps necessary in the development of a μP system using the EXORcisor.

11-2
Self-Evaluation Questions

Watch for the answers to the following questions as you read the chapter. They should help you understand the material presented.

1. Which μP signals should be monitored during debugging?
2. Why are 3-state drivers necessary in switch and light monitoring systems?
3. What are the advantages of ROM monitor systems?
4. What are pseudoregisters? What is their function?
5. What advantages does a Microcomputer Development System have over a MIKBUG or MINIBUG monitor system?
6. How does a logic analyzer help test μC systems?

11-3
μP System Design

Some designers build the hardware first; but without software, problems occur in verifying that all parts are operational and wired correctly. Other engineers will want to try out various software system concepts before the circuits are designed. To do this, an operating test system is required. The program under development must be loaded into the memory of an operating microcomputer and tested. This requires the use of special test programs in the system. These monitoring ROM programs are an indispensable part of system development. They allow the user's program to be executed at full speed, or stopped at any point, and stepped one instruction at a time while examining the progress. Changes or corrections are then easily made.

Any method of monitoring must include at least the ability to:

1. Read memory at any location.
2. Write into memory at any location.
3. Set the starting address into the PC.
4. Single step a program (run the program one instruction at a time) and observe its effect.
5. Run the program at full speed.

In the evolution of the µP, monitor systems have become more complex and more powerful. This chapter describes the features and capabilities of the most common monitoring methods.

**11-3.1
Rudimentary Monitor Systems**

The most elementary system to monitor a µP is to use switches (to control the address and other buses) and lights (typically LEDs) to indicate the state of the lines of these buses. Additional switches are needed to control the Read/Write line, set the starting address into the PC (RESET), and to single-step, or run the program. Typically, 3-state buffers are used to transfer control of the memory from the µP to the switches when reading or writing new data. A typical switch control circuit is shown in Fig. 11-1. When the WRITE switch is depressed a short pulse pulls down the R/W line (0 = Write), and the 3-state gates transfer the data from the data switches to memory at the address set on the address switches. When not activated, these gates present a high impedance to the lines and do not interfere with normal µP operation.

The 3-state receivers are left connected to the lines at all times to drive the LED displays since the inputs are always high impedance and do not overload the buses.

If this data and address display circuit is combined with the single-step circuit described in Sec. 8-7.2, the functions of a *basic* µP development system are provided. After manually entering the machine codes of the program using the switches, it can be executed one instruction at a time, by using the STEP switch or by being started in the run mode. These techniques have severe limitations that will be described, but they are still used by some experimenters or hobbyists.

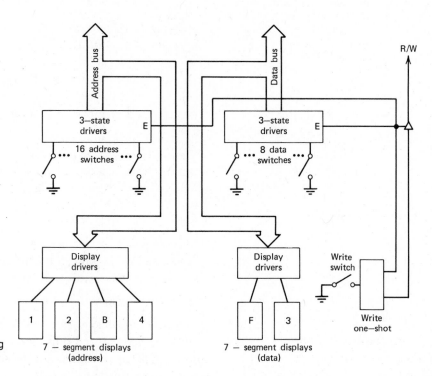

Figure 11-1 Light and switch monitoring of a μP.

<table>
<tr><td>11-3.2
Keyboards and 7-Segment Displays</td><td>Considerable improvement can be made in this HALT and STEP method of system monitoring by replacing the individual address and data switches with hexidecimally coded switches. These deal with four lines at a time and provide easier interpretation. A commercial version of this circuitry is known as the **MEX68SA** System Analyzer and is described in Sec. 11-11.8. Still greater improvement can be made by using a Keyboard as will be explained in the following sections.</td></tr>
<tr><td>11-3.3
Introduction to Monitor Programs</td><td>Total reliance on lights and switches to read or enter a program has two major drawbacks.</td></tr>
</table>

1. It is slow and tedious, especially for long programs. It is unwise to use this method for programs longer than about 100 lines because stepping through the program and keeping track of everything will be very difficult.

2. The main shortcoming is that the μP registers cannot be directly observed. (By use of the SWI, as will be explained, the register contents are available on the stack.)

For these reasons, a technique has evolved using the μP itself, with a special debug program, to fetch dynamically the register information and display it after the system runs each instruction of the user program in real time. Such debug program routines are normally combined with several utility functions into a ROM-based *monitor* or control program. When this ROM is included in a system, the functions desired are usually selected by means of commands on an operator terminal such as a CRT or TTY. In this way the operator can access instructions or segments of programs and, in effect, communicate in machine language (hexadecimal), with the system under development. The use of ROM monitor programs and a software approach to debugging is faster and cheaper than switches and lights. Instead of stepping through the program and observing the data and address buses, it is more informative to run the program one instruction at a time (or a subroutine at a time) while observing all registers after each step.

11-4
The MIKBUG Program

One of the first and simplest monitor programs provided for users of the **6800** family components is called MIKBUG. This ROM IC (part number **MCM6830L8**) is available from most parts distributers. Since this program was introduced before the ACIA was produced, it uses a PIA for input/output of the serial data needed for the operator terminal. The serial-to-parallel, and parallel-to-serial conversions are done in software. The functions provided by MIKBUG allow the user to:

1. Start a **6800** system (RESET).
2. Load memory, manually or from tape.
3. Display or change memory.
4. Display or change μP register contents.
5. Go to user's program.
6. Print or punch memory contents.
7. Service user's interrupt request (IRQ).
8. Service user's Non-Maskable interrupt (NMI).

These functions are described in the following paragraphs and are also explained in the Engineering Note EN100 referenced in Sec. 11-15. They enable a designer to test his software and other hardware that may be included on the same μP bus.

11-4.1
RESTART

If the MIKBUG ROM is installed in a **6800** system with the necessary scratch pad RAM at A000 and a PIA, as shown in Fig. 3.3 of EN100, it provides all of the above features, including the ability to start the system when the RESTART button is pressed. This MIKBUG ROM resides at E000 to E1FF but because address lines

A10 to A12 are not used, the ROM also appears at FE00 to FFFF and, in particular, the top 8 bytes respond to the **6800** vectors at FFF8 to FFFF. MIKBUG has a RESET routine that initializes the system and starts it running in the MIKBUG control loop. This action can be initiated by the RESTART button on a system, as was done on the **MEC6800** Evaluation Module I and the **MEK6800-D1** Kits that used this monitor program, or automatically when power is applied, if suitable start-up circuitry is provided. When the program starts, it does a CR, a LF, prints an * on the terminal, and waits for an input command.

11-4.2
Memory Display/Change

Any location in memory can be displayed and, if it is RAM, changed by the "M" command. This can be done after a program is loaded from tape or in order to manually enter a program. An M, followed by an address, will print the contents of that location. Note that four address digits must be entered even if they are zeros. The data can be left as is, or changed by appropriate actions. Figure 11-2 shows a typical memory display/change function. If, after opening the location and observing the 8-bit data (two hex characters), it is desired to change it, a space is entered followed by the new hex data to be stored. The system stores it and prints the next address and its contents. It then waits for the next operator response. In Fig. 11-2, the contents (20) of location 0000 was changed to FF, and the contents of 0001 (FE), was changed to AA. This displayed the contents of location 0002, which is 02. Since the operator did not want to change that and, instead, wanted to see the next byte, he entered a period (any character except a space). The contents of location 0003 were then displayed (which happened to be another 02). This time the memory display/change was terminated by entering a space followed by a nonhex character (a period). The program then returned to the MIKBUG command loop as indicated by the asterisk (*) on the last line.

11-4.3
Display μP Registers

To verify and monitor software performance, it is often necessary to display the contents of the μP registers. This display can be initiated by inserting an SWI instruction, (using the M command) into

Figure 11-2 Display/change memory function.

```
*M 0000
*0000 20  FF
*0001 FE  AA
*0002 02  .
*0003 02  .
*
```

any OP code location and then running the program. The program is started using the G command (see Sec. 11-4.4) and runs until the SWI is encountered. The Software Interrupt service routine (which is entered after the μP registers are stored on the stack) moves the register contents to locations in the MIKBUG RAM called *pseudo-registers,* and then prints them on the terminal. The SWI (OP code 3F) is usually inserted in a program at some point after a small portion of the program has been completed (i.e., after the initialization of a PIA, or perhaps after the buffer has been cleared). If the GO command is then used, the program will run up to the SWI instruction, print the contents of the μP registers, and return to MIKBUG. This is called *inserting a breakpoint* and effectively stops execution of the user's program at a specific point. Breakpoints are frequently used to troubleshoot μP systems.

The Register Display command (R) allows the user to examine the contents of the registers. MIKBUG's response to an R command is shown on the top line of Fig. 11-3a where we see:

*R F0 00 22 0100 0B12 A042

The * means MIKBUG is *ready for a command* and the R, typed by the operator, means *display registers.* Note that R is the only

```
 R F0 00 22 0100 0B12 A042
*M 0162
*0162 BD   3F
*0163 DO   .              NOTE: All operator entries are under-
*M A048                   lined. CRs, LFs, and *s are
*A048 0B   00             done by MIKBUG. The first entry
*A049 12   20             is a space in some cases.
*A04A FC   .
*R F0 00 22 0100 0020 A042
*G F0 00 0F 0100 0162 006A
*M 0162
*0162 3F   BD
*0163 DO   .
*
```

                                    (a)

```
0020 86 0F     START  LDA A #$F
0022 B7 0FC5          STA A $FC5
0025 7E 015F          JMP $15F

.... .. ....
015F 8E 0071          LDS #$71   SET STACK
0162 BD D08F          JSR $D08F  INIT SCREEN
0164 BD ....          etc.
```

Figure 11-3 Example of breakpoint operation in MIKBUG.
(a) Implementation of breakpoint
(b) Segment of user's program

                                    (b)

character on the line typed by the operator. The contents of the registers are then displayed in the following order along the line.: CC, B, A, X, PC, SP. In this example the condition codes are F0, B contains 00, and so on.

Example 11-1

A segment of a user program is shown in Fig. 11-3b. It starts at location 20. Describe the methods used with the MIKBUG program to perform breakpoint testing of this user's program and system. Location 0162 is chosen for the first SWI location.

Solution

Figure 11-3a shows the MIKBUG commands and responses.

a. Assuming the user's program has been loaded into memory and MIKBUG has just returned to the control loop as indicated by the printing of an asterisk (*), the R command is typed. This displays the values stored in the pseudoregister locations as a result of the last SWI software interrupt.

b. On lines 2, 3, and 4, location 162 is examined and changed from the JSR (OP code BD) to a SWI (3F).

c. The next step is to set the starting address. The PC pseudoregister locations A048 and A049 are changed to 00 and 20, respectively. (These locations are identified in EN100; see references in Sec. 11-15.)

d. On line 9, the register contents are reexamined and it will be seen that only the PC has changed.

e. The user program is then run by entering the G command. As shown, the registers are redisplayed on the same line, with no perceptible delay since the execution up to the SWI is at full clock speed. Note that accumulator A has changed from 22 to 0F as a result of the first line of the user program, and the SP is now at 006A, which is correct because it was set to 71 by the instruction at location 015F and then decremented 7 times by the SWI.

The SWI is then replaced by the JSR at location 162 to restore the user program for further testing, as shown in the last lines of Fig. 11-3a.

Obviously, if the program did not reach this SWI, it is because some instruction in that segment of the program did not perform as expected. The operator may then have to reload the program (since it probably ran away, and may have altered some of the instructions). He would then go back to the last SWI that was properly executed. A SWI can be placed after each instruction (instead of after the next group of instructions) and the program reentered until the faulty or omitted instruction is found.

11-4.4
GO to User's Program

The G command is used to run a program. It will pick up the contents of the pseudoregisters and insert them into the μP registers. The program then starts running from the address restored to the PC. Therefore, to start the program at a selected location, it is only necessary to enter the desired address into locations A048 and A049 using the M command, prior to using the G command. This is also shown in Fig. 11-3a where the address is changed to 0020 (and verified by typing R).

11-4.5
Servicing User's NMI and IRQ

Many systems under development need the ability to test response to any of the interrupts. Some way must be provided to change the vectors to accommodate different user's programs. This is done in MIKBUG by two routines that get their ultimate service routine addresses from entries in the scratch RAM. Locations A000 and A001 are used to store the user's IRQ vector, if needed. A006 and A007 are used for the NMI vector. When the correct addresses are entered in these locations and an interrupt occurs, the μP will jump to the service routines indirectly. The IRQ mask bit must not be set for it to respond.

11-4.6
Punch/Print Memory Contents

The MIKBUG program is designed to be used with an operator terminal similar to a TTY and equipped with tape features as described in Chapters 7 and 9 (see also Sec. 11-6). When the program has been corrected (by using M to change the instructions) or is patched as suggested in Sec. 6-7.1 to eliminate errors, it can be saved on tape by using the Punch (P) command. This will cause a tape to be produced on the TTY or TI cassette terminal, and will simultaneously print the object codes. A DC2 ASCII control character (see Appendix E) is sent to the terminal by MIKBUG to turn the punch ON or start the record function. The tape will begin at the address that has previously been stored in locations A002 and A003 (Fig. 11-4) using the M command and will continue until it reaches the address in A004 and A005. A DC4 will then stop the tape. This

```
*M A002
*A002 F7  00
*A003 6E  01
*A004 99  00
*A005 EE  10
*A006 A0  .
*P
S1130001AA0202020202020202020202020202AC79
*
```

Figure 11-4 Typical print/punch contents of memory function.

example shows only a one line program that is not typical. The tape will be formatted as described in Table 7-3, except that an S0 or an S9 line will not be generated by the MIKBUG routine.

11-4.7
LOAD Function

MIKBUG also includes a loader function that reads an object tape and puts the machine code into a RAM. This tape can be one that has previously been punched out (or recorded) by the P command described above, or it can be an output tape from an assembler program (see Sec. 7-9). The program must have been properly assembled with the ORG statement set to an address that matches the RAM module location. The load routine starts the tape reader (by outputting a DC1), and stores the bytes received from the tape in those locations specified in the tape format. The loader also verifies the checksum to detect any errors in reading or a faulty tape. The loader routine turns OFF the reader and returns to the MIKBUG control loop when it reads the S9 termination line (tapes made by MIKBUG do not have an S9 at the end and therefore will not exit from the loader routine). An S9 can be typed or the RESET button can be used to return to the command loop. To LOAD a tape, it is placed in the reader and an "L" is typed, to start it. Figure 11-5 shows the operator entries and the resultant printout on the terminal. When the S9 is detected the program returns to the MIKBUG command loop and prints *. Checksum errors will print a "?", followed by an * on the next line.

11-5
Other Monitor Systems

Several more powerful and more complex monitor ROMs are now in use. Table 11-1 shows some of them and identifies the functions included in these ROMs. The most significant of the features of these new ROMs are discussed below.

MINIBUG III is perhaps one of the most important of the improved ROMs because it adds commands (functions 10, 11, 12) to:

Trace user program (run-one-instruction).
Continue after a breakpoint.
Insert, display, or remove breakpoints.

```
*L  S11300207CC466047EE0FF00F631FED57C54DC60BF
S1030000FC
S9
*
```

Figure 11-5 LOAD function of MIKBUG.

MINIBUG III contains a breakpoint table. It is only necessary to enter the "V" command to enter addresses to the table, and the "U" command to remove a breakpoint. Up to eight breakpoints can be stored at one time and the "B" command will print their addresses.

An "N" command provides for running one instruction at a time. This should not be confused with HALT and STEP operation since running-one-instruction actually runs the user program instruction at full clock speed and simply does an SWI afterward to return to the display register routine and print out the registers. The processor is not HALTED at any time. The T command (followed by a number) will trace that many instructions and print the registers after each one.

MINIBUG III was first made available in a module known as Evaluation Module 2. It provides the ACIA circuitry, and a crystal clock for control of the µP as well as of the communications baud rate. It includes everything to make up a system but the power supply. Only 256 bytes of user memory is provided, however.

Micromodule 1A is a currently produced stand-alone **6800** system and is shown in Fig. 11-6. It has 1K of RAM and room for four 1K EROMs. A MICRObug monitor ROM with functions identical to MINIBUG III is available as shown in Table 11-1. A serial port for a standard operator terminal uses an ACIA and RS232C.

11-6
Terminal Requirements for
ROM Monitor Programs

All of the ROMs described so far have been written to work with a keyboard/printer terminal equivalent to the ASR33 teletypewriter (TTY). This terminal was the standard of the industry for many years, and its 20 mA interface and ASCII protocol is still used in most communications and computer equipment. Recently, however, several alternative terminals have been offered. One, is the TI 733ASR, which has equivalent functions including program storage on tape. (Cassettes are used in place of paper tape.) It is quieter and faster but is about three times as expensive as a TTY.

Users (particularly the hobbyists), have tried to find less expensive ways to test and operate µP systems. One popular device, with several manufacturers providing kits, is the CRT terminal. It is also possible to buy video interface modules, in kit form, to work with a commercial TV set.

When a CRT terminal is used in place of a tape terminal, loading and/or saving programs are no longer possible because of the lack

Table 11-1
ROMS Available for 6800 Showing Functions Included

Function	MEX68EX12 Exbug 1.2 (F000-FBFF)	MCM6830L7 Minibug (FE00-FEFF)	MCM6830L7 Mikbug (E000-E1FF)	MEC68MIN2 Minibug II (E000-E3FF)	MEC68MIN3 Minibug III (E000-E3FF)	In MEK6800D2 Kit Only J-Bug (E000-E3FF)	M68MM08A Microbug (FC00-FFFF)
1. Load programs	X	X	X	X	X	X	X
2. Print contents of memory (ASCII)	X		X	X	X		X
3. Punch contents of memory on tape (ASCII)	X		X	X	X		X
4. Display and/or change memory	X	X	X	X	X	X	X
5. Display and/or change MPU registers	X	X	X	X	X	X	X
6. Reinitialize	X	X	X	X	X	X	X
7. Run user program	X	X	X	X	X	X	X
8. Use coresident assembler/editor	X		X	X	X		X
9. Change terminal speed	X			X	X		X
10. Trace user program	X				X		X
11. Continue user program after trace or breakpoint	X				X	X	X
12. Insert, display, and/or remove breakpoints	X				X	X	X
13. Search tape for specific title	X						
14. Verify program loaded into memory	X						
15. Stop on address	X						
16. Calculate offset for relative branches	X					X	
17. Provide scope trigger at selected address	X						

of the tape facility. To overcome this disadvantage, several techniques have been used. One is to use an audio cassette recorder/player and a tone modulating scheme to convert the digital information to audio. One such modulating method is called the *Kansas City Standard,* named after a committee that met there to establish the standard. It makes use of a tone frequency shift method similar to that used in the 103 type modems. A Floppy Disk System can be used with the CRT and is very popular for professional systems. Its

Table 11-1 (Continued)
ROMS Available for 6800 Showing Functions Included

Function	MEX68EX12 Exbug 1.2 (F000-FBFF)	MCM6830L7 Minibug (FE00-FEFF)	MCM6830L7 Mikbug (E000-E1FF)	MEC68MIN2 Minibug II (E000-E3FF)	MEC68MIN3 Minibug III (E000-E3FF)	In MEK6800D2 Kit Only J-Bug (E000-E3FF)	M68MM08A Microbug (FC00-FFFF)
18. Abort from user program	X					X	
19. Disk interface	X						
20. Use macro-assembler	X						
21. Decimal, octal, hex conversions	X						
22. Search for specific bit pattern	X						
23. Trace to specified address	X						
24. Execute specified number of instructions	X						
25. Start user program from autostart	X						
26. 1200 or 2400 Baud TI operation	X						
27. Stop after encountering breakpoint "N" times	X						
28. Punch/load binary formatted tapes				X			
29. Test selected portion of memory				X			
30. Load memory from tape	X				X	X	X
31. Store memory on tape	X				X	X	X
32. Trace one instruction	X				X	X	X
Device marking	SCM44507,8,9	MCM6830L7,8		SCM44506	SCM44503	SCM44520	SCM37501
ACIA or PIA addresses required	FCF4-5	FCF4-5	8004-8007	8008-9	8008-9	8008-9	8408-9
RAM addresses required	FF00-FFFF	FF00-FF7F	A000-A07F	A000-A07F	A000-A07F	A000-A07F	380-3FF

added cost can often be justified by the dramatic improvement in operating speed. An assembler that takes about 25 minutes to load from tape can be loaded in about 5 seconds with the disk system.

11-7
The Motorola D2 Kit

The **MEK-6800-D2** Kit, shown in Fig. 11-7 is another approach to the operator terminal problem. This is a very popular kit used in many schools and colleges. The kit consists of two boards. One contains the μP and the other ICs required to make up the μC system. The second board is a separate keyboard/display module that includes

Figure 11-6 M68MM01A monoboard microcomputer 1A for use with MICROBUG.

a keypad and LED display. The LED display consists of four address and two data digits. Seven segment units capable of displaying hexadecimal characters (0 through F), are used. The keypad has 16 numerical keys (labeled 0 through F) for entry of hexadecimal data, and eight command keys with the following functions:

M—Examine and/or change memory. Entering an address from the keyboard followed by M causes the contents of that location to be displayed in the data LEDs. New data can then be entered via the keypad. Pressing G after an M command causes the contents of the next location to be displayed.

E— Escape (Abort) from operation in process, and wait for the next command.

R—Display μP registers. Typing an R causes the high byte of the PC to appear in the data display. The G key then displays the rest of the registers in the following order PC (LOW), X (HIGH), X (LOW), A, B, CC, SP (HIGH), SP (LOW).

G—Go, following an address entry, starts the execution of a program.

P— Punch (record) data from memory to magnetic tape.

L— Load memory from magnetic tape.

N—Run-one-instruction.

V—Set (and remove) breakpoints.

This module also includes interface circuitry for using a standard audio cassette tape recorder as an off-line magnetic storage medium.

The keyboard/display module is used in conjunction with a monitor program called JBUG (Table 11-1) that is supplied in a **6830** masked programmed ROM. JBUG provides routines for the operator interface through the hex keyboard/display and for the cassette interface. The audio cassette interface has been provided in place of the TTY connection because it is so much less expensive. Unfortunately however, the standard Motorola Assembler/Editor programs can no longer be used.

Function 16 (calculate offset) is a very useful addition since it helps in the installation of patches or software modifications by automatically calculating the 2s complement number for the relative address instructions. The ability to ABORT (function 18) from any function is also an important advantage in several debugging situations.

The Trace as its called in the D2 manual, is basically the same as run-one-instruction described previously but is accomplished in the D2 by means of a hardware counter, rather than by using the SWI instruction. As a result, Trace will work in ROM as well as RAM. Also the Trace can follow an ABORT or breakpoint without the need to reset registers.

Optionally, the keyboard/display module can be replaced with an RS232 or 20 mA interface and a tape equipped terminal. If the ROM is then replaced with MINIBUG 2 or 3, a standard Editor/Assembler tape can be used for program development.

The **MEK-6800-D2** Evaluation Kit II Manual and Application Note AN-771 referenced in Sec. 11-15 explain how to operate the kit and list a number of kit expansion techniques. The kit is an excellent learning tool and can be modified in several ways to do some of the system development tasks but it is not a μP Development System.

Figure 11-7 The MEK6800D2 kit.

11-8
μP System Development and
Testing Instrumentation

Because of the unique problems of designing and debugging μP systems, new concepts in test instrumentation have evolved.

In digital logic design, one is usually concerned with only one or two signals at a time. In the case of a μP, however, changes in the state of the signals occur on 8 data lines, 16 address lines, and several control lines at the same time. Several separate instruments have been created specifically for μP system testing. Most can be separated into two classes: Logic Analyzers and μP Development Systems. Microcomputer Development Systems are primarily used during the early stages of software development, while Logic Analyzers are used when the prototype hardware is first turned ON but will not run for some reason. Some μP Development Systems can do the whole job when equipped with a User System Evaluator (USE) (Sec. 11-11.7), a Systems Analyzer module (see Sec. 11-11.8) and augmented by a good dual channel Cathode Ray Oscilloscope (CRO). Likewise, some Logic Analyzers are versatile enough to be able to perform some software debugging as well. Logic Analyzers are described in Sec. 11-13.

11-8.1

µP Development Systems

The monitor ROM systems previously described all have limitations that make them rather difficult to use. They are not very efficient in finding hardware bugs. They cannot readily incorporate additional hardware to emulate the user's system, which is essential for early development.

To overcome the problems presented by earlier evaluation kits and modules, µP Development Systems have been created. These are similar to the MIKBUG and MINIBUG systems previously described but have more advanced software features for displaying and changing registers, and entering data, as well as special hardware features to aid the designer. Each of the major manufacturers of µPs has introduced such an instrument for their products, and most of them will support several different µP types. Although all µP development systems provide the ability to develop and debug software, not all of them provide a full hardware emulation capability or the ability to evaluate prototype or production hardware.

The Motorola µP Development System is called the EXORciser. The EXORciser is a modularized expandable development system that contains all the common ingredients of a microcomputer, and offers a versatile means to emulate any unique system. The Debug module includes the EXbug monitor or control program that is 3092 bytes long. The features include the User System Evaluator (USE) for testing prototypes. It was originally built around the **6800** family of parts but now also supports the **6801, 6802, 6809, 141000, 3870, 10800,** and **2900** µP components. The EXORciser is shown in Fig. 11-8. It is expensive compared to the monitor systems of Sec. 11-5 but not as expensive as a Logic Analyzer. So much engineering time can be saved by using its many features that it is often economical in the long run. The EXORciser and its EXbug control program are described in the following sections to show how a µP Development System works and how it is used in designing µP systems.

11-9
The EXBUG Program

EXBUG is a program written to control the EXORciser. It is stored in three **6830** ROMs, and contains routines for handling and debugging software. Several of its features also serve to debug the hardware.

Figure 11-8 The EXORciser.

The EXORciser uses a data terminal, such as a TTY, to communicate with the Debug system and with the system under development. All addresses and data are entered via the keyboard, and all status or data displays are printed (or displayed on a CRT) in ASCII-hex characters. Bytes and words are used rather than 1s and 0s. In addition to providing a keyboard and printer, the terminal (if equipped for paper or cassette tape) also provides a means to save the software programs and to load them back into memory, when required. Co-resident Editor/Assembler programs that run in the EXORciser are available for use either with tape terminals or floppy disks. The least expensive way to work with the Editor or Assembler is with a paper tape terminal such as a TTY or a cassette terminal such as a TI 733ASR. Floppy disk systems can be used where greater speed and flexibility are needed.

EXbug enables the user to do the following.

1. Search a tape for a specific file.   SRCH
2. Load the program from tape into RAM.   LOAD
3. Verify that the memory matches the tape.   VERF
4. Punch (record) the contents of memory on tape.   PNCH
5. Print (display) the contents of memory.   PRNT
6. Use MAID (Motorola Active Interface Debug) to test and
   debug both software and hardware.   MAID

The first four commands are not used with floppy disk systems.

11-9.1
MAID

The major debugging routines within EXBUG are in a subroutine called MAID. A list of MAID commands is shown in Table 11-2.

11-9.2
Memory Display/Change

Figure 11-9 shows a typical memory display/change printout as it would appear on a terminal. This figure illustrates how the user can examine the contents of memory locations and change them if necessary. The characters typed by the operator are underlined in Fig. 11-9 for clarity. MAID commands (LF, CR, or ↑), used after each input, are shown bracketed at the right. When the system is turned on, the "EXBUG 1.2" message is printed. The operator then types MAID and receives an *, indicating the system is awaiting another input.

When the operator types a location followed by a / (400 in Fig. 11-9), the contents of that location are displayed. The operator then has four options. He can type:

1. Two hex digits followed by a line feed (the fourth line of Fig. 11-9, for

Table 11-2
MAID Program Control Commands

Maid Command	Description
n/	Display the contents of memory location n and enable the EXORciser to change the contents of this memory location.
LF*	Displays the contents of the next sequential memory location and enables the EXORciser to change the contents of this memory location. (LF—Line Feed character)
↑	Display the contents of the previous sequential memory location and enable the EXORciser to change the contents of this memory location. (↑—up arrow character or SHIFT key and N character)
CR*	Return the displayed contents to memory and accept next command. (CR—Carriage Return character)
n;O	Calculate the address offset (for relative addressing mode instructions).
n;V	Enter a breakpoint at memory location n.
$V	Display the memory location of each breakpoint.
n;P	Continue executing from the selected breakpoint until this breakpoint is encountered n times.
n;U	Remove the breakpoint at memory location n.
;U	Remove all the breakpoints.
n;W	Search for the n bit pattern.
$M	Display the search mask.
;G	Execute the user's program starting at the auto restart memory location.
n;G	Execute user's program starting at memory location n.
$R	Display/change the user's program registers.
;P	Continue executing from the current program counter setting.
;N	Trace one instruction.
N	Trace one instruction.
n;N	Trace n instructions.
$T	Set the trace mode.
;T	Reset the trace mode.
$S	Display and set the stop-on address compare *or* Scope trigger pulse.
;S	Reset the stop-on-address compare *or* Scope trigger pulse.
	Switch S-2 determines which selected.
#n=	Convert the decimal number n to its hexadecimal equivalent.
#$n=	Convert the hexadecimal number n to its decimal equivalent.
#@n=	Convert the octal number n to its hexadecimal equivalent.

*Operator-entered commands that are nonprinting characters.

EXBUG 1.2 <u>MAID</u>
*800/00 <u>12</u>   (LF)
NO CHANGE
*400/01 <u>24</u>   (LF)
0401/89   (LF)
0402/05 <u>23</u>   (LF)
0403/1F   (↑)
0402/23 <u>66</u>   (LF)
0403/1F   (CR)
*

Figure 11-9 Examine or change memory operation.

example). The equivalent data value will be stored into that location of memory. EXbug then types the next address followed by a / and the contents of that location.

2. Only a line feed (LF). EXbug does not change the memory location but proceeds to the next location.

3. An ↑ , which causes EXbug to back up and display the previous location.

4. A carriage return (CR), which causes EXbug to exit from the display/ change command, back to MAID (* printed), to await another command.

This procedure should be contrasted with the Memory display/change methods for MIKBUG (Sec. 11-4.2). It will be seen that EXbug is simpler to use, and allows backing up in memory.

In EXbug, if the operator attempts to change a location where there is no memory or where ROM is used, EXbug prints ''NO CHANGE'' followed by a CR, a LF and an *, to indicate it is ready for the next command. In Fig. 11-9 this occurred when an attempt was made to change location 800.

Example 11-2

What are the contents of locations 400 through 403 after the commands shown in Fig. 11-9 are entered?

Solution

By examining the figure we find:

a. Location 400 was changed from 01 to 24.

b. Location 401 contained an 89 and was not changed.

c. Location 402 was first changed from 05 to 23. Then after examining location 403, the operator returned to 402 (by typing an ↑), and changed its contents from 23 to 66.

d. The contents of 403 (1F) were unchanged.

11-9.3
Register Display/Change

The μP registers can also be changed by means of MAID commands as shown in Fig. 11-10. In the figure the PC was changed from an initial value of 106 to 100, X was changed to 2345, the contents of A were unchanged and B was changed to 44. Note that these changes are actually made on locations in the EXbug RAM called *pseudo-registers*. The μP register values are saved here and reinserted into the μP registers prior to the execution of the next instruction.

EXbug is easier to use than MIKBUG because the registers are identified by letters for ease of use and there is no need to call the memory change routine. The $R command first displays the registers and then permits an easy change by typing new values, or allows bypassing registers by using a LF. The command can be terminated at any time with a CR that is consistently used to end any MAID command. Further simplification occurs because there is no need to enter leadings 0s in any EXBUG command.

11-9.4
Run and Trace Commands

The N command allows the system to run a single instruction and then print the contents of the registers. This is not to be confused with HALT and STEP. The instruction is executed at full clock rate and the program control then returns to EXbug and prints the registers. It does not HALT at any time. The command 5;N will run five instructions, printing the register contents after each instruction. This can be a valuable tool to rapidly see whether each instruction does what the operator expected. The operation of the N command is shown in Fig. 11-11. First, the registers are displayed by using the $R command. The PC is changed to 10 and the index register (X) is changed to 0000 and is followed by a CR, as shown by the underlined entries. The CR always returns control to MAID (∗), and awaits the next command. The command 3;N causes three instructions to be executed. The printout of Fig. 11-11 clearly shows the register contents after each instruction.

```
EXBUG 1.2 MAID
*$R
P-0106 X-4000 A-04 B-00 C-C4 S-FF91
P-0106 100          (LF)
X-4000 2345         (LF)
A-04
(LF)
B-00 44             (CR)
*                   Note: ( ↑ ) does not work
```

Figure 11-10 Examine or change the μP registers.

```
EXBUG 1.2 MAID
*$R
P-001D X-000F A-0F B-00 C-D0 S-0050
P-001D 10     (LF)
X-000F  0     (CR)
*3;N
P-0013 X-0000 A-0F B-00 C-D0 S-0050
P-0015 X-0000 A-00 B-00 C-D4 S-0050
P-0016 X-0000 A-00 B-00 C-D4 S-0050
*$T
END ADDR 001D 17
*10;G
P-0013 X-0000 A-00 B-00 CD0 S-0050
P-0015 X-0000 A-00 B-00 C-D4 S-0050
P-0017 X-0000 A-00 B-00 C-D4 S-0050
*;T
*
```

Figure 11-11 Run-one-instruction or trace functions.

Example 11-3

The instructions for the program being executed in Fig. 11-11 are not shown. How many bytes make up each instruction?

Solution

From the printout we see that the PC was set to 10 but then went to 13, then to 15, and finally to 16. Therefore, the first instruction was 3 bytes long, the second 2 bytes, and the third instruction had only 1 byte.

Figure 11-11 also shows the operation of the *Trace* command. The underlined entry $T is used to initiate the trace. The system immediately prints "END ADDR XXXX" (the address might be anything). The operator then enters the particular address at which he wants the trace to stop (17 in this case). An * is printed as a result of the CR and EXbug waits for the next command. The trace is started by entering "10;G". Register displays are then printed at full printer speed until address 17 is reached. An * is then printed to show that the function is done. The operator then entered ";T" to clear the trace function so that it will not print the next time the Go (n;G), or proceed (;P) commands are used.

**11-9.5
Breakpoints**

Up to eight breakpoints can be set in EXbug. Once breakpoints are set, the program is started and runs until it encounters one of the *breakpoint addresses*. It then causes an EXbug routine to be entered, which displays the μP registers as stored after the last user instruction was executed and returns control to MAID. The operator can then examine memory before continuing the trace through the program.

Multiple breakpoints can be set at one time so as to catch the program no matter which branch it takes.

The breakpoint function is one of the most useful functions to rapidly find problems in a system. It allows segments or sections of the program to be executed (in real time) until a section is found which does not run, or runs improperly. At this point, the N command is used to step through that section, one instruction at a time, until the error is located.

Breakpoints involve the U, V, and P commands, as shown in Fig. 11-12. A sample program, shown in Fig. 11-12a, is a simple routine to bring in four letters from the keyboard. These letters also appear in the printout and must not be confused with the commands. The steps in this process are:

1. The first breakpoint is entered at location 20 (20;V) and the program is started at address 10 (10;G). It is assumed the program is already in memory.
2. The program waits in the input loop until the A is typed. It then immediately "breaks" and prints the registers. The A register contains 41, which is the ASCII code for A. The PC register shows where it stopped (ready for the next instruction). The X register shows where the letter is stored.
3. A breakpoint is now inserted at 2A and the one at 20 is removed (20;U).
4. The program is started again with ;P, which proceeds from the address in the PC register, until the breakpoint at 2A is encountered. The only register change other than the PC was X, which was decremented.
5. The next command illustrates the "loop through breakpoint" feature. The 3;P is the *loop through breakpoint* command. The ASD are the typed characters. This allows the program to go around the loop three times (in this case, as each character is typed), and then to *break* again. None of the previously described Monitor ROMs have this feature.
6. The last character typed is in the A register, and the X register has been decremented back to address 000B.
7. At this point the breakpoints are displayed by the $V command and cleared by the ;U command, as confirmed by a repeat of the V command.

There are many more similar functions included in EXbug, and the student is referred to the EXORciser manual referenced in Sec. 11-15 for additional details.

**11-10
EXORciser Hardware
Features**

A block diagram of the EXORciser is shown in Fig. 11-13. As seen by the arrows along the left edge, it contains two systems working together; the *Debug* system and the *User*'s system. The Debug sys-

```
00001                            NAM    EXORT
00002                     *       PROGRAM TO INPUT FOUR CHARACTERS
00003                     *       USES EXBUG'S INCH ROUTINE
00004                            OPT    O         OBJECT OPTION
00005 0008                       ORG    8
00006 0008 0008                  RMB    8         LOCATIONS TO SAVE CHARACTERS
00007 0010 8E 0050               LDS    #$50      SET STACK
00008 0013 86 00      START      LDA A  #0
00009 0015 97 08                 STA A  8
00010 0017 86 0F                 LDA A  #$F
00011 0019 97 09                 STA A  9
00012 001B DE 08                 LDX    8         LOAD X WITH $000F
00013 001D BD F012   INPUT       JSR    INCH      INPUT CHARACTER
00014 0020 A7 00                 STA A  0,X       STORE IN MEM
00015 0022 A1 00                 CMP A  0,X       VERIFY
00016 0024 26 06                 BNE    EXIT
00017 0026 09                    DEX
00018 0027 8C 000B               CPX    #$B       LIMIT REACHED?
00019 002A 26 F1                 BNE    INPUT     NO- LOOP TIL DONE
00020 002C 7E F564   EXIT        JMP    $F564     RETURN TO EXBUG
00021      F012      INCH        EQU    $F012     EXBUG'S INPUT ONE CHAR
00022                            END
TOTAL ERRORS 00000
```

(a)

```
EXBUG 1.1 MAID
*20;V
*10;G
A
P-0020 X-000F A-41 B-F0 C-C0 S-0050
*2A;V
*20;U
*;P
P-002A X-000E A-41 B-F0 C-C0 S-0050
*3;PASD
P-002A X-000B A-44 B-F0 C-C4 S-0050
*$V
0000 002A 0000 0000 0000 0000 0000 0000
*;U
*$V
0000 0000 0000 0000 0000 0000 0000 0000
*
```

(b)

Figure 11-12 Insert, display, and
remove breakpoint function.
(a) Sample program
(b) EXbug breakpoint procedures

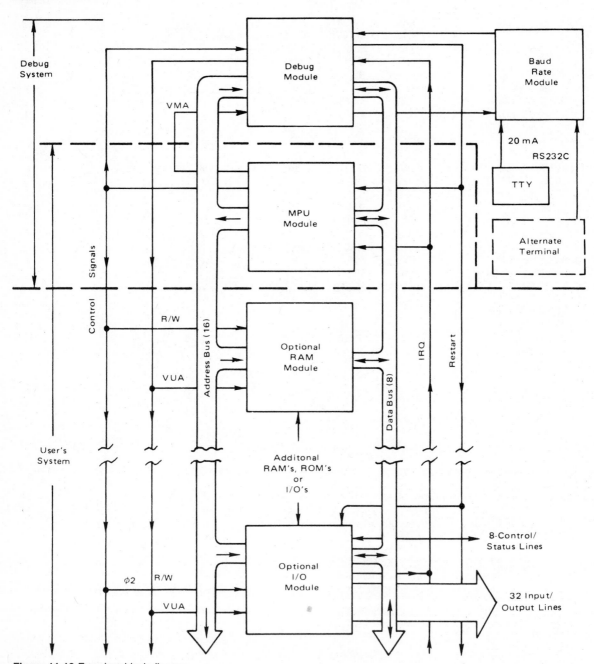

Figure 11-13 Exorciser block diagram.

tem consists of the MPU and the Debug modules. The User's system can either be external hardware or can be *emulated* by a set of modules plugged into other slots in the EXORciser.

11-10.1
The Debug System

The Debug system is designed to work alternately with the User's system to monitor its progress. This allows the user to quickly identify and correct any hardware or software problems that may occur during the execution of his program. These two plug-in modules plus the baud rate module, constitute a complete operating **6800** μP system with many unique hardware and software features intended to aid the designer.

The MPU module is a printed circuit card that contains a **6800** μP, an auto-restart circuit, (to provide an orderly startup when the power is applied), and a 1 MHz clock circuit with the ability to work with slow memories and to refresh dynamic memories. A switch allows an external clock to be used (down to 100 kHz). The interface to the EXORciser bus is provided by **MC6880/8T26** 3-state driver/ receivers (see Sec. 8-4.3). All this provides a module with the **6800** μP functions and essentially unlimited bus drive capability.

The rest of the Debug system is contained on the Debug module (except for the baud rate clock). This module has the 3 EXbug ROMs as well as 256 bytes of RAM, and the serial I/O used for the data terminal. In addition, several special hardware circuits are included such as the cycle counter used to provide the *run-one-instruction* feature and the *stop-on-address* comparator circuit, both of which will work even through the user's program is in ROM.

When the EXORciser is turned ON, it automatically starts up and prints the message "EXBUG 1.2", if a TTY or other 110 baud terminal is used. An entry can be made to accommodate either 30, 120, or 240 character per second terminals, such as the TI 733ASR. The DEC LA-30, or the GE Terminet 30 will only work at 30CPS.

11-10.2
The User's System

Figure 11-13 shows that the MPU module is used as part of both the Debug and User's system. The **6800** μP on the module acts as the user's μP when the User's system is assembled in the EXORciser chassis. The remaining 12 slots are used to accommodate the memory or I/O modules needed to *emulate* the rest of the User's system.

11-10.3
Memory Modules

When starting a μP design, users are often confronted with several problems:

1. They do not know how much memory will be required by the final system.
2. They are not sure where it should be placed in the 64K memory space available.
3. Designers do not know how much ROM and how much RAM will be needed in the final configuration. Since the ROM must be emulated by RAM, in order to test or change the program, it is convenient to use RAM exclusively during the system design phase.

Figure 11-14 shows the total memory map of the **6800** μP. Because of the organization of various memory ICs, it is logical to divide the 65536 byte map into blocks of 1024 bytes each, as shown. Most memory chips are multiples, or submultiples of that size. Mod-

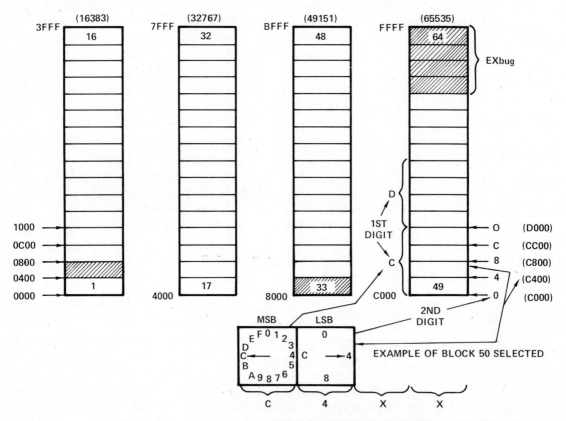

Figure 11-14 Memory map, showing 2K memory module address switching.

ules that have blocks of 1K (1024), 2K, 4K, 8K, 16K, or 32K are useful for ROM emulation, particularly if they can be assigned to any location in the available space. The 2K static memory module, which is one of the modules available for use in the EXORciser, is shown in Fig. 11-15, and the address switching scheme it uses is shown in the lower right of Fig. 11-14. It has two 1K blocks of memory that can be switched in 1K steps to occupy any block location indicated in the map. Other EXORciser memory modules are also provided in 8K configurations (with 4K blocks), 16K modules (with 8K blocks), and 16K in one block.

11-10.4
I/O Modules

In emulating many systems, there is a basic need for both a serial I/O module that uses the **6850** ACIA, and a parallel I/O module equipped with **6820** or **6821** PIAs. Figure 11-16 shows the PIA module. This module contains two **6820** PIAs and associated circuitry. The same addressing switches are used as in the memory

Figure 11-15 The 2K RAM module.

Figure 11-16 The PIA module.

modules but in this case, four switches are used for each PIA to accommodate all the possible assignments. Since each PIA occupies 4 locations in memory, this allows the PIAs to be placed at any address from 0000 to FFF4.

11-11
Use of the EXORciser in
System Development

Through its ability to *emulate* a user's system hardware and to debug the interfaces to external devices, as well as to test his software, a μP development system greatly reduces the time required for an engineer to construct a working model of his system. Instead of designing and building a prototype, the engineer can set up the test system to represent functionally his system using the plug-in optional modules previously described. The EXORciser can also be used to test existing hardware (see Sec. 11-11.7).

11-11.1
Peripheral Interfacing

Many external devices can be interfaced with PIAs and use TTL compatible signals. An I/O module (see Fig. 11-16) may be plugged into the EXORciser, and its PIA I/O pins wired to the user's peripheral device via a flat ribbon cable. (If the user circuits are not TTL compatible, level converters are installed.) The user can then test the hardware interface by using EXbug's Display/Change memory command (described in Sec. 11-9.2).

Since PIA registers resemble memory locations in **6800** systems (see Sec. 8-13), storing a data word in the PIA data register (assuming it has been programmed as an output port), puts signal levels on the output lines in accordance with the data word stored (i.e., 1s are HIGH and 0s are LOW). If, for example, Data line 0 is connected to a motor control circuit so it runs when the line is HIGH, a data word of 01 (or any word with Bit 0 SET), will start the motor. When testing with an EXORciser, if the desired result does not happen, an oscilloscope (CRO) or meter is used to observe the signals on the lines to the external devices and wires exchanged or the data word changed to correct the problem.

Once the proper words have been determined so that the control functions work properly, the sensing of external information, in the form of data read from the PIA's *input* data register, can also be analyzed. The bits of these words are the result of the data levels on the lines from the sensor hardware. After all the input/output data words are correlated with the hardware, a routine can be entered into memory in machine language, using EXbug, to "exorcise" the external hardware. When this test program is running properly, a complete program can be written and assembled in the EXORciser using the resident Editor/Assembler programs. The program for this user hardware subsystem would then be loaded into memory and tested by using breakpoints or "run-one-instruction" methods (see Sec. 11-9.4 and 11-9.5).

This same technique would be repeated for other subsystems and their additional peripheral units until a complete system is assembled. The entire process is shown in Fig. 11-17. The development system is shown with a TTY. This combination of equipment, with its paper tape, probably incurs the lowest cost for this design task. Other setups with cassettes or a floppy disk system are much faster and quieter. Figure 11-17 shows that each step in the design process has feedback paths so the designer can loop back any number of times to improve the hardware or software until the desired performance is achieved.

The engineer now has an operating model of his or her system using the development system hardware with a minimum amount

PROCEDURE FOR DESIGNING AND VERIFYING A SYSTEM USING
THE MOTOROLA M6800 MICROCOMPUTER

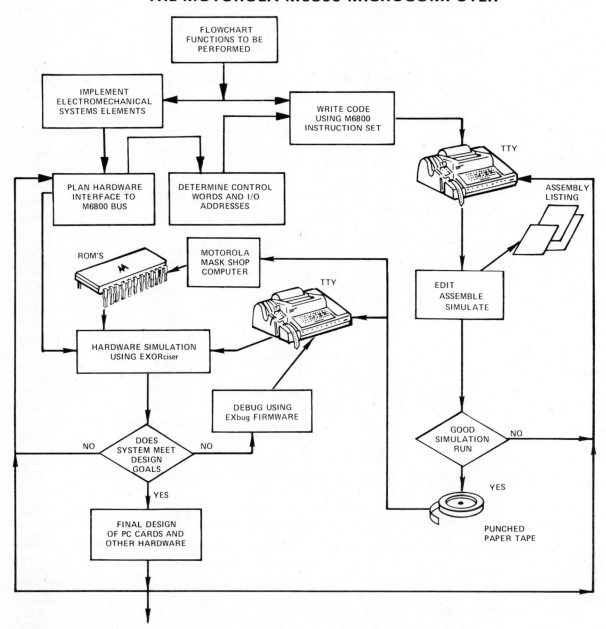

Figure 11-17 System design procedure.

of time spent on prototype construction. The programmer can now finalize his routines. The advantages to the programmer are that he can verify his I/O programming steps by testing them before he has final hardware, and this setup permits him to debug the resulting object code on a real-time basis.

11-11.2
EXORciser Memory Configuration

The EXORciser memory map is shown in Fig. 11-18a. The Debug system memory is not configured in the same way as a conventional **6800** system. The very top of memory is RAM (two-**6810s**), in contrast to ROM or PROM, that would normally be used. This is done so that the interrupt vectors can be changed for test purposes to suit any user's requirements. (A small PROM that contains the RST vector is switched in to get EXbug started.) The initialization routine then sets the RAM interrupt vector locations to values used by EXbug. IRQ is always masked and is not used by EXbug. The use of the interrupt vectors by the user is described in Sec. 11-11.5. The Debug system occupies the top 4096 bytes of the 65,536 available, which leaves 61,440 bytes for the user. This configuration is used so that user system interrupt handling can be evaluated and debugged. If the user feels that a portion of the program must reside in the top 4K (the only legitimate reason for this is that the 61440 bytes will be exceeded), and he wishes to use EXbug to debug it, it is recommended that that portion be assembled at some lower address, say 7000, debugged, and then reassembled at the originally planned location.

11-11.3
System Address Selection

Not all 16 address lines are needed in most **6800** systems. Usually, as few lines as possible are used in order to keep the decoding simple. Consider, for example, the system shown in Fig. 11-19, which contains only an EPROM, a RAM, and a PIA. Here, only lines A15 and A14 are used and only A15 is really required for the PROM. The addressing scheme is shown at the right of each IC. The starting address of the RAM (when all Ys are 0) can be an address starting with 0, 1, 2, or 3, a second digit of 0 to F, and a third digit of 0 or 8. (For example, 0000, 0080, 1A00, or 3F80.) PIA addresses would start with 4, 5, 6, or 7, and the PROM address with C, D, E, or F (when A14 is also used). Note that the PROM can be programmed to run at CXXX, and still respond to FXXX. This makes it possible to test the program without interfering with EXbug, and yet, in a final system configuration, where the PROM will actually have re-

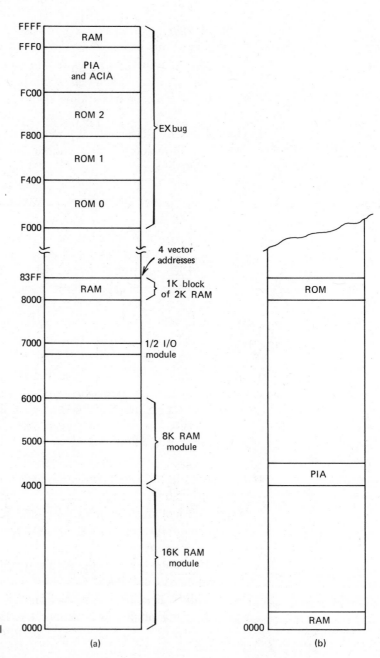

Figure 11-18 Memory map for a typical user system.

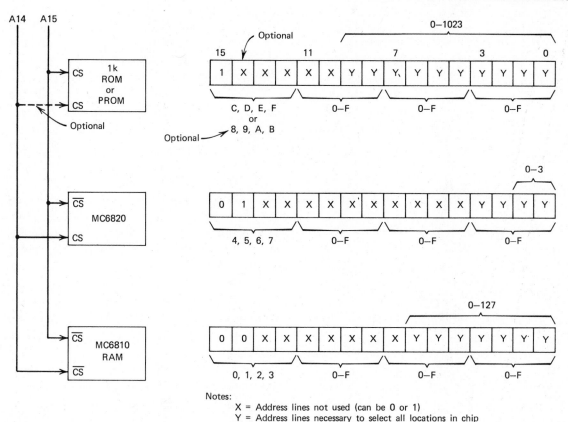

Notes:
X = Address lines not used (can be 0 or 1)
Y = Address lines necessary to select all locations in chip

Figure 11-19 Typical Small system addressing.

dundant decoding, the top eight locations *will be* accessed by the **6800** μP interrupt functions.

11-11.4
Steps in the Development
of a Program

When a program is to be initially tested in an EXORciser, one of the plug-in RAM modules is used with the address switches set for CXXX, (or D or E) and the basic program is debugged, including the interrupt service routines, by the run-one-instruction and/or breakpoint methods (Sec. 11-9.5). Redundant responses do not occur because the test system modules are fully decoded, which means the interrupt vectors are *not* accessible from the top of this memory module by the μP, and must be tested as described below.

11-11.5
Interrupt Testing

When completing the final stages of system emulation or prototype testing, it is desirable to test the final program as it works in the final system. Once the program has been debugged so that it runs properly in RAM, the vectors should be installed at the top of the highest memory block used. EXbug's "top-of-memory" address (located at FF00 and FF01), must be changed to the actual top address occupied by the vectors (i.e., C3FF, for the preceding example). The ABORT button is then pressed. This serves to move the IRQ vector up to the Debug module RAM at FFF8 (and 9), and also allows the ;G command to be used to enter the user's program at the RESTART address. IRQ's caused by the user's hardware will now be vectored to the user's service routine.

NMI and SWI vectors must be inserted manually into the RAM at FFFC (and D) or FFFA (and B), using the memory display/change function. It must be noted, however, that this will inhibit the ABORT and *run-one-instruction* functions (that use NMI) or the *breakpoint* function if SWI is changed. Also, pushing RESTART will restore the original EXbug vectors.

11-11.6
Memory Assignments

When initially emulating a system or evaluating concepts, users need not be too concerned about where they locate their PIAs, or memory, as long as they are kept below F000. The optional RAM modules are used to emulate ROM and, since everything is fully decoded, there is no need to be concerned about redundant addresses. When finalizing the system and testing interrupt vectors (see Sec. 11-11.5), however, the memory map must be carefully planned.

Figure 11-18b illustrates a memory map of a test system with the entries for a typical user system included. The map should be prepared as follows.

a. Construct a basic memory map of the system. On this map indicate that the EXORciser is using memory addresses F000 through FFFF.

b. Assign the memory location for your ROMs or PROMs at the top of *your* memory (see Sec. 11-11.3).

c. Assign the memory addresses for the **6810** or other RAMs. It is recommended that the RAMs be placed below address 100 in memory, to realize the advantage of the direct addressing mode to save memory. (See Chapters 5 and 7.)

d. If the system is using **6821** (PIAs), assign four addresses for each PIA as described in Chapter 8.

e. If the system is using **6850** (ACIAs), assign two addresses for each ACIA, as described in Chapter 8.

11-11.7
Prototype or Production
Hardware Testing

Once designers have successfully emulated their systems in the EXORciser chassis, construction of a prototype can begin. By emulation, designers know exactly how much memory they need, how many output ports or lines will be required, and even what their clock circuits and decoding schemes must be. This information allows them to design a prototype that will be reasonably close to the final production units. They have not eliminated the need for a prototype altogether, but probably have bypassed several preliminary versions.

When construction is completed, the prototype must be tested to determine whether it performs as well as the emulation system did. For this purpose, the EXORciser is augmented by the addition of the *User System Evaluator* (USE). This subsystem consists of a USE processor module that replaces the MPU module, and a USE2B buffer and cable assembly. A third component consists of an intercept module that allows the System Analyzer (MEX68SA) to be added to the system. (This is optional and is discussed in Sec. 11-11.8.)

Figure 11-20 shows the MEX68USE User System Evaluator installed in an Exorciser and shows how it is interconnected to the user's prototype or production system. The user's **6800** is not used. Instead, the USE cable that terminates in a 40-pin DIP plug is plugged into the socket intended for the user's μP. The USE system functions as the user's μP and also provides the same debug capabilities in the prototype as previously used in the emulation. The interconnection of the two systems in this way creates one larger system that operates in real time with one μP. This larger system is driven by the user's clock to avoid the need for any special rearrangement of the user system for the purpose of testing it. With this arrangement, it is now possible to operate and test the system with all or part of the I/O, or memory, in either system. The memory can be RAM or ROM (or PROM), and the I/O can be the original emulated version using EXORciser modules or can be the newly constructed circuits on the prototype.

To develop a typical system the following steps might occur.

1. Only the clock circuitry of the prototype is installed and tested.
2. Once the clock is performing properly, one or more of the I/O chips are installed and the associated external peripheral is tested by using the EXbug's memory display/change routine just as in the original emulation (see Sec. 11-11.1).
3. After all of the I/O has been activated, and works correctly, testing continues by loading the program that was used in the emulation into one or more EXORciser RAM modules and verifying that everything works properly with the user's actual I/O interface circuits.
4. When satisfied that the program is correct, it is written into a PROM

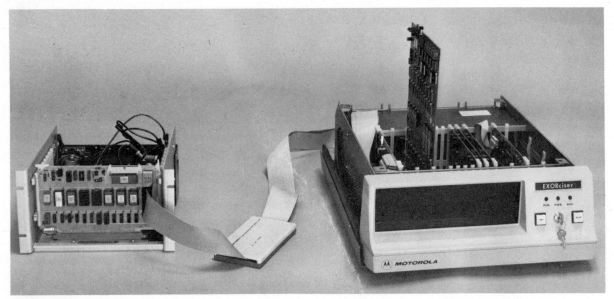

Figure 11-20 The User System
Evaluator (USE).

(using the PP3 PROM programmer module in the EXORciser), and the PROM is plugged into the proper socket of the prototype unit for final testing.

5. When power is applied to the EXORciser and the prototype, the system will start up in the EXbug program. All of the EXbug commands can be used to examine user memories (PROM or RAM) and test the I/O. When satisfied that everything is right, the user's PROM program can be executed using the G command of EXbug and the user system should perform normally. If the Debug module is disabled by the switch on top, operation of the RESTART button will fetch the vector from the user's PROM, and the user program will be entered directly.

6. When all the testing is done, the "umbilical cord" can be removed and the **6800** installed to allow the user's prototype to operate by itself.

11-11.8
The System Analyzer Module

Figure 11-20 also shows the MEX68SA System Analyzer module in use. This module has several unique characteristics that make it especially suitable for debugging prototypes. The EXORciser with its software approach to debugging, works well as long as the combined system will start and run EXbug properly. However, it frequently happens that a new prototype will not RESTART properly and therefore EXbug cannot be used.

The System Analyzer connects directly to the EXORciser buses and permits the user access to the operations that are being performed inside of the system. The System Analyzer has the following functions.

1. The ability to monitor and record 128 cycle-by-cycle sequences of processor operation, which includes the information on the address bus, data bus, four control signals (VMA, R/W, NMI, and IRQ), and four external signals (see Appendix C for instruction cycle information).
2. A trigger circuit that can initiate the capture of this data under selected compare conditions.
3. A LED display of the captured data.
4. A print function that can provide a hard copy (on a TTY) or display the data on a CRT terminal.

The data is stored in four **6810** RAMs that save the status on the buses during each Ø2 cycle. Switches are provided on the module to select the parameters that activate the trigger. This can be an address, a specific data word, any of four external TTL lines, or any combination of them. When triggered, the data is captured for 64 cycles prior to the trigger point and 64 cycles after it. In the window mode the program runs continuously. The "trace" mode also captures the data but halts the processor after the last cycle is stored.

The usefulness of the SA module can be realized if the prototype doesn't run when it is first turned on. When a start is attempted with the trigger address set at the RESTART vector, the few cycles of data captured may be enough to determine the reason. Frequently a study of the data reveals a shorted data or address line or an abnormality in VMA or R/W, for example. Once a suspicious line is identified, it can be further examined by using an oscilloscope or even an ohmmeter.

**11-12
Software Development
in the EXORciser**

The EXORciser can be used for software development at any time, even while in the middle of hardware debugging. Many engineers may choose to assemble their clock and I/O circuitry on the prototype board, or boards, and get it working with their peripherals before the programming is finalized. In these cases it is desirable to be able to edit and reassemble the program without dismantling the hardware setup. This is possible by installing one or more of the Dynamic RAM Memory modules into the EXORciser as follows.

1. If a tape terminal is being used (as described in Sec. 7-5), with the Co-resident Editor/Assembler programs, a minimum of 8K of RAM (MEX6815-3) is needed with its address switches set for 0 and 1, (so as

to have memory from 00 to 1FFF). The Editor/Assembler resides in this range with 744 bytes remaining for the editor buffer or assembler symbol table (see Chapter 7).

2. If the EXORdisk 2 floppy disk system is chosen, with the standard Editor and Assembler programs, a minimum of 16K of RAM (MEX6816-1), is needed with its address switch set for 0, to provide memory from 0000 to 3FFF.

With either of these arrangements, the editing and assembling process can be carried on in the EXORciser without disturbing the prototype hardware or the program in the 2K memory. (The IRQ must be inhibited.) The USE feature, whereby the memory in the EXORciser has priority over any memory (or I/O) in the user system at the same address allows this to work.

Any of the features of the EXbug program can be used at any time. For example, the Trace and Breakpoint functions are fully usable to run through programs in memory in either system. Trace will work with PROM (or ROM) and, although breakpoints will not work in ROM, the Stop-on-Address will, and does essentially the same job. These allow testing in real time (i.e., no-wait states are required, and the instructions are executed at the user's clock rate, including all I/O).

11-13
Use of Logic Analyzers

As mentioned in Sec. 11-8, Logic Analyzers are a new family of instruments designed to troubleshoot μP systems. They are an expansion of the multichannel cathode ray oscilloscope (CRO), and provide simultaneous displays of the data or address lines. Rather than displaying the data in a voltage verses time mode, it is often more useful to have data expressed as digital words in either 1s and 0s or, even better, as hexadecimal digits. Microprocessors require the analysis of combinations of signals rather than of one or two.

The Tektronix 7D01 Logic Analyzer is an example of a plug-in module for the 7000 series CRO mainframe, that has 16 channels. It is shown in Fig. 11-21. Used with the DF1 or DF2 Display Formatter, it provides five ways to look at the logic: timing, mapping, and state table displays in binary, hexadecimal and octal. The DF2 has two additional modes; IEEE 488/GPIB (General Purpose Interface Bus), and ASCII. The system includes a 4096-bit memory and a word recognizer for triggering. Typically, the analysis would begin by using the *mapping mode*. In this mode, the first two characters of a hexadecimal word determine the vertical location of a dot while the last two digits indicate the horizontal position (i.e., 0000 is the

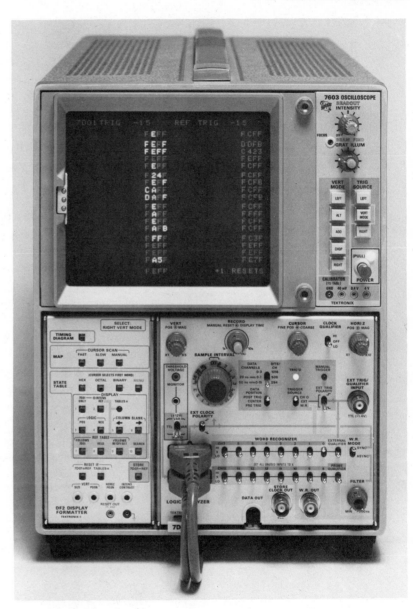

Figure 11-21 Tektronix 7D01 with DF1 display formatter. Reproduced by permission of copyright owner, Tektronix, Inc. All rights reserved.

upper left corner and FFFF is the lower right). If the 16-bit probes are connected to the address lines, the μP activity can be monitored by observing the dots displayed. Since each area of memory is identifiable, it can be determined where the μP system is spending its time. If an I/O port is being used to input data from a terminal, for example, the PIA or ACIA address and the RAM address where the data is stored will be active.

Once the problem area is located with mapping, the mode can be changed to the *state table* mode to locate the faulty bit or bits in the program itself. In this mode the captured data is displayed in binary or hexadecimal so that the I/O port address can be readily identified. The display might be one of the 16 addresses prior to the fault, so that it can be determined which devices were being accessed just before it went wrong.

Hewlett-Packard also makes a number of Logic Analyzers such as the 1611A shown in Fig. 11-22. This unit is of particular interest to **6800** users because it has a **6800** *personality module* that tailors the instrument to display in a format very familiar to **6800** designers. The system connects into the user's system either by a 40-pin clothespin-type clip or by replacing the μP with a 40-pin DIP plug and cable like the USE module. The **6800** is reinstalled in the probe body. The analyzer captures 64 cycles of address, data, and 8-bits of information that is gathered by means of an external probe. A triggering circuit is set up from the instruments keyboard to trigger when a selected address, data, or external data event occurs. A switch selects hexadecimal or octal for display of the captured cycle-by-cycle program flow. Of particular interest is the ability to convert the OP codes into mnemonics, as shown in Fig. 11-23. Although only 16 cycles of information are displayed at a time the window can be scrolled so that all 64 steps are seen. The trigger point is identified by inverting the video. A comparison with the MEX68SA will show

Figure 11-22 Hewlett-Packard 1611A Logic Analyzer. Reproduced by permission of Hewlett-Packard.

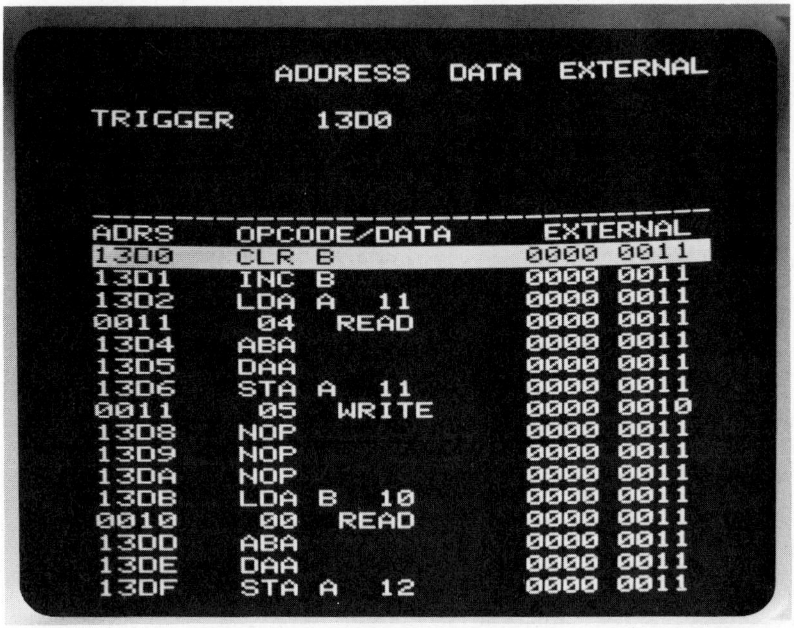

Figure 11-23 Photo of H-P 1611A screen display showing **6800** mnemonics.

a marked similarity in the data captured except that it is 64 cycles instead of 128, and the H-P information can be displayed in mnemonic form.

Other exclusive features include the ability to delay the trigger up to 65,472 cycles, and the calculation of execution times between two keyboard selected events.

Once a fault is found in the execution of the software or in the user's **6800** hardware, a CRO or other device is usually required to pinpoint the problem.

11-14 Summary

The problems of designing and testing μPs were described, and the evolution of the ROM monitor program concept for μP debugging was shown. Two classes of instrumentation, the Logic Analyzer and the μP Development System, were described. The EXORciser and its EXbug program were discussed to illustrate how μP designers use this type of instrument to emulate and later test prototypes or production versions of their design. Finally, Logic Analyzers and their application were explained.

11-15 References

Harrington, Wayne, *AN 771—MEK6800D2 Microcomputer Kit System Expansion Techniques,* Motorola Semiconductor Products, Inc., Box 20912, Phoenix, Arizona 85036.

Hewlett-Packard, *Functional Analysis of the Motorola* **M6800** μ*P System*. App. Note 167-9, Hewlett-Packard, 1501 Page Mill Rd., Pala Alto, California 94304.

Hewlett-Packard, *1611A Logic State Analyzer,* Technical Data, 1 September 76, Hewlett-Packard, 1501 Page Mill Rd., Palo Alto, California 94304.

Hewlett-Packard, *The Role of Logic State Analyzers in* μ*P Based Designs*. App. Note 167-13, Hewlett-Packard, 1501 Page Mill Rd., Palo Alto, California 94304.

Motorola, *Evaluation Module II User's Guide,* Motorola Semiconductors, Inc., Box 20912, Phoenix, Arizona 85036.

Motorola, *MEK6800D2 Manual,* 2nd Edition, Motorola Semiconductor Products, Inc., 3501 Bluestein Blvd., Austin, Texas 78721.

Motorola, *MICROBUG Operating Procedures Preliminary Info 1977,* Motorola Microsystems, 3102 No. 56th St., Phoenix, Arizona 85018.

Motorola, *MINIBUG III Operating Procedures Preliminary Info. 1977,* Motorola Microsystems, 3102 No. 56th St., Phoenix, Arizona 85018.

Motorola, *M68ADS1A Development System,* Motorola Microsystems, 3102 No. 56th St., Phoenix, Arizona 85018.

Motorola, *M68MM01A Monoboard Microcomputer 1A—1977,* Motorola Microsystems, 3102 North 56th Street, Phoenix, Arizona 85018.

Motorola, *M6800 EXORciser User's Guide,* 2nd Edition, M68PRMD(D), May 1977, Motorola Semiconductor Products, Inc., Box 20912, Phoenix, Arizona 85036.

Motorola, EN100 Engineering Note 100.

Tektronix, *Debugging a* μ*P Based Process Control System,* App. Note #57K3-1, Tektronix, Inc., P.O. Box 500, Beaverton, Oregon 97077.

Tektronix, *DF2 Display Formatter for the 7D01 Logic Analyzer,* A-3813-1 1/78, Tektronix, Inc., P.O. Box 500, Beaverton, Oregon 97077.

Tektronix *Troubleshooting a* μ*P,* Appl. note #57K1.0, Tektronix, Inc., P.O. Box 500, Beaverton, Oregon 97077.

Wray, William, The EXORciser and Its Uses, 1975, WESCON paper presented San Francisco, September 16–19, 1975.

**11-16
Glossary**

2900 Four-bit slice bipolar μP.

3870 A one-chip "F8" μC.

6802 A **6800** μP that includes a clock and 128 bytes of RAM.

10800 Four-bit ALU slice bipolar LSI.

141000 A CMOS 4-bit, one-chip μC.

Bipolar PROM TTL ROM that is programmed by blowing out fuse-type links.

Breakpoint Software technique to halt the program at a specified address. Used for debugging.

Co-resident Noninterfering programs resident in memory at the same time (e.g., Editor/Assembler).

CRT terminal Terminal that displays on CRT (cathode ray tube), (a TV tube) instead of printing.

Debugging Trouble-shooting or analyzing programs or hardware.

EROM, or EPROM Electrically programmable but μV light erasable ROM.

Firmware ROM or PROM.

Interrupt Vector An address pointing to the interrupt service routine.

LF, CR Line feed and carriage return functions of data terminal.

Memory Map Diagram of the full addressable range of memory locations.

Microprocessor Development System An instrument designed to aid in the design of μP systems.

Module Printed circuit card of standard size with specific functions implemented in TTL or MOS ICs.

Real Time Executing at the normal clock rate of (1 MHz) (not slowed down).

ROM Monitor Program Program to load, dump, change, or debug a user's program.

Run-one-instruction Software technique whereby a single instruction is executed in real time and the registers are then displayed.

TI terminal ASR733 Texas Instruments Silent 700 data terminal with cassettes.

TTY ASR33 Teletypewriter.

USE User System Evaluator. Module and cable that is added to EXORciser to interconnect it to a user's hardware, in order to test it.

Chapter 12 Other Microprocessors

This chapter provides a brief description of μP or μC products other than the **6800**. Some are **6800** related, but those that are not are either in common use or have advanced features that make them potentially useful. Space limitation prevents us from mentioning all of the available μPs, but the **6800**'s prime competitor, the **8080A** series is described briefly. As we have needed an entire book to describe a single μP, the reader will realize that we cannot provide equal coverage to the many other μPs. Instead, an overview is presented to give the reader a feel for the differences between these μPs and the **6800** and their capabilities. The reader is advised to consult the manufacturers' literature for detailed information on these other μC products.

Watch for the answers to the following questions as you read the chapter. They should help you understand the material presented.

1. What features are provided in the **6801** μC and **6809** μP that are not present in the **6800**?
2. What is position-independent machine language and why is it important?
3. What new instructions are offered in the **6801**?
4. Why would a system's designer choose the **3870** or **141000** μCs?
5. What are the differences between the **6800** and **8080A**?
6. Where are microprogrammed systems used?

Previous chapters discussed the **6800** μP exclusively. During 1977 and 1978, Motorola introduced several new μPs and μCs, such as the **6801, 6802, 6805,** and **6809**. These are NMOS IC chips that combine the features of several chips. They are improved new products and all of them, except the **6805**, have been designed to be upwardly compatible with the **6800**. The **6805** is a low-cost version of a μC (it includes ROM, I/O, and a timer). Most of the basic characteristics of all these devices are the same as the **6800** and, except for the **6805**, the new versions will run the same programs and follow the same hardware design rules. Programmers or engineers familiar with the **6800** can readily use them with little reeducation. The **6801** and **6802** use the same 8-bit instruction set and object codes as the **6800**, and the **6809** (which is the highest performance of the 8-bit μPs), is compatible at the *source* or *mnemonic level* (i.e., the **6800** source listings can be assembled with the **6809** assembler to produce a usable program). Since the hardware is all bus compatible, these new components can be interconnected with any of the **6800** family I/O, memory, or peripheral chips.

The **6802** has a processor that is the same as the **6800's**. The **6801** has improved architecture that provides 21 additional OP codes (10 instructions), and shortens the execution cycle times of many existing instructions. The **6809** is the most advanced of the new designs and not only has many new instructions but also has a second Stack Pointer, a second Index Register, and a Direct Page Register. Among the new instructions are 16-bit operations, which significantly enhance the performance. The **6809** instruction set contains about the same number of assembly-language instructions as the **6800**, yet many of them are much more powerful. Combining existing **6800** instructions into more general and versatile **6809** instructions has made room for the new ones. Each of these new components are described in this chapter along with other μPs of different manufacturers. Bit-slice designs are also described briefly.

12-3.1
The 6802/6846 Combination

The **6802** μP and a companion chip, the **6846** ROM-I/O-Timer, were introduced late in 1977. These two chips together form a *complete* μC since they combine the functions of six of the original **6800** family members (Fig. 12-1a). The **6802** includes an oscillator circuit (similar to the **6875**), 128 bytes of RAM, (the equivalent of a **6810**), and a μP with functions identical to the **6800**. The **6846** contains a 2K ($\times$8) ROM, a timer (or counter), and an I/O port (an I/O port is a group of I/O lines, usually 8, and is therefore able to input or output a byte at a time). The interconnections between these two chips are shown in Fig. 12-1b. The pin assignments of the **6802** are very similar to those of the **6800** as shown in Fig. 12-1c. The DMA feature of the **6800** was sacrificed because of the need for additional pins to accommodate the on-board RAM and clock. A comparison of pinouts shows that TSC, DBE, and Ø1 were removed, and RAM enable (RE), EXtal (EX), Xtal (X), Memory Ready (MR), Enable (E), and V_{CC} Standby were added. In the **6802**, 32 bytes of the RAM

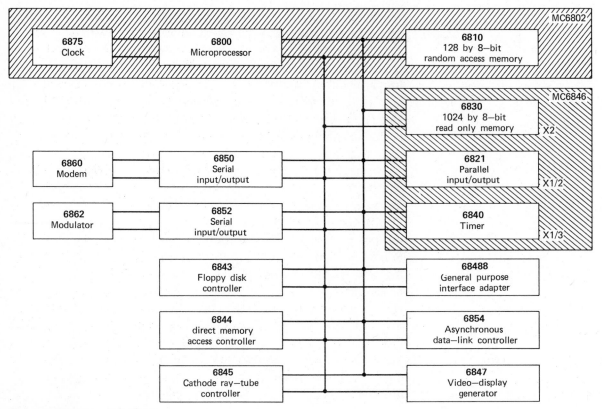

Figure 12-1 (a) The **6802/6846** two-chip µC showing functions.

can be used to retain information (by using a battery), thus providing a nonvolatile memory. The system is still expandable to 64K bytes and retains all the other **6800** features such as 5 V only operation.

The **6802** µP signals (or pins) that differ from those of the **6800** µP are listed below:

RAM Enable (RE) This signal controls the on-chip RAM. If taken low at least 3 cycles before V_{CC} falls below 4.75 V, it will disable the RAM and protect any data in the 32-byte portion that is supported by a battery.

EXtal (EX) and Xtal (X) These are for a parallel resonance quartz crystal to control the internal oscillator. A 4 MHz (or 3.59 MHz Tv) crystal can be used since it is divided by 4 internally, and is less expensive than the 1 MHz crystal normally used. Pin 39 (EXtal) can be driven from an external TTL oscillator if a separate clock is required.

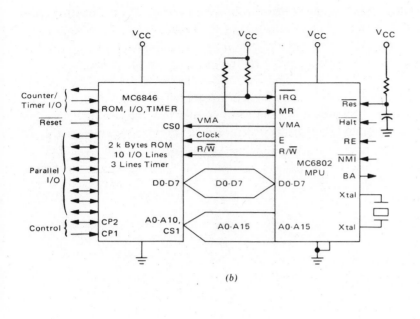

Figure 12-1 (b) Two-chip μC
interconnections.
Figure 12-1 (c) **6802/6800** pinouts.

Enable (E) This is the output of the divide-by-4 clock and is a single phase TTL-compatible signal used to drive the rest of the system. It is equivalent to the **6800** Ø2 clock. This signal is stretched by the Memory Ready signal.

Memory Ready This is used, as described in Sec. 8-7, to stretch the Ø2 clock integral multiples of half periods to allow use of slow memories. It is a TTL signal and allows normal operation when high.

V_{CC} **Standby** This pin supplies the dc voltage (battery or V_{CC}) to the 32 bytes of RAM. When properly used with the RE signal, retention of data during power down is guaranteed.

The student should study the data sheets referenced in Sec. 12-15 for more details.

12-3.2
The 6846 ROM-I/O-TIMER

The **6846** provides three important features for this two-chip μC combination. As seen in Fig. 12-1a, it includes 2 K bytes of mask programmable ROM equivalent to two of the original **6830** components, an 8-bit bidirectional I/O port similar to the B side of a **6821**, and a timer-counter function similar to one third of a **6840**. Figure 12-2 shows the block diagram of the **6846**.

The polarity of the ROM select pins (CS0 and CS1) is specified by the user when he provides the program for the mask.

12-3.3
The 6846 Timer

The timer may be programmed to operate in modes that fit a wide variety of applications. The **6846** is fully bus compatible with other **6800** system components and its registers are accessed from the μP by any of the memory-referencing instructions such as LOAD or STORE. In typical applications, the timer will be preset to the desired

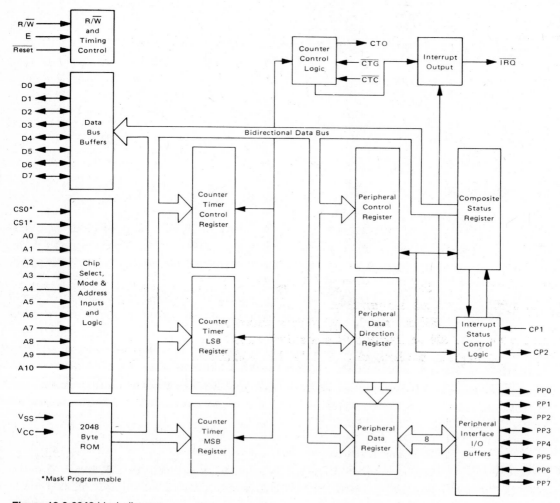

Figure 12-2 6846 block diagram.

count by storing two bytes of data into the counter latch. This data is then transferred into the counter during a counter initialization cycle. The counter decrements on each subsequent clock cycle (which may be the system Ø2 or an external clock) until one of the several preset conditions causes it to halt or recycle. Thus the timer is controllable by external events or μP programs. (See the **6846** data sheet referenced in Sec. 12-15 for precise details of the timer operation.)

12-3.4
The 6846 Peripheral Port

The peripheral port of the **6846** is similar to the B side of a PIA. As seen in Fig. 12-2, it contains 8 Peripheral Data lines (PP0-PP7), two Peripheral Control lines (CP1 and CP2), a Data Direction Register, a Peripheral Data Register, and a Peripheral Control Register. This latter register is very much like the control part of the control/status register of the **6821** PIA because it controls the operating modes of the CP1 and CP2 lines as well as a reset function.

The port also directly affects two bits (CSR1 and CSR2) of the Composite Status Register. The Composite Status Register (CSR) is a read only register that is shared by the timer and peripheral data port of the **6846**. Three individual interrupt flags in the register are set directly via the appropriate conditions in the timer or peripheral port. The composite interrupt flag and the IRQ output respond to these individual interrupts only if corresponding enable bits are set in the appropriate control registers.

12-4
The 6801 μC

The **6801** is a third generation single-chip μC whose internal configuration is shown in Fig. 12-3. This chip contains all elements of a μC including 2K of ROM, 128 bytes of RAM, a clock, a 16-bit timer, a serial I/O port, 31 parallel programmable I/O lines, and an improved **6800** μP. The **6801** is architecturally compatible with the **6800** family, so that it works with any of the **6800** peripheral components. The 2K ROM normally resides at F800 to FFFF, but can be specified at mask time to be at C800, D800, or E800. This ROM normally includes the interrupt and restart vectors from FFF0 to FFFF (see Table 12-1), but these can be external as determined by the mode. The 128-byte RAM is located at addresses 0080 to 00FF (optionally at A080) while the onboard timer and I/O are allocated the first 20 locations. Table 12-2 shows the memory map assignments for these registers. As can be seen they represent a combination of control and data registers for the parallel and serial I/O ports and a

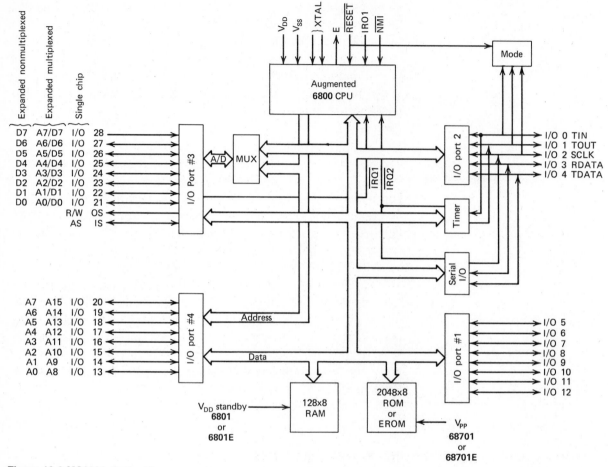

Figure 12-3 MC6801 single-chip
microcomputer.

timer, similar to those used by PIAs, ACIAs, and **6840** or **6846**
timers. The rest of the 64K of memory space can be accessed in the
multiplex modes. As with the **6802**, the internal oscillator includes
a divide-by-4 circuit to permit use of inexpensive crystals. A mask
option (**6801E**) allows the chip to be driven from an external TTL
compatible clock source. The internal oscillator also supplies the E
signal for any devices on the external buses.

To accommodate all these features the **6801** has many signal pins
that are *multiplexed*. This means that *each pin can provide up to
three different signals* depending on the *mode* selected.

Each line of Fig. 12-3 is marked with the two or three possible

Table 12-1
6801 Interrupt and Restart Vectors

	Vector		Interrupts Description
Highest priority	FFFE	FFFF	Restart
	FFFC	FFFD	Nonmaskable interrupt
	FFFA	FFFB	Software interrupt
	FFF8	FFF9	Interrupt request ($\overline{\text{IRQ1}}$)
	FFF6	FFF7	Timer input capture (IRQ2)*
	FFF4	FFF5	Timer output compare (IRQ2)
	FFF2	FFF3	Timer overflow (IRQ2)
Lowest priority	FFF0	FFF1	Serial I/O (IRQ2)

*IRQ2 is an internal interrupt.

Table 12-2
Register and I/O Port Memory Address for **6801**

Hex Address	Register
00	Data direction 1
01	Data direction 2
02	I/O port 1
03	I/O port 2
04	Data direction 3
05	Data direction 4
06	I/O port 3
07	I/O port 4
08	TCSR
09	Counter high byte
0A	Counter low byte
0B	Output compare high byte
0C	Output compare low byte
0D	Input capture high byte
0E	Input capture low byte
0F	I/O port 3 C/S register
10	Serial rate and mode register
11	Serial control and status register
12	Serial receiver data register
13	Serial transmit data register
14	RAM/EROM control register
15-1F Reserved	

identities it may have when the various modes are selected. For example, the line in the upper right of the figure, is either I/O line 0, or Tin (timer in), while the upper left line can be either address line A7, data line D7, or I/O line 28, depending on the mode selected. The I/O lines are arranged in four ports, as shown in Fig. 12-3. Port 2 consists of five lines. The serial I/O and timer I/O can use this port. An *address strobe* samples the address at the proper time, preventing any conflict between address and data. A simple reset circuit is provided that uses a Schmitt trigger to guarantee proper start-up after the type of power down condition that results from a power failure. The designer need only use a simple RC pull-up on the reset pin. The **6801** also has a powerful interrupt capability. Eight interrupts are provided, with one being under software control.

The designer has three 16-bit timer functions available. One controls inputs, one is for outputs, and the third serves as a 16-bit overflow. All functions are performed with the aid of an internal 16-bit free running counter that may be read by the **6801** μP. In the case of inputs, this setup, plus a bit-edge detector, allows the designer to measure the input pulse widths used in critical timing operations between processors. Each time an edge is detected the count from the counter is read into an input-capture register in the **6801** for use by the **6801** μC in computing the pulse width. The input edge-detector may also generate an interrupt to the μP to inform it that new data is available.

The serial-I/O (part of port 2), included in the **6801**, is intended for I/O expansion and serial communication. As Fig. 12-4 shows, the **6801** can communicate with simple serial I/O devices, such as shift register latches. In essence, this port is a very low-cost interface for the addition of low-speed peripherals, since in this mode the data is synchronously clocked into or out of the peripherals.

The remaining I/O ports (1, 3, and 4) handle 8 lines each, with port 3 also including two control lines. All can be used as general-purpose 8-bit data entries under control of a data direction register in the **6801** μC. The third port can also be used to perform special functions under control of an input strobe (IS) that strobes data into its input port. It may also generate an output strobe (OS) that can

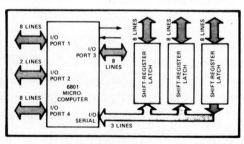

Figure 12-4 6801 serial I/O.

Table 12-3
New Instructions for the **6801**

ADDED INSTRUCTIONS

In addition to the existing M6800 instruction set, the following new instructions are incorporated in the MC6801 microcomputer.

ABX	Adds the 8-bit unsigned accumulator B to the 16-bit X-Register taking into account the possible carry out of the low order byte of the X-Register.	IX←IX + ACCB
ADDD	Adds the double precision ACCD* to the double precision value M:M+1 and places the results in ACCD.	ACCD←(ACCD) + (M:M+1)
ASLD	Shifts all bits of ACCD one place to the left. Bit 0 is loaded with zero. The C bit is loaded from the most significant bit of ACCD.	
LDD	Loads the contents of double precision memory location into the double accumulator A:B. The condition codes are set according to the data.	ACCD←(M:M+1)
LSRD	Shifts all bits of ACCD one place to the right. Bit 15 is loaded with zero. The C bit is loaded from the least significant bit of ACCD.	
MUL	Multiplies the 8 bits in accumulator A with the 8 bits in accumulator B to obtain a 16-bit unsigned number in A:B. ACCA contains MSB of result.	ACCD←ACCA * ACCB
PSHX	The contents of the index register is pushed onto the stack at the address contained in the stack pointer. The stack pointer is decremented by 2.	↓(IXL), SP←(SP) - 1 ↓(IXH), SP←(SP) - 1
PULX	The index register is pulled from the stack beginning at the current address contained in the stack pointer +1. The stack pointer is incremented by 2 in total.	SP←(SP) + 1; Msp → IXH SP←(SP) + 1; Msp → IXL
STD	Stores the contents of double accumulator A:B in memory. The contents of ACCD remain unchanged.	M:M + 1←(ACCD)
SUBD	Subtracts the contents of M:M + 1 from the contents of double accumulator AB and places the result in ACCD.	ACCD←(ACCD) - (M:M + 1)

*ACCD is the 16 bit register (A:B) formed by concatenating the A and B accumulators. The A-accumulator is the most significant byte.

then load data into an external device. This can do the useful job of providing a handshake capability between μPs and peripherals. In the expanded multiplexed modes (to be explained) port 3 is *time multiplexed* to provide both data and the most significant 8-bits of the address bus. The **6801** has 8 operating modes. It can stand alone as a one-chip controller, can serve as a central processor controlling memory and peripheral devices, or it can communicate with several other **6801s** under the control of a central **6800** series μP.

12-4.1

6801 **Instruction Improvements**

The **6801** instruction set is both source and object *compatible* with current **6800s**, and **6800** programs will run on the **6801** *without* modification. The **6800** instruction set has been augmented, however, by 10 new instructions (21 OP codes), as shown in Table 12-3. Table 12-4 shows that modifications have also been made to *shorten* the execution of many existing instructions. The **6801** instruction set is therefore a *superset* of the **6800** set.

Additions to the **6801** set include six 16-bit operations on the double accumulator (D). The double accumulator is a 16-bit accumulator made up of the A accumulator (which forms the 8 most significant bits of D), and the B accumulator (that forms the 8 least significant bits). Instructions using the double accumulator are load, store, add 16 bits, subtract 16 bits and shift the double accumulator right or left. (Table 12-3). Three other new operations manipulate the index (X) register as follows.

1. Push X register (onto the stack).
2. Pull X register (from the stack).
3. Add B accumulator to X register.

The push and pull of the index register enhances the **6801's** ability to handle *reentrant* as well as *position-independent* code and allows quick temporary storage of the index register.

The Compare Index Register (CPX) instruction is also modified to set properly all of the condition codes bits, so that *less than* or *greater than* decisions can be made. The instruction to add accumulator B to X, greatly reduces the time to modify addresses in the index register. Perhaps the most interesting new instruction for the **6801** is an 8-by-8-bit *unsigned multiply* that provides a 16-bit result in 10 microseconds. This instruction is 20 times faster than an implementation in **6800** software. The multiply instruction, along with the one for adding accumulator B to the index register, makes real-time table lookup and interpolation three to four times faster than before.

The **6801** has *eight* modes of operation. These are selected by switches, jumpers, or logic connected to pins 8, 9, and 10. During RESET, this hardware determines the TTL levels on these pins that are also the three LSBs of port 2. The levels are *latched* as indicated by the three MSBs of port 2s I/O register, which is located at address $0003 in the **6801's** memory map. They are latched when RESET goes high. Bidirectional couplers may be needed if these lines are to be used with external peripherals. Table 12-5 shows how the modes relate to the pin levels and describes the system configuration selected in each case.

The **6801** is capable of three basic modes.

1. **Single chip mode.** In this stand alone mode, the ports are all configured as I/O and as seen in Table 12-5, *all* RAM and ROM are internal. Since this provides 2K bytes of ROM and 128 bytes of RAM, many complete systems can be implemented.

2. **Expanded nonmultiplexed mode.** As shown in Figure 12-5, this mode of the **6801** will directly address **6800** peripherals with no external logic. Port 3 becomes the data bus, and port 4 is the address bus (A7–A0) (see Note 6 of Table 12-5). Port 2 can be parallel I/O, serial I/O, timer, or any combination thereof. Port 1 is parallel I/O only. Port 4 can address up to 256 locations but if fewer addresses are enough, the extra lines can be used as inputs for other signals.

3. **Expanded multiplexed mode.** When used in the expanded multiplexed mode, the **6801** *multiplexes* its 8-bit bus address lines A0–A7 with data lines D0–D7 (see Fig. 12-3 again). These lines are brought out of the third port, while the fourth I/O port provides address lines A8–A15. The first and second ports can still be used for I/O functions. Thus, at the expense of some I/O capability, the designer has all 65 kilobytes of address space available to him, except for those sections that are occupied by internal functions. With the addition of an 8-bit latch (see Fig. 12-6) up to 16 address lines are provided for expanding the system to the full memory map.

For multiprocessor applications, the **6801** architecture allows operation in several ways: programmable peripheral control, handshaking, and serial I/O. Each way lets the μPs communicate at a different speed and has different advantages and disadvantages, depending on the hardware configuration.

As a multiprocessor programmable peripheral controller (shown

Table 12-4
Instruction Execution Times for the **6801**

	ACCX	Immediate	Direct	Extended	Indexed	Inherent	Relative
ABA	•	•	•	•	•	2	•
ABX	•	•	•	•	•	3	•
ADC	•	2	3	4	4	•	•
ADD	•	2	3	4	4	•	•
ADDD	•	4	5	6	6	•	•
AND	•	2	3	4	4	•	•
ASL	2	•	•	6	6	2	•
ASLD	•	•	•	•	•	3	•
ASR	2	•	•	6	6	2	•
BCC	•	•	•	•	•	•	3
BCS	•	•	•	•	•	•	3
BEQ	•	•	•	•	•	•	3
BGE	•	•	•	•	•	•	3
BGT	•	•	•	•	•	•	3
BHI	•	•	•	•	•	•	3
BIT	•	2	3	4	4	•	•
BLE	•	•	•	•	•	•	3
BLS	•	•	•	•	•	•	3
BLT	•	•	•	•	•	•	3
BMI	•	•	•	•	•	•	3
BNE	•	•	•	•	•	•	3
BPL	•	•	•	•	•	•	3
BRA	•	•	•	•	•	•	3
BSR	•	•	•	•	•	•	•
BVC	•	•	•	•	•	•	3
BVS	•	•	•	•	•	•	3
CBA	•	•	•	•	•	2	•
CLC	•	•	•	•	•	2	•
CLI	•	•	•	•	•	2	•
CLR	2	•	•	6	6	2	•
CLV	•	•	•	•	•	2	•
CMP	•	2	3	4	4	•	•
COM	2	•	•	6	6	2	•
CPX	•	4	5	6	6	•	•
DAA	•	•	•	•	•	2	•
DEC	2	•	•	6	6	2	•
DES	•	•	•	•	•	3	•
DEX	•	•	•	•	•	3	•
EOR	•	2	3	4	4	•	•
INC	2	•	•	6	6	•	•
INS	•	•	•	•	•	3	•

	ACCX	Immediate	Direct	Extended	Indexed	Inherent	Relative
INX	•	•	•	•	3	•	
JMP	•	•	•	3	•	•	
JSR	•	•	5	6	•	•	
LDA	•	2	3	4	•	•	
LDD	•	3	4	5	•	•	
LDS	•	3	4	5	•	•	
LDX	•	3	4	5	5	•	•
LSLD	•	•	•	•	•	3	•
LSL	•	•	•	6	6	2	•
LSR	2	•	•	6	6	2	•
LSRD	•	•	•	•	•	3	•
MUL	•	•	•	•	•	10	•
NEG	2	•	•	6	6	2	•
NOP	•	•	•	•	•	2	•
ORA	•	2	3	4	4	•	•
PSH	3	•	•	•	•	3	•
PSHX	•	•	•	•	•	4	•
PUL	4	•	•	•	•	4	•
PULX	•	•	•	•	•	5	•
ROL	2	•	•	6	6	2	•
ROR	2	•	•	6	6	2	•
RTI	•	•	•	•	•	10	•
RTS	•	•	•	•	•	5	•
SBA	•	•	•	•	•	2	•
SBC	•	2	3	4	4	•	•
SEC	•	•	•	•	•	2	•
SEI	•	•	•	•	•	2	•
SEV	•	•	•	•	•	2	•
STA	•	•	3	4	4	•	•
STD	•	•	4	5	5	•	•
STS	•	•	4	5	5	•	•
STX	•	•	4	5	5	•	•
SUB	•	2	3	4	4	•	•
SUBD	•	4	5	6	6	•	•
SWI	•	•	•	•	•	12	•
TAB	•	•	•	•	•	2	•
TAP	•	•	•	•	•	2	•
TBA	•	•	•	•	•	2	•
TPA	•	•	•	•	•	2	•
TST	2	•	•	6	6	2	•
TSX	•	•	•	•	•	3	•
TXS	•	•	•	•	•	3	•
WAI	•	•	•	•	•	9	•

Table 12-5
6801 Mode Selection

MODE	I/O 22(7) PC2	I/O 21 PC1	I/O 20 PC0	ROM	RAM	Interrupt Vectors	Bus Mode	Operating Mode
7	H	H	H	I	I	I	I	Single Chip
6	H	H	L	I	I	I	MUX[6]	Multiplexed/Partial Decode
5	H	L	H	I	I	I	NMUX[6]	Non-Multiplexed/Partial Decode
4	H	L	L	I[2]	I[1]	I	I	Single Chip Test
3	L	H	H	E	E	E	MUX[4]	Multiplexed/No RAM or ROM
2	L	H	L	E	I	E	MUX[4]	Multiplexed/RAM
1	L	L	H	I	I	E	MUX[4]	Multiplexed RAM & ROM
0	L	L	L	I	I	I[3]	MUX[4]	Multiplexed Test

Legend: I—internal
E—external
MUX—multiplexed
NMUX—nonmultiplexed
L—logic ''0''
H—logic ''1''

Notes:

1. Internal RAM is addressed at $XX80.
2. Internal ROM is disabled.
3. $\overline{\text{RESET}}$ vector is external for 2 cycles after $\overline{\text{RESET}}$ goes high.
4. Addresses associated with ports 3 and 4 are considered external in modes 0, 1, 2, and 3.
5. Addresses associated with port 3 are considered external in modes 5 and 6.
6. Port 4 default is user data input; address output is optional by writing to port 4 Data Direction Register.

in Fig. 12-7) the **6801** interconnects directly to any **6800** μP bus (**6800, 6802,** or **6809**) or to another **6801**, simply as a peripheral device. Here the **6801** acts as a slave, communicating through the

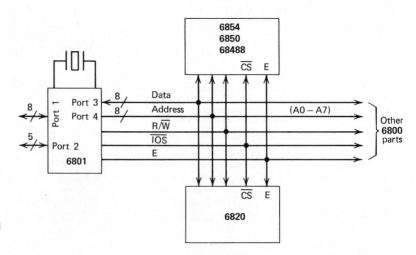

Figure 12-5 The **6801** in the expanded nonmultiplexed mode.

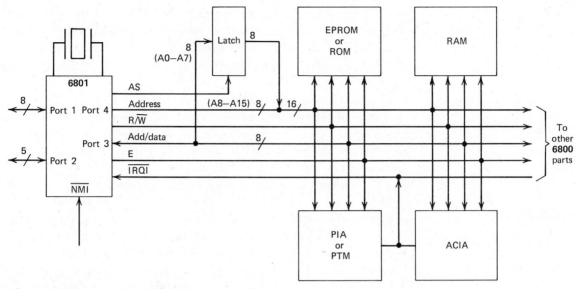

Figure 12-6 The expanded multiplexed mode of the **6801**.

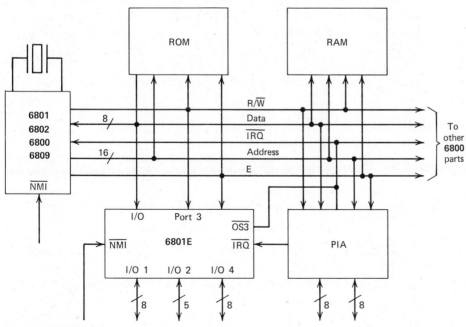

Figure 12-7 The **6801** as a programmable peripheral controller.

third I/O port on the master processor bus. Through this port, the processors can be made to talk to each other, and use the interrupt structure of each processor for handshaking. The other peripheral I/O ports (the first, second, and fourth) are available for peripheral control functions.

In the multiprocessor handshaking mode, shown in Fig. 12-8 two independent **6801s** may communicate over the 8-bit parallel bus from the third I/O port. The input strobe (IS) and output strobe (OS) may be used for *handshake* control. Since this port is the only one used for this mode, the other 21 I/O lines are still available for local functions, along with the IRQ and NMI interrupts.

Finally, in the multiprocessor serial mode (shown in Fig. 12-9), several **6801s** may communicate with each other over the single-wire I/O lines (bits 3 and 4 of port 2), with one processor being the master and the rest being slaves. Bit 2 of port 2 is used for clocking if the internal-clock-out, or external-clock-in options are used. I/O is handled with hardware shift registers on the **6801** chip; it is possible to achieve data transfer rates of up to 76 kilobaud between processors. This is the *fastest* **6801** multiprocessor mode and makes the most efficient use of the **6801's** general-purpose I/O pins in the first, second, and third I/O ports. When linked in this way, with MODEMs or other low noise transmission links, the **6801** locations may be physically remote from each other, and the number of locations is limited only by the minimum data transfer rate required for a particular application.

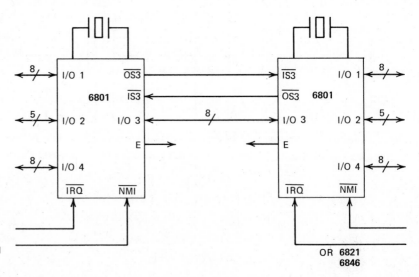

Figure 12-8 The **6801** in a handshaking arrangement.

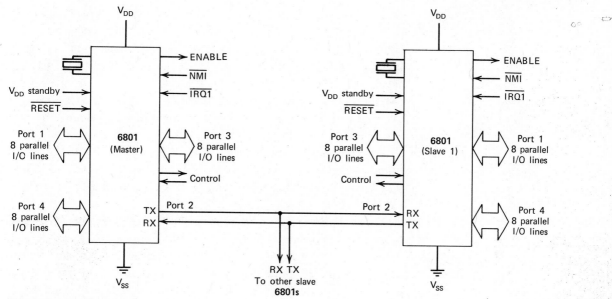

Figure 12-9 Multiprocessing interconnections using serial I/O.

12-5
The 6809 High
Performance μP

The **6809** was introduced in the fall of 1978. It is an advanced processor of the **6800** family and offers greater *throughput,* improved *byte-efficiency,* and the ability to handle new software methods. These include *position-independence, reentrancy, recursion, block structuring,* and high level language generation.

The **6809** is bus-compatible with the **6800** peripherals and is software-compatible with the **6800** at the source (mnemonic) level.

The **6809** object codes are not the same but a macro-assembler is provided that will generate **6809** machine codes from a **6800** source program. New instructions and more addressing modes have been added. The following sections point out the improvements inherent in the **6809**.

12-5.1
Hardware Features

The **6809** is similar to the **6800** in that it is also a 40-pin NMOS IC with the same basic bus architecture. The pin assignments include five new signals besides XTAL, EXTAL, and E that are the same as those used on the **6801** and **6802** devices. A third interrupt request input (FIRQ) and another processor status output (BS or Bus Status) have been added. A memory ready signal (MRDY) inhibits transitions of the on-chip clock an integral multiple of quarter (¼) bus cycles, as shown in Fig. 12-10. This line can be held low a maximum of 10 μsec to extend the data access time for slow memory applications. Also as shown in Fig. 12-10, a new clock signal called Q takes the place of phase 1 and leads E by 90 degrees. E is used similarly to phase 2 on the **6800**. It can also be seen that if MRDY is pulled LOW a minimum of 60 nsec before the end of a normal E cycle, it will prevent any level changes in either Q or E until the next quarter cycle after it is released.

The Q signal has no parallel in the **6800** but provides two additional timing edges at the ¼ and ¾ points in the cycle. Addresses will be valid with the leading edge of Q. As in the **6800**, data is latched on the falling edge of E.

A new bus request input (DMA/BREQ) provides for DMA and dynamic memory refresh. As shown in Fig. 12-11, a self-refresh feature will automatically refresh internal dynamic registers whenever DMA/BREQ is held longer than 14 cycles by executing 1 μP cycle. It will repeat every 17th cycle until DMA/BREQ is released.

The VMA signal (and its need for additional gating in chip selection) has been eliminated.

A revised RESET input requires only an RC delay to initialize the μP properly.

A third interrupt, Fast Interrupt ReQuest (FIRQ), has been added so that NMI, IRQ, and FIRQ are the hardware interrupt inputs available on the **6809**. When a logic zero is recognized at the FIRQ input, the **6809** places only the *program counter and condition code registers on the stack* prior to accessing the FIRQ vector. The IRQ or

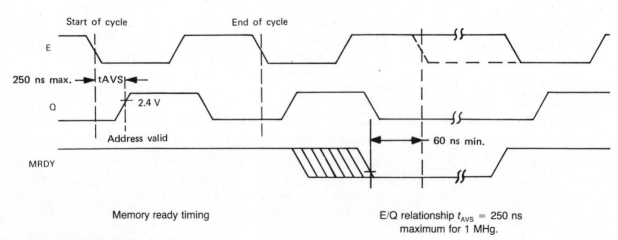

Memory ready timing

E/Q relationship t_{AVS} = 250 ns
maximum for 1 MHg.

Figure 12-10 MRDY timing.

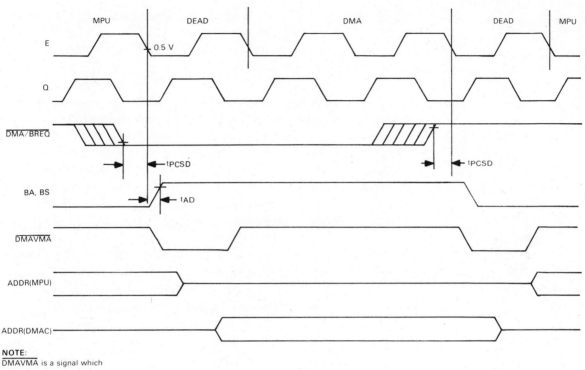

NOTE:
DMAVMA is a signal which
is developed externally, but
is a system requirement for DMA.

(a)

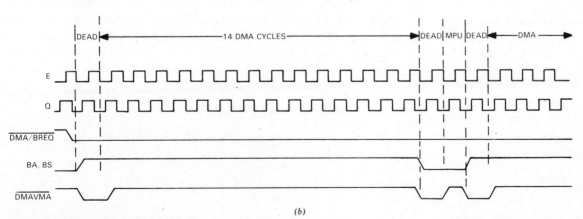

(b)

Figure 12-11 Auto-refresh DMA timing.
(a) Typical DMA timing (< 14 cycles).
(b) Auto-refresh DMA timing (> 14
    cycles).

NMI still put the content of *all* registers (same as **6800**) on the stack. Two software interrupts (SWI2 and SWI3) are also added. All interrupts are prioritized with NMI the highest, followed by SWI, IRQ, FIRQ, SWI2, and SWI3.

An Interrupt Acknowledge function (IACK) can be decoded from the Bus Status (BS) and Bus Available (BA) signals, as shown in Table 12-6, to indicate when a vector is being fetched for any of the interrupts (i.e., RESET, NMI, SWI, IRQ, FIRQ, SWI2, or SWI3). The SYNC instruction of the **6809** (see Sec. 12-8) causes the processor to halt and await an interrupt. The SYNC acknowledge condition shown in Table 12-6 can be detected to provide hardware feedback. This allows hardware devices to be synchronized with the IRQ, hence the name.

12-5.2
Programming Model

Three additional registers are provided in the **6809**; the Direct Page register (DP), User stack pointer (U), and a second index register (Y) (Fig. 12-12). Much greater flexibility of register usage is also provided by new addressing modes. In particular, the addition of indirect addressing, and enhancements of the indexed and relative addressing modes has increased the power of many instructions. These improvements will be described in the following paragraphs.

12-5.3
Accumulators

As in the **6800**, the A and B registers are general purpose 8-bit accumulators used for arithmetic and data manipulations. In general the two registers are identical in the **6809**, although some special purpose instructions apply to the A register only. Certain new instructions allow the A and B registers to be used together, as shown in Fig. 12-12, to form a *16-bit accumulator* known as the *D register*. The A accumulator is the MS byte. A number of 16-bit instructions (including *load, store, add,* and *subtract*) have been added. These

Table 12-6
Bus Condition Signals

BA	BS	
0	0	Normal (running)
0	1	Interrupt or RESET Acknowledge
1	0	SYNC acknowledge
1	1	HALT or Bus grant

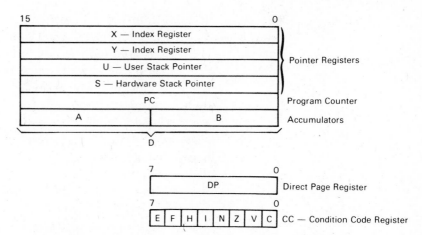

Figure 12-12 Programming model of the **6809** microprocessor.

double accumulator instructions have been provided with all the expanded addressing modes.

An example of the increased power of these instructions is given in the following example.

Example 12-1

a. Two 16-bit numbers are in memory locations F0, F1, F2, and F3. Write a **6809** program to add them and store the results in F4 and F5.

b. Compare the number of bytes and cycles with Ex. 5-11.

Solution

a. The program is shown in Table 12-7.

Table 12-7
6809 Program to Add Two 16-Bit Numbers

Addr	Code	Mnemonics	Cycles
1000	DC F0	LDD $F0	5
1002	D3 F2	ADDD $F2	6
1004	DD F4	STD $F4	5

b. The **6800** program (of Ex. 5-11) uses twice as many bytes (12 vs. 6) and requires 20 cycles instead of 16.

Note that the **6809** program is much simpler and faster.

12-5.4
Direct Page Register

The direct addressing concept is extended by use of the Direct Page (DP) register. The contents of this register appear as the high order bits (A8–A15) of *direct addressing* instructions, which allows direct addressing *anywhere* in memory. All bits of this register are cleared during RESET to insure **6800** compatibility. An assembler directive (SETDP) is used to make use of this feature. Table 12-8 shows the application of the directive as well as its effect on the assembly of typical instructions. For example, when the directive is acted upon by the assembler, the statements on lines 7 and 9 are assembled in the direct addressing form (two bytes) since they are in the $1A page, while line 8 is assembled as an extended instruction (three bytes). In lines 9 through 13, the > and < symbols are used to force the assembler to generate extended or direct addressing modes. Direct addressing is forced in lines 9, 10, and 13 (by <) as is extended addressing in lines 11 and 12 (by the >). The forcing of line 10 to assemble as a direct instruction is of dubious value since the DP register has not been previously set (to 1B), as is indicated by the assembler warning message. Line 14 is a repeat of the SETDP directive (to set the page to $1B). This directive can be used as many times as desired during an assembly. (This information is covered in detail in the **6809** Macro assembler reference manual listed in Sec. 12-15.) Note that if the programs of the previous Example 12-1 were changed, for example, to use locations at $10F0 through $10F5, for the data storage, the **6800** version would take 18 bytes and if the DP

Table 12-8
Effect of Direct Page Directive

```
PAGE   001  DIRPGE  .SA:0  DIRPGE

00001                               *    SET DIRECT PAGE DIRECTIVE
00002                              *THIS PROGRAM SHOWS THE EFFECT OF
00003                              *THE DIRECT PAGE DIRECTIVE IN ASSEMBLY
00004                              *OF A PROGRAM.
00005                                        NAM     DIRPGE
00006              001A        A             SETDP   $1A
00007A 0000 96     00          A             LDA     $1A00
00008A 0002 B6     1B00        A             LDA     $1B00
00009A 0005 96     00          A             LDA     <$1A00
****WARNING    002--00000
00010A 0007 96     00          A             LDA     <$1B00
00011A 0009 B6     1A00        A             LDA     >$1A00
00012A 000C B6     1B00        A             LDA     >$1B00
00013A 000F 9E     FF          A             LDX     <$1AFF
00014              001B        A             SETDP   $1B
00015A 0011 96     00          A             LDA     $1B00
00016                                        END
TOTAL ERRORS  00000--00000
TOTAL WARNINGS 00001--00010
```

register of the **6809** was set to $10, the **6809** program would still take only 6 bytes.

12-5.5
Condition Code Register

Bits 0 through 5 of the Condition Code register are identical to those of the **6800**, but bits 6 and 7 have been added (Fig. 12-12) for FIRQ handling. Bit 6 (F) is the mask bit for FIRQ, and bit 7 (E) controls the *ReTurn from Interrupt* (RTI) instruction to insure that the proper number of registers are pulled from the stack by the RTI instruction.

12-5.6
Stack Pointers

The hardware stack pointer (S) is used to store machine states during execution of subroutines and interrupts in the same way as in the **6800** (with a minor difference that is explained below). An additional user stack pointer (U) is provided in the **6809**, and is controlled by the user program, thus allowing arguments to be passed to and from subroutines with ease. Both S and U have the same indexed-mode addressing capabilities as the X and Y registers. This allows the **6809** to be used effectively as a *stack processor*, greatly enhancing its ability to support higher level languages. To facilitate use of the stack pointers in indexed-mode addressing, the registers always point to the last byte placed on the stack instead of to the next available byte as with the **6800** (Fig. 12-13).

Because of the additional registers in the **6809**, an interrupt causes more data to be written to the stack. This is shown in Fig. 12-13. Note that a FIRQ causes only the PC and CCR to be written, however, and is therefore much faster.

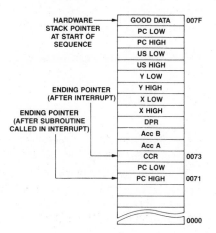

Figure 12-13 6809 stack operation.

12-6

Addressing Modes

Three new categories have been added to the addressing modes of the **6800** making a total of 9 for the **6809**, as listed below.

> Immediate
> Inherent
> Direct
> Extended
> Indexed
> Relative
> Extended indirect
> Indexed indirect
> Long relative

12-6.1

Immediate, Inherent, Direct, Extended, and Accumulator Modes

These modes are effectively the same as in the **6800**. See Sec. 12-5.4 for direct-mode added capability.

12-6.2

Indexed Modes

In the **6800**, the indexed mode of addressing provides for adding an offset to the index register to form an *effective address*, and this effective address is the value used to *access* memory locations. In the **6809**, this same feature exists, but several additional methods are available to generate the *effective addresses*. The offset can now be up to 16 bits, and can be an *expression* (such as a symbol plus a constant). The student is again referred to the assembler manual for a complete definition of the possible forms.

Five basic types of indexing are available. A *postbyte* (i.e., the byte immediately following the OP code) is used to specify the basic type as well as which pointer register is to be used.

1. In the *zero-offset* indexed mode the selected pointer register contains the *effective address*. This is the *fastest* indexing mode. Examples are:

> LDD 0,X
> LDA 0,X

As in the **6800**, the 0 can be omitted but the comma is required (i.e., LDD ,X).

2. The *constant offset* indexed mode adds a 2s complement offset to the contents of the pointer registers to form the *effective address*. The offset can be 8 or 16 bits. The 2s complement 8-bit offset value is in a single byte following the postbyte, and a 16-bit offset requires an additional byte. The assembler calculates the size of this offset. This mode is similar to the **6800** index mode except that several different registers are available for indexing in the **6809**.

Examples of constant-offset indexing are:

```
LDA  23,X
LDX  -2,S
LDY  300,X
LDU  CAT,Y
```

Note that the machine language could be up to five bytes for these instructions as follows:

OP code—One or two bytes (two for some lesser-used instructions)
Postbyte—One
Offset—One (for 8-bit) or two (for 16-bit)

3. A new indexing mode is *accumulator-offset*. This is similar to the previous mode except that a 2s complement value in one of the accumulators (A, B, or D), is added to the pointer register value to form the *effective address*. The postbyte shows *which* accumulator is used, and no additional bytes are needed. This mode is useful because the value of the offset can be calculated at run-time.

Some examples are:

```
LDA  B,Y
LDX  D,Y
LEAX B,X
```

4. Indexed addressing with *auto increment/decrement* is also possible. The data at the pointer register value is accessed *prior* to the increment (by 1 or 2) but, in decrementing, the address is *reduced* prior to the data access. This mode is useful for work with tables of single or double bytes (16-bits). The predecrement, postincrement nature of these modes allows X and Y to be used for stacks that behave identically to those using U or S.

Examples are:

```
LDA  ,X+
STD  ,Y++
LDB  ,-Y
LDX  ,--S
```

The **6809** assembler mnemonics are used here with the + and − indicating an increment or decrement (+ + is a double increment). For an example of autoincrementing and its use with the double accumulator, see the program shown in Table 12-9. Refer to the macroassembler manual identified in the references in Sec. 12-15 for details on the proper instruction syntax.

Example 12-2

The **6809** program of Table 12-9 adds two 16-bit vectors, one from Table A and one from Table B, and places the result in Table C. Explain specifically how the program of Table 12-9 works.

Table 12-9
Program to Add Two 16-Bit Numbers

```
M6800-M6809 CROSS-ASSEMBLER  2.2


00099                             ********** VECTOR ADDITION / 16-BIT **********
00100                             *
00101                             *     PERFORM AN ELEMENT-BY-ELEMENT ADDITION ON
00102                             *     TWO VECTORS OF N 16-BIT ELEMENTS EACH.
00103                             *     PLACE THE RESULT IN A DIFFERENT VECTOR.
00104                             *     LET N BE 20.
00105                             *
00106                             *     SETUP:      3 LN, 10 BY,  10 CY
00107                             *     OPERATION:  5 LN, 11 BY, 32*20=640 CY
00108                             *     TOTAL:      8 LN, 21 BY, 650 CY
00109                             *
00110                             **********************************************

00112 1077 8E   108E   3 ANBNCN LDX    #TABLEA
00113 107A 108E 10B6   4        LDY    #TABLEB
00114 107E CE   10DE   3        LDU    #TABLEC

00116 1081 EC   81     8 AN1    LDD    ,X++
00117 1083 E3   A1     9        ADDD   ,Y++
00118 1085 ED   C1     8        STD    ,U++
00119 1087 8C   10B6   4        CMPX   #2*20+TABLEA
00120 108A 26   F5     3        BNE    AN1

00122 108C 20   FE     3        BRA    *

00124 108E      0000     TABLEA FDB    $00,$01,$02,$03,$04
00125 1098      0005            FDB    $05,$06,$07,$08,$09
00126 10A2      0010            FDB    $10,$11,$12,$13,$14
00127 10AC      0015            FDB    $15,$16,$17,$18,$19
00128 10B6      0099     TABLEB FDB    $99,$98,$97,$96,$95
00129 10C0      0094            FDB    $94,$93,$92,$91,$90
00130 10CA      0089            FDB    $89,$88,$87,$86,$85
00131 10D4      0084            FDB    $84,$83,$82,$81,$80
00132 10DE      0000     TABLEC FDB    0,,,,,,,,,,,,,,,,,,,0
```

Solution

The program operates as follows:

1. The instructions on lines 112, 113, and 114 load the address of Tables A, B, and C (the table for the results) into the X, Y, and U registers. At this point, X contains 108E, Y contains 10B6, and U contains 10DE, as shown on lines 124, 128, and 132.
2. The instruction on lines 116, 117, and 118 cause the first two bytes of X (0001) to be added to the first two bytes of Y (9998). The result (9999) is stored in Table C. Note the use of the double registers for 16-bit addition.
3. Because of the autoincrement mode, X now contains 1090 (108E + 2), Y contains 10B8, and U contains 10E0.
4. X is now compared to 2*20 + Table A = $(40)_{10}$ + 108E = $(28)_{16}$ + 108E = 10B6. If they are equal, Table A is exhausted and the program stops. Otherwise it branches back and continues. Autoincrementing has taken care of properly incrementing the registers.

5. Still another indexing technique is *indexed indirect*. This is usable in all but the auto increment/decrement (by one) modes. An additional level of *indirect addressing* can be specified. The effective address is contained at the location specified by the index register plus any offset. In the example below, the A accumulator is loaded *indirectly* using an effective address calculated from the index register and an offset. Note that the square brackets indicate *indirect addressing*.

To start, X = $F000.

0100	LDA [10,X]	This instruction tells the **6809** that the address is in (X) + 10 = F010.
	. . .	
F010	FDB $F150	These locations contain the address of the data to be loaded into A.
	. . .	
F150	$AA	Accumulator A now = $AA.

Here are some examples of *indexed indirect* instructions.

```
LDA [ ,X]
LDD [10,S]
LDA [B,Y]
LDD [ ,X+ +]
```

Note: The zero has been omitted.

12-6.3
Relative Mode

Relative addressing involves adding a *signed constant* to the contents of the *program counter*. When used in conjunction with a branch instruction, this sum becomes the new program counter content if the branch is taken. (If the branch is not taken, the PC advances to the next instruction.)

Relative addressing differs from the **6800** because of two important additions. First the *constant offset* (which is a signed number) can be either 7 bits (± 128) or 15 bits (± 32768). This allows the program to branch to any location in the memory field, since in the latter case, the addresses wrap around (0000 is next after FFFF or FFFF is one less than 0000), and any location is therefore always less than 32768 bytes away, one way or the other. The second important addition to the relative mode is that it no longer is limited to branch instructions. In these cases, an *effective address*, which retains the *position-independent* nature of relative addressing, may be formed by adding a 7-bit or 15-bit offset to the program counter. This, in effect, is an indexed addressing mode with specific postbytes (8C, 8D, 9C, or 9D). The optional postbytes allow selection of the 7- or 15-bit offset for the *program counter relative* or *relative indirect* modes described below.

12-7
Program Counter Relative
Addressing

In addition to the normal function, the **6809** provides a mode allowing the program counter to be used as an index register. This is called the *Program Counter Relative* (PCR) mode and, as in relative addressing, the 8- or 16-bit signed offset is added to the current PC to create the *effective address*. Position-independent code can be more easily written than for other 8-bit μPs; for example:

```
LDA   CAT,PCR
LEAX  TABLE,PCR    (where CAT and TABLE are labels)
```

Since *program counter relative* is a form of indexing, an additional indirect addressing level is available, as follows:

```
LDA   [CAT,PCR]
LEAX  [TABLE,PCR]
```

12-7.1
Relative Indirect Mode

This addressing mode is, in effect, *indexed indirect* with the program counter used as an index register. One or two bytes (optionally) following the postbyte are used to provide a 7-bit or 15-bit offset. This signed number is added to the contents of the program counter, forming a pointer to consecutive locations in memory that contain the new effective address, for example:

```
LDA   [CAT,PCR]
LDU   [DOG,PCR]
```

12-7.2
Extended Indirect Mode

This addressing mode is actually another option of indexed indirect addressing. In this case, the *two bytes following* the *postbyte* are used as a *pointer* to consecutive locations that contain the new effective address.

12-7.3
Absolute Indirect Mode

This mode is exclusively used for *restart* and *interrupt* vectoring. Servicing of these conditions involves fetching the contents of a *dedicated* location in memory to be loaded into the program counter and, thus, it is not available for any locations other than the interrupt vectors.

12-8
6809 Instruction Set

A complete listing of the executable instructions is contained in Tables F1 to F5 in Appendix F. Some of the more unique instructions include *load effective address, synchronization with interrupt,* and *exchange registers.* These, along with others not available on the **6800**, are detailed in the following paragraphs.

Load Effective Address. (LEA-). Besides its obvious use, this instruction represents a convenient means of modifying any of the pointer (X, Y, S, or U) registers. The processor forms an effective address as dictated by the addressing mode, then loads this value into the designated register rather than outputting the data on the address lines. 2s complement addition of the A, B, or D (double accumulator) registers or an immediate (#) value, to X, Y, U, or S registers can be done. For example, LEAX D,X will add the signed number contained in the D register to the contents of the X register, then place this result into the X register.

Synchronize with Interrupt (SYNC). This instruction causes processing to discontinue until an interrupt input (NMI, IRQ, or FIRQ) is activated. When an interrupt occurs, and the associated mask is clear, the processor services the interrupt normally. If the interrupt mask is SET when the interrupt occurs, the processor exits the Sync Mode by continuing to the next instruction. The Bus Available (BA) output is activated during the Sync Mode. The instruction is particularly useful for synchronizing the program with a peripheral that uses or supplies data.

Exchange (EXG) and Transfer Registers (TFR). Both of these instructions use a postbyte to define the source and destination registers. The only restriction is that both source and destination must be similarly sized registers.

Push/Pull Register(s) (PSH-/PUL-). These instructions also use a postbyte to designate whether the register assigned to a particular bit is to be affected. Thus, a push instruction followed by a byte containing a 1 in bit 7 causes the program counter to be pushed onto a stack. Up to eight registers can be pushed or pulled with a single instruction.

Sign Extend (SEX). This instruction causes all bits in the A register to take on the value of the most significant bit of the B register.

Clear CCR and Wait (CWAI). This instruction is similar to the wait for interrupt used with the **6800**, but includes an immediate byte to clear condition codes if desired. The CWAI instruction can be used with any of the three interrupt lines, even though CWAI stacks all registers (except S). After stacking is complete, Bus Available (BA) is activated and the processor idles until an interrupt occurs.

Those familiar with the **6800** will note that some instructions are missing from the complement available with the **6800**. Provisions have been made to perform such operations in alternate ways when required. An example might be decrement X. This will not often be needed with the **6809** because of the autodecrement option with indexed addressing. If needed, however, the operation can be accomplished with an LEAX − 1,X instruction. Likewise, the **6800** instructions to clear/set various condition codes are replaced with ANDCC/ORCC. In this manner, the **6809** uses fewer instruction mnemonics (59 vs. 72) than the **6800**, yet is fully software compatible at the mnemonic level, as well as being considerably more powerful.

12-9
The 3870 μC

The **3870** is a complete 8-bit μC on a single MOS integrated circuit. Utilizing ion-implanted, N-channel, silicon-gate technology, and advanced circuit design techniques, the single chip **3870**, shown in functional block form in Fig. 12-14 provides a low cost replacement for discrete logic for controller applications.

It offers the following features.

Software compatible with F8 family
2048-byte mask programmed ROM
64-byte scratchpad RAM
32 bits (four 8 bit) I/O ports

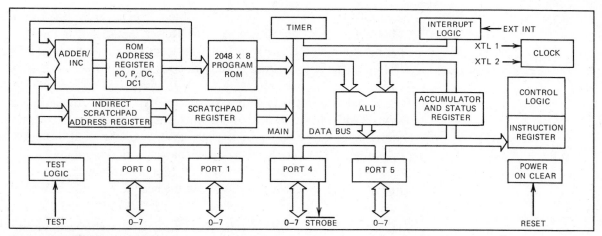

Figure 12-14 MC3870 single-chip microcomputer block diagram.

External interrupt
Crystal, LC, RC, external clock control
Low power (275 mW typ)
Single 5 V supply
Programmable binary timer

This 40-pin μC is very popular because of its low cost and available library of programs for controller applications. The need to evaluate system performance with a test program before the on-board mask programmable ROM can be specified presents some difficult problems. One solution to this problem is the **3870** Emulator Module for the EXORciser. This module contains three F8 family ICs (**3853, 3871,** and **3850**) that provide an accurate emulation of the **3870** but also permits RAM to be used in place of the **3870's** ROM. Thus, user programs can be debugged and tested before committing them to the masked ROM. Also, the program can be placed in an EPROM for extended testing and verification. Turn-around time for testing system concepts is thus shortened and development costs considerably reduced. Accompanying software includes an assembler to generate the object code and a debugging program very similar (in operation) to EXbug. Many identical commands (to the **6800's** EXBUG) make learning easy.

The system configuration for emulation testing is very much like the User System Evaluator (USE) described in Sec. 11-11.7 (i.e., a cable from the emulation module that terminates in a 40-pin plug is installed into the user's prototype system in place of the **3870** μC). This allows the user to use the EXORciser terminal to access his hardware through the I/O ports and to load programs into RAM for testing. After the program is fully debugged, and placed in the 2K EPROM, the module can be removed from the EXORciser and operated independently by simply supplying 5 volts to it. An additional associated μP (multiprocessor system) could then be developed (using another emulator board if necessary), until the total system is operational. The details of the **3870** characteristics are shown in the data sheet for the IC and in the **3870** Emulator Manual referenced in Sec. 12-15. These details eliminate the need to describe it further.

12-10
The 141000 **μC**

Although it is somewhat less sophisticated than the **3870**, this 4-bit single chip μC (shown in Fig. 12-15) nevertheless is more than adequate for a wide range of applications. It also features some unique advantages such as CMOS circuitry, which makes conventional 5 V or battery operation practicable. Forty-three basic instructions provide I/O, logic functions, or arithmetic processing, as in any larger computer. A 1024 × 8 ROM and a 64 × 4 RAM provide the on-chip memory requirements. The **MC141000** is source program (mnemonic) compatible (but not object code) with the well-known PMOS **TMS1000** unit. Since the **MC141000** is also a masked programmable part (like the **3870**), the same difficulty exists in developing a system. Again, an Emulator is available for the EXORciser.

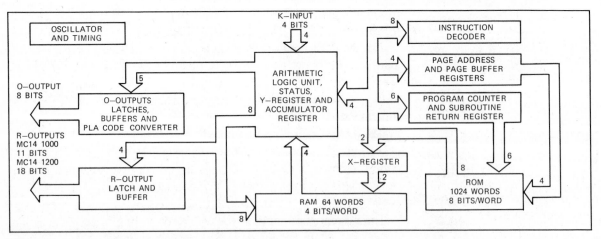

Figure 12-15 MC141000 single-chip 4-bit μC block diagram.

Details on this and the IC itself are listed in the data sheet for the **MC141000** and the **141000** Emulator manual referenced in Sec. 12-15.

12-11
The Intel μP Families

No book on μPs would be complete without mentioning the Intel **8080** and its associated family components. The **8080** was introduced before the **6800** and was the first of the 40-pin NMOS designs. Both the **6800** and the **8080** are enhancements of the Intel **8008** and are basically of the same generation. The **8080** has a 16-bit address bus and an 8-bit data bus and many instructions similar to those of the **6800**. There are significant differences however, in both architecture and software. Intel chose to remain compatible with a predecessor of the **8080**, the **8008**, which caused several design limitations. The **6800** is considered by many to be a cleaner or simpler design with a more straightforward instruction set. For example, the clock timing of the **8080** is more complex than that of the **6800**. The **6800** machine cycle is the same as a single clock period, whereas the **8080** machine cycle is made up of from 3 to 5 clock periods. The **8080** clock frequency is generally higher than the **6800**, but the **8080** takes more clock cycles than the **6800** to execute a similar instruction. The **8080A** is the currently available version and is electrically and functionally compatible with the **8080**.

12-11.1
The 8080A **Architecture**

Functions included in the **8080A** are basically the same as in the **6800**. It contains six 8-bit general purpose registers and an accumulator. The six registers can be addressed individually or in pairs. Five processor or ALU flags are provided. An external stack is used with a 16-bit stack pointer. In comparison to the **6800**, the extra registers and the ability to handle multiple-precision (16-bit) values is an advantage, but the availability of only one accumulator is a limitation. Another important difference is the use of unique I/O instructions and I/O read and write lines. As a result much less flexibility is realized because the many memory referencing instructions cannot be used as they are in the **6800** (e.g., ASR, COM, and BIT). The Intel manuals include circuits to provide this "memory mapped" capability but only 32 K of memory can be used. The Intel manual also implies that the clock timing is too complex to build with TTL logic and therefore requires the use of a **8224** clock generator component. Similarly the data and control buses are handled with an **8228** system controller. Still another difference from the

6800 is the fact the **8080A** requires 3.3 V for a logic 1 and its buses are therefore not TTL compatible. Pullup resistors are needed to work with many devices if they are directly on the bus. Last but not least of the hardware features is the requirement for three power supplies ($+5$, $+12$, and -5 V).

12-11.2
8080A WAIT, HOLD, and HALT States

The **8080A** has a built-in feature called WAIT. This is intended for use with slow memories or other devices. Its function is similar to that provided by the various clock circuits described for the **6800** in Sec. 8-7. WAIT is activated by pulling down the READY line. Data and address buses are not tri-stated in this mode. The HOLD state is very much like the WAI (WAIT) instruction in the **6800**, in that the μP is placed in a state of suspended animation; however, it is started by a signal on a pin of the μP, instead of by an instruction. The data and address buses are tri-stated during this state. HALT is initiated by an instruction but requires that READY be LOW prior to its execution. An interrupt is used to terminate the HALT condition.

12-11.3
The 8080A Instruction Set

Several instructions operate on the 16-bit contents of the BC, DE, or HL register pairs. These include 16-bit add, increment, or decrement. The instruction set of the **6800** is much easier to learn in the opinion of many experts. It has fewer basic types with more addressing options. One reason for greater difficulty with the **8080A** software may be the large number of one-of-a-kind instructions. The additional registers of the **8080A** make it possible to carry information from routine to routine more easily than the **6800**, but the limitations of one accumulator makes many other tasks more difficult and slower. The lack of a direct addressing mode requires more memory than would be necessary with the **6800**. The IN and OUT instructions are the major cause for differences in programming techniques.

12-11.4
Other Intel μPs

Like all other μP manufacturers, Intel has introduced new types of μPs that are the result of improvements in the technologies. One is the **8085**. This NMOS IC essentially combines the functions of the **8080**, **8224** (clock generator), and the **8228** system controller into a single chip. In order to provide expanded control functions, the low order address bits are multiplexed with the data bus. The LOW address lines (0–7) appear on the data bus at the beginning of each instruction cycle. The **8085** thus has 8 data/address lines and 8 address lines and, in order to access the full 64K of memory, address latches must be used. To accommodate this requirement, an *Address Latch Enable* (ALE) signal is provided and several new bus components have been introduced that feature built-in address latching.

Another Intel product is the **8048**. This is a single chip μC that contains a clock oscillator, 1024 bytes of mask programmed ROM, 64 bytes of RAM, an 8-bit timer/event counter and 27 I/O lines, in addition to the μP. An EPROM version is provided for ease in program development. A new instruction set is used in which over 70% are one-byte and the remainder are two-byte instructions. The software is not upward compatible from any previous μP and therefore does not have the advantages of the **6801**, for example. The **8048** has only 12 address lines available and thus the address map is limited to 4 K.

A number of other μPs and μCs have been recently introduced, such as the **8086** 16-bit μP, and the **8021** 8-bit μC that has 1K of ROM, 64 bytes of RAM, and 21 I/O lines in a 28-pin package. An 8-bit timer is also included.

**12-12
Microprogrammed Systems**

Throughout this book we have been discussing various types of μP or μC components that have the total computer architecture included in the masked integrated circuitry. These components are almost all fabricated using MOS technology, which provides the circuit density necessary to place all the functions on one or two chips. Because of the fixed architecture, the instruction sets are also fixed.

At the same time, another technique has been pursued by some engineers, in order to achieve special advantages. By keeping the many functions in discrete LSI blocks, and using state-of-the-art, low power Schottky integrated circuits, it is possible to build a variety of custom-designed computers with outstanding performance advantages. The principal advantage is greater speed of operation (or throughput). A second advantage is the ability to tailor the architecture or instruction sets to accommodate special requirements. The design is centered around LSI components called *bit-slices*. These are specialized arithmetic/logic units (ALUs) usually designed to manipulate 4 bits of the computer word, and arranged so that any number of them can be used together to form words of any size (multiples of 4). Other LSI components are used to provide the other functions needed. For example, devices to include the control functions such as sequencing and addressing control, or others that provide timing, are used frequently.

A concept often employed in bit-slice designs, is *microprogramming*. In a typical computer instruction, several tasks are usually performed. The more tasks, the more powerful is the instruction. If an instruction decoder is going to do several tasks simultaneously, it must have more gates or more inputs (i.e., more bits per control word). Each basic instruction usually consists of several *microinstructions* performed sequentially at *very high speed*. These microinstructions determine the functions performed by each basic instruction (i.e., the instruction set). In a microprogrammed computer, the microinstructions are usually stored in a ROM known as the Microprogram Control Store (MCS). This MCS memory is simply an N-word by M-bit ROM used to hold the microinstructions. A typical memory might be 48 bits per word and 512 words long.

12-12.1
A Microprogrammed Processor

Figure 12-16 shows the block diagram of a typical microprogrammed processor. Any processor generally includes four basic functions: data processing, memory and peripheral interfacing, timing, and main control. Data processing is accomplished by the ALU, accumulators, processor status register, and working storage. Memory and peripheral interface logic handles the buffering and address generation, required to exchange data with main memory, or I/O ports for communication to external terminals or bulk storage. Timing circuitry provides the proper sequencing for all devices. Finally, main control coordinates all functions and determines which operations occur and when they should occur. Each *microinstruction* is divided into groups of data called *control fields*. Each field is independent in that it controls a separate processor area; however, all fields are also interdependent in that all processor operations are parallel operations and are interactive. A sample microcode word is shown in Fig. 12-17. There are six fields to control different processor areas.

1. The first two fields are an Instruction Control (IC) field, and Next Address (NA) vector field. These control the microprogram address sequencer. The IC field determines the new address source—such as increment present address or jump to new address. If the instruction calls for a new address, the NA field supplies it.
2. The next two fields are the register/ALU (RALU) and modifier fields. These oversee the data processing operations. The ALU arithmetic and

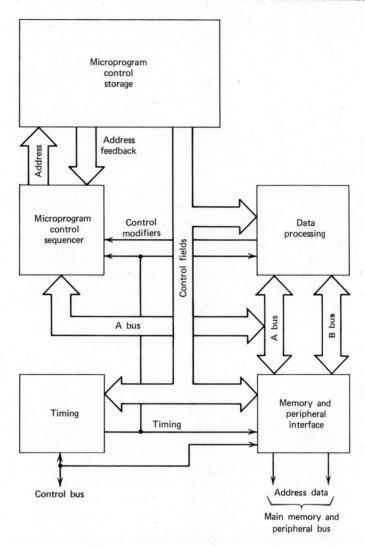

Figure 12-16 A microprogrammed processor.

logic functions are specified by the RALU bits. The modifier field interacts with the address sequencer for branches or shift functions, for example.

3. The final two fields are memory interface and timing, which cøntrol the

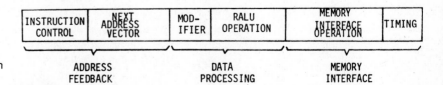

Figure 12-17 Sample microinstruction format.

processor interface with external buses. Memory address generation, data transfers, and control bus timing are managed by these bits.

During each microcycle, the data contained in these six fields determines the operation of each processor section. These parallel operations combine, forming one step of a larger *macroinstruction*. One macroinstruction may contain one, three, or fifty microinstructions. This is determined by the processor complexity or architecture.

It can be seen that the microprogrammed processor is flexible and powerful, but the designer now has two levels of hardware/software interface to contend with. The macroinstruction set must first be designed in terms of microinstructions, before higher level programming is done.

12-12.2
Development Tools for
Microprogrammed Processor Design

As in other system emulation hardware, a RAM is used to emulate a ROM that will ultimately be the Microprogram Control Store (MCS). This RAM must be configured to fit the word size required for the microcode words, and interconnected (via address and data probes) to the processor circuitry that has been assembled. Instruments for this purpose have been developed by American Micro Devices and by Motorola. The latter unit is for use with an EXORciser. It is called the MACE 29/800 Development System. A diagram of the MACE (and the interface to a user's system) is shown in Fig. 12-18. An EXORciser based system is shown in Fig. 12-19. It includes an EXorciser, a dual floppy disk, an operator terminal, and the MACE unit (shown connected to a user's system). MACE contains a number of 2K by 16-bit high speed memory modules (with probes) that can be configured to emulate the microprogram control store. These memory modules and their associated probes can be connected to work side by side for 32 bit, 48 bit (or wider), control words or can be cascaded to provide more words with less bits per word. A 2K $\times$ 64 bit configuration is shown in Fig. 12-20a, and a 16-bit by 8K word array, is shown in Fig. 12-20b.

12-13
Summary

The **6801, 6802, 6805,** and **6809** μPs and μCs were described, and it was shown that the previous chapters on the **6800** are applicable to these upward compatible components, which will work with the same software and emulating firmware tools as previously used. The **3870** and **141000** single-chip μCs were described as examples of low-cost, high-volume controller components. The Intel **8080A, 8085,** and **8048** μP systems were briefly compared to the **6800.** Finally the bit-slice techniques used for special purpose but obviously more expensive μCs were described.

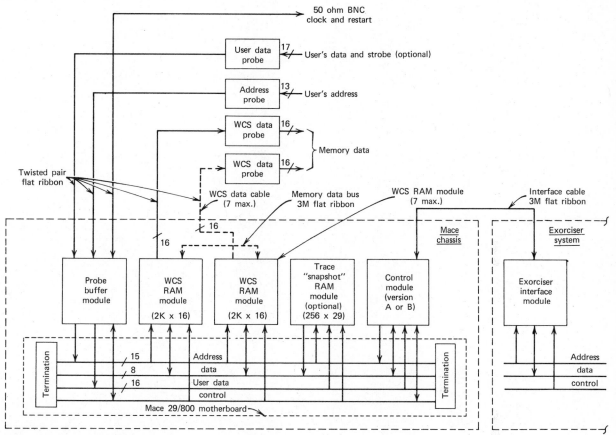

Figure 12-18 MACE 29/800 modular
bus and interconnection diagram.

12-14
Glossary

Arguments The mathematical variables associated with one routine that must be transferred to another.

Position-independent code Object code written with relative branch instructions such that it will operate correctly when located at any address.

Recursive code Each routine is capable of calling itself.

Reentrant code A technique of writing a subroutine such that the status can be saved while it is used by a higher priority program and then the original continued.

12-15
References

MC141000/MC141200 Product Preview NP-83, Motorola, Inc., 1977.

MC3870 Advance Information ADI-445, Motorola, Inc., June, 1978.

MC6801 Advance Information Data Sheet ADI-803R2, Motorola Semiconductor Products, Inc., 3501 Ed Bluestein Blvd., Austin, Texas 78721.

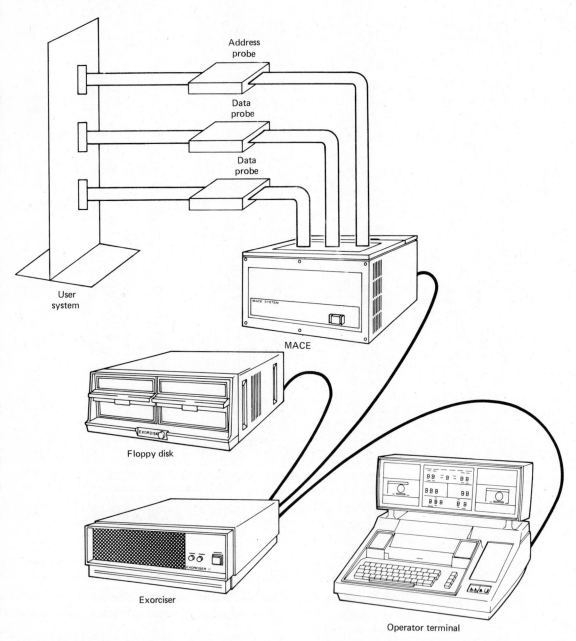

Address probe

Data probe

Data probe

User system

MACE

Floppy disk

Exorciser

Operator terminal

Figure 12-19 Exorciser based system.

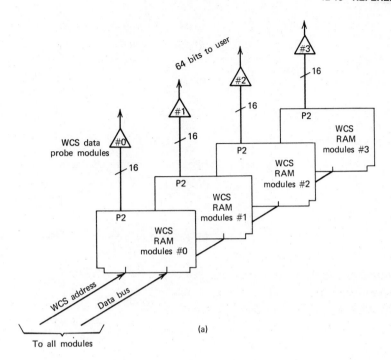

(a)

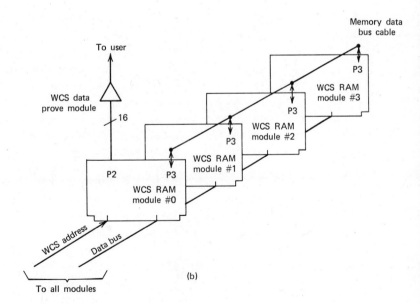

(b)

Figure 12-20 Optional memory module interconnections.
(a) 2K × 64 bit WCS memory array.
(b) 8K × 16 bit WCS memory array.

MC6805 Advanced Information Sheet ADI-811, Motorola, Inc., 1979.

MC6809 Advanced Information Sheet ADI-804-R1, Motorola, Inc., 1980.

MC6809 Macro Assemblers Reference Manual M68MASR(D), December, 1978.

MC6809 Motorola Microcomputer—Technical Training Manual, May, 1979, Motorola Semiconductor Products, Inc., P.O. Box 20912, Phoenix, Arizona 85036.

Systems on Silicon, Motorola Microcomputer Components, Motorola, Inc., Integrated Circuits Division, Mesa, Arizona.

MC6846 Advance Information ADI-473, Motorola, Inc., 1978.

12-16 Problems

12-1. **a.** Describe how to implement a circuit to use the 32 bytes of RAM in the **6802** μP with a battery to provide power failure recovery. Assume the **6846** combination shown in Fig. 12-1b.

    b. Write a routine for power failure detection as well as one for recovery.

12-2. **a.** Describe the connections to use the Timer of the **6846** to provide a real-time clock with 1 second updates. Use the μP crystal as a source.

    b. Write the initialization routines to set up the timer.

12-3. **a.** Assuming a **6801** system as shown in Fig. 12-6, describe the mode to be selected, and how its done.

    b. Assuming the ROM is really an EPROM, write a program to use the internal serial port to talk to an RS232 duplex terminal at 300 baud. Assume a 4.9152 MHz crystal. Include the initialization and I/O routines. Include external vectors in the top of the EPROM. Assume the EPROM resides at $E800.

12-4. **a.** Write the software to implement the **6801** timer. Connect pin 9 (timer out) to pin 4 (NMI) (with a 3.3K pullup), and program it to respond to periodic interrupts when the timer is enabled.

    b. Set up the output compare register to interrupt the system when a value is entered. What location is used for the service routine vector?

12-5. Write a routine to move a block of data using the ABX instruction. Write the same thing in **6800** language and compare the number of bytes as well as the cycle times.

12-6. How does the **6809** RTI instruction know when to restore only the PC and CC registers?

12-7. What happens when the DMA/BREQ line is pulled down while a program is being executed, and held down indefinitely?

12-8. What is the **6809** equivalent instruction for the **6801's** ASLD? How would the function be done in the **6809**?

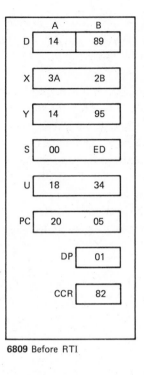

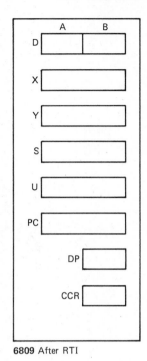

Figure 12-21 Register contents for Prob. 12-12.

6809 Before RTI

6809 After RTI

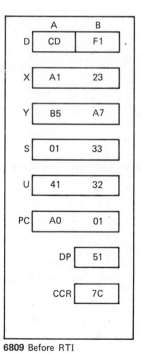

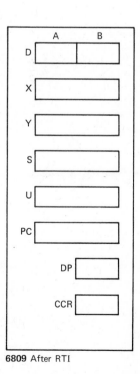

Figure 12-22 Register contents for Prob. 12-13.

6809 Before RTI

6809 After RTI

12-9. What is the difference between the **6800** TSX and **6809's** TFR S,X instructions? What has the change in the operation of the stack to do with it?

12-10. What **6809** instruction is equal to the **6800's** INX?

12-11. How can a ROM be programmed for a **6809** μP so that the ROM will execute properly when located at any absolute address?

12-12. The **6809** shown in Fig. 12-21 has just encountered an RTI instruction. Show the contents of the registers after execution of the RTI.

12-13. The **6809** shown in Fig. 12-22 has just encountered an RTI instruction. Show the contents of the registers after execution of the RTI.

12-14. Using a figure like 12-22, show the register contents after executing the instructions below. Use the instruction set summary or the **6809** Data Sheet to determine the address modes.

Hex Address	Hex Contents
1FB	1C
1FC	00
1FD	8E
1FE	02
1FF	0A
200	A6
201	1F
202	EE
203	9F
204	02
205	09
206	10
207	EE
208	98
209	02
20A	10
20B	8E
20C	02
20D	08
20E	1F
20F	8B
210	D6
211	03

After attempting to solve the problems, try to answer the self-evaluation questions in Sec. 12-2. If any of them still seem difficult, review the appropriate sections of the chapter to find the answers.

Chapter 13

Interfacing Techniques

13-1
Instructional Objectives

This chapter considers methods of connecting or interfacing digital and analog signals to the μP. Particular attention is paid to interfacing in an electrically noisy environment, as is often found in industry.

After reading the chapter, the student should be able to:

1. Use noise reduction techniques such as twisted pair wiring where necessary.
2. Properly ground systems.
3. Use input and output modules to isolate μCs from high power systems.
4. Use A/D and D/A converters to enable the μC to communicate with the analog world.
5. Explain the successive approximation technique for converting analog signals to their digital equivalents.

13-2
Self-Evaluation Questions

Watch for the answers to the following questions as you read the chapter. They should help you understand the material presented.

1. Why should the grounds for all circuits meet only at one common point?
2. What is the advantage of *twisted pair* wiring?
3. What are the advantages of input modules over direct TTL coupling? Under what circumstances must input modules be used?
4. What advantages do differential amplifiers have for the transmission of digital or analog signals?

13-3
Uses of μPs

Although the use of μPs for *business applications* is rapidly increasing, the majority are still used to *control industrial processes*. Automotive use alone could become a yearly market of approximately 10 million μPs.

The larger computer companies have been building business systems for some time, and recently many μP based designs have been introduced. These business μPs are usually prepackaged in a complete system (the Radio Shack TRS 80 and the Apple II are examples) with many software options. Most μP business or hobbyist systems use BASIC as their programming language.

Business systems present few interfacing problems. They use disks or cassettes for storage and CRTs or TTYs for data entry, all of which present a digital interface. Business systems generally operate in a quiet office environment where electrical noise or interference are minimal. Under these circumstances, direct TTL interfacing is satisfactory.

As opposed to these systems that work with bytes and the BASIC language, most *industrial control* applications use *bit manipulation* and assembly language programming. Each bit sent by the μP is a command to turn external devices ON or OFF, such as motors, solenoids, and relays. The bits received are the *status* of the input sensors, such as limit or pressure transducers. Because most industrial applications are unique, they present more difficult and challenging problems for the designer.

Systems to turn ON and OFF devices as a result of discrete events can be easily implemented by TTL or CMOS logic. But when *decisions* must be made based on a calculated result of inputs, the computing power of a μP is needed. Many μP systems must also accept a variable analog input signal or must output a similar changing control signal.

13-3.1
Real-World Electrical Interference

In a laboratory or business environment where the μP is close to the devices it is controlling, and no large power operated devices are used, there are usually no problems with electrical noise. If TTL connections are made to devices less than 30 feet (or 10 meters) away, and these devices are not connected to any external sources of voltage or ground, problems are usually minimal.

Frequently, however, this is not the case. In process control applications, for example, the equipment being controlled is often powered by high current dc or, more likely, by high power ac sources. Unless proper design techniques are used to interconnect the μC system to the power equipment, *large voltage pulses* (noise) induced into the μP or any associated digital circuits can cause malfunctions. In some cases, these pulses may be so powerful that the interfacing parts are even damaged. Since externally powered control equipment may produce transient voltages exceeding several thousands of volts, it is obvious that semiconductor devices, designed for 5 or even 12 V operation, can be damaged permanently.

13-4
Noise Reduction in
Digital Interfacing

The I/O devices discussed in previous chapters were TTL compatible, and an interfering pulse greater than about 1.2 V can cause false operation. When a μC is operated in an electrically noisy environment, special shielding and grounding precautions must be taken to prevent the introduction of *spikes* or *glitches*.

13-4.1
Ground Coupling

Improper grounding of digital circuits can cause severe noise problems. Depending on how circuits are wired, currents from several different circuits can flow through the same ground path and even if there is only a tenth-of-an-ohm (0.1 Ω) resistance in that path, can cause unwanted coupling. If the currents are large enough (a current of 10 A through 0.1 Ω produces a potential difference of 1 V), false operation can result. Figure 13-1a shows an example of improper grounding. The circuit of Fig. 13-1a uses two transistors to amplify the input signal V_{IN}. The problems occur because the ground line of transistor B is improperly connected to the ground of transistor A, rather than directly to the system ground. Assume the wire from the emitter of transistor A to the signal ground has a resistance of 0.1 Ω. If transistor B draws 10 A when it is ON, the emitter of A will be raised to 1.0 V, which will change its biasing dramatically and probably cause improper operation. Figure 13-1b shows the correct way to connect the grounds in order to eliminate any coupling because of the common ground path. If all grounds for a system are brought to *only one point* so that mutual resistance paths are avoided, coupling from this source is eliminated.

13-4.2
Capacitive and Inductive Coupling

Capacitive or inductive coupling between lines not actually connected can also result in interference. Since digital signals are pulses, and have changing levels like ac, either type of coupling can cause trouble.

Two lines parallel to one another on a PC card or in a ribbon cable, or the closeness of the metallic cabinet to the interconnecting

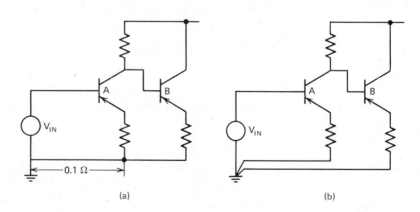

Figure 13-1 Proper ground
connections.
(a) Improper grounding
(b) Proper grounding

(a)

(b)

wiring, can act like a capacitor. Since the input impedance of some IC gates is as high as 100 kΩ, a capacitance of only a few pF (picofarads) can result in a signal large enough to cause trouble. This is called *crosstalk*. It is particularly troublesome when the coupling exists to a line or surface that is hundreds of volts above ground. Similarly, whenever there are large currents in wires, strong magnetic fields result, inductively producing currents in nearby wires. This inductive effect also results in interference.

13-4.3
Engineering Techniques for
Reduction of Coupling

Several techniques are used to avoid interference resulting from capacitive, inductive, or ground circuit coupling.

1. Capacitively coupled noise voltages are reduced greatly using electrostatic shielding. This consists of a grounded wire (or metallic screen) between the two circuits, or surrounding one of them. A coaxial cable (which is just that) is frequently used to carry digital signals whenever capacitive interference is possible.

2. Proper twisting of wires carrying heavy currents causes magnetic fields to nearly cancel each other, thus greatly reducing inductively generated interfering voltages. When combined with proper (right-angle) separation, this can effectively eliminate magnetic coupling.

Twisted pair wires are also used to reduce capacitive coupling. A ground wire is twisted with a signal wire and serves to provide electrostatic shielding and therefore reduce crosstalk.

3. The use of optical coupling, described below, is one of the most effective ways to minimize grounding problems.

13-4.4
Optical Coupling

As shown in Fig. 13-2, an *optical coupler* consists of a *light-emitting-diode* (LED), and a *phototransistor*. Because the information is transmitted optically (i.e., light from the LED shines on the phototransistor to turn it ON), the input circuit is electrically isolated from the output, and separate power sources are possible. When properly installed, common ground and capacitive coupling are both avoided. Various types of optical couplers are now available to provide this circuit isolation and some of them feature the ability to withstand up to 7500 V (RMS) between input and output.

13-5
Methods of Interfacing
Digital Devices

In order to connect the TTL signals of a μC to external control equipment, the following methods are used:

1. Direct TTL
2. Relays
3. Optically coupled dc circuits
4. Solid-state relays

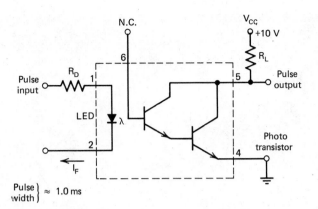

Figure 13-2 An optical coupler.

As stated previously, a direct TTL connection can be used only if external power or grounds are very carefully connected and in a noise-free environment such as a laboratory or office.

For years, relays have been used where isolation was needed between grounds and power sources. Many types of relays are available including a growing number of types that can be mounted on PC cards. Relay isolation qualities are excellent, but relays are mechanical devices and will wear out or require adjustment in time.

DC optical coupling is provided in single transistor or Darlington types, and can be used in many applications where ground isolation is needed and large dc voltages or currents are involved.

Solid-state relays are optically coupled circuits that usually include TRIACS or silicon-controlled-rectifiers (SCRs) to switch ac circuits. They also include zero-crossing detection circuits (the circuit is opened or closed only when the ac voltage is at the zero point of the cycle) to minimize the generation of transient noise signals.

All the previous devices are used as output ON-OFF switches where isolation between the μC circuits and the controlled equipment is required. All except the ac versions of solid-state relays can also be used to connect input signals into the μC.

13-5.1
Digital Output Modules

Figures 13-3 and 13-5 show commercially available modules using relays or optical couplers. Figure 13-3 shows a Burr-Brown MP702 digital output module for use with the **6800** μP. It is also known as an **M68MM13A** (or **B**) Motorola Micromodule. This output module is physically compatible with the EXORciser and other Micromodules. It uses miniature DIP reed relays to provide up to 600 V isolation protection. Figure 13-4 is a block diagram of the output

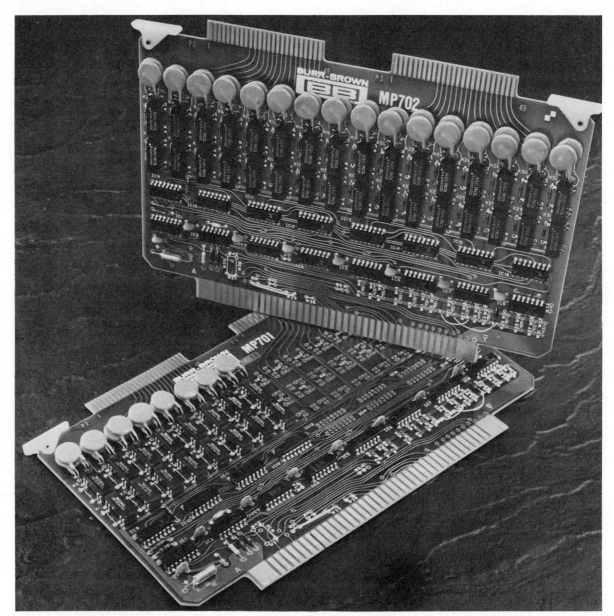

Figure 13-3 Digital output module.
Reproduced by permission of Burr-
Brown.

module. The address decoding and control logic cause these modules
to appear as memory locations when plugged into the μC buses.
Address bits A0 and A1 on **MM13A** and A0 on **MM13B** (which

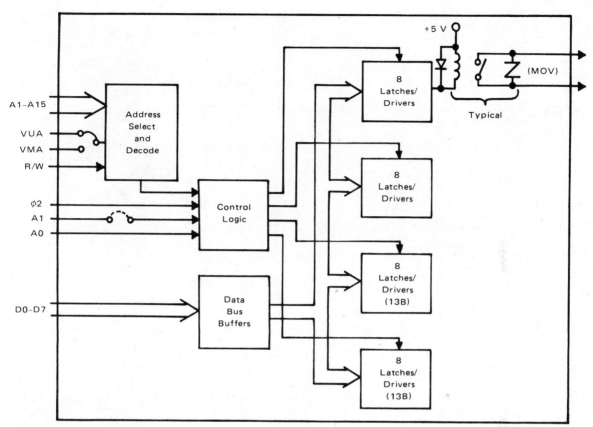

Figure 13-4 MP701/MP702 isolated digital output module block diagram. Redrawn from information supplied by Burr-Brown.

connect into the control logic) select which set of eight outputs are controlled. The remainder of the address lines are used to select the board itself. When data is written to that address, the "1s" turn ON the appropriate relays and the "0s" turn them OFF. Specifications for these modules can be found in the references (Sec. 13-10).

13-5.2
Digital Input Modules

Figure 13-5 shows a similar module (**MP710** or **M68MM13C** & **D**) used for input of digital (ON/OFF) signals. As shown in the block diagram of Fig. 13-6, these modules provide 24 isolated inputs using optically coupled circuits and can withstand voltages up to 600 V between the external wires and ground. These input circuits can also work with up to 84 Vdc or 168 Vac (peak to peak) between the wires. The circuit also provides the *wetting* voltages to work with

Figure 13-5 Digital input module. Reproduced by permission of Burr-Brown.

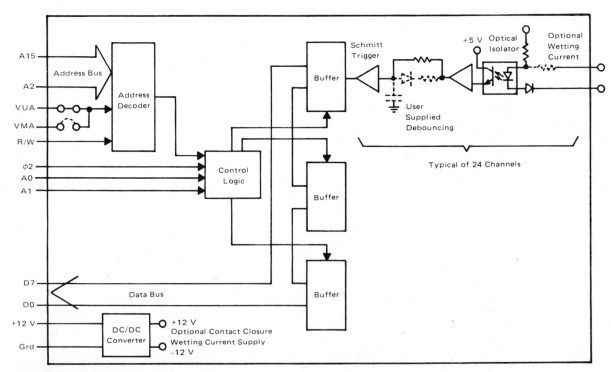

Figure 13-6 MP710 isolated digital input module block diagram. Redrawn from information supplied by Burr-Brown.

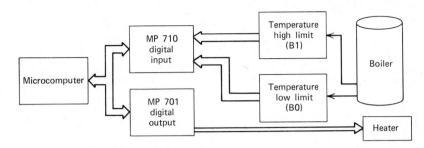

Figure 13-7 Temperature control subsystem. Redrawn from information supplied by Burr-Brown.

external contacts, typically used in limit, pressure, thermostat, or other similar switches. These modules are addressed in the same way as the output module described above.

13-5.3
Temperature Controller Application of Digital Modules

Figure 13-7 shows a simplified temperature controller subsystem using a μC with optically isolated digital inputs and reed-relay outputs. Temperature limit switches are used to provide the contact closures. The limit switch B1 closes when the temperature exceeds the HIGH limit, and the B0 switch closes when the temperature is too LOW, in accordance with Table 13-1.

Figure 13-8 shows the flow diagram of the system functions to be implemented in software.

Note that this is an extremely simple example and could easily have been implemented in discrete TTL logic. A μC might be used, however, because it can simultaneously perform other functions. It gives the designer a great deal of flexibility, and modifications can be easily made.

13-5.4
Mixture Controller Application Using Digital Modules

Figure 13-9 shows a mixture-control subsystem. Two solenoid valves control the flow of liquids into a vat. Two float switches close their contacts whenever levels *A* or *B* are reached. The μC starts a sequence with the vat empty. Valve *A* is opened until level switch *A* closes. Valve *B* is then opened until level *B* switch closes. The two

Table 13-1
Operation of Temperature Limit Switches

Input B1 / B0		Process Status	Control Action
0	0	Temperature acceptable	No change required
1	0	Temperature too high	Turn OFF heater
0	1	Temperature too low	Turn ON heater
1	1	Controller malfunction	Sound alarm

(Closed contacts = 1)

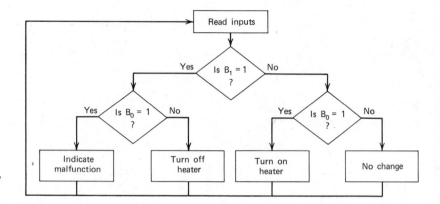

Figure 13-8 Flow diagram for temperature control system software. Redrawn from information supplied by Burr-Brown.

liquids are then mixed and drained out by devices not shown. Level *C* is monitored at all times and if ever reached, both valves are turned OFF, and an alarm is sounded.

Again this is a simple example just to show the application of the input/output modules. Students can use their imagination to elaborate on the design. For example, several more float sensors could be added and a high and low speed flow could be used by switching to low speed for "topping off" when a level just under the desired level is reached. Alternatively the mixture "recipe" could be changed by an operator entry to a control terminal, which selects different sensors.

13-5.5
Solid-State Relays

Figure 13-10 shows a solid-state relay capable of controlling motors or heaters or other ac operated devices. The functional block diagram is shown in Fig. 13-10a, and a picture of several typical units is shown in Fig. 13-10b. Solid-state relays are just another form of

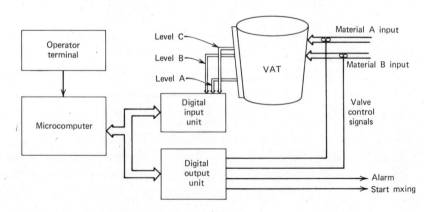

Figure 13-9 Mixture control system. Redrawn from information supplied by Burr-Brown.

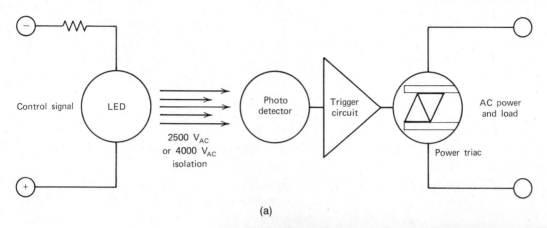

(a)

Figure 13-10 Typical solid-state relays.
(a) Functional block diagram.
(b) Solid-state relays.

(b)

optically coupled semiconductors, where the dc input to the LEDs controls TRIACs or SCRs (silicon-controlled rectifiers) to turn ac powered devices ON or OFF. Basic units are available that control up to 25 A with an isolated dc input of 1 to 10 mA. Depending on the sensitivity, they can be directly operated from a **6820** or **6821** PIA in some cases (the **6821** is rated at 3.2 mA). Three-phase motors of considerable power can be controlled with one TTL PIA output. It would be connected to the paralleled dc inputs of three solid-state relays (a driver transistor capable of up to 30 mA may be required). The three output circuits would be connected in series with each of the three ac power wires to the motor.

13-6
Analog Input/Output (I/O)
for μC Systems

Microcomputer systems must often generate analog (or variable), control voltages, and read (or *sense*) variable input voltages with high accuracy (possibly as high as 0.01%). In the fields of process control, industrial instrumentation, and medical electronics, a variety of physical parameters must first be converted to electrical analog signals and then translated to a digital equivalent in order to be compatible with and controllable by a μC system. Devices that perform these functions are called *transducers*. They convert heat, motion, and position, for example, to (or from) an electrical signal proportional to their magnitude. For example, a pressure transducer may consist of a diaphragm connected to a strain gage whose resistance varies as the diaphragm is deflected by the pressure. Using the strain gage as one arm of a resistance bridge, a voltage proportional to the pressure is obtained. This voltage is used as an input to an analog interface.

The output of an analog transducer can range from millivolts to volts, and can also be in the form of a varying current. Fortunately, some standardization exists and most transducers have outputs falling within five major voltage/current categories: high and low level voltages, and three current ranges.

High level voltage outputs may range up to several volts, generally not exceeding 10 V. Low voltages may be up to a few tens of millivolts, either positive or negative. Current ranges of most transducers are 0 to 20 mA, 4 to 20 mA, or 10 to 50 mA.

Frequently, it is possible to set up a typical analog input system that includes a number of transducers with types having similar output signal levels. In this case it is possible to use a *multiplexer* to switch the various transducers to the same input circuit (rather than using a duplicate amplifier and analog-to-digital converter for each channel). Each of the components used in the data acquisition system has unique characteristics that must be understood before specifying or constructing an interface. Overall speed, accuracy, and noise immunity must all be considered in any system.

13-6.1
Interface Problems with
Analog Signals

All the noise problems that affect digital inputs also affect analog signals. Since most analog signals are smaller than TTL digital signals, interference effects may be more severe. If a single wire and ground is used to input an electrical analog signal, the presence of noise is amplified by the same factor as the desired signal. This is shown in Fig. 13-11a.

Amplifiers with *differential* inputs are used extensively to separate the two signals. The circuit is designed so that the noise signal impressed in phase on both inputs of a differential amplifier will be rejected. Only voltages across the input are amplified. The voltage that is common to both lines is known as the *common-mode* voltage. Figure 13-11b shows the connections for *differential* inputs. The noise reduction achieved by this means is considerable, and is measured by the ratio of the *differential-mode gain* (DMG) to the *common-mode gain* (CMG). Generally this *common-mode rejection* ratio (CMRR) is expressed in decibels (dB) and is equal to 20 log DMG/CMG. See the article by Don Aldridge referenced in Sec. 13-10. Typically values of CMRR range from 70 to 120 dB.

13-6.2
Overvoltage Protection

The most devastating occurrence for an IC component is excessive voltage on any one of its pins. In industrial installations, long lines can easily come in contact with abnormal voltages. Therefore all inputs must be protected from damage from unexpected sources including lightning or power transients. Any protection technique,

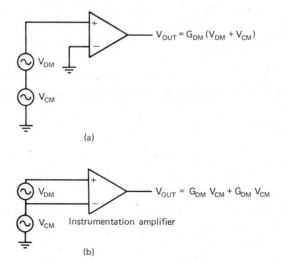

$$V_{OUT} = G_{DM} (V_{DM} + V_{CM})$$

(a)

$$V_{OUT} = G_{DM} V_{CM} + G_{DM} V_{CM}$$

Instrumentation amplifier

(b)

Figure 13-11 Single ended vs. differential input connections.
(a) Single-ended analog connection.
(b) Use of differential input amplifiers.

however, must not affect the accuracy in the normal range. This is usually done using a circuit similar to that shown in Fig. 13-12. Here, the maximum range of voltages is limited by diodes that conduct whenever their reverse bias is exceeded. To protect the diodes from damage in the event of an installation error or lightning stroke, a limiting resistor and a fuse are also used. The series resistance must be low compared to the amplifier's input impedance so as not to degrade accuracy.

13-6.3
Analog to Digital (A/D)
Conversion Techniques

A number of techniques are used to convert analog transducer outputs to digital signals. When it is desired to perform a fast conversion at a moderate price, successive approximation converters are almost always the choice. They use a *comparator* that adjusts a D/A converter until its output voltage closely approximates the analog input signal. When the closest match is found, the digital inputs to the D/A converter represent the unknown analog signal. This is shown in the graph of Fig. 13-13b for a 4-bit converter.

13-6.4
A/D Conversions Using the 6800

An A/D converter using the **6800** can be assembled as shown in Fig. 13-14. The DAC used is the **MC1408L-8** IC. This chip contains the FFs and ladder network necessary to produce the binary values of current used by the comparator. The 8-bit digital word is input by the DAC from the A side of the PIA. An internally compensated *operational amplifier* (**MC1741**) is used as a buffer for the input voltage and provides the proper current source to match the current output of the 1408 (through R1 and R2). The comparator is an **MLM301A**. This amplifier's output saturates if the input currents of the buffer and **1408** do not match, thus toggling the comparator. This output is sensed by PB7 of the PIA so that the software can readjust the DAC to obtain the desired match.

The program needed for this hardware setup is shown in Fig. 13-15.

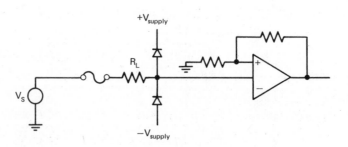

Figure 13-12 Overvoltage protection circuit.

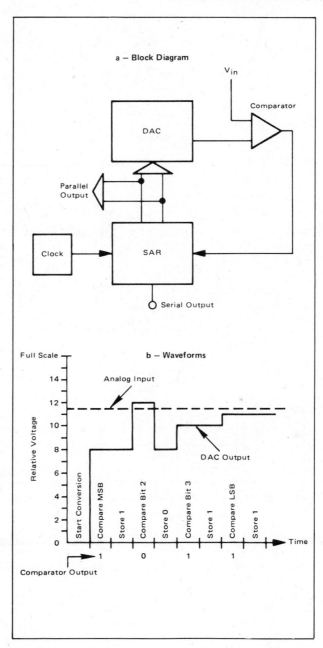

Figure 13-13 Four-bit successive approximation converter.

A similar A/D converter can be assembled using a Burr-Brown MP11 DAC unit as shown in Fig. 13-16. the MP11 contains two channels. Each channel has an 8-bit D/A converter, two operational

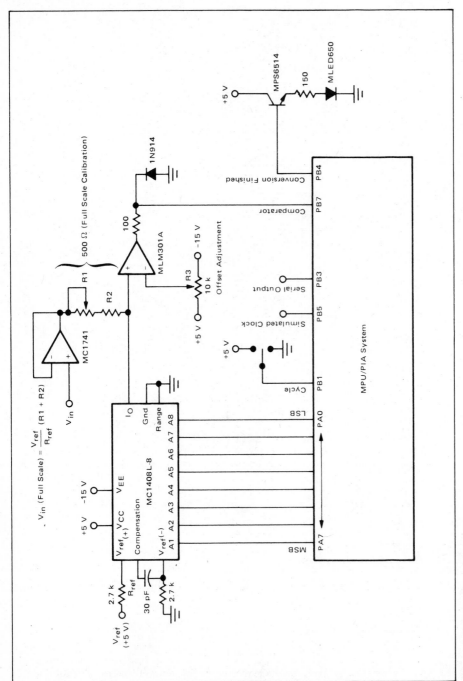

Figure 13-14 An 8-bit successive approximation A/D converter for the **6800** system.

amplifiers, a precision voltage reference, and a thin film network. Laser trimming for gain and offset errors is used and therefore no external adjustments are needed to obtain an absolute accuracy of ±0.2% typical over a +10 V output range. Moreover the analog output remains linear to within ±½ LSB. Settling time of 25 μs (within ±½ LSB) is also achieved. A program similar to Fig. 13-15 would be used.

13-6.5
Analog I/O Modules

Two modules that are designed to work with a **6800** system are shown in Fig. 13-17 and 13-18. The **M68MM15A/15A1** Analog *input* module block diagram is shown in Fig. 13-17. It accepts analog input signals that it converts to digital and makes them available on the μP bus. The data sheets referenced in Sec. 13-10 provide detailed specifications and programming information.

The **M68MM15CV** or **M68MM15CI** are companion analog *output* modules, and their block diagram is shown in Fig. 13-18. Each module has digital-to-analog converters (DACs), but the difference between them is that the CI module has 4 to 20 mA *current* output whereas the CV module provides various ranges of output *voltage*.

In any analog-to-digital (A/D) converter system, the method of handling the A/D conversion must be considered. The simplest method, after the process has been started, is for the program to check continually the *end of conversion* signal to determine when the conversion is finished. This is inefficient and wastes valuable μP time since nothing else is accomplished during this period.

A better method uses the μP's *interrupt* system to report the end of conversion. During the conversion time, other segments of the program can be executed until the end of conversion signal interrupts the μP. Although this approach may appear efficient, caution should be used when interfacing very fast analog to digital systems. The overhead time associated with servicing the interrupt may take the μP longer than the time required for the conversion. The net effect is that the overall throughput is slower than when looping and waiting for the end of conversion signal.

The analog system can be connected in such a way that it places the μP in a WAIT state during the conversion process. This provides the highest throughput speed for programmed data transfers while considerably reducing the electrical noise generated by the digital system. An additional benefit can be found in those processors, such as the **6800**, that can be halted in midcycle to wait for slow memory. With the **6800**, the entire conversion process is carried out during

PAGE 001   DWA12

```
00001                         NAM    DWA12
00002                         OPT    O
00003               *  8 BIT SUCCESSIVE APPROXIMATION A/D
00004               *  WRITTEN BY DON ALDRIDGE - MODIFIED BY W C WRAY
00005               *
00006 0020                    ORG    $20
00007 0020 0001     ANS    RMB    1          FINAL ANSWER MEMORY LOCATION
00008 0021 0001     POINTR RMB    1          TEMP MEMORY LOCATION
00009               *
00010 4004                    ORG    $4004      PIA MEMORY ADDRESS ASSIGNMENT
00011 4004 0001     PIA1AD RMB    1          A SIDE - DIRECTION/DATA REGIS
00012 4005 0001     PIA1AC RMB    1          A SIDE - CONTROL/STATUS     "
00013 4006 0001     PIA1BD RMB    1          B SIDE - DIRECTION/DATA     "
00014 4007 0001     PIA1BC RMB    1          B SIDE - CONTROL/STATUS     "
00015               *
00016               *  PIA1AD IS USED FOR DIGITAL OUTPUT TO THE DAC
00017               *  PIA1BD IS USED FOR A/D CONTROL
00018               *
00019               *           PIABD PIN ASSIGNMENTS
00020               *  PB7     PB6     PB5     PB4     PB3     PB2     PB1
00021               *  COMP    NC      SC      CF      SO      NC      CYCLE
00022               *
00023               *  COMP = COMPARATOR - NC = NO CONNECTION - SC = SIMU
00024               *  SO = SERIAL OUTPUT - CF = CONVERSION FINISHED
00025               *
00026 1200                    ORG    $1200      BEGINNING ADDRESS
00027               *
00028               *           PIA INITIALIZATION
00029 1200 7F 4005          CLR    PIA1AC     SELECT DIRECTION REGISTER
00030 1203 7F 4007          CLR    PIA1BC     "         "         "
00031 1206 86 7D            LDA A  #$7D       SET B DIRECTION FOR CONTROL S
00032 1208 B7 4006          STA A  PIA1BD
00033 120B 86 FF            LDA A  #$FF
00034 120D B7 4004          STA A  PIA1AD     SET ALL LINES AS OUTPUTS ON A
00035 1210 86 04            LDA A  #4
00036 1212 B7 4005          STA A  PIA1AC     LATCH DIRECTION AND DISABLE I
00037 1215 B7 4007          STA A  PIA1BC     "         "       "       "       "
00038               *
00039 1218 86 10     RSTART LDA A  #$10
00040 121A B7 4006          STA A  PIA1BD     SET CONVERSION FINISHED BIT
00041               *
00042               *           CYCLE TEST
00043               *
00044 121D B6 4006   CYCLE  LDA A  PIA1BD     GET B STATUS
00045 1220 84 02            AND A  #2         TEST BIT 1
00046 1222 27 F9            BEQ    CYCLE      IF ZERO, LOOP TIL PULSED
00047               *
00048 1224 7F 4004          CLR    PIA1AD     CLEAR OUTPUT REGISTER
00049 1227 7F 0021          CLR    POINTR     CLEAR TEMP LOCATION
00050               *
00051 122A 7F 4006          CLR    PIA1BD     RESET CONVERSION FINISHED BIT
00052 122D 0D              SEC
00053               *
00054 122E 76 0021   CONVRT ROR    POINTR     MOVE CARRY INTO MSB
```

PAGE 002 DWA12

```
00055 1231 25 E5          BCS   RSTART   IF CARRY SET - SET CONV FINIS
00056 1233 B6 4004         LDA A PIA1AD   RECALL PREVIOUS DIGITAL OUTPU
00057 1236 9B 21           ADD A POINTR
00058 1238 B7 4004         STA A PIA1AD   SET NEW DIGITAL OUTPUT
00059                *
00060                *      DELAY FOR COMPARATOR
00061                *
00062 123B 01              NOP
00063 123C 01              NOP
00064 123D 01              NOP
00065 123E 01              NOP
00066 123F B6 4006         LDA A PIA1BD   GET B STATUS
00067 1242 2B 10           BMI   YES      IF BIT 7 SET GO TO YES
00068                *
00069                *      LOW COMPARATOR LOOP
00070                *
00071 1244 B6 4004         LDA A PIA1AD   GET VALUE IN DATA REG
00072 1247 90 21           SUB A POINTR
00073 1249 C6 20           LDA B #$20     SERIAL OUT OF "0" - CLOCK SET
00074 124B F7 4006         STA B PIA1BD
00075 124E 5F              CLR B
00076 124F F7 4006         STA B PIA1BD   CLOCK RESET
00077 1252 20 10           BRA   END      FINISH
00078                *
00079                *      HIGH COMPARATOR LOOP
00080                *
00081 1254 B6 4004 YES     LDA A PIA1AD   GET DATA
00082 1257 01              NOP
00083 1258 01              NOP            DELAY
00084 1259 01              NOP
00085 125A C6 28           LDA B #$28     SERIAL OUTPUT OF "1" - CLOCK
00086 125C F7 4006         STA B PIA1BD
00087 125F C6 08           LDA B #8
00088 1261 F7 4006         STA B PIA1BD   CLOCK RESET
00089                *
00090 1264 B7 4004 END     STA A PIA1AD   OUTPUT TO DAC
00091 1267 97 20           STA A ANS      PLACE OUTPUT VALUE IN ANSWER
00092 1269 20 C3           BRA   CONVRT   GO AROUND AGAIN
00093                *
00094                      END
```

TOTAL ERRORS 00000

Figure 13-15 Program for successive approximation A/D converter.

the course of a single memory read instruction with the timing of the operation totally transparent to the programmer. For all of its merits, this method has one serious drawback. The μP is totally blind to any other outside events during the conversion. Where μP response times (for external events) are required to be shorter than the conversion time, this method cannot be used.

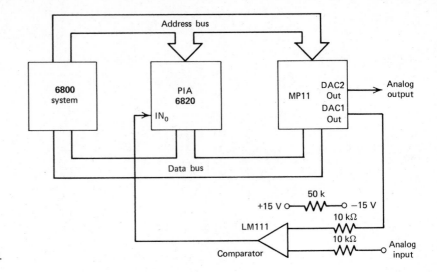

Figure 13-16 A simple A/D converter.

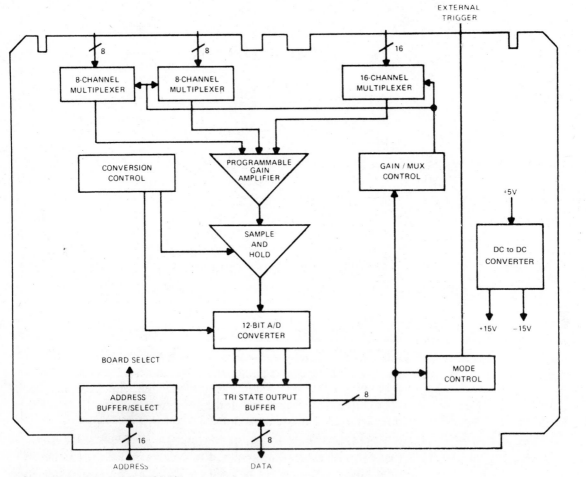

Figure 13-17 Micromodule 15A/15A1 block diagram.

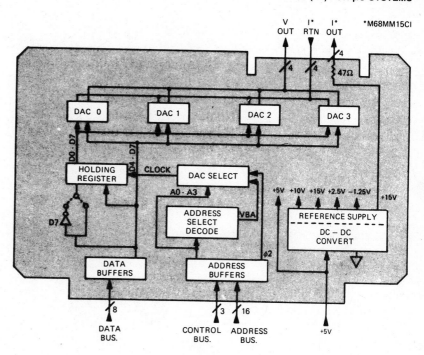

Figure 13-18 Analog output block diagram of the **M68MM15CV.**

When several channels are to be converted before the data is processed, or a block of channels must be continually scanned, direct memory access (DMA) should be considered as the interfacing method. Although more complicated from a hardware point of view, this method maximizes channel throughput with a minimum of software. In one mode of operation, a segment of memory can be continually updated by continuous automatic operation of the analog system and the transfer of digital data performed between processor cycles. Only a slight reduction in software execution speed is noticed, and the data is fetched from memory without regard to the details of operating the analog interface. Another mode of operation might allow several channels to be processed and then an interrupt generated to signal the software that the block of data is available.

Two programming examples for Micromodule 15A/15A1 are shown in Table 13-2. They illustrate some of the considerations described in the preceding paragraphs. Details of these modules are given in the references in Sec. 13-10.

13-6.6
Boiler Control with Analog Modules

An example of a typical microcomputer application might be found in a large process control facility. Large computers direct the overall operation of the plant through the activities of μC systems placed strategically throughout the plant. As shown in Fig. 13-19, one such

Table 13-2
Programming Examples for the MM15A Analog Module

a. Software Start-of-Conversion with busy test for End-of-Conversion.

```
         LDA  A  #%01000001      SELECT CHAN  1 - GAIN = 2
         STA  A  $9D00           OUTPUT TO GMAR  REG.
         LDA  A  #%00000100      START CONVERSION NO IRQ OR HALT
         STA  A  $9D01           OUTPUT TO CONTROL/STATUS REG.
TEST     BIT  A  $9D01           TEST BUSY BIT
         BNE  TEST               LOOP TILL BUSY = 0
         LDX     $9D02           LOAD X REG WITH DATA
```

b. External Trigger starts conversion - with IRQ at End-of-Conversion.

```
         LDA  A  #%10000010      SELECT CHAN 2 - GAIN = 4
         STA  A  $9D00           OUTPUT TO GMAR REG.
         LDA  A  $%01010100      ARM BUSY - ALLOW EXT TRIG TO STRT
         STA  A  $9D01           CONVERSION - ALLOW IRQ AT E-O-C

         (Run other program until an interrupt occurs)

IRQ      LDA  A  $9D01           SERVICE IRQ - READ STATUS
         BMI  ADATA              IF IRQF SET, READ DATA
         ...  .....              OTHER INTERRUPT POLLING
         RTI

ADATA    LDA  A  $9D02           LOAD  A   ACCUM WITH DATA HI
         LDA  B  $9D03           LOAD  B   ACCUM WITH DATA LOW
```

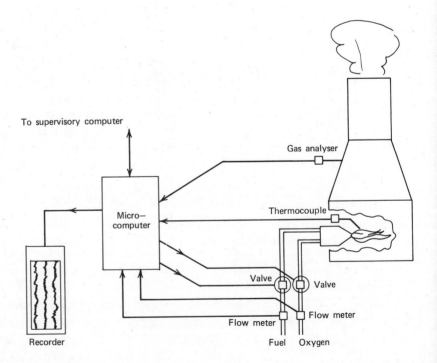

Figure 13-19 Boiler control with a μC and analog interface.

μC system might be assigned the sole task of monitoring the combustion in a boiler. Inputs would originate from flame-temperature transducers, effluent-gas analyzers, and fuel-flow meters. Outputs would control fuel and oxygen flow and drive a small strip-chart recorder to make a permanent record of the burner's operation. The main supervisory computer would direct the μC system to set the burner for a specified (desired) flame temperature. With this information, the μC's control algorithm would make the necessary adjustments to fuel flow and mixture, to attain the required temperature while maintaining minimum combustion pollutants and maximum fuel economy.

At the analog interface, the signals must undergo an A/D conversion before they are suitable for processing. Since there is more than one input, either multiple A/D converters are used or, if all transducers provide the same range of output, all inputs are connected to a single A/D converter through a multiplexer switch. This latter method is currently the least expensive and is almost universally used. However, before these low-level signals can go through the conversion process, they must be amplified since all modern A/D converter designs require inputs of several volts. A differential-input instrumentation amplifier is used for this purpose. Not only is amplification performed in such an amplifier but through the return of both signal lines from the transducers as a differential connection, high common-mode noise rejection can also be attained (Sec. 13-6.1). Electrically operated proportionally controlled fuel and mixture valves are adjusted through their voltage inputs. The analog output modules produce these voltages through a separate D/A converter for each transducer.

13-7 Remote Operation

When it is not convenient to locate the computer at the remote site but where the distance is too far to run low-level analog signals (greater than 100 feet), it is possible to use a system like the one shown in Fig. 13-20. Here, the digital information is transmitted *serially* over telephone lines by converting it to 20 mA current loop circuits. Similar 20 mA converter circuits would be used at both ends of the lines and the **6850** ACIAs would send and receive data at 2400 BPS, or more. This method can be used over lines up to several thousand feet long. The ACIA at the distant end would be used to convert the data back to parallel for connection to the analog modules.

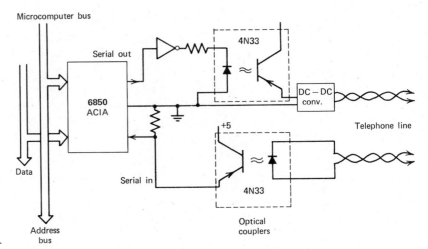

Figure 13-20 Serial digital transmission.

**13-8
Summary**

This chapter has shown how μCs can be interfaced to real-world control equipment, both for ON/OFF (digital) signals and for cases where analog signals are needed.

**13-9
Glossary**

ac Alternating current.

ACIA Asynchronous Communication Interface Adapter—the **6850** serial data component.

Analog Resembling the original. In electronics, it usually refers to a voltage that varies in direct relationship to some physical property.

DAC Digital-to-analog converter.

dc Direct current.

Digital A voltage or signal that has two states, 1 and 0, or ON and OFF.

DIP Dual-In-Line Package—a standard package for integrated circuits with pins on a 0.1 inch grid pattern.

Electrostatic shield A conductive screen placed between or around an electrical circuit to drain off unwanted charges.

Ground Earth potential—the point to which the frame or chassis is connected.

Multiplexer An electronic switch to select any of a number of inputs or outputs.

Optical coupling A semiconductor device that uses a light emitting diode (LED) whose output is detected by a phototransistor.

PC card Printed circuit (on a card).

Picofarad A unit of capacitance equal to 10^{-12} farads.

Reed relay Vacuum encapsulated contacts operated by magnetic field.

Solenoid valve Electrically operated valve, using dc magnetic actuator.

Solid-state relay Semiconductor devices connected so that the optically coupled output turns on a TRIAC or silicon-controlled rectifier (SCR) for control of ac motors, lights, and so on.

Successive approximation A technique of determining equality by comparing with progressively smaller values.

Transducer A converter to change physical parameters to electrical signals, or vice versa.

TRIAC A semiconductor device that can be "triggered" ON or OFF for control of ac powered units.

Wetting voltage A voltage impressed across contacts to assure that sufficient current will flow to break through any oxides or dirt.

**13-10
References**

Aldridge, Don, Applications Engineer, *Analog-to-Digital Conversion Techniques with the* **M6800** *Microprocessor System,* Application note AN-757, Motorola Semiconductor Products, Inc., P.O. Box 20912, Phoenix, Arizona 85036.

Barna, Arpad, and Dan I Porat, *Integrated Circuits in Digital Electronics,* Wiley, New York, 1973.

Burr-Brown, *Digital Output (Contact Closure) Microperipherals for Motorola Microcomputers,* **MP701, MP702,** PDS 381, Burr-Brown Research Corporation.

Burr-Brown *Microcomputer Digital Input System,* MP710, PDS 386, Burr-Brown Research Corporation.

Electronic Relays, *ERI All Solid-State and Reed-Coupled Solid-State Relays,* Catalog no. 257, Electronic Relays, Inc., 7106 W. Touhy Ave., Niles, Illinois 60648.

Kostopoulos, George K., *Digital Engineering,* Wiley, New York, 1975.

Morrison, Robert, Applications Engineer, *Data Acquisition and the Microcomputer,* Burr-Brown Research Corporation, International Airport Industrial Park, P.O. Box 11400, Tucson, Arizona 85734.

Motorola, M68MM15A/15A1 *High-Level A/D Module,* Micromodule 15A/15A1 **M68MM15A (D),** First Edition, Motorola Microsystems.

Motorola, M68MM15C *Analog Output Module,* Micromodule 15C, **M68MM15C (D),** First Edition, Motorola Microsystems, 3102 North 56th Street, Phoenix, Arizona 85018.

Teeple, C. R., *Isolated Digital Input/Output Microcomputer Peripherals Solve Industrial Problems,* Burr-Brown Research Corporation.

Chapter 14

**CRT
Display
Terminal
Application**

**14-1
Instructional Objectives**

This chapter introduces one of the end uses of μPs: a typical design of a CRT "intelligent terminal." When the chapter is completed, the student should be able to:

1. Design a video display circuit using **6800** family components.
2. Write the software necessary to provide the normal features expected in an operator terminal.
3. Understand CRT fundamentals and character generator functions.
4. Learn new techniques on how to speed memory access.
5. Realize the requirements for serial communications in distributed processing systems.

**14-2
Self-Evaluation Questions**

Students should watch for the answers to the following questions while reading the chapter. It will help them to understand the many uses of μPs.

1. Why should an operator terminal include serial communications interface?
2. What makes a terminal "intelligent"?
3. What are the advantages of a CRT terminal over a TTY?
4. How does the **MC6845** CRT controller IC simplify the design and improve performance of an operator terminal.
5. Why is the access time of the **6800** memories so important in a terminal design?
6. What are the advantages of programmable screen formatting and software cursor control?

**14-3
The 6800 μP in Data
Handling Applications**

Large central computers have been used extensively to implement data processing and some industrial process control systems. With the advent of μPs, however, the concept of *distributed processing* is being used more and more. The central processor (in some cases also a μP) is still used to direct the overall system operation, but several μPs are frequently used together to perform the individual

414

tasks. Operator control points are usually required and a man–machine interface is involved.

14-3.1
The CRT Terminal

Probably the most popular I/O (input/output) device for communications between humans and computers is the *CRT terminal*. It consists of a CRT (cathode ray tube) that displays alphanumeric or graphic information, either read from a computer's memory or received over a line from a distant system, a keyboard similar to a typewriter, and an interface for data transfer from the memory to the CRT. Figure 14-1 shows a typical CRT terminal.

Most business systems use CRT terminals for entering and examining data files and other information exchange. In large companies a number of CRTs are often interconnected within a plant or even between several plants in different cities using MODEMs and telephone circuits. Airline reservation systems, for example, make extensive use of CRT terminals. Sophisticated CRT terminals have editing and graphics capabilities.

The CRT terminal provides essentially the same functions as a TTY, and has several advantages. It is quiet, very fast, and generates no printed record (called hard copy) of the transactions. Sometimes a printed record of the data is required, but files are often accessed

Figure 14-1 A CRT terminal. The Motorola EXORterm.

just for information and the hard copy is unnecessary. Furthermore, the nuisance of constantly feeding paper into the machine is avoided.

CRTs can be used with μP Development Systems for debugging or editing programs and *hard copy* is not needed. Where it is required, as for assembly listings, a printer is often provided. The combination of a CRT and printer are preferred by many users but are more expensive than a TTY that does both jobs. A CRT terminal of this type contains several subsystems including a *keyboard encoder, video display circuitry,* and a *serial communications interface*. In the past these subsystems were interconnected on a common bus and used discrete logic to provide the necessary functions. A μP can provide these same functions, and many new ones such as editing commands or graphics are easily added.

14-3.2
CRT Fundamentals

A CRT is an evacuated glass tube that produces images by focusing an electron beam on phosphors, which coat the screen area of the device. The brightness of the display is determined by the current in the beam. The beam is directed by either electrostatic or magnetic deflection circuits built around the neck of the CRT. A display is created by systematically sweeping the beam across the entire surface of the screen while varying the intensity. In a typical CRT data terminal or in a home TV set, an electron beam starts in the upper left-hand corner and moves horizontally across the screen. This action is called a *horizontal scan*. The beam is then *blanked* (or turned OFF) to avoid interference with the display on the screen, and returned to the left side to start another scan. The time for this *horizontal retrace* is much shorter than the scan time. The horizontal scan rate for American TV and many data terminals is 15,750 Hz.

During the horizontal scans the beam is slowly moving down the screen until it reaches the bottom. At this point the beam has made *many horizontal scans* and *one vertical scan*. The beam is then blanked and rapidly returned to the top to start another *vertical scan* or *field*.

Two types of raster scanning are used in CRTs, *interlace* and *noninterlace*. Interlace scanning is used in broadcast TV and on some data monitors where high density data must be displayed. Two trips, or *fields* are made down the screen for one single picture or *frame*. One field starts in the upper left corner, and the second in the top center, overlapping or interlacing the two fields into a single frame. This is shown in Fig. 14-2 where the solid line indicates the visible trace for field 1 and the dotted line is the return. The second field is

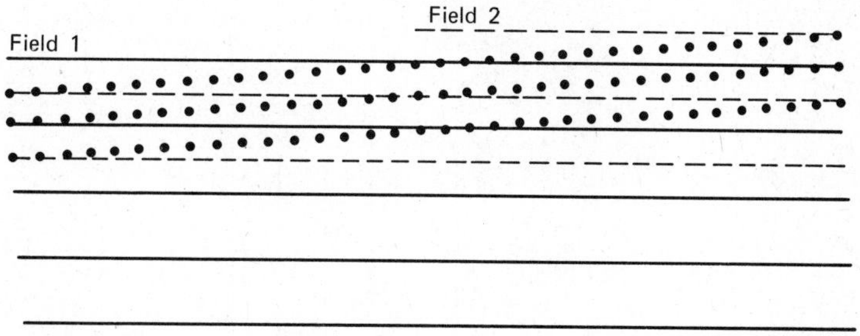

Field 1

Field 2

Figure 14-2 Interlaced scan.

indicated by the dashed lines. There are 262.5 horizontal lines per field and a total of 525 lines per frame. The field rate is 60 Hz, and the frame rate is 30 Hz.

The interlace method works well in TV applications where colors and shadings change gradually. In the display of characters however, noninterlaced scanning is more commonly used. In noninterlaced scanning the beam starts on the same scan line each time so that the frame refresh rate is 60 Hz.

Higher density displays are needed for some of the more advanced terminals and future developments will undoubtedly use the interlace method. To get more characters on the screen some data CRTs use a higher sweep frequency. The horizontal oscillator frequency can range from 15,720 Hz, which gives 262 scan lines per field, to 50,000 Hz, which gives 833 scan lines.

To generate a legible display, the horizontal and vertical oscillators must be kept in step with each other and with the displayed information. This is accomplished by generating a *horizontal sync* and a *vertical sync* signal. Each of these causes its oscillator to be reset and starts the beam over again at precisely the right time. As the beam scans off the edge of the screen, it must be blanked until it reaches the position where data is to be displayed. The beam must also be blanked during retrace both in the horizontal and vertical directions. The signal that controls the electron beam is called *"Blanking"* or *display enable*. Figure 14-3 shows the display and its controlling signals.

**14-3.3
Character Generation**

The most common method of generating characters is to create a matrix of dots, ''x'' dots (or columns) wide, and ''y'' dots (or rows) high. Each character is created by selectively filling in dots. As ''x'' and ''y'' get larger, a more detailed character can be created. Two common dot matrices are 5 × 7 and 7 × 9. Characters require some space between them, so they are placed in a character block that is

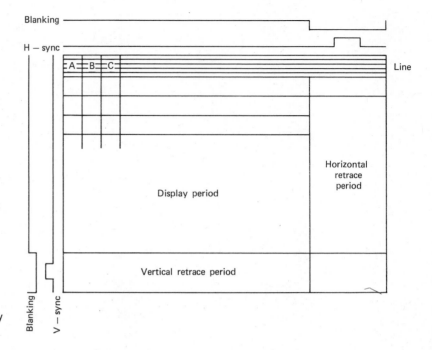

Figure 14-3 CRT display controlled by Hsync, Vsync, and Blanking.

larger than the character, as shown in Fig. 14-4. As the electron gun of the CRT scans one line across the screen, it displays the first row of dots for each character on that character line. On the next scan, the second row of dots and spaces for each character are displayed. This process continues until all ''y'' rows of the character have been

ROW SELECT
TRUTH TABLE

RS3	RS2	RS1	RS0	OUTPUT
0	0	0	0	R0
0	0	0	1	R1
0	0	1	0	R2
0	0	1	1	R3
0	1	0	0	R4
0	1	0	1	R5
0	1	1	0	R6
0	1	1	1	R7
1	0	0	0	R8
1	0	0	1	R9
1	0	1	0	R10
1	0	1	1	R11
1	1	0	0	R12
1	1	0	1	R13
1	1	1	0	R14
1	1	1	1	R15

Figure 14-4 A 7 × 9 dot matrix character in a 9 × 16 character block.

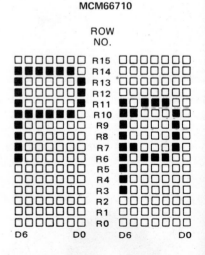

MCM66710

displayed, then repeats for every character line on the screen, as shown in Fig. 14-5.

This method of scanning is made easy by the use of a *character generation* ROM, which converts an ASCII encoded character into the dots required to display that character. The inputs to the ROM are the ASCII code of the desired character and the count for the row of dots. The lines of ASCII codes (one byte for each character) are normally stored in the display RAM and retrieved repeatedly as the rows of dots are being refreshed.

Figure 14-6 shows one of many patterns that are available in one type of these ROMs, the Motorola **MC66750**. It contains the full ASCII code of 128 character codes. These consist of both upper- and lower-case letters, numbers from 0 to 9, punctuation marks, and 32 control characters. Other simpler character generators are also available (such as the Signetics **2513**).

Control characters such as a *carriage return* or *line feed* are not normally displayable, but a feature of the full complement ROM like the **66750** is the ability to display a symbol or a dual character (as shown in the top two rows of Fig. 14-6) for each of the control codes.

These ROMs are usually used in the more advanced *intelligent* CRT terminals and software is used to select whether the control codes are sent or a display is generated. This option is very valuable when testing communications systems.

Most of the simpler ROMs like the Signetics **2513** or other 5 × 7 character generators do not display lowercase letters or control codes.

As seen in the boxes along the top and sides of Fig. 14-6, the seven address line (A0–A6) select the character. The four row select inputs (RS0–RS3) select the row of dots that make up the character. This is shown in more detail in Fig. 14-4.

Example 14-1

What output is obtained from a 66750 character ROM when the ASCII character is $41 (or A6. . . . .A0 is 1000001), and RS3. .RS0 = 0000?

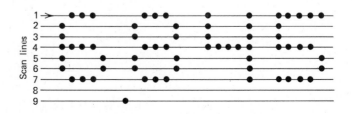

Figure 14-5 Dot matrix scanning using 5 × 7 characters.

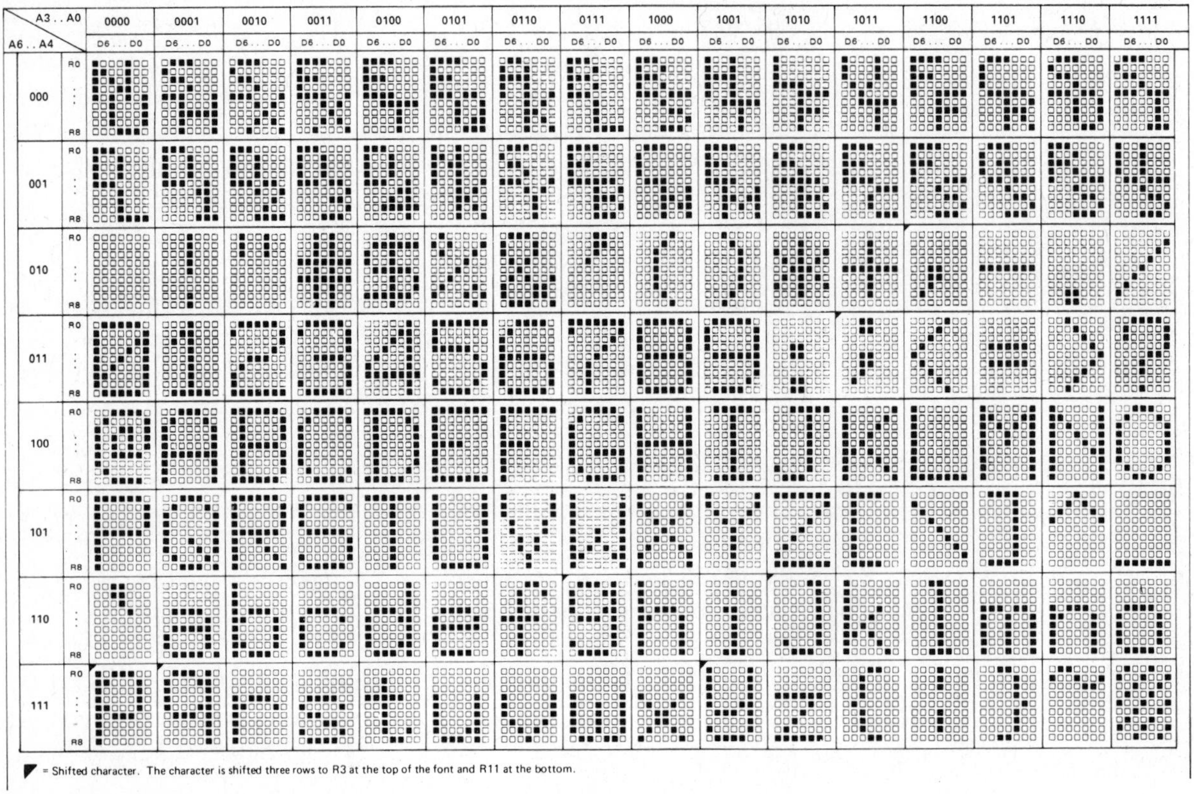

A6..A4 \ A3..A0	0000	0001	0010	0011	0100	0101	0110	0111	1000	1001	1010	1011	1100	1101	1110	1111
	D6...D0	D6...D0	D6...D0	D6...D0	D6...D0	D6...D0	D6...D0	D6...D0	D6...D0	D6...D0	D6...D0	D6...D0	D6...D0	D6...D0	D6...D0	D6...D0
000 (R0...R8)																
001 (R0...R8)																
010 (R0...R8)																
011 (R0...R8)																
100 (R0...R8)																
101 (R0...R8)																
110 (R0...R8)																
111 (R0...R8)																

▶ = Shifted character. The character is shifted three rows to R3 at the top of the font and R11 at the bottom.

Figure 14-6 MCM66750 pattern.

Solution

Figure 14-6 shows that for A3..A0 = 0001, the character is in the second column, and for A6, A5, A4 = 100 (the fifth row down), the character is "A." If the row select pins are all 0, the top row is selected. The ROM output code is **0011100**.

Figure 14-7 shows a typical character generator circuit. The 7-bit ASCII code is applied to the character ROM that then outputs one row of dots according to the count on the row select inputs. The output dots (0011100 for Example 14-1) are sent to a parallel-to-serial converter where it is shifted out to the CRT beam circuit to produce dots on the screen in the right place. Here two **7495s** are used in series to accommodate the 7-bits of each character row. Of course, the row and character selection must be synchronized with the scanning beam, and, as the row counter is appropriately incremented, the next row is put into the parallel side of the shift register.

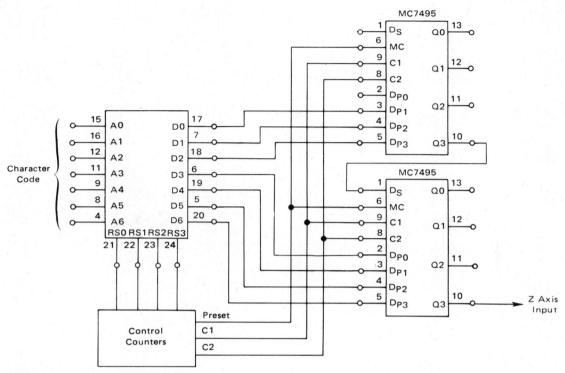

Figure 14-7 Method of serializing the dots.

14-4
The 6845 CRT Controller

Generating the scanning and blanking signals for the CRT, as well as those necessary to place the characters on the screen in the proper place is complex. Fortunately, these functions have been incorporated into an LSI μP peripheral IC known as a *CRT Controller*. The Motorola device for this purpose is the **6845** CRTC, and it is used as the interface from the μP bus to the video monitor (detailed information can be found in the Data Sheet referenced in Sec. 14-9).

A block diagram of a system that uses this CRT controller is shown in Fig. 14-8. In the figure, all of the system components associated with the video display and character generation are shown below the μP bus lines, and the components that make up the rest of the computer system are shown at the top of the diagram. Several EPROMs might be used to provide sufficient memory for the controlling program (depending on the number of features implemented). The RAM may also need to be increased to 1K or more. The I/O components shown allow for parallel keyboard input and serial com-

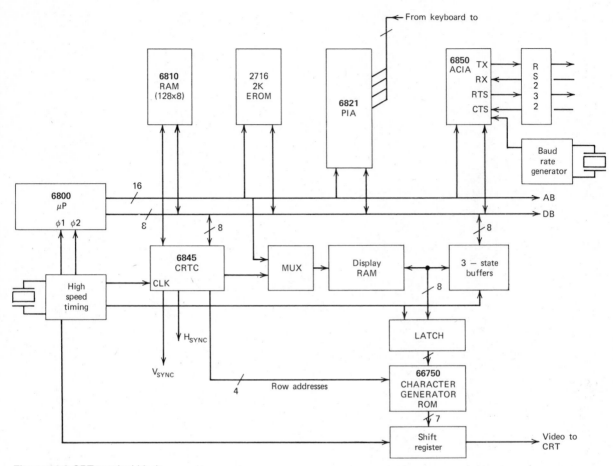

Figure 14-8 CRT terminal block diagram.

munication (perhaps via MODEMs from a remote site). If desired a **6852** Synchronous Serial Data Adapter might be substituted for the ACIA.

One of the requirements of a CRT data terminal is that the characters must be repeatedly rewritten on the screen every frame time. This is called *screen refresh*. In the implementation shown in Fig. 14-8, this is done by using a RAM array, which stores the characters in the format specified by the **6845**. This RAM is called the *display* or *refresh* RAM. The screen formats are programmable in the **6845** and almost any configuration can be provided [e.g., 24 lines of 80 characters (80 × 24), 64 × 16, 72 × 64, 132 × 20, etc.]. The number of characters capable of being stored depends on the display

RAM size. As shown in Fig. 14-8, the primary functions of the CRTC are to *generate refresh addresses, row selects* for the character ROM, and video monitor timing (*Hsync, Vsync*). The internal cursor register generates a *cursor output* when its contents compare to the current refresh address. *The cursor position indicates to the operator where the next character will be written.*

The **6845** CRTC contains 18 internal registers that must be initialized by the μP. The μP communicates with the **6845** registers through a buffered 8-bit data bus. These **6845** registers hold the basic system parameters such as the number of horizontal lines for each character row, number of lines per field, the cursor location, and whether interlaced or noninterlaced scan is desired.

Example 14-2
Sixty-four characters must be displayed on each line of a CRT. If standard TV sweep frequencies are used and 20% of the line is allowed for horizontal blanking and retrace, how much of the time is allowed for each character?

Solution
The standard TV display scan frequency is 15,750 Hz. This means each sweep takes 1/15750 = 63.49 μs. If 20% of this time is used for blanking and retrace, the displayable part of the line takes 50.79 μs. The time to display each character is therefore 50.79/64 = 0.79 μs or at a rate of 1.267 MHz.

If there are 80 characters on the line the rate must be 1.58 MHz. Unless multiplexing is used, the display RAM must be accessed at this rate.

All **6845** timing is derived from the CLK input. In alphanumeric terminals this corresponds to the character rate and is divided down from the video dot rate by a high speed external counter. The video signal to the display is the row of bits shifted out of the output shift register by the DOT high speed timing (see Fig. 14-8).

14-5
Memory Access Techniques

There is contention for the display RAM. Its output must be read and sent to the character ROM whenever the screen needs refreshing, but the RAM must also be accessed by the μP to enter or delete data from the screen. One way to handle contention is to refresh the screen from the RAM during Ø1 of the μP cycle and to allow R/W access to the RAM by the μP during Ø2 just as normally done with any **6800** system memory. This provides a transparent access (i.e., no flicker).

A video display circuit similar to Fig. 14-8 for use with a standard CRT monitor (or modified TV set) and a **6800** μP can be designed by using a **MC6845** CRT controller. The **6800** has a two-phase clock with a constant length cycle in contrast to that of other μPs. During Ø1 the **6800** presents the address to the bus and during Ø2, the data is either written to or read from any addressed device. By using faster memory devices, it is possible for the **6845** to separately access memory during the time when Ø1 is high without interfering with the normal Ø2 access by the μP. (See the display memory timing in Fig. 14-9.) For a 1 MHz **6800** system the memory must have an access time of 350 nsec or better, to complete the access during one phase of the clock.

At the higher data rates necessitated by 80 characters on a line, two characters must be read from the memory during Ø1 to keep memory access times in the range of 300 to 500 ns. To accomplish this the display memory is split into two blocks and interleaved to form an array 8 bits wide to the μP and 16 bits wide to the CRTC. (See Fig. 14-10.)

During the *first* character time of a scan, the CRTC accesses the first two memory locations. At the end of this character time 16 bits of data are latched into two 8-bit latches. This data represents addresses in the character generator of the characters to be displayed. During the *second* character time the data from the *even* memory block is applied to the character generator. At the end of the *second* character time the character generator's output data is loaded into the shift register. Also during the *second* character time the memory is

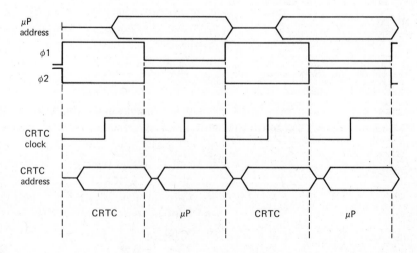

Figure 14-9 Display memory timing.

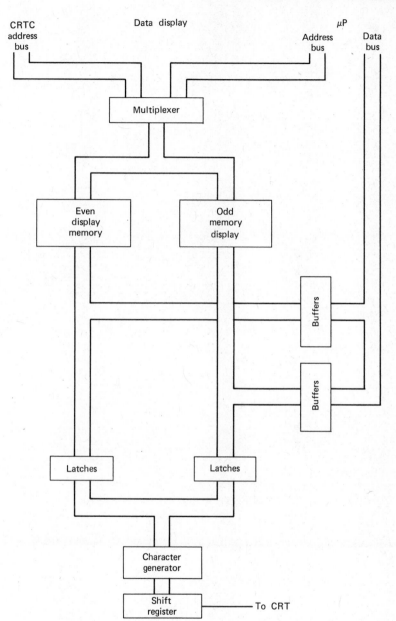

Figure 14-10 Block diagram showing interleaved memory.

available to the μP for access. Not until the *third* character time is the data for the *first* character shifted out onto the screen. This delay through the memory is known as *pipelining* and requires the blanking and cursor outputs also to be delayed by two character times. During

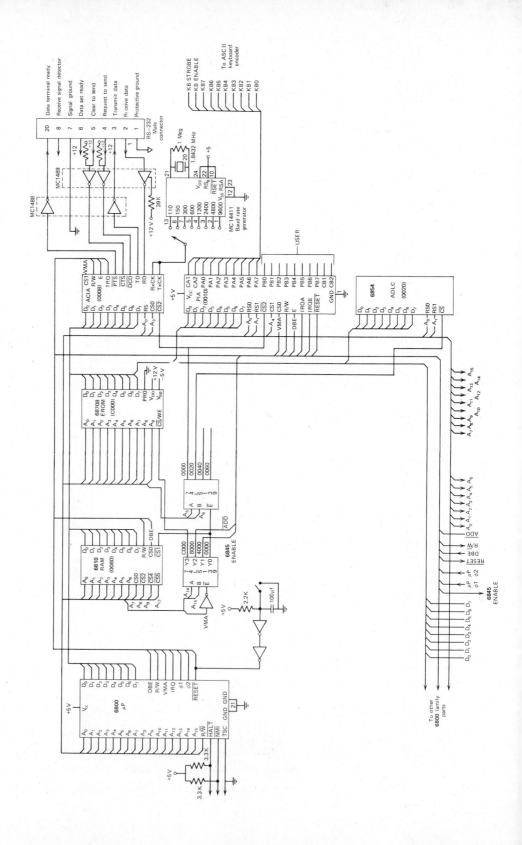

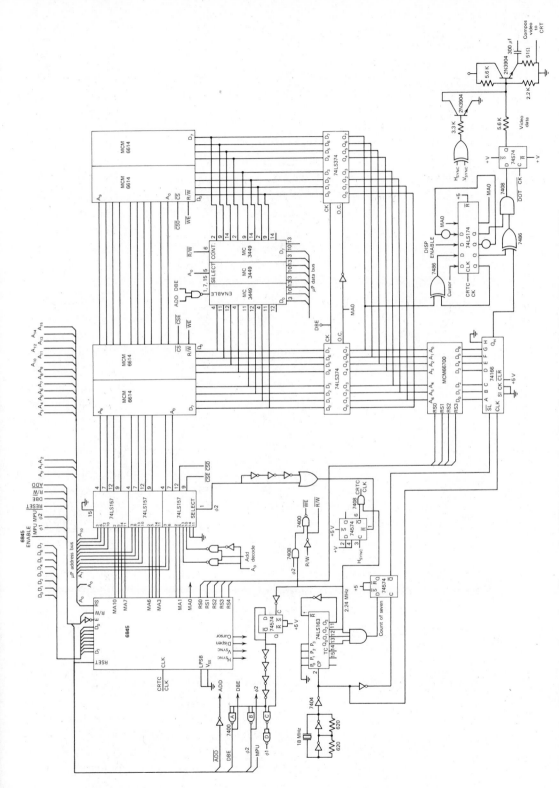

Figure 14-11 Schematic of complete μP controlled CRT data terminal. Note that all unmarked inverters are type 7404.

the *third* character time the data in the *odd* memory latch is applied to the character generator. In addition the CRTC is accessing the next two memory locations. This sequence of events continually repeats itself.

**14-5.1
A Practical CRT Design
Using the** 6845

Figure 14-11 is the actual implementation of the previous block diagram. This CRT data terminal system uses the character generator circuit, **6845** CRT controller, and memory access techniques previously described. It includes an ACIA with RS232 interface and selectable baud rates for serial I/O, and a PIA for use with a keyboard. Reference to the figure shows that the display memory access is implemented using three **74LS157s** to form a single multiplex bus switch for the RAM address lines. DBE (which is the same as Ø2) controls this switch and selects the CRTC during Ø1 and the µP during Ø2. Three **MC3449s** form a bidirectional data bus switch to the µP bus with the A0 line used to select the even/odd bank of memory. The R/W line controls the direction of the bidirectional buffers. Two **74LS374s** are used to latch the 16-bit data flowing to the CRT. The output of these latches are 3-state and are controlled by address line MA0. The *even* block of data is routed to the character generator when MA0 is low and vice versa. Data in the latches is delayed by one character time, so MA0 is also delayed by the **74LS174**.

All the timing for this CRT system is derived from a central 18 MHz oscillator. The frequency of this oscillator is at the *DOT clock rate* and is determined by the system parameters. The DOT clock is divided by 9 (7 dots + 2 spaces) to generate the *character clock* (9 dots per character block). A 3-input AND gate decodes the seventh count, which is delayed ½ clock time by the **74S74** and used to load the shift register (Fig. 14-12). Clocking for the **6800** is created by dividing the Q3 output of the counter by two. A nonoverlapping clock is generated by the series of gates shown above the oscillator. The ROM at C000 contains the CRTC program and all initialization.

**14-6
Software for the** 6845 **CRT
Controller**

The program written to work with the hardware described in the previous section is shown in Appendix D.

The **6845** CRTC and **6800** are designed for a hardware/software balance. Together, they provide the user with a basic CRT terminal. For instance, all keyboard functions, data movement, cursor movement, and editing are under processor control; whereas the CRTC

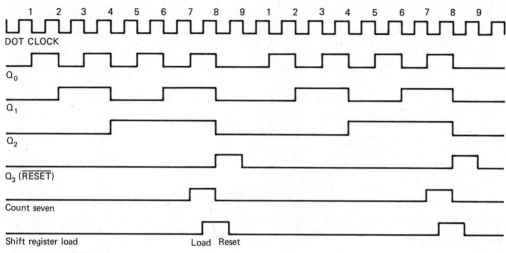

Figure 14-12 CRT system timing.

provides video timing, display memory addressing, hardware scrolling and paging, and light pen detection. Because of the CRTC, such things as block moves (to scroll and page the display) are not needed. In addition, powerful driver routines can be generated in a few hundred bytes of memory.

The software provides the following features.

User-defined display format
Carriage return
Line feed
Scroll up
Scroll down
Page up
Page down
Character decode
Memory clear
Keyboard input
Serial I/O
CRTC initialization

In order to maintain software flexibility, most of the commands were written as subroutines. A small control loop combines these subroutines into a useful terminal function. Other commands and subroutines may be added by expanding the command search table. Equate statements are given at the end of the listing and must be in accord with the hardware addresses used.

Figure 14-13 is an overall flowchart for the program shown in Appendix D. After reset, the ACIA (serial interface) and PIA (keyboard interface) are initialized. The display memory should be cleared before the CRTC is initialized to eliminate a flash of false data on the screen. The CRT initialization routine loads the contents of the CRT table (CRTTAB) into the 18 CRTC registers and clears the character and line counters.

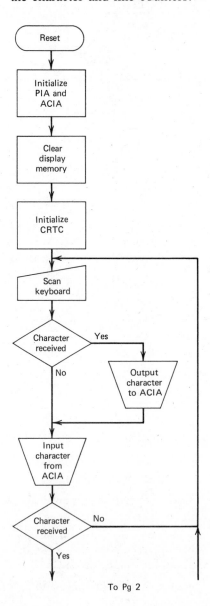

Figure 14-13 Flowchart for CRT program.

To Pg 2

The CRTC allows up to 105 displayed characters per line and up to 165 displayed character rows per field. (See the **6845** Data Sheet). CLINE equals the number of displayed characters per line and LSCREN equals the number of displayed character rows per screen, minus one. These two parameters and the other CRT initialization values determine the display format. They have been initially set for an 80 × 24 display, but can be easily changed to accommodate any format.

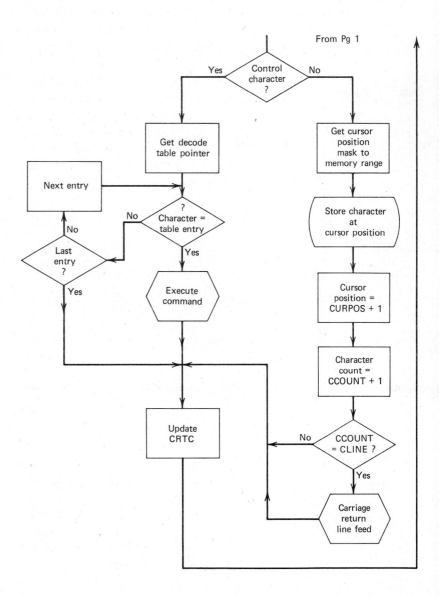

Upon completing the initialization, the processor enters a control loop that recognizes any of the control characters and calls the appropriate subroutines to implement the basic terminal functions. The first subroutine reads the keyboard and checks for a *keypress*. If a key was pressed the character is read and transmitted via the serial interface to another nearby RS232 terminal or via a modem to a distant terminal. Normally the system is operated in full duplex, which means that information typed on the distant keyboard is displayed locally on the CRT and vice versa. Sometimes the distant processor is arranged to echo back the character typed, or the local system is operated in half duplex, so the operator can see what he or she typed.

After checking the PIA for a keypress the ACIA is checked to see if a remote character has been received. In this control loop routine, the PIA and ACIA inputs are scanned alternately and continuously until a character is received. It must then be decoded to determine if it is a *displayable* character or a *control* character. If bits 5 and 6 of an ASCII character are zero, then the character is a control word; otherwise it is a displayable character. This is tested by ANDing the character with $60 and, if the result is zero, the program is branched to DECOD1. To keep track of where the next character is to be placed, several parameters must be retained. Since the CRTC requires binary addresses, two 16-bit binary numbers for both the *cursor position* and *starting address* are saved in RAM. Labels for these two are CURPOS and STARAD, respectively. In addition the number of characters per line must be retained to ensure that a carriage return and line feed are performed if the entered characters exceed the line length. The number of lines per screen must also be counted to determine if scroll up must be performed. Labels for the two counters are CCOUNT and LCOUNT, respectively.

When a displayable character is received, it is stored in the memory location pointed to by CURPOS. However CURPOS is a 16-bit counter and not an absolute memory location. Therefore, first the higher order address bits must be masked to the display memory size, then the correct high order address bits must be "ORed" to correctly position the character in the μP memory map. The cursor position counter (CURPOS) must be incremented as well as the characters per line counter (CCOUNT). If CCOUNT is equal to the line length, then a carriage return/line feed must be performed. After all the counters are updated the CRTC start address and cursor address register are updated.

If the input character is a control character, it must be examined to determine the command. This is accomplished by stepping through a decode table (DECTAB), comparing the character with table entries, and counting the entries. If a match is found, then the count equals the table entry. Another table containing addresses of each command routine (DECADD) is entered by stepping through entries and decrementing the entry count until it reaches zero. The address of the correct subroutines is available and the subroutine can be executed. Again the CRTC must be updated before returning to the control loop. Each of the subroutines will now be described.

14-6.1
Line Feed (Fig. 14-14)

The *line feed* subroutine will move the cursor to the same position in the next line. If the current line is the last line on the screen, a line feed will also cause a scroll up.

To perform a line feed the cursor position counter (CURPOS) and current line starting address pointer must be incremented by the number of characters per line (CLINE). This subroutine must be fast if

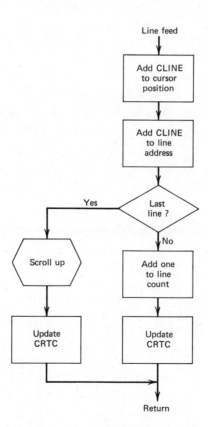

Figure 14-14 Flowchart for line feed subroutine.

the terminal is to run at 9600 baud. At this baud rate the characters are 1.04 milliseconds apart. However the ACIA is double buffered so that for a short burst the μP has slightly more than one character time to execute a line feed.

The line counter must also be checked to see if a scroll up is required. If not the line counter is incremented. Otherwise a scroll up is performed and the CRTC is updated.

14-6.2
Carriage Return (Fig. 14-15)

The carriage return subroutine moves the cursor to the beginning of the current line, clears the character counter (CCOUNT), and updates the CRTC.

14-6.3
Memory Clear (Fig. 14-16)

The memory clear routine stores an ASCII space (hex 20) into the memory address pointed to by memory start (MEMSTR), increments the pointer, loops back to store another space, and continues until the pointer reaches the memory end (MEMEND).

14-6.4
Scroll Up (Fig. 14-17)

The scroll up subroutine moves all data on the screen up one line and adds a new line to the bottom. The new line is not cleared. The cursor remains in the same character position.

14-6.5
Scroll Down (Fig. 14-18)

The scroll down subroutine moves all the data on the screen down one line and adds a new line to the top of the screen. The new line is not cleared. The CURSOR remains in the same character position.

14-6.6
Page Up (Fig. 14-19)

Page up subroutine calls the scroll up subroutine enough times to shift all the lines off and new ones on. The new lines are not cleared and the cursor remains in the same character position.

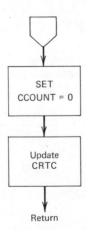

Figure 14-15 Carriage return software flowchart.

SET
CCOUNT = 0

Update
CRTC

Return

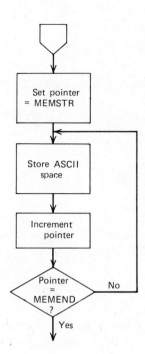

Figure 14-16 Memory clear subroutine.

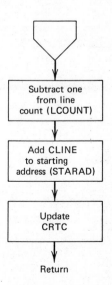

Figure 14-17 Scroll up subroutine.

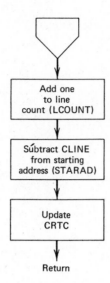

Figure 14-18 Scroll down subroutine.

14-6.7
Page Down (Fig. 14-20)

The page down subroutine calls the scroll down subroutine enough times to shift all existing lines off the screen and new ones on. The new lines are not cleared and the cursor remains in the same character position.

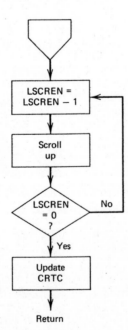

Figure 14-19 Page up subroutine.

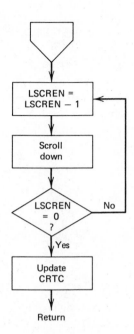

Figure 14-20 Page down subroutine.

14-7
Summary

A complete design of a practical CRT terminal has been discussed to illustrate applications of the various **6800** family components. This has included not only the description of the hardware needed to generate the video signal for display of alphanumeric data on the CRT monitor but also the software to complete the system design. The software and hardware also allow for keyboard input and serial data communications functions. Unfortunately, some portions of the design may appear overly complex, and complete details cannot be included in the space available. Many of the new IC peripherals fall in this category and would require a full chapter to explain adequately.

We regret that we could not have given additional complete system examples but, as seen in this chapter, this would have been difficult. Instead, in the previous chapters, we have tried to present basic principles of individual **6800** μP component applications, and have given examples so that the readers should, by the time they reach this chapter be able to assemble a system of their own design. It is strongly recommended that students procure the manufacturers literature and applications notes referenced in each chapter for more complete understanding.

14-8
Glossary

Alphanumeric Includes both letters and numbers.

Blanking The portion of the scan line that is inhibited because it is out of displayable area or is the retrace line.

Character Generator An ROM (usually NMOS) that serves as a lookup table for characters. With an input of the character code and the row address, it will provide the DOT bits for each row of the character matrix.

CRT Cathode ray tube—a special vacuum tube that produces images on its screen area.

DOT clock A timing signal that indicates the point on each scan line where a dot can be located.

Hsync The horizontal oscillator's synchronization pulse.

MODEM A MODulator/DEModulator used to translate signal parameters from data to audio and vice versa.

Shift Register An IC (usually FFs) in which the bits can be loaded in parallel and shifted out serially.

Video A signal intended for display on a CRT (TV) monitor.

Vsync The vertical oscillator's synchronization pulse.

14-9 References

Kister, Jack E., CRT Concepts and Implementations, Unpublished Application Note, Motorola Semiconductor Products, Inc., P.O. Box 20912, Phoenix, Arizona 85036.

Motorola, *MC6845 CRT Controller Data Sheet ADI—465,* Motorola Semiconductors, 3501 Ed Bluestein Blvd., Austin, Texas 78721.

Motorola, *MEX6845(D) CRTC Support Module User's Guide,* September, 1978, Motorola, Inc., Integrated Circuits Division, Microsystems, 3102 N. 56th Street, Phoenix, Arizona 85018.

14-10 Problems

14-1. What happens to the top line when the screen is scrolled up?

14-2. What would be required to use the scroll feature in a word processing system.

14-3. What is the difference between a half-duplex and full-duplex serial interface? How would an operator see what is typed?

14-4. Why is the terminal described called an intelligent terminal?

14-5. How much additional memory space is available for additional routines?

14-6. If a suitable CRT tube could be obtained, what would be the advantage to using interlaced scan?

14-7. a. What data would you save if a power failure feature were added?
  b. Which routines would need modification?
  c. Which routines would have to be added?
  d. What hardware additions are needed to add Power Failure Recovery?

14-8. Draw the flowcharts for adding the following routines and, if time permits, write the assembly language program.
   a. Insert character
   b. Delete character
   c. Insert line
   d. Delete line

After attempting to solve the problems, try to answer the self-evaluation questions in Sec. 14.2. If any of them still seem difficult review the appropriate sections of the chapter to find the answers.

Appendix A[1] Positive and Negative Powers of 2

2^n	n	2^{-n}
1	0	1.0
2	1	0.5
4	2	0.25
8	3	0.125
16	4	0.062 5
32	5	0.031 25
64	6	0.015 625
128	7	0.007 812 5
256	8	0.003 906 25
512	9	0.001 953 125
1 024	10	0.000 976 562 5
2 048	11	0.000 488 281 25
4 096	12	0.000 244 140 625
8 192	13	0.000 122 070 312 5
16 384	14	0.000 061 035 156 25
32 768	15	0.000 030 517 578 125
65 536	16	0.000 015 258 789 062 5
131 072	17	0.000 007 629 394 531 25
262 144	18	0.000 003 814 697 265 625
524 288	19	0.000 001 907 348 632 812 5
1 048 576	20	0.000 000 953 674 316 406 25
2 097 152	21	0.000 000 476 837 153 203 125
4 194 304	22	0.000 000 238 418 579 101 562 5
8 388 608	23	0.000 000 119 209 289 550 781 25
16 777 216	24	0.000 000 059 604 644 775 390 625
33 554 432	25	0.000 000 029 802 322 387 695 312 5
67 108 864	26	0.000 000 014 901 161 193 817 656 25
134 217 728	27	0.000 000 007 450 580 596 923 828 125
268 435 456	28	0.000 000 003 725 290 298 461 914 062 5
536 870 912	29	0.000 000 001 862 645 149 230 957 031 25
1 073 741 824	30	0.000 000 000 931 322 574 615 478 515 625
2 147 483 648	31	0.000 000 000 465 661 287 307 739 257 812 5
4 294 967 296	32	0.000 000 000 232 830 643 653 869 628 906 25
8 589 934 592	33	0.000 000 000 116 415 321 826 934 814 453 125
17 179 869 184	34	0.000 000 000 058 207 660 913 467 407 226 562 5
34 359 738 368	35	0.000 000 000 029 103 830 456 733 703 613 281 25
68 719 476 736	36	0.000 000 000 014 551 915 228 366 851 806 640 625
137 438 953 472	37	0.000 000 000 007 275 957 614 183 425 903 320 312 5
274 877 906 944	38	0.000 000 000 003 637 978 807 091 712 951 660 156 25
549 755 813 888	39	0.000 000 000 001 818 898 403 545 856 475 830 078 125
1 099 511 627 776	40	0.000 000 000 000 909 494 701 772 928 237 915 039 062 5
2 199 023 255 552	41	0.000 000 000 000 454 747 350 886 464 118 957 519 531 25
4 398 046 511 104	42	0.000 000 000 000 227 373 675 443 232 059 478 759 765 625
8 796 093 022 208	43	0.000 000 000 000 113 686 837 721 616 029 739 379 882 812 5
17 592 186 044 416	44	0.000 000 000 000 056 843 418 860 808 014 869 689 941 406 25
35 184 372 088 832	45	0.000 000 000 000 028 421 709 431 404 007 434 844 970 703 125
70 368 744 177 664	46	0.000 000 000 000 014 210 854 715 702 003 717 422 485 351 562 5
140 737 488 355 328	47	0.000 000 000 000 007 105 427 357 601 001 858 711 242 675 781 25
281 474 976 710 656	48	0.000 000 000 000 003 552 713 678 800 500 929 355 621 337 890 625
562 949 953 421 312	49	0.000 000 000 000 001 776 356 839 400 250 464 677 810 668 945 312 5
1 125 899 906 843 624	50	0.000 000 000 000 000 888 178 419 700 125 232 338 905 334 472 656 25
2 251 799 813 685 248	51	0.000 000 000 000 000 444 089 209 850 062 616 169 452 667 236 328 125
4 503 599 627 370 496	52	0.000 000 000 000 000 222 044 804 925 031 308 084 726 333 618 164 062 5
9 007 199 254 740 992	53	0.000 000 000 000 000 111 022 302 462 515 654 042 363 166 809 082 031 25
18 014 398 509 481 984	54	0.000 000 000 000 000 055 511 151 231 257 827 021 181 583 404 541 015 625
36 028 797 018 963 968	55	0.000 000 000 000 000 027 755 575 615 628 911 510 590 791 702 270 507 812 5
72 057 594 037 927 936	56	0.000 000 000 000 000 013 877 787 807 814 456 755 295 395 851 135 253 906 25
144 115 188 075 855 872	57	0.000 000 000 000 000 006 938 893 903 907 228 377 647 697 925 567 626 953 125
288 230 376 151 711 744	58	0.000 000 000 000 000 003 469 446 951 953 614 188 823 848 962 783 813 476 562 5
576 460 752 303 423 488	59	0.000 000 000 000 000 001 734 723 475 976 807 094 411 924 481 391 906 738 281 25
1 152 921 504 606 846 976	60	0.000 000 000 000 000 000 867 361 737 988 403 547 205 962 240 695 953 369 140 625
2 305 843 009 213 693 952	61	0.000 000 000 000 000 000 433 680 868 994 201 773 602 981 120 347 976 684 570 312 5
4 611 686 018 427 387 904	62	0.000 000 000 000 000 000 216 840 434 497 100 886 801 490 560 173 988 342 285 156 25
9 223 372 036 854 775 808	63	0.000 000 000 000 000 000 108 420 217 248 550 443 400 745 280 086 994 171 142 578 125
18 446 744 073 709 551 616	64	0.000 000 000 000 000 000 054 210 108 624 275 221 700 372 640 043 497 085 571 289 062 5
36 893 488 147 419 103 232	65	0.000 000 000 000 000 000 027 105 054 312 137 610 850 186 320 021 748 542 785 644 531 25
73 786 976 294 838 206 464	66	0.000 000 000 000 000 000 013 552 527 156 068 805 425 093 160 010 874 271 392 822 265 625
147 573 952 589 676 412 928	67	0.000 000 000 000 000 000 006 776 263 578 034 402 712 546 580 005 437 135 696 411 132 812 5
295 147 905 179 352 825 856	68	0.000 000 000 000 000 000 003 388 131 789 017 201 356 273 290 002 718 567 848 205 566 406 25
590 295 810 358 705 651 712	69	0.000 000 000 000 000 000 001 694 065 894 508 600 678 136 645 001 359 283 924 102 783 203 125
1 180 591 620 717 411 303 422	70	0.000 000 000 000 000 000 000 847 032 947 254 300 339 068 322 500 679 641 962 051 391 601 562 5
2 361 183 241 434 822 606 848	71	0.000 000 000 000 000 000 000 423 516 473 627 150 169 534 161 250 339 820 981 025 695 800 781 25
4 722 366 482 869 645 213 696	72	0.000 000 000 000 000 000 000 211 758 236 813 575 084 767 080 625 169 910 490 512 847 900 390 625

Table of powers of 2.

[1]George K. Kostopoulos. *Digital Engineering*. Copyright John Wiley & Sons, Inc. 1975. Reprinted by permission of John Wiley & Sons, Inc.

Appendix B The 6800 Instruction Set

Table B-1
Accumulator and Memory Instructions

OPERATIONS	MNEMONIC	IMMED OP	~	=	DIRECT OP	~	=	INDEX OP	~	=	EXTND OP	~	=	IMPLIED OP	~	=	BOOLEAN/ARITHMETIC OPERATION (All register labels refer to contents)	H	I	N	Z	V	C
Add	ADDA	8B	2	2	9B	3	2	AB	5	2	BB	4	3				A + M → A	↕	●	↕	↕	↕	↕
	ADDB	CB	2	2	DB	3	2	EB	5	2	FB	4	3				B + M → B	↕	●	↕	↕	↕	↕
Add Acmltrs	ABA													1B	2	1	A + B → A	↕	●	↕	↕	↕	↕
Add with Carry	ADCA	89	2	2	99	3	2	A9	5	2	B9	4	3				A + M + C → A	↕	●	↕	↕	↕	↕
	ADCB	C9	2	2	D9	3	2	E9	5	2	F9	4	3				B + M + C → B	↕	●	↕	↕	↕	↕
And	ANDA	84	2	2	94	3	2	A4	5	2	B4	4	3				A · M → A	●	●	↕	↕	R	●
	ANDB	C4	2	2	D4	3	2	E4	5	2	F4	4	3				B · M → B	●	●	↕	↕	R	●
Bit Test	BITA	85	2	2	95	3	2	A5	5	2	B5	4	3				A · M	●	●	↕	↕	R	●
	BITB	C5	2	2	D5	3	2	E5	5	2	F5	4	3				B · M	●	●	↕	↕	R	●
Clear	CLR							6F	7	2	7F	6	3				00 → M	●	●	R	S	R	R
	CLRA													4F	2	1	00 → A	●	●	R	S	R	R
	CLRB													5F	2	1	00 → B	●	●	R	S	R	R
Compare	CMPA	81	2	2	91	3	2	A1	5	2	B1	4	3				A - M	●	●	↕	↕	↕	↕
	CMPB	C1	2	2	D1	3	2	E1	5	2	F1	4	3				B - M	●	●	↕	↕	↕	↕
Compare Acmltrs	CBA													11	2	1	A - B	●	●	↕	↕	↕	↕
Complement, 1's	COM							63	7	2	73	6	3				M̄ → M	●	●	↕	↕	R	S
	COMA													43	2	1	Ā → A	●	●	↕	↕	R	S
	COMB													53	2	1	B̄ → B	●	●	↕	↕	R	S
Complement, 2's	NEG							60	7	2	70	6	3				00 - M → M	●	●	↕	↕	①	②
(Negate)	NEGA													40	2	1	00 - A → A	●	●	↕	↕	①	②
	NEGB													50	2	1	00 - B → B	●	●	↕	↕	①	②
Decimal Adjust, A	DAA													19	2	1	Converts Binary Add. of BCD Characters into BCD Format	●	●	↕	↕	↕	③
Decrement	DEC							6A	7	2	7A	6	3				M - 1 → M	●	●	↕	↕	④	●
	DECA													4A	2	1	A - 1 → A	●	●	↕	↕	④	●
	DECB													5A	2	1	B - 1 → B	●	●	↕	↕	④	●
Exclusive OR	EORA	88	2	2	98	3	2	A8	5	2	B8	4	3				A ⊕ M → A	●	●	↕	↕	R	●
	EORB	C8	2	2	D8	3	2	E8	5	2	F8	4	3				B ⊕ M → B	●	●	↕	↕	R	●
Increment	INC							6C	7	2	7C	6	3				M + 1 → M	●	●	↕	↕	⑤	●
	INCA													4C	2	1	A + 1 → A	●	●	↕	↕	⑤	●
	INCB													5C	2	1	B + 1 → B	●	●	↕	↕	⑤	●
Load Acmltr	LDAA	86	2	2	96	3	2	A6	5	2	B6	4	3				M → A	●	●	↕	↕	R	●
	LDAB	C6	2	2	D6	3	2	E6	5	2	F6	4	3				M → B	●	●	↕	↕	R	●
Or, Inclusive	ORAA	8A	2	2	9A	3	2	AA	5	2	BA	4	3				A + M → A	●	●	↕	↕	R	●
	ORAB	CA	2	2	DA	3	2	EA	5	2	FA	4	3				B + M → B	●	●	↕	↕	R	●
Push Data	PSHA													36	4	1	A → Msp, SP - 1 → SP	●	●	●	●	●	●
	PSHB													37	4	1	B → Msp, SP - 1 → SP	●	●	●	●	●	●
Pull Data	PULA													32	4	1	SP + 1 → SP, Msp → A	●	●	●	●	●	●
	PULB													33	4	1	SP + 1 → SP, Msp → B	●	●	●	●	●	●
Rotate Left	ROL							69	7	2	79	6	3				M (rotate left through carry)	●	●	↕	↕	⑥	↕
	ROLA													49	2	1	A	●	●	↕	↕	⑥	↕
	ROLB													59	2	1	B	●	●	↕	↕	⑥	↕
Rotate Right	ROR							66	7	2	76	6	3				M (rotate right through carry)	●	●	↕	↕	⑥	↕
	RORA													46	2	1	A	●	●	↕	↕	⑥	↕
	RORB													56	2	1	B	●	●	↕	↕	⑥	↕
Shift Left, Arithmetic	ASL							68	7	2	78	6	3				M (shift left)	●	●	↕	↕	⑥	↕
	ASLA													48	2	1	A	●	●	↕	↕	⑥	↕
	ASLB													58	2	1	B	●	●	↕	↕	⑥	↕
Shift Right, Arithmetic	ASR							67	7	2	77	6	3				M (arithmetic shift right)	●	●	↕	↕	⑥	↕
	ASRA													47	2	1	A	●	●	↕	↕	⑥	↕
	ASRB													57	2	1	B	●	●	↕	↕	⑥	↕
Shift Right, Logic	LSR							64	7	2	74	6	3				M (logical shift right)	●	●	R	↕	⑥	↕
	LSRA													44	2	1	A	●	●	R	↕	⑥	↕
	LSRB													54	2	1	B	●	●	R	↕	⑥	↕
Store Acmltr.	STAA				97	4	2	A7	6	2	B7	5	3				A → M	●	●	↕	↕	R	●
	STAB				D7	4	2	E7	6	2	F7	5	3				B → M	●	●	↕	↕	R	●
Subtract	SUBA	80	2	2	90	3	2	A0	5	2	B0	4	3				A - M → A	●	●	↕	↕	↕	↕
	SUBB	C0	2	2	D0	3	2	E0	5	2	F0	4	3				B - M → B	●	●	↕	↕	↕	↕
Subtract Acmltrs.	SBA													10	2	1	A - B → A	●	●	↕	↕	↕	↕
Subtr. with Carry	SBCA	82	2	2	92	3	2	A2	5	2	B2	4	3				A - M - C → A	●	●	↕	↕	↕	↕
	SBCB	C2	2	2	D2	3	2	E2	5	2	F2	4	3				B - M - C → B	●	●	↕	↕	↕	↕
Transfer Acmltrs	TAB													16	2	1	A → B	●	●	↕	↕	R	●
	TBA													17	2	1	B → A	●	●	↕	↕	R	●
Test, Zero or Minus	TST							6D	7	2	7D	6	3				M - 00	●	●	↕	↕	R	R
	TSTA													4D	2	1	A - 00	●	●	↕	↕	R	R
	TSTB													5D	2	1	B - 00	●	●	↕	↕	R	R

Condition code register bit positions: 5 4 3 2 1 0 = H I N Z V C

Table B-2
Index Register and Stack Manipulation

POINTER OPERATIONS	MNEMONIC	IMMED OP	~	#	DIRECT OP	~	#	INDEX OP	~	#	EXTND OP	~	#	IMPLIED OP	~	#	BOOLEAN/ARITHMETIC OPERATION	H	I	N	Z	V	C
Compare Index Reg	CPX	8C	3	3	9C	4	2	AC	6	2	BC	5	3				$X_H - M, X_L - (M+1)$	•	•	⑦	↕	⑧	•
Decrement Index Reg	DEX													09	4	1	$X - 1 \to X$	•	•	•	↕	•	•
Decrement Stack Pntr	DES													34	4	1	$SP - 1 \to SP$	•	•	•	•	•	•
Increment Index Reg	INX													08	4	1	$X + 1 \to X$	•	•	•	↕	•	•
Increment Stack Pntr	INS													31	4	1	$SP + 1 \to SP$	•	•	•	•	•	•
Load Index Reg	LDX	CE	3	3	DE	4	2	EE	6	2	FE	5	3				$M \to X_H, (M+1) \to X_L$	•	•	⑨	↕	R	•
Load Stack Pntr	LDS	8E	3	3	9E	4	2	AE	6	2	BE	5	3				$M \to SP_H, (M+1) \to SP_L$	•	•	⑨	↕	R	•
Store Index Reg	STX				DF	5	2	EF	7	2	FF	6	3				$X_H \to M, X_L \to (M+1)$	•	•	⑨	↕	R	•
Store Stack Pntr	STS				9F	5	2	AF	7	2	BF	6	3				$SP_H \to M, SP_L \to (M+1)$	•	•	⑨	↕	R	•
Indx Reg → Stack Pntr	TXS													35	4	1	$X - 1 \to SP$	•	•	•	•	•	•
Stack Pntr → Indx Reg	TSX													30	4	1	$SP + 1 \to X$	•	•	•	•	•	•

COND. CODE REG. columns: 5 4 3 2 1 0 = H I N Z V C

OPERATIONS	MNEMONIC	RELATIVE OP	~	#	INDEX OP	~	#	EXTND OP	~	#	IMPLIED OP	~	#	BRANCH TEST	H	I	N	Z	V	C
Branch Always	BRA	20	4	2										None	•	•	•	•	•	•
Branch If Carry Clear	BCC	24	4	2										$C = 0$	•	•	•	•	•	•
Branch If Carry Set	BCS	25	4	2										$C = 1$	•	•	•	•	•	•
Branch If = Zero	BEQ	27	4	2										$Z = 1$	•	•	•	•	•	•
Branch If ≥ Zero	BGE	2C	4	2										$N \oplus V = 0$	•	•	•	•	•	•
Branch If > Zero	BGT	2E	4	2										$Z + (N \oplus V) = 0$	•	•	•	•	•	•
Branch If Higher	BHI	22	4	2										$C + Z = 0$	•	•	•	•	•	•
Branch If ≤ Zero	BLE	2F	4	2										$Z + (N \oplus V) = 1$	•	•	•	•	•	•
Branch If Lower Or Same	BLS	23	4	2										$C + Z = 1$	•	•	•	•	•	•
Branch If < Zero	BLT	2D	4	2										$N \oplus V = 1$	•	•	•	•	•	•
Branch If Minus	BMI	2B	4	2										$N = 1$	•	•	•	•	•	•
Branch If Not Equal Zero	BNE	26	4	2										$Z = 0$	•	•	•	•	•	•
Branch If Overflow Clear	BVC	28	4	2										$V = 0$	•	•	•	•	•	•
Branch If Overflow Set	BVS	29	4	2										$V = 1$	•	•	•	•	•	•
Branch If Plus	BPL	2A	4	2										$N = 0$	•	•	•	•	•	•
Branch To Subroutine	BSR	8D	8	2											•	•	•	•	•	•
Jump	JMP				6E	4	2	7E	3	3				See Special Operations	•	•	•	•	•	•
Jump To Subroutine	JSR				AD	8	2	BD	9	3					•	•	•	•	•	•
No Operation	NOP										01	2	1	Advances Prog. Cntr. Only	•	•	•	•	•	•
Return From Interrupt	RTI										3B	10	1		⑩					
Return From Subroutine	RTS										39	5	1		•	•	•	•	•	•
Software Interrupt	SWI										3F	12	1	See Special Operations	•	•	•	•	•	•
Wait for Interrupt*	WAI										3E	9	1		•	⑪	•	•	•	•

*WAI puts Address Bus, R/W, and Data Bus in the three state mode while VMA is held low.

Table B-3
Jump and Branch Instructions

COND. CODE REG. columns: 5 4 3 2 1 0 = H I N Z V C

OPERATIONS	MNEMONIC	IMPLIED OP	~	#	BOOLEAN OPERATION	H	I	N	Z	V	C
Clear Carry	CLC	0C	2	1	$0 \to C$	•	•	•	•	•	R
Clear Interrupt Mask	CLI	0E	2	1	$0 \to I$	•	R	•	•	•	•
Clear Overflow	CLV	0A	2	1	$0 \to V$	•	•	•	•	R	•
Set Carry	SEC	0D	2	1	$1 \to C$	•	•	•	•	•	S
Set Interrupt Mask	SEI	0F	2	1	$1 \to I$	•	S	•	•	•	•
Set Overflow	SEV	0B	2	1	$1 \to V$	•	•	•	•	S	•
Acmltr A → CCR	TAP	06	2	1	$A \to CCR$	⑫					
CCR → Acmltr A	TPA	07	2	1	$CCR \to A$	•	•	•	•	•	•

CONDITION CODE REGISTER NOTES: (Bit set if test is true and cleared otherwise)

1 (Bit V) Test: Result = 10000000?
2 (Bit C) Test: Result = 00000000?
3 (Bit C) Test: Decimal value of most significant BCD Character greater than nine? (Not cleared if previously set.)
4 (Bit V) Test: Operand = 10000000 prior to execution?
5 (Bit V) Test: Operand = 01111111 prior to execution?
6 (Bit V) Test: Set equal to result of N⊕C after shift has occurred.
7 (Bit N) Test: Sign bit of most significant (MS) byte = 1?
8 (Bit V) Test: 2's complement overflow from subtraction of MS bytes?
9 (Bit N) Test: Result less than zero? (Bit 15 = 1)
10 (All)   Load Condition Code Register from Stack. (See Special Operations)
11 (Bit I) Set when interrupt occurs. If previously set, a Non-Maskable Interrupt is required to exit the wait state.
12 (All)   Set according to the contents of Accumulator A.

Appendix C Table of Cycle by Cycle Operation for Each 6800 Instruction

Table 8 provides a detailed description of the information present on the Address Bus, Data Bus, Valid Memory Address line (VMA), and the Read/Write line (R/W) during each cycle for each instruction.

This information is useful in comparing actual with expected results during debug of both software and hardware as the control program is executed. The information is categorized in groups according to Addressing Mode and Number of Cycles per instruction. (In general, instructions with the same Addressing Mode and Number of Cycles execute in the same manner; exceptions are indicated in the table.)

TABLE 8 – OPERATION SUMMARY

Address Mode and Instructions	Cycles	Cycle #	VMA Line	Address Bus	R/W Line	Data Bus
IMMEDIATE						
ADC EOR ADD LDA AND ORA BIT SBC CMP SUB	2	1 2	1 1	Op Code Address Op Code Address + 1	1 1	Op Code Operand Data
CPX LDS LDX	3	1 2 3	1 1 1	Op Code Address Op Code Address + 1 Op Code Address + 2	1 1 1	Op Code Operand Data (High Order Byte) Operand Data (Low Order Byte)
DIRECT						
ADC EOR ADD LDA AND ORA BIT SBC CMP SUB	3	1 2 3	1 1 1	Op Code Address Op Code Address + 1 Address of Operand	1 1 1	Op Code Address of Operand Operand Data
CPX LDS LDX	4	1 2 3 4	1 1 1 1	Op Code Address Op Code Address + 1 Address of Operand Operand Address + 1	1 1 1 1	Op Code Address of Operand Operand Data (High Order Byte) Operand Data (Low Order Byte)
STA	4	1 2 3 4	1 1 0 1	Op Code Address Op Code Address + 1 Destination Address Destination Address	1 1 1 0	Op Code Destination Address Irrelevant Data (Note 1) Data from Accumulator
STS STX	5	1 2 3 4 5	1 1 0 1 1	Op Code Address Op Code Address + 1 Address of Operand Address of Operand Address of Operand + 1	1 1 1 0 0	Op Code Address of Operand Irrelevant Data (Note 1) Register Data (High Order Byte) Register Data (Low Order Byte)
INDEXED						
JMP	4	1 2 3 4	1 1 0 0	Op Code Address Op Code Address + 1 Index Register Index Register Plus Offset (w/o Carry)	1 1 1 1	Op Code Offset Irrelevant Data (Note 1) Irrelevant Data (Note 1)
ADC EOR ADD LDA AND ORA BIT SBC CMP SUB	5	1 2 3 4 5	1 1 0 0 1	Op Code Address Op Code Address + 1 Index Register Index Register Plus Offset (w/o Carry) Index Register Plus Offset	1 1 1 1 1	Op Code Offset Irrelevant Data (Note 1) Irrelevant Data (Note 1) Operand Data
CPX LDS LDX	6	1 2 3 4 5 6	1 1 0 0 1 1	Op Code Address Op Code Address + 1 Index Register Index Register Plus Offset (w/o Carry) Index Register Plus Offset Index Register Plus Offset + 1	1 1 1 1 1 1	Op Code Offset Irrelevant Data (Note 1) Irrelevant Data (Note 1) Operand Data (High Order Byte) Operand Data (Low Order Byte)

APPENDIX C   TABLE OF CYCLE BY CYCLE OPERATION FOR EACH 6800 INSTRUCTION

Address Mode and Instructions	Cycles	Cycle #	VMA Line	Address Bus	R/W Line	Data Bus
INDEXED (Continued)						
STA		1	1	Op Code Address	1	Op Code
		2	1	Op Code Address + 1	1	Offset
	6	3	0	Index Register	1	Irrelevant Data (Note 1)
		4	0	Index Register Plus Offset (w/o Carry)	1	Irrelevant Data (Note 1)
		5	0	Index Register Plus Offset	1	Irrelevant Data (Note 1)
		6	1	Index Register Plus Offset	0	Operand Data
ASL LSR		1	1	Op Code Address	1	Op Code
ASR NEG		2	1	Op Code Address + 1	1	Offset
CLR ROL		3	0	Index Register	1	Irrelevant Data (Note 1)
COM ROR	7	4	0	Index Register Plus Offset (w/o Carry)	1	Irrelevant Data (Note 1)
DEC TST		5	1	Index Register Plus Offset	1	Current Operand Data
INC		6	0	Index Register Plus Offset	1	Irrelevant Data (Note 1)
		7	1/0 (Note 3)	Index Register Plus Offset	0	New Operand Data (Note 3)
STS		1	1	Op Code Address	1	Op Code
STX		2	1	Op Code Address + 1	1	Offset
		3	0	Index Register	1	Irrelevant Data (Note 1)
	7	4	0	Index Register Plus Offset (w/o Carry)	1	Irrelevant Data (Note 1)
		5	0	Index Register Plus Offset	1	Irrelevant Data (Note 1)
		6	1	Index Register Plus Offset	0	Operand Data (High Order Byte)
		7	1	Index Register Plus Offset + 1	0	Operand Data (Low Order Byte)
JSR		1	1	Op Code Address	1	Op Code
		2	1	Op Code Address + 1	1	Offset
		3	0	Index Register	1	Irrelevant Data (Note 1)
	8	4	1	Stack Pointer	0	Return Address (Low Order Byte)
		5	1	Stack Pointer − 1	0	Return Address (High Order Byte)
		6	0	Stack Pointer − 2	1	Irrelevant Data (Note 1)
		7	0	Index Register	1	Irrelevant Data (Note 1)
		8	0	Index Register Plus Offset (w/o Carry)	1	Irrelevant Data (Note 1)
EXTENDED						
JMP		1	1	Op Code Address	1	Op Code
	3	2	1	Op Code Address + 1	1	Jump Address (High Order Byte)
		3	1	Op Code Address + 2	1	Jump Address (Low Order Byte)
ADC EOR		1	1	Op Code Address	1	Op Code
ADD LDA		2	1	Op Code Address + 1	1	Address of Operand (High Order Byte)
AND ORA	4	3	1	Op Code Address + 2	1	Address of Operand (Low Order Byte)
BIT SBC		4	1	Address of Operand	1	Operand Data
CMP SUB						
CPX		1	1	Op Code Address	1	Op Code
LDS		2	1	Op Code Address + 1	1	Address of Operand (High Order Byte)
LDX	5	3	1	Op Code Address + 2	1	Address of Operand (Low Order Byte)
		4	1	Address of Operand	1	Operand Data (High Order Byte)
		5	1	Address of Operand + 1	1	Operand Data (Low Order Byte)
STA A		1	1	Op Code Address	1	Op Code
STA B		2	1	Op Code Address + 1	1	Destination Address (High Order Byte)
	5	3	1	Op Code Address + 2	1	Destination Address (Low Order Byte)
		4	0	Operand Destination Address	1	Irrelevant Data (Note 1)
		5	1	Operand Destination Address	0	Data from Accumulator
ASL LSR		1	1	Op Code Address	1	Op Code
ASR NEG		2	1	Op Code Address + 1	1	Address of Operand (High Order Byte)
CLR ROL		3	1	Op Code Address + 2	1	Address of Operand (Low Order Byte)
COM ROR	6	4	1	Address of Operand	1	Current Operand Data
DEC TST		5	0	Address of Operand	1	Irrelevant Data (Note 1)
INC		6	1/0 (Note 3)	Address of Operand	0	New Operand Data (Note 3)

APPENDIX C   TABLE OF CYCLE BY CYCLE OPERATION FOR EACH 6800 INSTRUCTION

Address Mode and Instructions	Cycles	Cycle #	VMA Line	Address Bus	R/W Line	Data Bus
EXTENDED (Continued)						
STS STX	6	1	1	Op Code Address	1	Op Code
		2	1	Op Code Address + 1	1	Address of Operand (High Order Byte)
		3	1	Op Code Address + 2	1	Address of Operand (Low Order Byte)
		4	0	Address of Operand	1	Irrelevant Data (Note 1)
		5	1	Address of Operand	0	Operand Data (High Order Byte)
		6	1	Address of Operand + 1	0	Operand Data (Low Order Byte)
JSR	9	1	1	Op Code Address	1	Op Code
		2	1	Op Code Address + 1	1	Address of Subroutine (High Order Byte)
		3	1	Op Code Address + 2	1	Address of Subroutine (Low Order Byte)
		4	1	Subroutine Starting Address	1	Op Code of Next Instruction
		5	1	Stack Pointer	0	Return Address (Low Order Byte)
		6	1	Stack Pointer − 1	0	Return Address (High Order Byte)
		7	0	Stack Pointer − 2	1	Irrelevant Data (Note 1)
		8	0	Op Code Address + 2	1	Irrelevant Data (Note 1)
		9	1	Op Code Address + 2	1	Address of Subroutine (Low Order Byte)
INHERENT						
ABA DAA SEC ASL DEC SEI ASR INC SEV CBA LSR TAB CLC NEG TAP CLI NOP TBA CLR ROL TPA CLV ROR TST COM SBA	2	1	1	Op Code Address	1	Op Code
		2	1	Op Code Address + 1	1	Op Code of Next Instruction
DES DEX INS INX	4	1	1	Op Code Address	1	Op Code
		2	1	Op Code Address + 1	1	Op Code of Next Instruction
		3	0	Previous Register Contents	1	Irrelevant Data (Note 1)
		4	0	New Register Contents	1	Irrelevant Data (Note 1)
PSH	4	1	1	Op Code Address	1	Op Code
		2	1	Op Code Address + 1	1	Op Code of Next Instruction
		3	1	Stack Pointer	0	Accumulator Data
		4	0	Stack Pointer − 1	1	Accumulator Data
PUL	4	1	1	Op Code Address	1	Op Code
		2	1	Op Code Address + 1	1	Op Code of Next Instruction
		3	0	Stack Pointer	1	Irrelevant Data (Note 1)
		4	1	Stack Pointer + 1	1	Operand Data from Stack
TSX	4	1	1	Op Code Address	1	Op Code
		2	1	Op Code Address + 1	1	Op Code of Next Instruction
		3	0	Stack Pointer	1	Irrelevant Data (Note 1)
		4	0	New Index Register	1	Irrelevant Data (Note 1)
TXS	4	1	1	Op Code Address	1	Op Code
		2	1	Op Code Address + 1	1	Op Code of Next Instruction
		3	0	Index Register	1	Irrelevant Data
		4	0	New Stack Pointer	1	Irrelevant Data
RTS	5	1	1	Op Code Address	1	Op Code
		2	1	Op Code Address + 1	1	Irrelevant Data (Note 2)
		3	0	Stack Pointer	1	Irrelevant Data (Note 1)
		4	1	Stack Pointer + 1	1	Address of Next Instruction (High Order Byte)
		5	1	Stack Pointer + 2	1	Address of Next Instruction (Low Order Byte)

Address Mode and Instructions	Cycles	Cycle #	VMA Line	Address Bus	R/W Line	Data Bus
INHERENT (Continued)						
WAI		1	1	Op Code Address	1	Op Code
		2	1	Op Code Address + 1	1	Op Code of Next Instruction
		3	1	Stack Pointer	0	Return Address (Low Order Byte)
		4	1	Stack Pointer — 1	0	Return Address (High Order Byte)
	9	5	1	Stack Pointer — 2	0	Index Register (Low Order Byte)
		6	1	Stack Pointer — 3	0	Index Register (High Order Byte)
		7	1	Stack Pointer — 4	0	Contents of Accumulator A
		8	1	Stack Pointer — 5	0	Contents of Accumulator B
		9	1	Stack Pointer — 6 (Note 4)	1	Contents of Cond. Code Register
RTI		1	1	Op Code Address	1	Op Code
		2	1	Op Code Address + 1	1	Irrelevant Data (Note 2)
		3	0	Stack Pointer	1	Irrelevant Data (Note 1)
		4	1	Stack Pointer + 1	1	Contents of Cond. Code Register from Stack
	10	5	1	Stack Pointer + 2	1	Contents of Accumulator B from Stack
		6	1	Stack Pointer + 3	1	Contents of Accumulator A from Stack
		7	1	Stack Pointer + 4	1	Index Register from Stack (High Order Byte)
		8	1	Stack Pointer + 5	1	Index Register from Stack (Low Order Byte)
		9	1	Stack Pointer + 6	1	Next Instruction Address from Stack (High Order Byte)
		10	1	Stack Pointer + 7	1	Next Instruction Address from Stack (Low Order Byte)
SWI		1	1	Op Code Address	1	Op Code
		2	1	Op Code Address + 1	1	Irrelevant Data (Note 1)
		3	1	Stack Pointer	0	Return Address (Low Order Byte)
		4	1	Stack Pointer — 1	0	Return Address (High Order Byte)
		5	1	Stack Pointer — 2	0	Index Register (Low Order Byte)
		6	1	Stack Pointer — 3	0	Index Register (High Order Byte)
	12	7	1	Stack Pointer — 4	0	Contents of Accumulator A
		8	1	Stack Pointer — 5	0	Contents of Accumulator B
		9	1	Stack Pointer — 6	0	Contents of Cond. Code Register
		10	0	Stack Pointer — 7	1	Irrelevant Data (Note 1)
		11	1	Vector Address FFFA (Hex)	1	Address of Subroutine (High Order Byte)
		12	1	Vector Address FFFB (Hex)	1	Address of Subroutine (Low Order Byte)
RELATIVE						
BCC BHI BNE BCS BLE BPL BEQ BLS BRA BGE BLT BVC BGT BMI BVS	4	1	1	Op Code Address	1	Op Code
		2	1	Op Code Address + 1	1	Branch Offset
		3	0	Op Code Address + 2	1	Irrelevant Data (Note 1)
		4	0	Branch Address	1	Irrelevant Data (Note 1)
BSR		1	1	Op Code Address	1	Op Code
		2	1	Op Code Address + 1	1	Branch Offset
		3	0	Return Address of Main Program	1	Irrelevant Data (Note 1)
	8	4	1	Stack Pointer	0	Return Address (Low Order Byte)
		5	1	Stack Pointer — 1	0	Return Address (High Order Byte)
		6	0	Stack Pointer — 2	1	Irrelevant Data (Note 1)
		7	0	Return Address of Main Program	1	Irrelevant Data (Note 1)
		8	0	Subroutine Address	1	Irrelevant Data (Note 1)

Note 1.   If device which is addressed during this cycle uses VMA, then the Data Bus will go to the high impedance three-state condition. Depending on bus capacitance, data from the previous cycle may be retained on the Data Bus.
Note 2.   Data is ignored by the MPU.
Note 3.   For TST, VMA = 0 and Operand data does not change.
Note 4.   While the MPU is waiting for the interrupt, Bus Available will go high indicating the following states of the control lines: VMA is low; Address Bus, R/W, and Data Bus are all in the high impedance state.

Appendix D Program for a CRT Terminal

```
00001                        NAM    CRT
00002              *   THIS IS A PROGRAM TO SUPPLY THE BASIC DRIVER
00003              *   ROUTINES FOR A CRT TERMINAL USING THE 6845
00004              *   AN EXECUTIVE IS PROVIDED TO PERFORM
00005              *   THE FUNCTIONS OF A DUMB TERMINAL
00006              *   OCT 29, 1978
00007              *
00008                        OPT    O,NOG
00009 B000                   ORG    $B000
00010              *
00011              *   ENTER HERE ON POWER SEQUENCE
00012              *
00013 B000 8E 00FF RESET     LDS    #STKADD  INITIALIZE STACK
00014 B003 86 03             LDA A  #$03     RESET ACIA
00015 B005 B7 0008           STA A  ACIACR
00016 B008 86 15             LDA A  #$15     1 STOP BIT - NO PARITY
00017 B00A B7 0008           STA A  ACIACR   INITIALIZE ACIA
00018 B00D 4F                CLR A
00019 B00E B7 0010           STA A  PIA1AD   PIA1A DDR INPUTS
00020 B011 86 04             LDA A  #$04     CA1 NEG. INPUT
00021 B013 B7 0011           STA A  PIA1AC   PROGRAM KEYBOARD PIA
00022              *
00023              *   ROUTINE TO CLEAR DISPLAY MEMORY
00024              *
00025 B016 CE 8000 CLEAR     LDX    #MEMSTR  GET STARTING MEMORY ADDR
00026 B019 86 20             LDA A  #$20
00027 B01B A7 00   CLEAR1    STA A  0,X      STORE A SPACE
00028 B01D 08                INX             NEXT LOCATION
00029 B01E 8C 87FF           CPX    #MEMEND  COMPARE WITH MEMORY END
00030 B021 26 F8             BNE    CLEAR1
00031              *
00032              *
00033              *   ROUTINE TO INITIALIZE CRTC
00034              *   ADDRESS $4000
00035              *
00036 B023 CE B154 CRTIZ     LDX    #CRTTAB  POINT TO CRT INIT TAB
00037 B026 4F                CLR A
00038 B027 B7 4000 CRT1      STA A  CRTCAR   SELECT REGISTER
00039 B02A E6 00             LDA B  0,X      GET VALUE
00040 B02C F7 4001           STA B  CRTCDR   PROGRAM VALUE
00041 B02F 08                INX             NEXT VALUE
00042 B030 4C                INC A           NEXT REGISTER
00043 B031 81 10             CMP A  #$10     LAST REGISTER?
00044 B033 26 F2             BNE    CRT1
00045 B035 CE 8000           LDX    #MEMSTR  INITIAL CURSOR POS.
00046 B038 FF 0082           STX    CURPOS
00047 B03B FF 0080           STX    STARAD   INITIAL START ADDR.
00048 B03E FF 0086           STX    LINEAD   STARTING ADD. THIS LINE
00049 B041 CE 0000           LDX    #0
00050 B044 FF 0084           STX    CCOUNT   CLEAR CCOUNT & LCOUNT
00051              *
00052              *   CONTROL LOOP
00053              *
00054 B047 BD B0CF CONTRO    JSR    INCHP    SCAN KEYBOARD
```

PAGE 002   CRT


```
00055 B04A 24 02              BCC    CONT1    NO INPUT
00056 B04C 8D 74              BSR    OUTCH    TRANSMIT CHAR
00057 B04E 8D 63     CONT1    BSR    INCHS    CHECK SERIAL PORT
00058 B050 24 F5              BCC    CONTRO   NO INPUT
00059 B052 8D 02              BSR    DECODE   TEST CHAR.
00060 B054 20 F1              BRA    CONTRO   GET NEXT CHAR
00061                *
00062                *  SUBROUTINE TO DECODE CHARACTER
00063                *
00064 B056 85 60     DECODE BIT A  #$60      CONTROL CHAR ?
00065 B058 27 27              BEQ    DECOD1   YES - CONTROL CHAR
00066 B05A F6 0082            LDA B  CURPOS   GET CURSOR POSITION MSB
00067 B05D C4 1F              AND B  #$1F     MASK TO 8K
00068 B05F F7 008C            STA B  CUTEMP   SAVE IN TEMP
00069 B062 F6 0083            LDA B  CURPOS+1 GET LSB
00070 B065 F7 008D            STA B  CUTEMP+1 SAVE IT
00071 B068 FE 008C            LDX    CUTEMP   GET CURPOS MASKED TO 8K
00072 B06B A7 00              STA A  0,X      WRITE CHAR.
00073 B06D FE 0082            LDX    CURPOS   GET CURSOR POSITION
00074 B070 08                 INX             BUMP CURSOR POSITION
00075 B071 FF 0082            STX    CURPOS   SAVE CURSOR POSITION
00076 B074 7C 0084            INC    CCOUNT
00077 B077 B6 0084            LDA A  CCOUNT   GET CHAR THIS LINE
00078 B07A B1 B164            CMP A  CLINE    LAST CHARACTER?
00079 B07D 2A 69              BPL    CRLF     YES -
00080 B07F 20 1C              BRA    UPDATE   UPDATE CRTC
00081 B081 CE B165   DECOD1 LDX   #DECTAB-1  POINT TO DECODE TAB
00082 B084 5F                 CLR B
00083 B085 5C       NEXT1    INC B           COUNT ENTRY
00084 B086 08                 INX            NEXT ENTRY
00085 B087 8C B16C            CPX    #DECEND
00086 B08A 27 10              BEQ    DECOD    LAST ENTRY?
00087 B08C A1 00              CMP A  0,X      THIS ENTRY
00088 B08E 26 F5              BNE    NEXT1
00089 B090 CE B16A            LDX   #DECADD-2 POINT TO ROUTINE TAB
00090 B093 08       NEXT2    INX
00091 B094 08                 INX            NEXT ENTRY
00092 B095 5A                 DEC B          COUNT ENTRIES
00093 B096 26 FB              BNE    NEXT2
00094 B098 EE 00              LDX    0,X      GET ROUTINE ADD.
00095 B09A AD 00              JSR    0,X      GOTO SUBROUTINE
00096 B09C 39       DECOD    RTS             BACK TO CONTROL
00097                *
00098                *  SUBROUTINE TO UPDATE THE CRTC
00099                *  A & X REGISTERS ARE DESTROYED
00100                *
00101 B09D 37       UPDATE PSH B            SAVE B REG
00102 B09E C6 0C             LDA B  #$0C     POINT TO CTRC START ADD.
00103 B0A0 CE 0080           LDX    #STARAD  POINT TO DISPLAY VAR.
00104 B0A3 A6 00    UDATE1 LDA A  0,X       GET DATA
00105 B0A5 F7 4000           STA B  CRTCAR   SELECT REGISTER
00106 B0A8 B7 4001           STA A  CRTCDR   PROGRAM VALUE
00107 B0AB 08                INX             NEXT VALUE
00108 B0AC 5C                INC B           NEXT REGISTER
```

PAGE 003   CRT

```
00109 B0AD C1 10          CMP B   #$10     LAST REG.?
00110 B0AF 26 F2          BNE     UDATE1   NEXT VALUES
00111 B0B1 33             PUL B            RESTORE B REG.
00112 B0B2 39             RTS
00113                *
00114                *  SUBROUTINE TO SCAN ACIA
00115                *  IF CARRY SET, CHAR. IN A REG.
00116                *  B & X REGISTERS SAVED
00117                *
00118 B0B3 37       INCHS  PSH B           SAVE B REG.
00119 B0B4 F6 0008         LDA B   ACIACR   GET STATUS REG
00120 B0B7 56               ROR B           TEST DATA READY BIT
00121 B0B8 24 06            BCC     INCHS1
00122 B0BA B6 0009          LDA A   ACIADR   GET CHARACTER
00123 B0BD 84 7F            AND A   #$7F     MASK OFF PARITY
00124 B0BF 0D               SEC             SET CARRY IF INPUT
00125 B0C0 33       INCHS1  PUL B           RESTORE B REG
00126 B0C1 39               RTS
00127                *
00128                *  SUBROUTINE TO OUTPUT A CHAR IN A REG.
00129                *  B & X REGISTERS SAVED
00130                *
00131 B0C2 37       OUTCH  PSH B           SAVE B REG.
00132 B0C3 F6 0008 OUTCH1 LDA B   ACIACR   GET ACIA STATUS
00133 B0C6 56               ROR B
00134 B0C7 56               ROR B
00135 B0C8 24 F9            BCC     OUTCH1   DATA REG. EMPTY?
00136 B0CA B7 0009          STA A   ACIADR   OUTPUT DATA
00137 B0CD 33               PUL B           RESTORE B REG.
00138 B0CE 39               RTS
00139                *
00140                *  SUBROUTINE TO SCAN PIA1A (KEYBOARD)
00141                *  IF CARRY SET, CHAR IN A REG.
00142                *
00143 B0CF F6 0011 INCHP  LDA B   PIA1AC   GET STATUS REG.
00144 B0D2 58               ASL B           CHECK FOR DATA
00145 B0D3 24 07            BCC     INCHP1   NO DATA?
00146 B0D5 B6 0010          LDA A   PIA1AD   GET DATA
00147                *  IF KEYBOARD IS NOT COMPLEMENTED REPLACE NEXT
00148                *     INSTRUCTION WITH A NOP.
00149 B0D8 43               COM A           COMPLEMENT DATA
00150 B0D9 84 7F            AND A   #$7F     STRIP PARITY
00151 B0DB 0D               SEC             SET CARRY
00152 B0DC 39       INCHP1 RTS
00153                *
00154                *  SUBROUTINE TO CARRIAGE RETURN
00155                *  ALL REGISTERS DESTROYED
00156                *
00157 B0DD FE 0086 RTURN1 LDX     LINEAD   GET STAR. ADD THIS LINE
00158 B0E0 FF 0082         STX     CURPOS   SAVE IT
00159 B0E3 7F 0084         CLR     CCOUNT   CLEAR CHAR/LINE COUNTER
00160 B0E6 20 B5           BRA     UPDATE   UPDATE CRTC
00161                *
00162                *  SUBROUTINE TO CRLF
```

PAGE 004   CRT

```
00163                      *
00164 B0E8 8D F3   CRLF    BSR    RTURN1
00165                      *
00166                      *  SUBROUTINE TO LINE FEED
00167                      *  ALL REGISTERS DESTROYED
00168                      *
00169 B0EA CE 0080 LFEED   LDX    #STARAD  POINT TO DISPLAY VARIBLE
00170 B0ED A6 03           LDA A  3,X      GET CURPOS LSB
00171 B0EF BB B164         ADD A  CLINE    ADD CHAR/LINE
00172 B0F2 A7 03           STA A  3,X      SAVE IT
00173 B0F4 24 02           BCC    LFEED1   CHECK CARRY
00174 B0F6 6C 02           INC    2,X      ADD CARRY TO MSB
00175                      *
00176                      *  ROUTINE TO ADVANCE LINE START ADDR
00177                      *
00178 B0F8 A6 07   LFEED1  LDA A  7,X      GET LINEAD LSB
00179 B0FA BB B164         ADD A  CLINE    ADD CHAR/LINE
00180 B0FD A7 07           STA A  7,X      SAVE IT
00181 B0FF B7 008D         STA A  CUTEMP+1 SAVE IT IN TEMP
00182 B102 A6 06           LDA A  6,X      GET LINEAD MSB
00183 B104 89 00           ADC A  #0       ADD CARRY
00184 B106 A7 06           STA A  6,X      SAVE IT
00185                      *
00186                      *  ROUTINE TO CHECK FOR LAST LINE ON SCREEN
00187                      *
00188 B108 CE 0080         LDX    #STARAD  POINT TO DISPLAY VARIABLE
00189 B10B A6 05           LDA A  5,X      GET LINES THIS SCREEN
00190 B10D B1 B165         CMP A  LSCREN   LAST LINE?
00191 B110 26 04           BNE    LFEED2
00192 B112 6C 05           INC    5,X      COUNT LINE
00193 B114 20 05           BRA    SCROLU   SCROLL UP
00194 B116 6C 05   LFEED2  INC    5,X      COUNT LINE
00195 B118 7E B09D         JMP    UPDATE
00196                      *
00197                      *  SUBROUTINE TO SCROLL UP
00198                      *  A & X REGISTERS DESTROYED
00199                      *
00200 B11B CE 0080 SCROLU  LDX    #STARAD  POINT TO DISPLAY VARIBLE
00201 B11E 6A 05           DEC    5,X      SUB1 FROM LINE COUNT
00202 B120 A6 01           LDA A  1,X      GET STARTING ADD. LSB
00203 B122 BB B164         ADD A  CLINE    ADD, CHAR/LINE
00204 B125 A7 01           STA A  1,X
00205 B127 24 02           BCC    SCROL1
00206 B129 6C 00           INC    0,X
00207 B12B 7E B09D SCROL1  JMP    UPDATE   UPDATE STARTING ADD.
00208                      *
00209                      *  SUBROUTINE TO SCROLL DOWN
00210                      *  A & X REGISTERS DESTROYED
00211                      *
00212 B12E CE 0080 SCROLD  LDX    #STARAD  POINT TO SCREEN VARIABLE
00213 B131 6C 05           INC    5,X      ADD 1 LINE TO LINE COUNT
00214 B133 A6 01   SCROD1  LDA A  1,X      GET STARTING ADD. LSB
00215 B135 B0 B164         SUB A  CLINE    CHAR/LINE
00216 B138 A7 01           STA A  1,X      SAVE IT
```

PAGE 005   CRT

```
00217 B13A 24 03          BCC    SCROD2    CHECK BORROW
00218 B13C 7A 0000        DEC    0.X       SUB. BORROW FROM MSB
00219 B13F 7E B09D SCROD2 JMP    UPDATE    UPDATE START ADD.
00220                *
00221                *  SUBROUTINE TO PAGE DOWN
00222                *  ALL REGISTERS DESTROYED
00223                *
00224 B142 F6 B165 PAGEDN LDA B  LSCREN    GET LINE/SCREEN
00225 B145 8D E7 PAGED1   BSR    SCROLD    SCROLD DOWN 1 LINE
00226 B147 5A             DEC B            COUNT LINE
00227 B148 2C FB          BGE    PAGED1    LAST LINE?
00228 B14A 39             RTS
00229                *
00230                *  SUBROUTINE TO PAGE UP
00231                *  ALL REGISTERS DESTROYED
00232                *
00233 B14B F6 B165 PAGEUP LDA B  LSCREN    GET LINE/SCREEN
00234 B14E 8D CB PAGEU1   BSR    SCROLU    SCROLL UP 1 LINE
00235 B150 5A             DEC B            COUNT LINES
00236 B151 2C FB          BGE    PAGEU1
00237 B153 39             RTS
00238                *
00239                *  THIS TABLE CONTAINS THE CRTC INITIAL
00240                *  CONDITIONS. TO CHANGE FORMATS THIS
00241                *  TABLE MUST BE CHANGED
00242                *
00243 B154 67      CRTTAB FCB    103,80,86,06  HORIZONTAL SECTION
00244 B158 1A             FCB    26,00,24,25  VERTICAL SECTION
00245 B15C 00             FCB    00,10     INTERLACE,MAX RASTER
00246 B15E 00             FCB    00,10     CURSOR SIZE & BLINK
00247 B160 01             FCB    1,0       CURSOR LOCATION
00248 B162 01             FCB    1,0       START ADDRESS
00249                *
00250                *  THESE ARE TWO PARAMETERS THAT FORMAT
00251                *    THE SCREEN THEY ARE SET AT 80 BY 24
00252                *
00253 B164 50      CLINE  FCB    80        NUMBER OF CHAR. LINE
00254 B165 17      LSCREN FCB    24-1      LINES PER SCREEN-1
00255                *
00256                *  THIS TABLE IS SEARCHED FOR A CONTROL
00257                *   CHARACTER. TO ADD COMMANDS, ADD TO
00258                *    THIS TABLE. IF DIFFERENT CODES
00259                *   ARE REQUIRED CHANGE HERE.
00260                *
00261 B166 0A      DECTAB FCB    $0A       LINE FEED
00262 B167 0D             FCB    $0D       CARRIAGE RETURN
00263 B168 05             FCB    $05       SCROLL UP - CONTROL E
00264 B169 04             FCB    $04       SCROLL DOWN - CONTROL D
00265 B16A 03             FCB    $03       PAGE UP - CONTROL C
00266 B16B 02             FCB    $02       PAGE DOWN - CONTROL B
00267      B16C   DECEND  EQU    *
00268 B16C B0EA   DECADD  FDB    LFEED
00269 B16E B0DD           FDB    RTURN1
00270 B170 B11B           FDB    SCROLU
```

```
                      PAGE   006   CRT


              00271 B172 B12E          FDB      SCROLD
              00272 B174 B14B          FDB      PAGEUP
              00273 B176 B142          FDB      PAGEDN
              00274                *
              00275                *  THESE EQUATES DEFINE THE BEGINNING AND ENDING
              00276                *  ADDRESSES FOR THE DISPLAY MEMORY CLEAR ROUTINE
              00277      8000     MEMSTR EQU    $8000      DISPLAY MEM. START ADDR
              00278      87FF     MEMEND EQU    $87FF      DISPLAY MEM. END ADDR
              00279                *
              00280                *  STACK INITIALIZATION LOCATION
              00281      00FF     STKADD EQU    $FF        STACK INITIAL LOCATION
              00282                *  THESE ARE THE I/O EQUATES THEY MUST
              00283                *  MATCH THE HARDWARE USED
              00284      4000     CRTCAR EQU    $4000
              00285      4001     CRTCDR EQU    $4001
              00286      0010     PIA1AD EQU    $0010
              00287      0011     PIA1AC EQU    $0011
              00288      0012     PIA1BD EQU    $0012
              00289      0013     PIA1BC EQU    $0013
              00290      0008     ACIACR EQU    $0008
              00291      0009     ACIADR EQU    $0009
              00292 0080              ORG       $0080
              00293 0080 0002     STARAD RMB    2
              00294 0082 0002     CURPOS RMB    2
              00295 0084 0001     CCOUNT RMB    1
              00296 0085 0001     LCOUNT RMB    1
              00297 0086 0002     LINEAD RMB    2
              00298 0088 0002     STEMP  RMB    2
              00299 008A 0002     CTEMP  RMB    2
              00300 008C 0002     CUTEMP RMB    2
              00301                   END


              TOTAL ERRORS 00000
```

Appendix E # ASCII Conversion Chart

The conversion chart listed below is helpful in converting from a two-digit (two-byte) hexadecimal number to an ASCII character or from an ASCII character to a two-digit hexadecimal number. The example provided below shows the method of using this conversion chart.

Example

		Bits						
		MSB ←				→ LSB		
ASCII	Hex #	6	5	4	3	2	1	0
T	54	1	0	1	0	1	0	0
?	3F	0	1	1	1	1	1	1
+	2B	0	1	0	1	0	0	1

Bits 0 to 3 Second Hex Digit (LSB)	Bits 4 to 6 First Hex Digit (MSB)							
	0	1	2	3	4	5	6	7
0	NUL	DLE	SP	0	@	P		p
1	SOH	DC1	!	1	A	Q	a	q
2	STX	DC2	"	2	B	R	b	r
3	ETX	DC3	#	3	C	S	c	s
4	EOT	DC4	$	4	D	T	d	t
5	ENQ	NAK	%	5	E	U	e	u
6	ACK	SYN	&	6	F	V	f	v
7	BEL	ETB	'	7	G	W	g	w
8	BS	CAN	(	8	H	X	h	x
9	HT	EM	)	9	I	Y	i	y
A	LF	SUB	*	:	J	Z	j	z
B	VT	ESC	+	;	K	[	k	{
C	FF	FS	,	<	L	/	l	/
D	CR	GS	-	=	M	]	m	}
E	SO	RS	.	>	N	∧	n	≈
F	SI	US	/	?	O	—	o	DEL

6809

Instruction
Set

Table F-1
8-Bit Accumulator and Memory Instructions

Mnemonic(s)	Operation
ADCA, ADCB	Add memory to accumulator with carry
ADDA, ADDB	Add memory to accumulator
ANDA, ANDB	And memory with accumulator
ASL, ASLA, ASLB	Arithmetic shift of accumulator or memory left
ASR, ASRA, ASRB	Arithmetic shift of accumulator or memory right
BITA, BITB	Bit test memory with accumulator
CLR, CLRA, CLRB	Clear accumulator or memory location
CMPA, CMPB	Compare memory from accumulator
COM, COMA, COMB	Complement accumulator or memory location
DAA	Decimal adjust A-accumulator
DEC, DECA, DECB	Decrement accumulator or memory location
EORA, EORB	Exclusive or memory with accumulator
EXG R1, R2	Exchange R1 with R2 (R1, R2 = A, B, CC, DP)
INC, INCA, INCB	Increment accumulator or memory location
LDA, LDB	Load accumulator from memory
LSL, LSLA, LSLB	Logical shift left accumulator or memory location
LSR, LSRA, LSRB	Logical shift right accumulator or memory location
MUL	Unsigned multiply (A x B → D)
NEG, NEGA, NEGB	Negate accumulator or memory
ORA, ORB	Or memory with accumulator
ROL, ROLA, ROLB	Rotate accumulator or memory left
ROR, RORA, RORB	Rotate accumulator or memory right
SBCA, SBCB	Subtract memory from accumulator with borrow
STA, STB	Store accumulator to memory
SUBA, SUBB	Subtract memory from accumulator
TST, TSTA, TSTB	Test accumulator or memory location
TFR, R1, R2	Transfer R1 to R2 (R1, R2 = A, B, CC, DP)

NOTE: A, B, CC, or DP may be pushed to (pulled from) either stack with PSHS, PSHU, (PULS, PULU) instructions.

Table F-2
16-Bit Accumulator and Memory Instructions

Mnemonic(s)	Operation
ADDD	Add memory to D accumulator
CMPD	Compare memory from D accumulator
EXG D, R	Exchange D with X, Y, S, U or PC
LDD	Load D accumulator from memory
SEX	Sign Extend B accumulator into A accumulator
STD	Store D accumulator to memory
SUBD	Subtract memory from D accumulator
TFR D, R	Transfer D to X, Y, S, U or PC
TFR R, D	Transfer X, Y, S, U or PC to D

Table F-3
Index Register/Stack Pointer Instructions

Mnemonic(s)	Operation
CMPS, CMPU	Compare memory from stack pointer
CMPX, CMPY	Compare memory from index register
EXG R1, R2	Exchange D, X, Y, S, U, or PC with D, X, Y, S, U or PC
LEAS, LEAU	Load effective address into stack pointer
LEAX, LEAY	Load effective address into index register
LDS, LDU	Load stack pointer from memory
LDX, LDY	Load index register from memory
PSHS	Push any register(s) onto hardware stack (except S)
PSHU	Push any register(s) onto user stack (except U)
PULS	Pull any register(s) from hardware stack (except S)
PULU	Pull any register(s) from hardware stack (except U)
STS, STU	Store stack pointer to memory
STX, STY	Store index register to memory
TFR R1, R2	Transfer D, X, Y, S, U or PC to D, X, Y, S, U or PC
ABX	Add B accumulator to X (unsigned)

Table F-4
Branch Instructions

Mnemonic(s)	Operation
BCC, LBCC	Branch if carry clear
BCS, LBCS	Branch if carry set
BEQ, LBEQ	Branch if equal
BGE, LBGE	Branch if greater than or equal (signed)
BGT, LBGT	Branch if greater (signed)
BHI, LBHI	Branch if higher (unsigned)
BHS, LBHS	Branch if higher or same (unsigned)
BLE, LBLE	Branch if less than or equal (signed)
BLO, LBLO	Branch if lower (unsigned)
BLS, LBLS	Branch if lower or same (unsigned)
BLT, LBLT	Branch if less than (signed)
BMI, LBMI	Branch if minus
BNE, LBNE	Branch if not equal
BPL, LBPL	Branch if plus
BRA, LBRA	Branch always
BRN, LBRN	Branch never
BSR, LBSR	Branch to subroutine
BVC, LBVC	Branch if overflow clear
BVS, LBVS	Branch if overflow set

Table F-5
Miscellaneous Instructions

Mnemonic(s)	Operation
ANDCC	AND condition code register
CWAI	AND condition code register, then wait for interrupt
NOP	No operation
ORCC	OR condition code register
JMP	Jump
JSR	Jump to subroutine
RTI	Return from interrupt
RTS	Return from subroutine
SWI, SWI2, SWI3	Software interrupt (absolute indirect)
SYNC	Synchronize with interrupt line

Index

457